Praise for *Labyrinth of Ice*

"Every page sh   vivalist instinct. There is
never a dull mo   ic. Highly recommended!"
                                   ouglas Brinkley, author of
                                   and the Great Space Race

"A must-read for armchair adventurers everywhere. Buddy Levy's research is
thorough and his writing fast-paced, making for an epic page-turner."
— Martin Dugard, #1 *New York Times* bestselling author

"A page-turner that tells in fascinating detail the story of Lt. Adolphus
Greely—who ranks as one of the nineteenth century's most intrepid and
ruthless explorers—and the two dozen men of his command who battled the
Arctic elements and each other to try to survive one of the most harrowing
voyages of discovery ever recorded." — Tom Clavin, *New York Times*
bestselling author of *Dodge City* and *The Heart of Everything That Is*

"No one brings the narratives of history to life more brilliantly than Buddy
Levy. With laser accuracy, keen intelligence, exhaustive research, exhilarating
detail, and genuine compassion, he takes us on wondrous journeys so packed
with stunning moments of heroism, hope, fear, and survival that we feel that
we are witnessing the events not in the past, but in the present. . . . Moments
of unimaginable human endeavor, folly, and sacrifice become something
more than myth, more than legend, more than history itself: they become an
unforgettable part of our own reality." — Kim Barnes,
author of *In the Kingdom of Men* and the Pulitzer Prize finalist
In the Wilderness: Coming of Age in Unknown Country

"Buddy Levy, noted for bringing a fine novelist's sense of storytelling to his
narrative histories, tells this difficult but fascinating story with a compassion
and vividness often lacking in works of this nature. . . . *Labyrinth of Ice* is a
remarkable book. It should not be missed." — *Anchorage Daily News*

"An engaging, superbly written, and meticulously researched chronicle of the Greely expedition that proves it is one of the most engaging adventure narratives ever. With cinematic prose, great economy of language, and vivid descriptions, Levy places readers in the middle of the action and makes them see the snow, feel the hunger and the tension, and hear the cracking of the ice. . . . *Labyrinth of Ice* reads like an outstanding script for an action movie. A riveting, engaging read packed with superhuman feats, incredible journeys, amazing discoveries, tension, heartbreak, and constant danger. It is also a true tale—and that makes it a book that demands to be read." —NPR

"An armchair explorer's dream—all the drama, all the fear, all the steadfastness that fans could want. Unexpectedly, Levy manages also to carve out important space in the narrative for Greely's wife, Henrietta, who was key to the rescue. An invaluable addition to polar history." —*Booklist*

"Levy's masterful use of primary sources from Greely and others creates a highly detailed narrative that brings the men and their expedition to life. This gripping book is a testament to the bravery and sheer doggedness of men determined to survive despite harsh conditions." —*Library Journal*

"Evocative, deeply researched . . . the result is an intense historical adventure with modern-day relevance for the climate change debate." —*Publishers Weekly*

"A graphic tale of horrific deprivation that is sure to be the benchmark account." —*Kirkus Reviews*

"A gripping account of historical adventure and horror that maintains tension from beginning to end, despite the conclusion having been known for more than 130 years. Perfect for fans of Nathaniel Philbrick and Erik Larson." —*Shelf Awareness*

"[With] all the ingredients for a harrowing armchair adventure." —*Lewiston Tribune*

"Levy paints with pathos a picture of the expedition's members, from commander to the lowliest private. In these portraits-in-miniature, their character and personalities reveal both the best and worst of humans in crisis: heroism, grit, selflessness, but also dishonesty, disobedience, and callous self-regard. It is a tale as old as time, but never gets old in the telling—and Levy does it superbly. *Labyrinth of Ice* takes the reader to the forbidding Farthest North in the best way possible as we avidly turn the pages, sipping hot tea from a cozy, warm chair."
　　　　　　　　　　　　　　　　　　　　　　　　—*Open Letters Review*

"*Labyrinth of Ice* is another masterful narrative by America's premier historiographer of harrowing, character-baring expeditions into the unknown. A tour de force of vivid detail and voluminous research!"　　　—Alex Shoumatoff,
　　　　　　　　　editor of DispatchesfromtheVanishingWorld.com

"Buddy Levy's *Labyrinth of Ice* is riveting. It's a true tale of unparalleled discovery, endurance, survival, and patriotism, set in one of the world's most unforgiving places: the Polar North. Levy writes history with a novelist's timing and describes the stunning landscapes with precise, imagistic language. A gripping, unforgettable story."　　　　　　　　　　—Erik Weihenmayer,
　　　　　　　　　global adventurer, speaker, and author

ALSO BY BUDDY LEVY

No Barriers: A Blind Man's Journey to Kayak the Grand Canyon

Geronimo: Leadership Strategies of an American Warrior

*River of Darkness: Francisco Orellana's Legendary Voyage
of Death and Discovery Down the Amazon*

*Conquistador: Hernán Cortés, King Montezuma, and the
Last Stand of the Aztecs*

American Legend: The Real-Life Adventures of David Crockett

Echoes on Rimrock: In Pursuit of the Chukar Partridge

LABYRINTH
of ICE

The Triumphant and Tragic
Greely Polar Expedition

Buddy Levy

ST. MARTIN'S GRIFFIN
NEW YORK

The Library of Congress has cataloged the hardcover edition as follows:

Names: Levy, Buddy, 1960– author.
Title: Labyrinth of ice : the triumphant and tragic Greely polar expedition / Buddy Levy.
Description: First edition. | New York : St. Martin's Press, 2019. | Includes bibliographical
references and index.
Identifiers: LCCN 2019034039 | ISBN 9781250182197 (hardcover) | ISBN 9781250182203 (ebook)
Subjects: LCSH: Lady Franklin Bay Expedition (1881–1884) | Greely, A. W. (Adolphus Washington),
1844–1935. | Arctic regions—Discovery and exploration—American.
Classification: LCC G670 1881 .L48 2019 | DDC 910.9163/27—dc23
LC record available at https://lccn.loc.gov/2019034039

ISBN 978-1-250-78206-9 (trade paperback)

Our books may be purchased in bulk for promotional, educational, or business use. Please contact
your local bookseller or the Macmillan Corporate and Premium Sales Department at 1-800-221-7945,
extension 5442, or by email at MacmillanSpecialMarkets@macmillan.com.

First St. Martin's Griffin Edition: 2021

D   10 9 8 7 6

For John Larkin—aka Juan Alarcón . . . aka Johnny Morocco

Confidant and coconspirator

Adventure brother and boatbuider

Literary critic and adviser

Truest of true friends

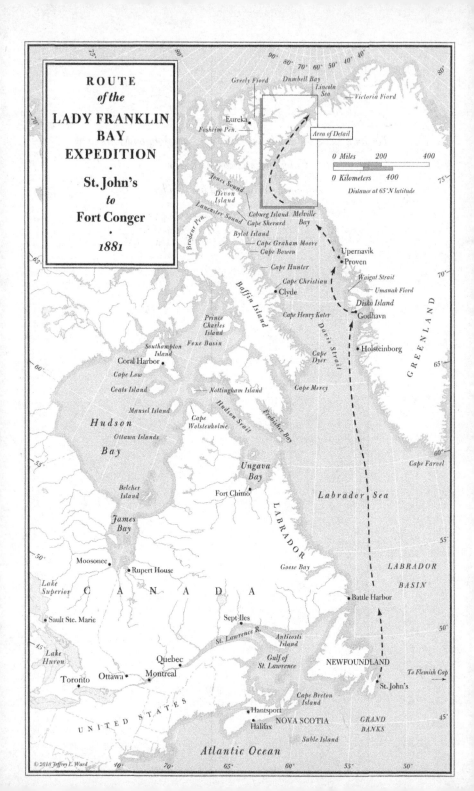

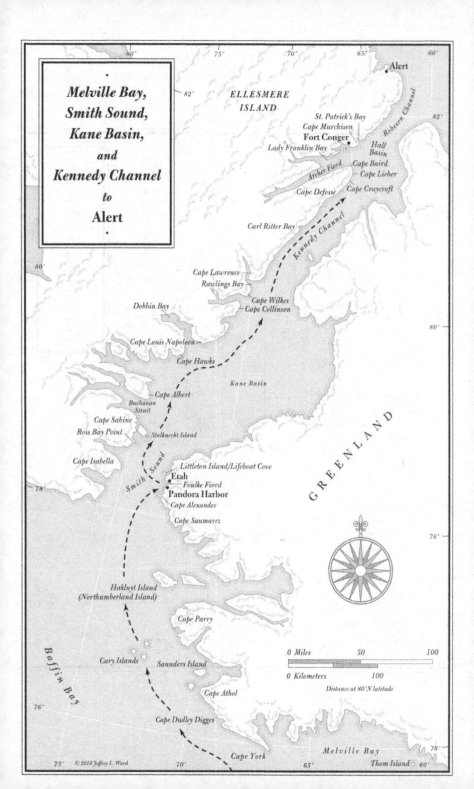

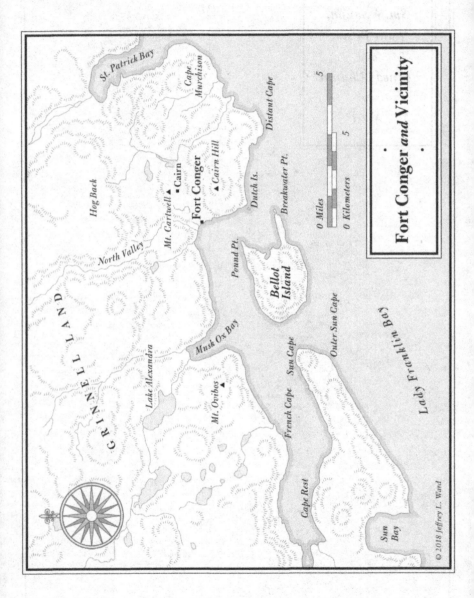

Fort Conger and Vicinity

St. Patrick Bay

Cape Murchison

Distant Cape

Cairn

Cairn Hill

Fort Conger

Mt. Cartmell

Dutch Is.

Breakwater Pt.

Hog Back

North Valley

Pound Pt.

Bellot Island

GRINNELL LAND

Lake Alexandra

Musk Ox Bay

Mt. Ovibos

Sun Cape

Outer Sun Cape

French Cape

Lady Franklin Bay

Cape Rest

Sun Bay

0 Miles   5

0 Kilometers   5

© 2018 Jeffrey L. Ward

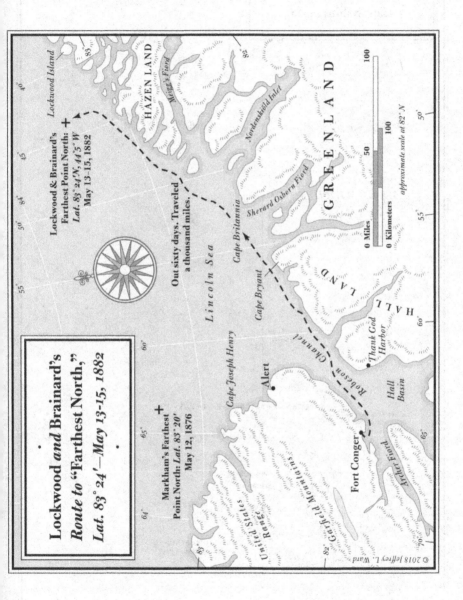

Lockwood *and* Brainard's
Route to "Farthest North,"
Lat. 83° 24'—May 13-15, 1882

Lockwood & Brainard's
Farthest Point North:
Lat. 83° 24'N, 44°5" W
May 13-15, 1882

Out sixty days. Traveled
a thousand miles.

Markham's Farthest
Point North: Lat. 83° 20'
May 12, 1876

Lockwood Island

HAZEN LAND

Meig's Fiord

Nordenskiöld Inlet

Sherard Osborn Fiord

G R E E N L A N D

Cape Britannia

Cape Bryant

Lincoln Sea

Cape Joseph Henry

Alert

H A L L   L A N D

Thank God Harbor

Hall Basin

Robeson Channel

Fort Conger

Archer Fiord

United States Range

Garfield Mountains

approximate scale at 82° N

0 Miles   50   100

0 Kilometers   100

© 2018 Jeffrey L. Ward

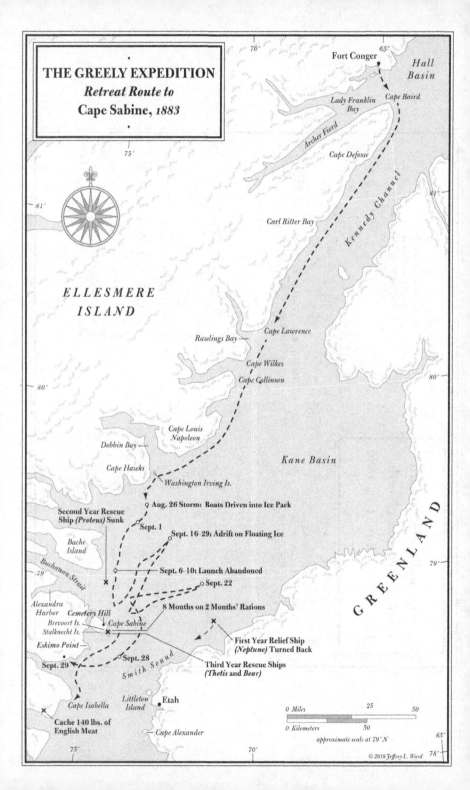

By many paths and by many means mankind has endeavored to penetrate this kingdom of death.

—Fridtjof Nansen, Arctic explorer

CONTENTS

❧❧❧

THE CREW OF THE LADY FRANKLIN BAY EXPEDITION

(Also Known as the Greely Expedition)

❧❧❧

1st Lt. Adolphus W. Greely—Fifth Cavalry, acting signal officer

2nd Lt. Frederick F. Kislingbury—Eleventh Infantry, acting signal officer

2nd Lt. James B. Lockwood—Twenty-Third Infantry, acting signal officer

Octave Pavy—Physician and naturalist

Sgt. David L. Brainard—Company L, Second Cavalry, U.S. Army

Sgt. William H. Cross—General Service, U.S. Army

Sgt. Hampden S. Gardiner—Signal Corps, U.S. Army

Sgt. Edward Israel—Signal Corps, U.S. Army, astronomer and meteorologist

Sgt. Winfield S. Jewell—Signal Corps, U.S. Army

Sgt. David Linn—Company C, Second Cavalry, U.S. Army

Sgt. David C. Ralston—Signal Corps, U.S. Army

Sgt. George W. Rice—Signal Corps, U.S. Army, expedition photographer

Cpl. Joseph Elison—Company E, Tenth Infantry, U.S. Army

Cpl. Nicholas Salor—Company H, Second Cavalry, U.S. Army

Pvt. Jacob Bender—Company F, Ninth Infantry, U.S. Army

Pvt. Henry Biederbick—Company L, Second Cavalry, U.S. Army

Pvt. Maurice Connell—Company B, Third Cavalry, U.S. Army

Pvt. William A. Ellis—Company C, Second Cavalry, U.S. Army

Pvt. Julius Frederick—Company L, Second Cavalry, U.S. Army

Pvt. Charles B. Henry—Company E, Fifth Cavalry, U.S. Army

Pvt. Francis Long—Company F, Ninth Infantry, U.S. Army

Pvt. Roderick R. Schneider—First Artillery, U.S. Army

Pvt. William Whisler—Company F, Ninth Infantry, U.S. Army

Jens Edward—Native Greenlander, hunter and dog driver

Thorlip Frederik Christiansen—Native Greenlander, hunter and dog driver

LABYRINTH
of ICE

Members of Greely Expedition 1881–84.

Seated left to right: Private Maurice Connell, USA; Sergeant David L. Brainard, USA; 2nd Lieutenant Frederick F. Kislingbury, USA; Lieutenant Adolphus W. Greely, USA; 2nd Lieutenant James B. Lockwood, USA; Sergeant Edward Israel, USA; Sergeant Winfield S. Jewell, USA; Sergeant George W. Rice, USA. *Standing left to right:* Private William Whisler, USA; Private William A. Ellis, USA; Private Jacob Bender, USA; Sergeant William H. Cross, USA; Private Julius Frederick, USA; Sergeant David Linn, USA; Private Henry Biederbick, USA (Acting Hospital Steward); Private Charles B. Henry, USA; Private Francis Long, USA; Sergeant David C. Ralston, USA; Corporal Nicholas Salor, USA; Surgeon Octave Pavy; Sergeant Hampden S. Gardiner, USA; Corporal Joseph Elison, USA. *(Courtesy of Naval History and Heritage Command)*

PROLOGUE

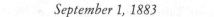

September 1, 1883

Expedition commander Lt. Adolphus W. Greely stood on the edge of the ice floe listening to the constant groan and roar of the ice pack, a sound so eerily hideous that it had come to be known by Arctic explorers as "the Devil's symphony." Not even the howling wind—which was pushing out to sea the small ice floe Greely and his twenty-four men were stranded on, away from their destination—could drown out the weird and terrible sound of the pack: ice grinding against ice, shearing and shrieking and wailing, an ever-present reminder of their desperate vulnerability in this colossal and hostile environment. He and his men were mere specks, adrift on a small island of sea ice moving at the mercy of the tide and winds. Two of their boats had been hauled up onto the ice, and a third—the ten-thousand-pound steam launch *Lady Greely*—had been made fast to the side of the floeberg with ice anchors.

Greely consulted with his meteorologist, who took readings through the blowing snow. It was 11°F.* No polar party had ever recorded a lower temperature this early in the year. Greely surveyed the desolate surroundings between Ellesmere Island and Greenland: To the west, on the Ellesmere Island

---

* Unless otherwise noted, all temperatures are rendered in Fahrenheit.

side of the lower Kane Basin, were rugged, rocky cliffs, and beyond them the snowcapped Victoria and Albert Mountains rose high above. To the east were foggy fiords and mist-shrouded peaks rising from the Greenland shore. Everything and everyone—all the gear and boats and men—were encrusted with a veneer of frost.

They had made it to within thirty miles above Cape Sabine, the location where Greely—through prearranged and explicitly written military orders—had instructed relief ships to deposit food for his expeditionary force. But for the last few days they had been drifting slowly away from land and back toward the north, away from shore and the food cache that Greely hoped would be their salvation. His men were exhausted from three weeks of nearly constant motion, their hands raw and bleeding inside their sealskin mittens from pulling at the oars and from hauling the boats on and off icebergs every day—or sometimes every hour. Their shoulders were sore and blistered from the drag ropes. Men shivered, nearly hypothermic, as they fought for sleep bivouacked directly on the ice or hunkered in the bottoms of their uncovered small craft. Greely took his trusted sergeant, David Brainard, aside and they carefully inventoried their dwindling stores. Counting the various meats, including pemmican, bacon, and beef—plus the hardtack bread—there were rations for perhaps fifty days, maybe a week longer if the hunters could shoot seals, walruses, or bears.

The expedition had already been through tremendous trials. Together, more than two hundred miles to the north, they had been confronted by and survived every possible challenge: attacks by wolves; hurricane-force winds; temperatures approaching 100° below zero; and near insanity brought on by the months of total darkness. Following orders, three weeks earlier Greely had commanded his men to abandon the comforts of Fort Conger—which they had built above an inlet at the far northeastern shore of Ellesmere Island. They had turned away from the fort's coal-burning cookstove, its fireplace, insulated walls, and protective roof—and a year's supply of food—and traveled by boats into the ice-choked seas, heading south toward Cape Sabine. Navigating the roiling chop and massive bergs through mist and fog, sleet and snow, and dying autumn light had been treacherous. And although Greely would not admit it, his poor eyesight was making navigation nearly impossible. He needed a better set of eyes to do the ice piloting.

Ultimately, with ice pressing in on them from all sides, Greely had made the decision to commit the boats and men to the mercies of the floes, with the forlorn hope that tides and winds would propel them south to Cape Sabine. If that failed, they would abandon everything not essential and attempt to cross ice bridges from floe to floe until they reached land. Some of Greely's men disagreed with him, muttering that his decisions were madness and amounted to suicide. One of the men said he feared "another Franklin disaster." The expedition doctor scribbled furiously in his journal: "It is terrible to float in this manner, in the snow, fog, and dark. This seems to me like a nightmare in one of Edgar Allan Poe's stories." And in many ways, it was.

Early on the afternoon of September 1, 1883, Greely's two Greenlandic hunters brought in two seals. While one of the cooks struggled to light an alcohol stove in the high Arctic winds, the native Greenlanders skinned and cleaned their kill—doling out the raw hearts, lungs, and intestines to the famished expedition members, who chewed hungrily at the entrails. A few of the weaker men hovered nearby, then knelt at the bodies of the slain seals, taking turns lapping at the warm blood still spouting from the bullet holes.

Just then, with men gnawing on seal offal and wiping blood from their chins, Sergeant Brainard sprinted from the edge of their floe and screamed for everyone to prepare for impact. A giant iceberg was thundering toward them from the north. Men looked up to see a mass of white upon them and then felt a shuddering jolt of impact from the collision. The immense pressure of the striking pack tore great rifts in their small berg, splitting its surface into canyons. They scurried wildly, leaping over deep fissures, hurrying to secure food and boats and gear as the ice rent and ruptured underfoot.

Frozen rubble from the colliding floe fractured like glass around them, some of the pieces the size of their whaleboats. Commander Greely stood in stupefied awe as the five-ton *Lady Greely*, squeezed by unimaginable pressure, rose out of the water and up the iceberg's wall, suspended there. Everyone stared, mouths agape, expecting the boat to splinter like firewood. But it did not break.

It was held aloft, pushed up by the ice, for hours until the winds and tides shifted, releasing the pressure and easing it back down into the sea.

Commander Greely ordered all of the *Lady Greely*'s remaining contents brought up onto what remained of their floe to be lashed down. They would abandon it if they must. The ice floe on which they rode had been torn in two, and all the men ducked and shuddered from the blasting wind and the wailing, menacing roar of the pack. Their small ice island now pitched and spun as they drifted out to sea at the mercy of the winds and tides, with no way to predict or control when or if they would ever reach land again.

1

The Lady Franklin Bay
Expeditionary Force

July 9, 1881—Labrador Basin,
North Atlantic Ocean

Lt. A. W. Greely, commander of the Lady Franklin Bay Expedition, rode at the bow of the two-hundred-foot-long steamship *Proteus*, his vision fixed on the northern horizon. He wore a double-breasted, boiled-wool peacoat with thick fur at the collar and cuffs. He and his crew were bound for the top of the world, to one of the last regions yet unmarked on global maps. As the inlet narrowed near the strait of Belle Isle, they passed great protruding shapes of ice rising from the sea. Some resembled immense white-blue anvils, and some looked like the wind-scoured sandstone towers he'd seen in the American Southwest. Most of the icebergs* he could not describe, or compare to phenomena he had ever witnessed before in nature. He observed them and everything else, squinting through his oval spectacles at the breathtaking expanse,

---

* Generally speaking, an *iceberg* is a massive piece of ice of dramatically varying shape that has broken away from a glacier and may be afloat or aground. An *ice floe* is any relatively flat piece of sea ice of twenty yards or more across, subdivided by size ranging from small (twenty to one hundred yards across) to giant (more than six miles across). A *floeberg* is a large to massive piece of sea ice, comprising hummocks and pressure ridges, which has separated from the ice pack.

trying to visualize what lay ahead. The combination of ice, rock, and water appeared to have some vague kind of course he might plot his way through. As the *Proteus* plowed into the wind-chopped Labrador Sea, massive slabs of glacial ice cleaved off the shore and crashed into the sea, spewing freezing brine over the gunwales and frosting his sharp narrow face and pointed black beard.

His heart raced with anticipation, but his mind was much burdened. Less than a week earlier, on July 2, at the Baltimore and Potomac Rail Station in Washington, D.C., President James A. Garfield had been shot twice at point-blank range—once in the shoulder and once in the back, the second shot lodging near his pancreas—and now, with family and physicians huddled around him, he fought for his life at the White House. Greely's heart was heavy at this news, with the uncertainty of how another presidential assassination—should Garfield not recover—would rock the Republic. And he already missed his young family, his wife of just three years, Henrietta, and their two infant daughters, Antoinette and Adola. But the call of adventure—and possibly international fame—had lured him toward the Arctic on a voyage of exploration and discovery that would last at least two years, should all go as planned. However, Greely was savvy enough to know that Arctic journeys never went as planned. He had spent years studying the history of Arctic exploration and the quest for the Northwest Passage, and he understood the dangers and stark realities: He steered toward a harsh, ice-bound labyrinth where crew losses of 50 percent or more were the norm. But Greely had some hard bark on him, a war-earned toughness coupled with an uncanny sense of *the thing to do now*, and he hoped his men had it too. They'd better: A. W. Greely would allow no disorder. This was sovereign. He'd started following orders when he was seventeen, then nicknamed "Dolph" by his friends. He'd been weaned on discipline. Now he was the one giving the orders, and he demanded a strict, unwavering adherence to them, and to discipline generally.

Poor weather and northwesterly gales slammed into the *Proteus,* slowing progress, but within a week they'd steamed into the Davis Strait, where they encountered their first pack ice.

Greely was fascinated and awed by the ice, noting in his journal that *the greater part of the ice ranged from three to five feet above the water, and was deeply grooved at the water's edge, evidently by the action of the waves. Above and below the surface of the sea projected long tongue-like edges. . . . The most delicate tints of blue mingled quickly and indistinguishably into those of rare light green, to be succeeded later as the water receded from the floe's side by shades of blueish white.*

They passed more bergs, some jutting fifteen feet from the water, the ice rising in giant hummocks and pinnacles. Greely contemplated the threefold mission at hand: First, he was to set up the northernmost of a chain of a dozen research stations around the Arctic, to simultaneously collect magnetic, astronomical, and meteorological data. This was part of a revolutionary scientific mission named the International Polar Year (two years, really)—a global effort to record data at the farthest reaches of the world to better understand the earth's climate. Second, Greely would search for and hopefully rescue the men of the lost USS *Jeannette*, which had vanished two years earlier during an attempted voyage to the North Pole. Greely had known Lt. Cdr. George W. De Long, the expedition's leader, very well. He would try his best to find him. Third—though definitely not last—Greely secretly intended to reach the North Pole; or, should he fall short, to attain Farthest North, an explorer's holy grail of the highest northern latitude, which had been held by the British for three hundred years.

At thirty-seven, tall, sinewy, and strong, Greely had earned his current command through two decades of army service, surviving some of the bloodiest battles in the nation's history. At Antietam in 1862, as part of the Nineteenth Massachusetts Regiment, Greely took a bullet to the face that fractured his jaw, knocked out several teeth, and left him unconscious as his regiment retreated. When he came to, a Confederate soldier stood over him and tried to capture him, but Greely fought his way to safety, though he was struck in the thigh by another musket ball during his escape. As Greely received treatment and then recovered in a field hospital cot, he witnessed a macabre sight: Piled up high against the side of the house were the amputated arms and legs of soldiers, both

Union and Confederate, stacked like cordwood. The Union lost 12,410 men that day, the most of any single day in the Civil War.

From then on, Greely wore a full beard to cover the scars from his wound, and as well to hide the reminder of the atrocities he'd witnessed.

He'd worked his way up the army ranks since he was an enlisted teen, eventually being posted out West to construct telegraph lines throughout the hostile Indian frontier. During this duty, through careful observation, he'd become an expert in telegraphy, electricity, and meteorology. Eventually, through his leadership skills and his abilities, he'd convinced the Signal Corps and the highest brass of the U.S. Army—as well as Secretary of War Robert Todd Lincoln (Abraham Lincoln's son, who signed his orders)—that he had the "stuff." He would lead this mission, formally named the Lady Franklin Bay Expedition in honor of Lady Jane Franklin. Her husband, the legendary Sir John Franklin (and his crew of 129), had vanished seeking the Northwest Passage in 1845. Lady Franklin sponsored numerous expeditions to find him.

But everyone knew the current voyage was in fact the Greely Expedition, and A. W. Greely was in charge.

The *Proteus*—christened and launched new in 1874 out of Dundee, Scotland—was a 467-ton, iron-prowed steamer designed for the sealing trade. It was built to last a half century or longer if well maintained. The ship was commanded by Capt. Richard Pike, one of the most experienced ice navigators in Newfoundland. Pike coursed northward with unusual speed for the season, clipping through the normally ice-choked waters of the Davis Strait. Cutting through dense fog and wave chop, the sturdy steamship made land at the windswept western shores of Greenland at Godhavn (now Qeqertarsuaq), Disko Island. Through lifting fog, Greely and his men saw mountains rising up from the sea some three thousand feet, and along a secure, landlocked harbor and tranquil cove sat a native settlement under Danish control. As the *Proteus* anchored, Greely heard a cannon fire a salute signaling their arrival, and soon afterward Sophus Krarup-Smith, the Danish royal inspector of North Greenland, came aboard.

Inspector Krarup-Smith had been about to depart for his annual assessment of Upernavik to the north, but out of courtesy he delayed leaving to host Greely and his men and to offer any provisions, intelligence, and assistance that the expedition required. Krarup-Smith welcomed the men into his home, which was surprisingly elaborate given its remoteness: There was a grand piano, a small billiard table, "a well-filled book-case, carpets, pictures, and many other evidences of civilization and even elegance." Krarup-Smith and his wife served Greely and two of his lieutenants—Kislingbury and Lockwood—an elaborate welcome dinner that included fresh salmon, larded eider ducks, and delicate Arctic ptarmigan, all served with excellent European wines. They also sampled seal meat, which some of the men found unpalatable because of its coarse, dark, and oily appearance. Greely relished it as juicy and tender, "with a slight sweetish taste."

They remained in Godhavn for five days. Greely observed that the Inuit houses were built of stone and turf, lined with wood, so low that he could hardly stand up inside. He was impressed by their ingenuity in using stretched seal intestines for windows. Greely scouted the area, characterizing it as "all mountains and sea," the cliffs thrusting a few thousand feet straight up from the water. Though he found breaks in the cliffs that gave way to low, sloping valleys and brooks lined with vegetation, mostly he was awed by the region's "grandeur and desolation."

There was also expedition business to attend to. Greely purchased a team of twelve Greenlandic sled dogs, the pack snarling and vicious. He would need these animals, as well as Greenlandic sled drivers he still had to enlist, for his intended sorties toward the North Pole. Greely also bartered for a large quantity of *mattak*—the skin of the white whale—which he'd learned from reading previous expedition logs was "antiscorbutic"*—important in helping to prevent scurvy.

On July 20 a Louisiana-born Frenchman, Dr. Octave Pavy, arrived from nearby Ritenbenck, where he'd spent the preceding year serving as naturalist

---

* At the time, though scurvy was known as a dietary deficiency, it was not completely understood. It was known that citrus fruits like lemons and limes appeared to combat the disease, so mariners began taking them on extended voyages (resulting in the origin of the British expression "Limeys"). It was not until the 1930s that the Hungarian-born Albert Szent-Györgyi isolated vitamin C, for which he was awarded the Nobel Prize in Physiology or Medicine in 1937.

in an ambitious colonization attempt organized by U.S. Army captain Henry Howgate. But funding for that mission had failed to make it through Congress, and now Greely was free to hire Pavy as a contract surgeon. He was experienced in treating ailments typical of the severe northern region. Greely oversaw his signing of the oath of service that very day. Pavy was also to serve as chief naturalist and taxidermist in charge of preserving and recording all specimens procured.

They sailed north once more, stopping at Upernavik, at the time the most northerly settlement in the world. There Greely purchased ten suits of sealskin clothing fashioned for Arctic expeditionary work. He also hired two sturdy and able Greenlandic sledge drivers from a small nearby coastal settlement. They were said to be skilled hunters and kayakers. One was named Thorlip Frederik Christiansen; his mother was a Greenlandic Inuit,* his father a Dane. Greely's men quickly nicknamed him "Eskimo Fred." His full-blooded Greenlander friend was named Jens Edward. Though neither of them could speak English, Pavy, who'd been on Greenland for the last year, helped translate at the beginning. They loaded their kayaks and hunting gear and climbed aboard.

Thus provisioned, Greely ordered Captain Pike to steam the *Proteus* ahead toward the dreaded Melville Bay, a three-hundred-mile-wide body of turbulent water known as a "mysterious region of terror." The bay's churning, swirling currents were much feared by whalers, and Greely had read that in one season alone, nineteen ships were lost there, some blown off course and capsized in the howling, freezing gales, others crushed and splintered between massive bergs. They plowed through thin "pancake ice" barely an inch thick and marveled at the massive floating icebergs gleaming white and blue-green in the per-

---

* The people of this region of Greenland, and particularly those of northwestern Greenland, were Greenlandic Inuit, descendants of the Thule people who spread across the Arctic from Alaska around AD 1000–1400 and were the most northerly people in the world. Explorers who first came into contact with these people referred to them variously as Etah, Arctic Highlanders, Polar Eskimo, or Eskimo—the last being the American usage. More specifically the inhabitants as far north as Melville Bay are commonly referred to as West Greenlanders; the indigenous inhabitants of the Canadian territories (Ellesmere Island) are called Inuit; and the northernmost of these peoples are Inughuit, meaning "great and powerful human beings." (Sources: Lyle Dick, *Muskox Land*, pp. xix and 61, and David Damas, *Handbook of North American Indians*, vol. 5, p. 593.)

petual sunlight. But that year, one of the fairest summers in memory, the waters of Melville Bay remained remarkably open, and on July 31, lookouts sighted Cape York. Captain Pike had navigated the watery graveyard in an unheard-of thirty-six hours, the fastest crossing then on record. Greely was pleased with the speed, but he privately wondered whether such open waters were an anomaly. What if the sound was not as open when the ship to relieve him attempted to pass through?

Just past Cape York, Greely anchored at the Cary Islands, twenty miles off the Greenland coast. Winds gusted, and he clasped his records tightly. They showed that English captain Sir George Strong Nares had cached significant provisions here during his 1875–76 expedition. Greely sent Doctor Pavy and Lieutenant Kislingbury, his second in command, ashore, and sure enough, at a small cove on the southern tip of the island they found a cairn, and nearby 3,600 rations in good condition. They secured and covered these for the future, should they or other explorers need them. Nares had also left behind a sturdy whaleboat that the men wanted to take, as it was in serviceable condition, but Greely ordered them to leave the craft, reckoning it might just save some imperiled whaler's life one day—or their own lives. They noted the location of the cache in their journals and moved on. Greely, emboldened by the open water, directed Captain Pike to take them past Cape Sabine on the coast of Grinnell Land—the central section of Ellesmere Island—where Nares had recorded having a sledging depot and had cached a few hundred pounds of canned beef.

They pressed on, easing into the Smith Sound narrows as lookouts scanned ahead for ice. They saw polar bears and flipper seals and many walruses. Eider ducks and small black-and-white arctic auks called dovekies winged along the shore. The prevalence of game seemed a good omen to Greely and his men, and they shot some animals and birds en route, increasing their considerable larder. Smith Sound had been discovered by the fabled English navigator William Baffin in 1616 and was thought to be the gateway to the "Open Polar Sea," the hypothesized ice-free sea surrounding the North Pole. The narrows linking Baffin Bay to the Kane Basin were aptly referred to as the "Northern Pillars of Hercules," and believed to be the most likely route to the North Pole. Where the sound bottlenecked between Littleton Island on western Greenland

and Cape Sabine off eastern Grinnell Land, the gap was a mere twenty-three miles. Surveying the craggy shorelines, Greely determined that under the right conditions, it would not take much to completely clog this narrow funnel of a waterway.

The *Proteus* reached Cape Hawks midmorning on August 3. Dense fog descended, and they crawled forward with great caution at half speed. Greely scribbled in his journal: "We met an impenetrable icefield at 10 P.M. and the *Proteus* butted against it. We are at the entrance of Lady Franklin Bay." Pike anchored the ship to the ice pack off Cape Baird, a headland of Bellot Island that guards Lady Franklin Bay. But he was forced to disengage when winds and shifting ice began to buffet the *Proteus* toward the south, away from their destination. For a week they were driven backward a total of about forty miles. Greely was dumbfounded by the power of the wind and the pack, amazed by how helpless they were, even in a powerful, nearly five-hundred-ton steam sealer. They were entirely at the mercy of nature.

As they retreated, Greely watched the ice and the water, mesmerized by schools of white beluga whales being chased by swordfish. The size of the beluga—between twelve and twenty feet—impressed Greely, as did their appearance. They had, he noted, a "smooth, unwrinkled hide, which is of a waxy-white color in adults, but of a light grayish brown in the young." The larger of these creatures could yield nearly a thousand pounds each of blubber and meat. Yellowish-white narwhals—the so-called unicorns of the sea, named for their long, straight, up-to-ten-foot-long "tusk"—also swam past in great numbers.

Finally the winds shifted in Greely's favor and blew hard to the west, the ice beginning to split and fissure, with "leads"—lanes of navigable water—opening in the frozen sea. Leads, as noted by Sergeant Brainard, who was learning to study them carefully, were "impermanent and tricky affairs. They open and they close without a sign of warning. A lead may remain open for a week, or it may close in an hour." Leads are the Arctic navigator's map, and often his lifeline, in a frozen sea. Now Captain Pike drove at full steam through the splintery web of leads, snaking and cutting in a northerly direction until, on August 11, 1881, as the morning fog lifted, they entered the western mouth of Lady Franklin Bay, which was for the moment relatively clear of ice.

Greely ordered Pike to make anchor and dispatched Lieutenant Lockwood ashore to ascertain the existence of a deep and productive coal seam reported by Nares in 1875. Lockwood returned from his reconnaissance to report that the coal seam was easily accessible and of excellent quality, and further, that he'd killed three musk-oxen from a large herd. Game seemed plentiful, and the nearby shores of the bay appeared suitable for establishing their station. Beyond the shore in all directions, mountains rose up to three thousand feet, gently curving at their summits like the backs of hogs. Many of the mountaintops—like those of three-mile-long Bellot Island—were covered even in summer with snow drifts. The great harbor there at the foot of the mountains, with more than twenty square miles of enormous ice floes, was named Discovery Harbor for Nares's ship, HMS *Discovery*. The harbor was, Greely observed, "hemmed in at every point by precipitous walls, which ranged from hundreds to thousands of feet in height."

In order to get close enough to unload their considerable stores—which included all the precut timber needed to build a sixty-five-foot longhouse—Pike began ramming through ice that ranged from two to ten feet thick. He would reverse the ship a few hundred yards, then throttle full steam ahead, bashing the ice with the iron bow, plowing through as far as half—and sometimes even the entire length—of the ship. As the *Proteus* thrust forward, Pike and Greely urged the men to run fore and then aft, causing a rocking motion to aid in breaking the ice and also to keep the ship from becoming "beset" or "nipped"—the Arctic whalers' expression for getting trapped in the ice.

After seven hours of ramming through rotting harbor ice, the *Proteus* rested within one hundred yards of the shore. Beyond the ice foot, and within thirty yards of the water's edge, was a flat, scrubby bluff scoured by wind, ice, and sea. This was the place. Greely dubbed the spot Fort Conger, after Michigan senator Omar Conger, who had supported the expedition from the start. They had made a remarkable seven hundred miles in just six days of actual steaming (discounting the week they were blown south). Here they would build their scientific station and spend the next two years collecting data, venturing forth into the unexplored northern Lincoln Sea, and attempting to reach the North Pole.

⌒⌒⌒

Greely stepped onshore and strode up a small hill covered with saxifrage—small, purple-blooming flowers growing in tufts between rocks. Gulls and terns soared and hovered on the wind along the shore. A freshwater brook rushed down a steep slope just past the lichen-covered plateau. The place looked promising, and they would have everything they would need. The air was cold, fresh, salty, and bracing. He paused to look back as the men began unloading the *Proteus*. Ice was beginning to pack and encroach in Discovery Harbor, as well as beyond, to the west in the Kennedy Channel. From somewhere out in the bunched and knuckled hills came the plaintive howl of a wolf. Adolphus Greely, adjusting his spectacles and gazing at the three tall masts of the *Proteus* piercing the horizon, had cause for both excitement and trepidation. For as his men lowered the whaleboats, and the twenty-eight-foot steam launch dubbed the *Lady Greely*, it occurred to him that they were 250 miles north of the last known Eskimo settlement, and more than 1,000 miles north of the Arctic Circle. They were, in fact, now the most northerly colony of human inhabitants in the world. They were being left, quite literally, at the far end of the earth.

Unloading the *Proteus* at Discovery Harbor. *(G. W. Rice, photographer / Library of Congress)*

Building Fort Conger. *(G. W. Rice, photographer / Library of Congress)*

2

Fort Conger

There was no time to waste in disembarking. Some open leads remained that the *Proteus* could use in its departure, but ice was closing in fast. Greely ordered the men to work around the clock in four-hour shifts, made possible by the summer's perpetual daylight. He knew that very soon—in just two months, by mid-October—the skies would go dark and the sun would not return again for 130 days, so every day was critical in building the fort and setting up the weather stations.

They had enough food for a three-year stay, should that be necessary, including nearly thirty thousand rations (a ration being one day's allotment of food for one man) of various meats—including pork and pemmican (a high-calorie mixture of dried meat, melted fat, and often berries), bacon, ham, and mutton—as well as canned salmon, cod, and crabmeat. Greely had brought along some forty thousand rations of beans and rice, plus two thousand pounds of potatoes packed in five-pound cans, and mixed vegetables in two-pound cans, including pickles, onions, and beets. There were preserved peaches, molasses and syrup, canned pork and beef, as well as foods known to thwart scurvy: immense quantities of dried fruits, damsons and other plums, and cranberry sauce. They also brought many casks of rum, whose restorative properties were considered more necessity than luxury.

Greely carefully supervised the unloading of the two hundred scientific instruments, which were of paramount importance. His station would be the northernmost of a network of research stations circumscribing the Arctic. The global effort—which sought to understand everything from brutal weather to the frozen seas to the aurora borealis (northern lights) to magnetic fields—included twelve countries manning fourteen circumpolar stations. The idea had sprung from the revolutionary mind of the Austro-Hungarian Karl Weyprecht, an intrepid explorer and physicist. He had journeyed to the Far East, North America, Mexico, and the West Indies before finally casting his gaze to the Far North, and on a North Pole expedition (1872–74) led by him and fellow Austro-Hungarian officer and explorer Julius von Payer, they'd discovered Franz Joseph Land (named for the Hapsburg emperor Franz Joseph I), a glaciated archipelago of nearly two hundred islands lying off the northern coast of Russia in the Barents Sea.

Weyprecht had died in March 1881 of tuberculosis, and Greely was deeply disappointed that the visionary man would not live to see the outcome of his grand circumpolar idea. But Greely also felt a keen responsibility to carry out his experiments dutifully, so he took interest as Sgt. Edward Israel, the expedition's astronomer and meteorologist, unpacked and cataloged hygrometers, barometers, galvanometers, anemometers, chronometers, magnetometers, and two sets of "Thermometers for Solar Radiation" (tested by Yale University), as well as numerous mercury thermometers. One of the heaviest pieces of scientific equipment was the one-hundred-pound brass cylindrical gravity pendulum. Made by Professor Charles Sanders Peirce of the U.S. Coastal Survey (he was also a respected philosopher, mathematician, and logician), it was designed to measure gravitational forces with great precision.

To do their work Greely and his men would need shelter, and for this purpose he'd brought along a double-walled, prefabricated wooden structure, a lengthy, barrack-like longhouse measuring sixty-five feet long, twenty-one feet wide, and fourteen feet tall. It was the first of its kind. No sooner had Greely chosen the site for the fort than the carpenters launched into work, and within only a few twenty-four-hour shifts, they had the rafters raised and were ready for roofing with tar paper. The double walls of half-inch-thick boards (between which was a foot of airspace for insulation) were coated with extra-heavy tar paper to absorb the sun's rays when there was sun, and to provide further protection against the winter's bitter cold, which would plunge to –75° or even colder.

Greely helped cart the last of the cargo from the *Proteus* and supervised Fort Conger's construction. There would be a number of outbuildings for the storage and use of scientific observation equipment, an astronomical observatory, as well as tarped lean-tos adjoining the fort to house sledges, sledge-building equipment, and supplies for the dog teams. As the tethered dogs yapped, barked, and snarled, Greely listened to the hammering of floorboards and siding, impressed by the carpenters' skill at framing doors and windows, and by other enlisted men's ability to fit out a full kitchen with range, stoves, and a boiler, and to fashion bunk beds, shelving, and even a bathroom with a bathtub. When he told them that it would soon be 75° below zero, they hammered double time. By the last week of August—less than two weeks after their arrival—the fort was nearly completed.*

Some days before, the *Proteus* had attempted to depart, but heavily bunched wind-blown ice in Lady Franklin Bay stopped it near Dutch Island, in view of Fort Conger and a nearby fifteen-hundred-foot rise called Cairn Hill, so named for the cairn and records left there by Nares during his expedition of 1875. The communication method of leaving notes in cairns had become prevalent and trusted among Arctic explorers. Cairn Hill was a convenient promontory from which to scan in all directions, and on a clear day, one could see all the way across the Hall Basin and Robeson Channel to Greenland, some twenty miles

---

* In 1898 the American explorer Robert Peary, during a sledge trip through the region in which he later claimed to have reached the North Pole (the claim is still disputed), suffered severe frostbite that required the amputation of eight toes. He came across Fort Conger and found it in solid shape (though it appeared, he claimed, to have been hastily abandoned). He spent several weeks recovering there, which may well have saved his life. He eventually stayed there a year and a half, using the longhouse built by Greely and his men for shelter as a base for his forays toward the North Pole. Peary also used wood and other materials left by Greely to build a three-hut settlement on the site.

to the east. Knowing the *Proteus* would depart any day, Greely and all his men scribbled last-minute letters to their loved ones and families for Captain Pike to carry back to the United States.

With the fort now livable, Greely mustered his men to impart general orders for the duties and living conditions at Fort Conger. More than six feet tall, thin but wiry strong, Greely was a stern and commanding presence, his eyes—framed by his spectacles—intelligent and fierce. His voice resounded with firmness of purpose; his words were clear and definite. When pensive, or when balancing on the cusp of a major decision, he'd pull at the tip of his long, bushy, pointed black beard. Though this was his first Arctic exploration, he'd experienced the battlefields of the Civil War and the American Southwest, where in the early to mid-1870s he'd worked in Indian country for the Signal Corps as the country's top meteorologist, building immense strings of telegraph lines. Once, in the badlands of the Dakota Territory, stuck in a blizzard and almost buried by deep snow, he'd spent three days huddled under a wagon wrapped only in a thin canvas blanket, the howling winds preventing him from starting a fire. He'd survived, and when the storm cleared, he had made his way back to the Powder River and continued inspecting the lines: He got the job done.

Now Greely surveyed his mustered corps. To call them unconventional for such a mission would be a gross understatement. For starters, they were army instead of navy, unusual for nautical duty. But they were under the direction of the U.S. Department of War, and since most of the men were from various branches of the army—either Signal Corps, Cavalry, or Infantry—he was confident in their abilities to follow orders. The problem was that Greely had no nautical experience either. But as with everything he'd ever done, he believed that his preparation and ability to adapt on the fly would be enough. It always had been.

He'd known his second in command, Lt. Frederick Kislingbury, since 1874, when the lieutenant had assisted him building telegraph lines across the southwestern plains. Kislingbury had heard about the Arctic expedition and written Greely a persuasive letter, citing his willingness to learn, his endurance and patience, and his ability to lead troops through hardships. Kislingbury was a deadeye with a rifle, which would be useful. Early on, however, Greely noted that Kislingbury was prone to melancholy, and that he had the annoying habit of preening, combing his mustache constantly, sometimes a half dozen times a day. Such dedicated grooming struck Greely as overly concerned with self-image, which wouldn't do him a lot of good up here.

Lt. James B. Lockwood was nearly thirty, a well-trained career officer who came from a distinguished military family. His father, Henry Hayes Lockwood, had risen to the rank of general during the Civil War. James Lockwood was tough, ready, able, and possessed a biting humor that was useful for breaking tension during difficult times. He was dutiful, fit, and came highly recommended.

Dr. Octave Pavy, the surgeon whom Greely had signed at Godhavn, Greenland, for one hundred dollars a month, was a Louisiana Creole, born in New Orleans to a French plantation owner. He'd studied medicine, as well as painting and sculpture, at the University of Paris, and he perpetually smoked a pipe, running his hand over his broad, high forehead as he slicked back his hair. He'd once conceived of a scientific North Pole expedition with the French explorer Gustave Lambert, but the Franco-Prussian War—in which both Pavy and Lambert served—squelched that plan when Lambert died in battle in 1871. After returning to the United States, Pavy remained fascinated by the Arctic, and had signed on to American captain Henry Howgate's ill-fated colonization mission of 1880 and had remained in the North to continue his scientific studies after Howgate's damaged ship, the *Gulnare*, was forced to return home. Pavy's understanding of Arctic history and lore was matched only by Greely's, and he was the only man among them—other than the Greenlanders, Jens and Fred—who'd spent any time in the frozen North. Greely hoped he'd be able to manage the Frenchman's ego and arrogance.

The Greenlanders, Jens and Fred, were remarkably able, serving as sledge drivers, hunters, fishermen, and scientific assistants. They did their work with a whistle and a smile, chatting in their native Inuit language with each other and Pavy. They were tough and compliant, though somewhat given to moodiness. Still, Greely expected a great deal from these young men and would rely on their local knowledge as much as he could in all manner of work and exploration. Along with Pvt. Roderick Schneider as an assistant, they were generally in charge of the sled dogs.

Of the nineteen enlisted men, the highest-ranked noncommissioned man was Sgt. David L. Brainard, whom Greely had entrusted as supply chief, though in this outfit, men were expected to wear many hats. Only twenty-four years old, physically fit and dashing—with a well-trimmed handlebar mustache and piercing eyes—Brainard had been wounded in the Montana Territory in the Battle of Little Muddy Creek in 1877 (part of the Great Sioux War of 1876–77), suffering gunshot wounds to his right hand and right cheek. He had also fought in the Nez Percé and Bannock Wars under then-colonel Nelson A. Miles—who would go on to chase Sitting Bull all the way to the Canadian border and later be instrumental in hunting down, and ultimately bringing in, the Apache legend Geronimo. Brainard's youth and wry sense of humor belied his war-hardened toughness, and Greely intended to exploit the man's evident grit.

Four civilian specialists had signed on and were now standing at attention, noncommissioned officers chosen for their particular expertise. Sgt. William Cross, who wore a beard as long and bushy—but not quite as pointy—as Greely's, was a machinist at the Washington Navy Yard who'd enlisted as engineer of the expedition's steam launch. The expedition photographer was Sgt. George W. Rice, a young, energetic, and highly educated Nova Scotian. He spoke and read French and had enrolled to study law at Columbia University in New York when he volunteered for the Lady Franklin Bay Expedition. He had garnered an assignment from *The New York Herald* to write about and photograph his Arctic experiences, but he was equally driven by the opportunity to become the first Canadian to photograph the high northern region.

Greely beamed when he looked on the face of the brassy, beardless, twenty-two-year-old Sgt. Edward Israel. He admired his pluck. The youngest of the expedition, Israel had been a senior at the University of Michigan when his astronomy professor recommended him for the journey. Near him stood Winfield Jewell, a robust and seasoned former member of the Signal Corps who'd spent a winter atop freezing Mount Washington in New Hampshire, known for some of the most brutal weather in the East. He'd be the chief meteorologist. Jewell was assigned two assistants, Sergeants Ralston and Gardiner.

The rest of the crew were men recently recruited from the American frontier. Cavalrymen and foot soldiers toughened by the plains, they came recommended to Greely for their hardiness, their skills in carpentry and mechanics, and their willingness to endure long hours—or more likely days on end—without complaint. They were men built for and inured to living afield.

At ease, men—but not too much ease.

Greely outlined specific duties and strict orders for everyone. The scientists were to take detailed readings and measurements, documenting as many as five hundred per day including temperature, wind speeds, barometric pressure, gravitational forces, tidal observations, ice depths, and other meteorological work that only Israel and Greely fully understood. Others were broken into teams and assigned various projects that included digging coal from the rich seam four miles from Fort Conger, scouting and charting the regions in the vicinity of Discovery Bay and its environs, and trail cutting in the immediate vicinity of the fort. Some men, like Kislingbury, who was an excellent rifle shot, were sent out hunting.

Jens and Fred continued to work with the dogs, and Greely attempted a few trips with teams and sledges, but on the advice of the Greenlanders he halted sledge work for a few months until the entire area would be snow covered and frozen. The "young ice" of the frozen sea was particularly dangerous before it froze solid, being thin, breakable, and, as Greely observed, "covered with a moist, saline efflorescence, beautiful to the eye, but which binds and impedes the passage of a sledge much the same as wet sand checks the movement of an engine on the rails." This problem, coupled with the danger of breaking through the young ice and either drowning or becoming severely frostbitten, persuaded him to send scouting parties out on foot instead. Greely dispatched Lockwood and two others on a two-day trek inland to the area around St. Patrick Bay. They encountered small musk-ox herds in valleys rimmed by sheer cliffs higher than one thousand feet. There was a narrow gulch cutting through the cliffs, which Lockwood suggested he explore later in the autumn.

Doctor Pavy and Sergeant Rice were sent scouting to the north, with instructions to go as far as they could toward Cape Joseph Henry, around a brawny headland on the uppermost end of Ellesmere Island along the shores of the Lincoln Sea. They would search for any signs or traces of the missing steamship *Jeannette*, which had sailed from San Francisco in July 1879, captained by navy man George W. De Long. De Long's plan—supported and financed by the gallivanting and wealthy *New York Herald* publisher James Gordon Bennett, Jr.—had been to sail through the Bering Strait and follow the warm, north-flowing Pacific Current—known as the Kuroshio, Japanese for "Black Current"—all the way to the North Pole. But the *Jeannette* remained missing. Last seen by American Arctic whalers, the steamship had belched plumes of black smoke as it was engulfed by mist and fog near Herald Island, off Russia's northeastern coast. Pavy and Rice found no sign of the *Jeannette*, but Rice broke through ice and froze his foot, suffering the first severe frostbite of the expedition. With Doctor Pavy's medical aid, however, Rice recovered quickly.

The bunkhouse stood as a beacon of life and safety on that scrubby plateau. Inside its sturdy walls Fort Conger was well ordered and functional, with the four officers sharing a room, heated by a potbellied stove, at one end of the long dwelling. Greely's quarters were comfortably fitted out with a bed—which sat atop an ammunition chest that doubled as a clothes dresser—a rocking chair, and a small library with the hundreds of books, charts, maps, and exploration logs he'd brought along. He devoted much time to these, studying and contemplating. On the wall he hung an American flag that Henrietta had sewn for him or one of his men to unfurl and fly should they, God willing, reach Farthest North or the North Pole. Here, staining his fingers with ink late into the night—the ink often freezing at the tip of his pen—Greely wrote long letters to Henrietta and his young girls, Antoinette and Adola.

Next to the officers' quarters, a hall led to both the kitchen and outdoors. In the middle of the building was a washroom that also served as a workroom for charting scientific observations. The enlisted men slept in two-tiered bunks along the walls, which took up much of the remaining room of the longhouse. Mess tables stretched in a long line down the center of the barracks. A large coal stove spat and crackled in the main area.

∽∽∽

Because of the close proximity of the men—and especially that of the officers, who shared a room—Greely had ample time to speak with and observe them. Since their arrival, he had noticed that Lieutenant Kislingbury routinely missed the mandatory 7:30 a.m. call for breakfast. The man had been a half hour late three days in a row, at first merely holding up breakfast, but a few times he had missed it entirely, sleeping past 9:00 a.m., then slinking in, eating quickly, and retiring to bed until dinner. It seemed unusual behavior to Greely, and Kislingbury was alone among them in these habits and practices. On a couple of occasions he'd boarded the *Proteus*, which still lay trapped by ice in the harbor, and retired to a stateroom, where Greely learned that he spent hours penning long letters.

Greely wrote letters, too, but he reasoned that officers must rise for breakfast at the same time as the enlisted men. Officers were duty bound to present a good example to the men. Greely said as much, taking Kislingbury aside and giving him a firm dressing-down. It didn't matter whether he ate breakfast—he simply had to be up and assembled with everyone else; this was an order. Greely firmly reminded the second lieutenant that orders must be obeyed by everyone. Kislingbury argued bitterly that it made no sense that officers be forced to rise at the same time as the men. Greely eyed him hard, then said calmly but with an edge that if he couldn't follow commands, perhaps he should resign his post and depart with the *Proteus*. He would tolerate no disobedience. With that, Kislingbury stormed off in anger.

Greely pondered what to do. He felt sorry for Kislingbury. He knew the man was troubled. Kislingbury had first written to him from the Dakota Territory, where he was stationed, practically begging to go. He was distraught, pleading to be allowed to come along as a salve against his recent griefs. He had lost two wives and a sister to epidemics within three years and was left alone to care for four young boys. Evidently his family would take the boys in his absence—they'd be looked after. He'd written that to go would be hard, and he'd miss his children terribly, but that "my children will love me better when I return and will be proud of the father who dared to brave the dangers we have read about of a sojourn in the Arctic regions." Greely had taken a chance on him, convinced by Kislingbury's heartfelt appeal that the expedition would be "a godsend for me now, a chance to wear out my terrible sorrow."

But instead of easing his anguish, the stark barrenness of this place seemed to have driven Lieutenant Kislingbury further into darkness. When Greely reprimanded him for sleeping late and missing breakfast, Kislingbury slunk back to the stateroom on the *Proteus* and wrote a letter stating that he felt Greely had no confidence in him and his abilities, and continuing: "The only thing I feel left for me to do is be asked to be relieved from duty." He asked Doctor Pavy to deliver the letter to Greely.

Greely was in a tough spot. His resources at the outpost were limited, and not only was Kislingbury a fine marksman who would be a useful and productive hunter, he was scrappy and relished the rigors of difficult fieldwork. But if the man was going to balk at orders, well, that wouldn't do. It boded poorly. After dinner on August 26, Greely assembled Pavy and Lockwood some distance from the longhouse to witness a formal meeting with Kislingbury. Greely read Kislingbury's entire letter aloud. He gave the second lieutenant a chance to stay, on the condition that he obey all orders and with a good attitude.

But Kislingbury wanted to go. So that was that. Greely drafted an official order, stating: "Lieutenant F. Kislingbury, 11th Infantry, acting signal officer, is at his own request relieved from his duty as a member of this Expedition, returning by the steamship *Proteus* to St. John's, Newfoundland, will report without delay to the CSO of the Army, Washington, D.C."

That evening Kislingbury eyed the steaming stacks of the *Proteus* and packed quickly. It was around seven o'clock. For the last six days the *Proteus* had remained icebound, sitting at anchor between Fort Conger and Dutch Island, two miles distant. Kislingbury requested and was granted the assistance of two men to help carry his bags and gear down the broken ground to the hummocked ice foot along the shore. But as they made their way over the jumbled ground, slowed by all the trunks and boxes, Kislingbury heard a freight-train-like belch and chuff, and saw thick black plumes of smoke rising from the funnel of the *Proteus* as it spewed boiler steam. Captain Pike, having spotted a worthy lead—a dark seam between ice floes that ran like a river—was picking up speed and racing for it.

Kislingbury broke into a run, sprinting down the shoreline and the ragged ice foot, where sea converged with land. The two men helping could not keep up, so they dropped the bags and crates and ascended through the boulders of Cairn Hill to get a better view. Kislingbury became a small figure in the distance, yelling out, his voice absorbed by the vast expanse, his arms little windmills flailing wildly as he desperately tried to hail the ship. But the *Proteus* was at full steam now, running hard out of the pack, cleaving through the ice and bearing toward Kennedy Channel.

As a cold wind hammered their rocky outcrop, the men stared at the horizon, watching the steamer run northeastward and then vanish beyond Distant Cape a few miles away. For a time they saw nothing, neither ship nor man, until finally they spotted a lone figure stumbling awkwardly toward them, moving over the craggy ground alongshore, dragging his bags slowly back to the fort.

The *Proteus* steaming away from Fort Conger, leaving Lieutenant Kislingbury behind. *(G. W. Rice, photographer / Library of Congress)*

3

Preparing for Darkness

It is the unknown which awes and terrifies.
—*Adolphus Greely, Three Years of Arctic Service*

As Kislingbury staggered back to the station, despondent and forlorn, Greely knew he now faced an uncomfortable conundrum. He had a persona non grata in the midst of his men. Always efficient and thorough, Greely immediately redrafted Lieutenant Kislingbury's orders, modifying them to state that he "should not be considered a member of this expeditionary force but as temporarily at this station awaiting transportation." The lieutenant could give no orders to any of the men, and was essentially relegated to the status of a guest—one who was, in Greely's words, to "proceed from this place to St. John's by the first visiting steamship."

Like it or not, Kislingbury would be with the expedition for the next year at least, when a resupply ship was scheduled to return the following summer. He would try to make the best of it, and perhaps, he figured, if he made himself useful hunting, he could win his way back into Greely's good graces and Greely would revoke the order and reinstate him to active duty.

On August 28, a Sunday, Greely called for the first day off since their arrival. His thinking was that despite their being cut off from the rest of the world, some semblance of civil society should prevail. There would be no work or games on Sundays. Every Sunday morning the Sabbath would be observed by everyone, unless they had religious differences that prevented them from hearing him read Psalms. After formal services the men were free to go hunting or tramping around the station as they wished. Such diversion every week, Greely believed, would "provide a break in the monotony of our life, and thus be conducive both to mental and physical health."

In the evenings Greely retired to his quarters in the longhouse to study maps and charts of the region and to read and reread his orders and plans for their proposed two-year stay, as well as the planned relief missions. He'd sent written copies of these orders and relief plans back to Washington with Captain Pike on the *Proteus*, and they were all based on conversations he'd had with his military commanders and the chief security officer before departure. But still, it was good to be overprepared and to have a sense of clarity in a mission.

The plan scheduled relief-resupply ships for the summers of 1882 and 1883. As a contingency, should the first fail for any reason to reach Fort Conger, it was to cache supplies and correspondence on the northeast coast of Ellesmere Island, and also to establish a depot of cached food rations on Littleton Island, off the west coast of Greenland. If the second, 1883, relief ship failed to make it all the way to Fort Conger, it was instructed to land all of its stores and provisions as well as a relief party of men at Littleton Island, and to be fully prepared for a winter's stay. In the event that no relief arrived by the end of the second summer, Greely would depart with his men and head south, using the motorized launch the *Lady Greely* and three whaleboats, plus a dinghy. They would retreat, scouring the shores, hoping to find food caches or relief ships and men along the coast of Ellesmere Island as far south as Cape Sabine, or at Littleton Island, both some 250 miles south of Fort Conger. He'd gone over it multiple times, and it seemed a well-reasoned plan, allowing for multiple contingencies. Greely was a man who liked clearly written and adhered-to contingency plans. Their absence might result in disorder—even anarchy and death.

Comfortable in his corner quarters at his desk, Greely pored over and contemplated the charts and reports of the difficult Nares Expedition of 1875–76. The British explorer Sir George Strong Nares had been the first person to navigate successfully through the narrows between northern Ellesmere Island and northern Greenland (the channel was subsequently named the Nares Strait) to the Lincoln Sea. On the *Alert*, Nares had reached 82°N but foundered, was beset in pack ice, and forced to winter aboard the ship. Many of his men suffered from scurvy, but when the ice broke up the following summer, Nares was able to make a successful retreat. They'd left some caches and depots in the area, which Greely had encountered, and some detailed records of the region, though most of these were limited to the coastline. Now, before the winter darkness set in, Greely wanted to continue his explorations of the interior, going to places where no man had been before.

Another rationale for the autumn forays was to set up food and equipment caches and depots of his own, for use in the spring when even-more-ambitious exploring would be possible, with nearly twenty-four-hour daylight and frozen waters for good sledging. Caches of food and equipment were explorers' lifelines, gifts left from prior expeditions that could invigorate, sustain, and keep them alive. Greely well knew the history and lore of the Arctic; he'd read everything ever written and published, and he reread the considerable volumes—his Arctic library—he'd brought along. Two things stuck in his mind: One was that during the Nares Expedition, a sledging party commanded by Albert Hastings Markham had set a new record of Farthest North, making it to 83°20′26″N, as close to the North Pole as any man had ever been. This mark sustained English dominance of a record they'd now held for three centuries, and though Greely's men didn't know it just yet, he intended to break it. They were here for science, yes, but national pride burned in Greely as deeply as in any man alive, and he'd go as far as he needed to go—all the way to the North Pole—to garner laurels for his country and for himself.

And, should he or any of his men reach the North Pole and live to tell of it, he would have new scientific information for the world as well. The mysteries and theories about that uncharted place had swirled for centuries. The beliefs held—and there were numerous speculative maps, from those of the Flemish cartographer Gerardus Mercator, published in 1595, to that of the American naval officer Silas Bent, of 1872—that the top of the world was open, with warm and navigable waters, the so-called Open Polar Sea. The idea was that a thick ring of ice rimmed the pole, but if it could just be broken through by a powerful ship with a reinforced hull, it would be clear sailing to the top of the world. Some maps even showed it to be a tropical paradise there, complete with palm trees. Such tantalizing, if wildly imaginative, ideas had led many explorers— including most recently George De Long aboard the *Jeannette*—on epic quests in search of this Arctic grail. Greely knew from Nares's logs and reports of less than a decade before that at least as far as 83°N, ice still prevailed, and Markham had found a frozen polar sea rather than an open one. But beyond that, no one really knew for sure.

Throughout September and early October, Greely dispatched men on foot, as well as with dogs and sledges, and in boats when open leads allowed, in all directions from Fort Conger. A number of these were targeted to the north, along the coast of the Robeson Channel. Lockwood established a cache to the north, near Cape Murchison, which they called Depot A. Later Lockwood and five men, hauling about 150 pounds per man, set up Depot B at Cape Beechy, some twenty miles north of Fort Conger. Rice followed behind, bringing more supplies and food to cache. Between them, Lockwood and Rice were gaining valuable experience in sledging.

Pavy and Rice went even farther north, past Wrangel Bay to Lincoln Bay. They bore heavy packs and tents through rugged inland valleys and past small lakes filled with small fish called Arctic char. At Lincoln Bay, about thirty miles from the fort, they discovered an English cache; some of it was in disarray, torn apart by polar bears and strewn by violent winds. But they also found nearly one thousand rations of "beef, curry paste, onion powder and matches in perfect condition." During this long journey Rice buckled over, disabled by an attack of what Pavy diagnosed as "acute rheumatism." Snow fell, and the temperatures dropped to 17°. Rice was unable to proceed, so Pavy set up a tent, got him into a sleeping bag, and, leaving him with food and water, struck out for Fort Conger. On Pavy's arrival Greely sent Brainard and ten men to assist Rice. Brainard found him shivering and sick, "his legs swollen to double size," but revived him with "hot coffee, sauterne wine, and the needful medicines to make him comfortable." The relief party wrapped him in thick buffalo robes and placed him in a makeshift stretcher made from a sled. Working together, they descended steep cliffs and eventually arrived safely back at Fort Conger, where within ten days Rice was fully recovered and eager to return to the field.

The hunters, including Jens, Fred, and Kislingbury, had tremendous success. Musk-oxen were plentiful, as were ptarmigan, though these birds' plumage turned white with the arriving snows, making them nearly impossible to spot against the white backdrop. Many of the bird species began to depart for the south as it turned colder, but by early October 1881, the expedition had taken, skinned, and dressed "twenty-six musk-oxen, ten ducks, a hare, two seal, and a ptarmigan." They hung the musk-oxen from large wooden game stands resembling tepee frames. In all, they were able to put up for winter an astounding six thousand pounds of fresh meat, as well as plenty of scrap meat and offal for the dogs.

Despite the initial awkwardness with Kislingbury, the men were working well together, and Greely was pleased with their efforts. There had been some minor injuries—including one involving the commander himself, when he tripped moving across a scree slope of loose rocks, and badly twisted his knee, which took a few weeks to heal. Both Lockwood and Rice had experienced minor frostbite from breaking through ice and freezing their feet, and the party was learning to take great care to avoid becoming soaked in the cold conditions, which could be deadly. The autumn forays had in the main been successful, exceeding Greely's hopes: "Four depots had been established to the northward," he wrote, "the condition of the [Nares] stores at Lincoln Bay ascertained, points previously unknown reached toward the interior, over three tons of fresh meat obtained by the hunt." Additionally they'd learned much about the sledging conditions and the various other equipment, information that would be highly valuable come spring. They'd hauled tons of coal from the nearby seam, and the finished longhouse offered warmth, comfort, and safety in this stark and forbidding place.

But in the waning light of early October, during which time Greely noted that "the sun shines but little, and feebly," they had their first encounters with wolves. A large band of nearly twenty—it was hard to count them in the low light against the dusky hillsides—appeared one evening very near the house. Their gaunt forms slunk nearby, moving like ghosts through the Arctic fog. Some of them, according to Greely, "appeared to be as large as calves." The pack came silently, then disappeared as one into the mist, the echoes of their distant howls the only trace left of them. Jens and Fred watched the sled dogs carefully, worried they'd be attacked.

One evening Jens and Cpl. Joseph Elison—at just five feet four one of the shortest men on the expedition—were taking some readings at the observation hut. Located about one hundred yards from the house at the end of a winding trail, it was a small, roofed wooden structure housing scientific instruments that were monitored and recorded numerous times each day, these duties divided equally between the men. They scribbled entries into notebooks, including relative humidity, temperature, and wind speed, also noting that the ground around the fort was covered with about three inches of crusty snow. As they finished their work and headed for the rear entry of the main house, they heard the dogs barking aggressively. Jens went ahead, trying to hush the dogs, when, from out of the twilight, a wolf leaped from an overhanging rock and took him down. Jens was carrying his bolt-action rifle, and as he tried to fight off the wolf with it, two more wolves attacked, tearing at his legs with their fangs. Jens fired a wild round as he struggled, smashing at one wolf with the rifle butt. Quickly and instinctively, as a wolf bit him through his parka hood, Jens worked the bolt, chambered another bullet, and blew a round into the snarling animal.

Elison was some yards behind, fighting off three other wolves that had knocked him to the ground and were tearing at his neck and shoulders. At the explosive report of the second gunshot, all the wolves scattered, and men came running from the barracks at the commotion and gunfire. They assisted Jens and Elison inside, stepping warily past the mangy dead wolf on the snow just near the house. Doctor Pavy had Jens and Elison remove their heavy fur clothing and found them cut and bruised around the legs and neck but otherwise uninjured—though obviously traumatized. The thickness of their clothing and Jens's quick action with the rifle had likely saved their lives.

After that encounter Greely sent Kislingbury out to follow the wolves' tracks and blood signs in the snow, and the lieutenant fired on and brought down one more wolf with his rifle. But the pack was stealthy, and few individuals ever came into rifle range again. So Greely, concerned for his men as well as the dogs, laid out poisoned meat, hoping to destroy as many of the rogue pack as he could. But they were intelligent and wary, and despite their hunger they showed "much craft and caution in approaching the poisoned meat, and would touch none." Greely experimented with various poisons and added portions of good meat along with the poisoned, "and eventually four wolves and a fox were poisoned, and the rest disappeared for that season at least."

By early October 1881 there was so little sunlight that lamps were required indoors. Greely ordered the men to practice a detailed and organized fire drill, which could mean their very survival given their remoteness. Back in September they'd had a close call when the large hospital tent, which doubled as a toolshed and carpenter's shop, caught fire. Men scrambled to douse the flames with water and fire extinguishers, but their efforts failed, and the tent and its contents burned to the ground. The smoldering heap prompted Greely to institute regular fire drills, and to divide and separate stores and pieces of equipment widely around the encampment, so that a single fire could not destroy everything at once.

During the first weeks of October, leading up to the darkness, Greely ordered teams to bank and wall up the longhouse as further protection and insulation against the coming winter, which he knew from explorers' journals to be much harsher than any winters any of the men had ever experienced. About a three-foot distance from the house, the men built a six-foot-high wall of ice by cutting and stacking blocks, then coating them with wetter snow, which served to seal the wall. In the space between the ice wall and the house, they shoveled dry, looser snow and dirt as an insulating layer.

None of the men, including the Greenlanders, had ever spent a winter this far north, so none knew exactly what to expect. Lieutenant Kislingbury, sipping on his daily one-ounce issue of lime juice to thwart scurvy, sat at a desk in the captain's quarters and read over a letter he'd written to his sons. He told the boys he was so far north that the ice was everywhere, and he'd even spotted Santa Claus, and that he'd made a deal that Santa deliver gifts to them. Then he got serious, adding: "Papa has but one thing he dreads, and that is *the long night* . . . 130 days of darkness will be trying."

The long night. The continuous darkness had driven some Arctic explorers to madness. Greely knew he must guard against that at all costs. He must keep the men busy to stave off boredom and depression and perhaps even insanity. Having never experienced an Arctic winter, Greely wrote: "It is the unknown which awes and terrifies."

On October 14 just after midday, most of the men assembled outside to get one last glimpse of the sun. There was a silent restlessness moving through them, a low current of unease. Greely strode to the top of a hill just north of the longhouse to watch for one last appearance. He stood quiet and alone for some time, then saw a few beams bursting through the cloud cover and gleaming atop the Hogback's snow-covered summit. He watched, awestruck, as the moving clouds, lit by the sun, seemed to catch fire with bursts of orange and red. And for a moment the orange-red rays touched down, lighting up the outer bay and the harbor, intensified by the "rosy, curling columns of vapor rising in the dense, cold air." Then, as quickly as the rays had come, they transformed into a gloom that unfurled across the landscape like a flat, lead-colored gray blanket. The sun was gone, giving way to "the long night," the polar effect of perpetual twilight.

Lieutenant Greely's corner quarters at Fort Conger. *(Library of Congress)*

Arctic wolf that attacked the men at Fort Conger. *(G. W. Rice, photographer / Library of Congress)*

Dr. Octave Pavy and Greenlander Jens skinning a seal. *(G. W. Rice, photographer / Library of Congress)*

Musk-ox near Fort Conger. *(G. W. Rice, photographer / Library of Congress)*

4

The Long Night

The monotony of the Arctic night produces
strange effects on white men.
—David L. Brainard, *The Outpost of the Lost*

At first Greely was glad that the sun had finally gone. Just as when the *Proteus* finally sailed away, it gave their situation a kind of definitiveness, leaving them without looming expectations.

As the temperatures plunged to an average of –24° in November, Greely continued to send out a few sledging parties. Pavy and a pair of dog sledge teams added to the stores of Depot C at Wrangel Bay, and Lockwood, along with eight men, made an unsuccessful attempt to cross the Robeson Channel at Cape Beechy. He returned within a week, reporting that the water there was not completely frozen, and therefore impassable by sledge.

Within three weeks of the sun's departure, Greely stopped all lengthy excursions, and the men settled in at Fort Conger for the winter. The scientific readings and measurements would proceed daily, with ten readings hourly recorded at the "observers' hut." Another hut had been built nearby to record air pressure, dew point and temperature, the speed and direction of the wind, as well as auroral activity. One difficult job was mounting an anemometer and self-registering thermometer on the summit of Mount Campbell, which rose to 2,100 feet above the sea on neighboring Bellot Island.

Assisted by Lockwood, Greely also instituted a triweekly school, with regular courses in mathematics, English grammar and spelling, and geography, as well as meteorology. Greely gave readings and lectures on a multitude of subjects, including storm cycles, the nature of magnetism, and the history of polar explorations, as well as personal recollections of the Civil War. Doctor Pavy was invited to speak, and although he had war tales of his own, the commander urged him to talk primarily on medical subjects. Pavy also taught French to a few of the men.

Another amusing diversion was the creation by Lockwood—with the editorial assistance of Sergeant Rice and Private Henry—of a biweekly newspaper titled *Arctic Moon*, whose purpose was to be "a guide by day and a light by night that will shine for the public good." The paper was hectographed (using a gelatin duplicator, or "jellygraph") and distributed as being written by "the finest minds of the country." It contained comical, serious, and maudlin articles, which the men found to be a great amusement. They also played numerous games, including checkers and cards, and engaged in heated debates on any and all topics, ranging from the philosophical to the mundane, including which fire department was better, New York's or Chicago's. Someone even created an Anti-Swearing Society, complete with a recording secretary, that imposed a penalty of extra chores and duties for every curse word recorded.

Although the polar winter was devoid of sun, it was not devoid of light. Every two weeks the men were transfixed by the appearance of the magical northern lights, or aurora borealis, a phenomenon of bright and sometimes dancing lights that result from collisions between gaseous particles in the Earth's atmosphere with charged particles released from the sun's atmosphere. The men witnessed many variations in color, due to the types of colliding particles. Greely noted displays that were "grand and magnificent in the extreme," including "lances of white light, having perhaps a faint tinge of golden or citron color, which appeared as moving shafts or spears," and one that looked like "a pillar of glowing fire, from horizon to horizon through the zenith, showing at times a decidedly rosy tint, and later a Nile-green color." Sometimes while watching this spectacle, men would see the ghostly outline of polar bears traversing the shore and the ice foot, and Greely was reminded of the wolf attack. The men would need to be always alert, for danger lurked everywhere.

On November 10, 1881, Corporal Elison ran screaming from the newly built carpenter's tent and outside into the –32° temperature, his hair, eyebrows, and beard on fire. He'd been filling a gasoline lamp before it had been properly extinguished, and the lamp burst into flames, igniting the tent, some of its contents, and Elison himself. Luckily the men in the longhouse heard his cries and followed their fire drill to the letter, first dousing Elison and then the tent with extinguishers, then smothering the flames inside with blankets. Some contents of the carpenter's tent were destroyed, but fortunately none of the men who responded got frostbite, though it was dangerously cold, and they retreated quickly back to the main house. Despite losing his eyebrows, beard, and part of his hair, Elison was no worse for wear, though after the fire and the recent wolf attack, he was somewhat shaken.

The first Thanksgiving at Fort Conger proved memorable indeed. After being mostly fort-bound for weeks, Greely organized a series of races, contests, and competitions. All the men participated in one way or another, either as contestants, judges, or coaches. Illuminated all day by a series of auroral streamers of fluctuating brilliance, the men competed in snowshoe races, footraces, sled-dog races, and finally, a shooting competition. The snowshoe race measured four hundred yards, and although Private Henry had a good lead at one hundred yards, he was a big man of over two hundred pounds, and the distance proved too great. Sergeant Brainard passed him easily, crossing the line first, with Ralston and Gardiner right on his heels.

Jens and Fred each took a team of seven dogs and raced from the fort to Dutch Island and back, a round-trip distance of about four miles, which Fred won handily. The one-hundred-yard dash resulted in a three-way tie, with Private Ellis prevailing in the runoff. Later in the afternoon Greely orchestrated a very original shooting competition by placing a lighted candle in a box at twenty-five yards' distance, the candle illuminating a target inside the box. Jens and Sergeant Cross both shot well, but Private Henry stunned everyone by shooting fifteen out of a possible fifteen. He was declared the clear victor, and the games concluded as it was dinnertime.

To enhance morale Greely took great care to make celebrations like birthdays and holidays special for the men. A birthday celebrant was exempt from duties that day and could choose the dinner that evening from the entire store of foods and desserts, which were considerable. The celebrant was also allotted a quart of rum, and it became the tradition to pass it around, sharing the spoils with all the men. As they'd arrived by a large and powerful steamship, their original food stores were remarkably varied and delectable, so the first Thanksgiving menu was elaborate, as follows: "Oyster soup, salmon, ham, eider ducks, devilled crab, lobster-salad, asparagus, green corn, several kinds of cake and ice-cream, dates, figs, and nuts." Greely and the other officers sipped Sauternes from his private supply, and he gave "a moderate amount of rum . . . to the men in the evening, which contributed much to the merriment of the day." During the meal, prizes were distributed to the winners of the day's events, and the evening concluded with concertina and violin music and singing.

The levity and joy of Thanksgiving were tempered late in the month by the expedition's first serious injury. On November 30, Sergeant Gardiner was on duty making tidal observations. In recent days this task had proved bitingly cold and difficult, for the slope leading down to the tidal gauge was steep and icy. Descending by lantern light, with the ice floes in the bay beyond grinding and thundering against one another, Gardiner slipped and fell, tumbling down the frozen trail and breaking his left leg. Doctor Pavy set the break, and Private Biederbick, who often served as Pavy's nurse and assistant, attended to Gardiner well. Gardiner was laid up for a couple of months, but eventually the bone knit and healed well.

The festivities of Thanksgiving gave way to a period of dark doldrums, and between then and Christmas, Greely began to notice a number of the party succumbing to the weight of monotony—the seemingly interminable sameness of things. Trivial arguments sparked up and flamed into full-blown shouting matches. Some men were constantly touchy and irritable, and others completely lost their appetites, becoming lethargic, not wanting to rise from bed. At this time Brainard noted in his journal: "The effect on the men of the continued darkness is very apparent. Many of them are depressed, while others growl for slight, if any reason."

The monotony produced "strange effects" on the Greenlanders as well. On the morning of December 13, snow fell from foreboding, black skies. When Jens failed to show up for breakfast, Greely immediately grew concerned. Private Long had seen Jens washing up, but no one had seen him since. For the last few days Greely had noticed that both Jens and Eskimo Fred were uneasy and restless, and he spoke to them both individually, as he put it, "to restore these Greenlanders to a cheerful mental condition." Greely knew that Jens had a wife and three children at home, and he might well have been homesick—that was understandable, and Greely felt the same pangs daily for his dear Henrietta and their girls. Greely had showed Jens pictures of his own daughters, Antoinette and Adola, to illustrate that he was also a father who missed his family. He had also given Jens some treats of nuts, figs, and tobacco to try to cheer him up, but nothing seemed to work. Jens still said he felt "bad, no good."

Sergeants Brainard and Rice, using lanterns, struck out and walked in a half mile semicircle—Brainard north of the fort and Rice to the south. Jens's tracks were found in the snow heading southward toward Dutch Island and the Robeson Channel. Brainard, Rice, and Private Whisler went together and followed the tracks while Doctor Pavy rigged up a sledge and a dog team and sped off after them.

The going was difficult in the dark, especially near the ice foot of the Robeson Channel. Here the undulating ice of the direct shoreline was punctuated by enormous masses of pressed-up ice, frozen boulders and knobs that were driven and packed into the shore by giant ice floes pushed by winds and currents. Huge formations—some dangling icicles that hung like great frozen stalactites—made travel treacherous. About six miles from the fort, Rice tripped over buckled ground and slammed down hard onto a jagged slab of ice. Knocked briefly unconscious by the fall, when he came to he realized that the others in the sledge were far ahead, and his right shoulder was severely injured; he couldn't lift his arm. It must have been either dislocated or broken, Rice figured. He hurried as best he could, following the sledge-runner tracks under dim candlelight and finally caught up with Pavy, Whisler, and the dogs.

Doctor Pavy wrapped Rice's damaged arm in a sling and sent him back under the care of Private Whisler, while he and Brainard continued chasing after Jens. What Pavy failed to notice was that in his zeal to help pursue Jens, Whisler had left the fort without the proper clothing. At first Whisler helped Rice along, supporting him as they stumbled and groped through the freezing darkness, the temperatures plunging to –30°. It was very slow travel, and by the time they reached Distant Cape—still more than ten miles from Fort Conger— Whisler began to complain of extreme cold. Rice recalled: "He began to talk incoherently, and by the time we were halfway to Dutch Island, he was delirious." Whisler flopped down onto the ice and said he would go no farther.

Meanwhile, Brainard and Pavy had kept following Jens's tracks, moving relatively fast with the dogs. About five more miles around the coast toward the northeast, a half mile from Cape Murchison, Brainard saw a slight figure trudging along through the darkness. He called out to Jens, with Pavy translating that they meant no harm. Jens was silent, sullen, and offered no explanation for why he'd wandered off. Reluctantly, with some coaxing and assurances from Pavy and Brainard, he agreed to return to Fort Conger.

Ahead of them, Rice and Whisler struggled through their own ordeal. Rice, who'd originally needed Whisler's assistance to walk, was now the one guiding Whisler back toward the fort. Cold winds lashed snow at their faces, and Whisler stumbled and fell, babbling gibberish.

"He was continually falling down and could hardly resist the temptation to remain on the ice," Rice remembered. "I attempted to lead him, and having no light, our footing was so uncertain that I was continually jarred by missteps which caused me to suffer intensely from my shoulder. I had to cajole, coax and command Whisler at every step to get him along. I began to fear for his life."

By great good fortune, Pavy, Brainard, and Jens arrived just then with the sledge. Pavy assessed Whisler's condition and recommended he ride in the sledge, but Jens broke his silence, yelling: "No, in sledge he die! He run behind sledge, keep warm!" So Whisler scuffed and stumbled at a slow jog for a couple of miles until his core temperature rose; as they neared the station, however, his legs gave out and they lifted him into the sledge. Pavy ran the dogs as fast as he could, driving Whisler the last of the way to Fort Conger in the sledge.

Once they were all inside the warmth of the fort, Pavy examined Rice's shoulder and found the fracture "not complete, but the bone evidently cracked, and ligature injured." When the other men heard the story of how Rice—with the use of only one arm—had led Whisler back over many miles, for eight hours in –30 to –40° temperatures, they had newfound respect for the scrappy Canadian. Greely was duly impressed, noting, "He would have perished from the cold had it not been for Sergeant Rice's judicious and persistent efforts." Of Whisler's condition, Greely added: "The exposure affected Private Whisler's mental faculties . . . it was several hours after his return to the station before Whisler was entirely in his right mind."

It appeared that the men's mental malaise—and especially the Greenlanders'—was more dangerous than anything physical. In trying to understand what had prompted Jens to walk away, Greely learned, through discussions with Pavy, who could comprehend some of the Greenlanders' language, that Inuit lore and mythology had played a role. He may have been trying to find or appeal to *Torngarsuk*, an extremely powerful sky god who sometimes took the form of a great bear. Intriguingly, he also sometimes took the form of a one-armed man. Jens's people had a deep belief in shamanism, including shape-shifting, so it's safe to assume that his motivations were driven by these beliefs.

Two days after the ordeal with Jens, Eskimo Fred stormed into the officers' quarters screaming and holding a large wooden cross; he said it was protection against the men who planned to shoot him. He muttered, "Good-bye, good-bye," to Greely, and apparently intended to walk away alone to die in the snow. Doctor Pavy, speaking in calm tones in Fred's language, managed to discourage him from leaving.

Greely was now deeply concerned about the Greenlanders, noting: "I am quite in despair as to how Fred and Jens are to be managed." Though the soldiers had always treated Jens and Fred with respect, Greely took them aside and reinforced that no poking fun, jokes, or any remarks that might be taken as slights toward the two would be tolerated.

⌒⌒⌒

Greely was himself prone to melancholy during this time, though he vowed not to show it to his men. He wrote lengthy and passionate letters to Henrietta, exclaiming:

> *It would never do that the commander should show signs of homesickness. He of all men must have the least to say and betray the fewest signs of ever thinking of it.... When I get back to you, have no fear that I shall ever be willing to leave you again. One such separation is enough for a lifetime.*

But Greely had come north with a purpose, with the responsibility of scientific discovery and the chance to achieve international fame, and he wanted his dutiful wife to understand that it had not been in vain. He went on:

> *I miss you so much, my darling ... and yet with all my yearnings and inward sighings for you I cannot bring myself to regret coming here. I shall at least have made my mark in the world and shall go down in history as one of the Arctic leaders who has met in a measure of success.*

The Arctic grail of Farthest North was never far from his mind.

By the winter solstice on December 21, the mood throughout the encampment seemed to lighten with the promise of the coming sun. Lockwood wrote joyously in his journal: "The backbone of winter is broken!" Greely also paused to comment poetically on the coming light: "The sun tonight turns northward in its course, and in a few days, darkness will give place to returning light, which, as with many other blessings, has never been fully appreciated until it took flight." Brainard's twenty-fifth birthday fell on the solstice, and he appeared chipper as well: "Relieved of all duties and made out bill of fare for dinner. Another welcome offering—a quart of rum for the birthday punch."

Greely wanted to keep spirits lifted among his men, so he helped plan an elaborate Christmas meal and celebration. First he had Brainard oversee building the last of the outdoor ice wall and embankment, which entailed shoring up the exterior adjacent to the officers' quarters. That done, he set teams to deep-cleaning the entire inside of the fort, including swabbing and then scraping the floors, the latter made necessary by ice forming on the floor after mopping, as well as from condensation. The commander wanted the place in tip-top condition for the festivities.

Preparations for the Christmas feast began days before the twenty-fifth. Julius "Shorty" Frederick (so named for being just over five feet, and roly-poly), who continued as the primary cook, received assistance from Private Long as a kind of sous-chef, so elaborate was the planned meal. When Frederick learned that plum pudding had been added to the menu at the last minute he initially panicked, unsure whether he had the skill or the ingredients to pull off the dessert; Greely grinned and informed the frazzled cook that Mrs. Greely had thoughtfully sent an entire case along with the expedition for the very occasion of their first Christmas.

As the cooks labored in the kitchen, clanking pans and using all the burners, oven ranges, and hot water boilers, Brainard and Rice—the latter with his shoulder still heavily bandaged—took the lead in decorating, hanging military standards (guidons) and other flags, as well as any and all colorful cloth that could be hung or draped festively.

Since Christmas fell on a Sunday, Greely held a midmorning service of Psalms reading, which was emotional, for all the men thought of their loved ones back home. The rest of the day was spent in leisure or eager anticipation of the meal. The editors of *Arctic Moon* made hectograph copies of the menu for distribution, providing a fancy flourish. Greely offered eggnog, moderately enhanced by rum, and many of the men made toasts to their family members.

The menu—given their unique status as the most northerly inhabitants in the world—was a wonder and a delight, consisting of eight courses and including the following concoctions: "Mock-turtle soup, salmon, fricasseed guillemot, spiced musk-ox tongue, crab-salad, roast beef, eider-ducks, tenderloin of musk-ox, potatoes, asparagus, green corn, green peas, cocoanut-pie, jelly-cake, plum-pudding with wine-sauce, several kinds of ice-cream, grapes, cherries, pineapples, dates, figs, nuts, candies, coffee, chocolate." Mrs. Greely's plum pudding—served with a wine sauce—was a resounding success, in part because it was accompanied by cigars as well as candies and chocolates from Huyler's, the most famous confectioner in New York City.

The fantastic Christmas feast set the tone for the big party and variety show that was scheduled for the twenty-sixth, for which the men had been rehearsing a week. As Brainard put it: "We have decided to keep the festivities going for three days." The ringleaders of the events, the self-titled Lime Juice Club, made the tongue-in-cheek announcement, hectographed as a playbill, that they would perform at the Dutch Island Opera House, "for one night only, and that dog-chariots could be ordered at 10pm." The admission fee was in tobacco, "the current coin of Grinnell Land."

The bawdy and off-color variety show opened with an Indian Council, then a War Dance and pow-wow, with Whisler playing Chief "Freeze-to-Death" surrounded by eight other "braves." This performance led into a racy female impersonation by Pvt. Roderick Schneider, who, during one of their stops on Greenland coming up, had acquired the entire embroidered outfit of an "Eskimo belle," including a woman's hood. Not being very tall, he'd managed to "squeeze himself into the garments." He'd taken extra time to closely shave his entire face and even applied "makeup." Private Henry sang comic songs in different accents and dialects, followed by Jewell, the chief meteorologist, with the finale. Jewell strode onto the stage and announced with great sincerity that he was to give a "select reading." He produced a leather case, opened it with panache and a flourish, and then produced a large volume. While the crowd waited anxiously—expecting Dickens or some Christmas-related prose—Jewell brandished and hung on the wall an aneroid barometer and read for the men the day's meteorological data. The men laughed uproariously, slapping their knees and buckling over with tears in their eyes.

The warmth and levity inside the fort were juxtaposed with the stark reality of the world just outside the walls of their sturdy shelter. During the month of December, the mean temperature was –32°, with a low of –52°. Greely of course maintained all scientific study and readings, though this duty was certainly not looked forward to by the men. And some of the men, mainly Jens, Fred, Brainard, and Kislingbury, kept up their hunting, though game was scarce—a few hares and a fox here and there, with the wolves howling from some great, safe distance.

On New Year's Eve, Greely sanctioned another party, which included a gun salute outdoors, an impromptu footrace between Biederbick and Schneider to Dutch Island and back—about four miles total—both receiving extra rum as a prize. This was followed by storytelling, revelry, and music by the "tin pan orchestra," in which men banged pots and pans from the kitchen, using metal spoons and other utensils as drumsticks. The party went on until 3:00 a.m.

Early on the morning of January 16, 1882, Greely watched with fascination as the barometer fell quickly and a brisk southwest gale started to blow, first at just four miles per hour, but increasing every hour. By 11:00 a.m. it was blowing nearly twenty, and Greely, sensing a significant storm cycle forming, ordered readings taken every fifteen minutes. By noon the wind had shifted to the northeast and was howling at fifty miles per hour. Greely ordered two men at a time, buttressing each other in the gale, to take readings while shielding each other's faces from the biting snow. Tidal readings were also done in pairs, Greely employing a "buddy system" because of the dangers involved of falling down the steep embankment, as had happened to Gardiner.

By afternoon the freak storm became like a hurricane, with winds screaming at sixty-five miles per hour. It took six of the strongest men, all roped together, to make it to the observation huts to take the readings. Brainard said they were driven back by the wind's force, and "the air was so full of snow which adhered so firmly that a full cast of the face could be taken after a few moments exposure." Inside, Greely worried whether Fort Conger would survive the storm: "The house shook and creaked in an alarming and ominous manner. Every instant I expected that the roof would be twisted or torn off, and the whole building blown into the harbor. . . . The violence of the wind for over an hour kept us in a state of suspense as to what would be our fate." In the next few hours, the sustained, violent wind gave way to intermittent gusts that hammered at the walls at up to ninety miles per hour.

The next day, under clear and calm skies, Greely and teams went out to assess the damage. Because of excellent roof building, and also as a result of the reinforced, double ice and earth walls surrounding the fort, the house was mostly unscathed. But a number of the outlying tents had been blown to smith-ereens, "their contents carried away and buried in the snow. Some were not found at all. The snow drifts were a problem," noted Brainard. They shoveled through a number of them to find buried articles, tools, and gear. One of the anemometer spindles had sheared off in the storm, and they discovered that its cups had blown several miles into the harbor. The men spent the next week or so repairing the damage done by the extraordinary gale.

The storm was so severe that it had blown the snow completely off all the surrounding mountaintops. The prevailing winds had also driven a great deal of snow into densely packed drifts all around the fort and into any low depres-sions in the ground, so that the men were now conveniently able to cut blocks to build a snow house to be used as an outdoor freezer outside the main house. As the men worked, laughing and humming songs of home, Greely noticed something in the air, in the skies, the beginnings of an auroral display unlike any he'd seen before. Great towering arches—"bright, beautiful, and well de-fined, extended from the western horizon to the east"—then shifted from arches to "streamers," then "from streamers to patches and ribbons and back again to arches," spanning, as Greely put it, "the entire heavens."

The display was wondrous and surreal, a sublime play of color and light. Perhaps, Greely thought, they were going to make it through this first winter after all. Spring, and light, were now just a little more than a month away. For some of his men, Greely understood, the light could not come soon enough. Jens had developed some symptoms that looked like scurvy, and others ap-peared grim and sickly, "their pallid complexions taking on a greenish tinge." Greely left the house and marched toward the harbor—he wanted to check on the tides and the condition of the ice himself. The sky was weird, foreboding, and portentous, and as he crunched across the frozen ground, "the new moon appeared, a narrow crescent which, strange to say, was exactly the color of blood."

Greely Expedition member near the hogbacked mountains of Grinnell Land (Ellesmere Island).
(G. W. Rice, photographer / Library of Congress)

5

Farthest North

Lieutenant Kislingbury and Private Whisler crossed the thick harbor ice and ascended Mount Campbell on Bellot Island. Reaching the summit at 2,100 feet, they had an unimpeded 360-degree panorama and they took it all in, exhaling deep breaths in the air. It was good to be out of the stuffy, lamplit longhouse. They watched the hazy horizon with great expectation until finally, they saw it. Just before noon on February 28, 1882, the thin outline of a glowing orb pierced the southern skyline and hung there, like a wafer pasted in the air. Though faint, the sight was glorious: It was the first time they had seen the sun in 137 days.

Down at Fort Conger, Greely ran into the house calling out with excitement, encouraging everyone to come outside and look. "Now is the time! Come out, you can get the best view of the sun." For Greely the scene was profound. "All our hearts re-echoed that exclamation of 'blessed sun,' while thanking God that to us in health and strength the sun had reappeared, and our first Arctic winter had ended." Now the days would get increasingly longer through spring, and Greely was fired by this knowledge. It was time to send out sledging parties in earnest and to see just what his men were made of.

The men were definitely ready for even some symbol of warmth, as February had been the coldest month ever recorded in the Arctic, at an average of –52°. It was so cold that the sled dogs—nearly immune to the cold—would raise one foot after the other, lifting them off the bare ground "as if it burned them." To find warmth they would sleep on the tossed-out ashes from the fireplace and cookstove.

Since early February, expedition preparations had been under way. The main room of the fort had been converted into a temporary shop, and the carpenters toiled away fabricating backup and replacement sledge runners and stays. Shorty Frederick, the main leatherworker/"seamster," stitched together untanned sealskin boots lined with buffalo, bear, or reindeer skin. He also knitted and repaired many pairs of woolen mittens, as well as the crucial three-man buffalo-fur-lined sleeping bags they'd be taking to the north. The three-man bags were necessary for weight and space purposes, and also because the men would need to sleep together to produce enough body heat to avoid becoming hypothermic and freezing to death in the biting cold. Men skilled in metalwork fabricated and fixed numerous cylindrical field cookstoves. These fireproof tin vessels, as well as alcohol-burning lamps, could melt ice into drinking water in fifteen minutes, and would be vital for making hot teas and warming stews.

All members of the party made certain that their field clothing was in suitable order. During the first winter many had tried out both seal and fur clothing but found these "about as convenient and comfortable as a coat of [chain mail]." These sealskin suits also produced too much sweat during the exertion of pushing or running behind sledges, and excessive perspiration was potentially deadly, freezing inside the garments. They found that the best outfits, even for the coldest temperatures, comprised a double layer of woolen undergarments, with the outer layer of thicker, boiled wool. To prevent snow from sticking, on top of these woolens men wore a smooth shell garment of army-issued "stable frocks and overalls," which could be removed and dried at the end of a long day's trek.

With the arrival of spring, Greely wrote long food and gear lists, basing the amounts—down to precise ounces of meat, fuel, and tent weights—on ledgers and records from the previous expedition logs of explorers like Lewis Beaumont, Charles Hall, Elisha Kane, and George Nares. Lockwood—whom Greely was beginning to trust more and more each day, impressed by his grit and tenacity afield—was hankering to get adventuring, and he studied and traced regional maps. During these long evenings in the officers' quarters, sometimes with curtains drawn for a bit of privacy, Greely and Lockwood started speaking in earnest about a concerted spring attempt at the fabled Farthest North.

By late March, Greely had written explicit orders for two separate teams to make lengthy, concerted forays northward. They were to use the four depots previously established as bases, as well as rely on a few caches known to have been left by earlier British expeditions. Greely made no secret of his goals for these teams. Yes, they were to look for any signs of the vanished *Jeannette* and commander De Long, combing the coast and the Arctic sea for clues about the missing naval officer, one of Greely's personal friends. Greely had with him, tucked away among his personal belongings at Fort Conger, a handwritten letter from Mrs. De Long to deliver personally should they rescue him. But the principal goal of their assaults was to "explore the mystic north and, if possible, beat Commander Markham's claim of the highest latitude ever reached by a human being."

Doctor Pavy would lead one team, with a dog team pulling the sledge christened *Lilla*. They would have the support of a number of men as far as Lincoln Bay. Pavy's charge was to skirt the east coast of Grinnell Land and then strike north to determine what existed past Cape Joseph Henry. Land or sea? No one knew.

Lockwood would depart some days later, accompanied by Brainard and Eskimo Fred, with a number of others in support. Lockwood's orders from Greely were direct—and daunting:

> *You are charged with the full control and arrangement of the most important sledging and geographical work of this expedition—that of exploring the northeast coast of Greenland. . . . The energy and discretion already displayed, plus your endurance and broad experience (tested by nearly two hundred miles of field work this season)—this has prepared you with the ability to withstand temperatures lower than 90 degrees below zero. . . . The object of this work will be to explore the coast of Greenland near Cape Britannia.*

Greely added that at the farthest point obtained, Lockwood was to collect samples and specimens. And last, when he'd gone as far north as he could humanly survive, he was to take a full day to determine his position accurately. Greely threw in an extra monetary incentive as well: a team reward of nine hundred dollars for making Farthest North, plus an additional five hundred for Lockwood as the expedition leader. The subtext was crystal clear: Beat Markham's record!

By the end of March preparations had nearly been completed for an April 3–4 departure date. Brainard left in an advance team, dragging sledges named for Arctic legends: *Hayes, Kane, Hall,* and *Beaumont.* Each man bore nearly eighty pounds, and they'd pick up more gear at Depots A and B—so they'd be lugging 130 pounds each. Lockwood left the next day with two men and eight dogs.

After trying numerous different sledge types and designs during the previous fall's excursions, Greely and the men determined that the Hudson Bay sledges—which weighed just thirty-five pounds unloaded—were the lightest and most durable. They also handled deep, soft snow well. One of the sledges for the attempt at Farthest North was dubbed the *Antoinette,* named for the commander's elder daughter. That sledge also flew a small American flag knitted and sewn by Henrietta Greely. On April 3, to a chorus of cheers echoing around Fort Conger, the expedition party headed out, comprising one dog sledge and three other fully loaded sledges, carrying about two thousand pounds, to be hauled by seven men.

As Lockwood's party began their journey, Pavy's team were struggling. They broke a sledge runner early on, forcing Rice and Jens to return to Fort Conger to pick up a replacement. Then Pavy encountered open water at Cape Joseph Henry, halting his northern progress. His party returned on May 3, 1882, after more than a month of difficulty and privation, but in the end they had not managed to explore any land on northern Ellesmere Island that had not already been discovered by the Nares Expedition. Any shot at Farthest North now rested on the shoulders of Lockwood's team.

The ambitious plan involved crossing the frozen Robeson Channel to the east and skirting the western coast of Greenland bearing north, using the depots en route, then establishing a main base camp at Polaris Boat Camp on Newman Bay. The support parties would congregate there, accumulating the tons of food (including dog food), fuel, survival gear, and backup sledge runners and other equipment they'd need for the final push into the unknown. And the weather, they hoped, would be tolerable. On April 3, Greely wrote in his journal that the temperature had risen to 1.2° above zero, officially heralding the arrival of spring. This was a welcome change, for remarkably, the temperature had been below zero for an astounding 160 consecutive days.

On April 16 the entire party headed out, striking from Boat Camp toward Cape Bryant more than sixty miles to the northwest. Because they were leaving behind a base camp and needed everything with them now, they'd increased their loads to ninety-three pounds per dog and 182 pounds per man. Crossing Newman Bay, they found the hard ice superb sledding. They flew, "rushing along as if propelled by steam," Brainard said. But the smooth sailing didn't last long. Snow began falling between the Gap Valley and Repulse Harbor, and the temperature plunged to −40°. Rough ice and snow as thick and heavy as sand severely slowed their progress, and eventually one of their sledges was so broken it had to be abandoned.

The days in the continuous light were long and arduous, the leather of the drag ropes searing into the men's shoulders as they heaved and hauled the loads. The coast they traveled was gouged by numerous bays. Snow accumulated in great drifts before them, concealing hummocks of ice as well as gravel and sharp rocks that cracked the wooden sledges or tipped them over. Each day became a series of leapfroggings, with the entire team having to leave one sledge behind, move forward a few miles, then go back for the other sledge. Gales blew so hard that Brainard said the wind "made the flying snow feel like gravel thrown in our faces." Lieutenant Lockwood set the pace and the example, backtracking often three or four times over the same track, and after eleven days of such toil, they finally reached Cape Bryant on April 27.

Lockwood and Brainard assessed the condition of the men and the equipment. Two of the support group—Linn and Ralston—were snow-blind, suffering temporary vision loss as their corneas had been burned by the intensity of the highly reflective snow and ice. Eskimo Fred had been ill for the last two days, skipping meals, and he needed to rest. They plied him with hot brandy and soon he was fast asleep and snoring loudly, so they hoped he'd feel rejuvenated when he awoke. Two of the three remaining sledges were in rough shape, so Lockwood made the decision: The rest of the support party would return to Polaris Boat Camp and wait while he, Brainard, and Fred, when he was rested, would take the *Antoinette* and go on toward the north, toward Cape Britannia and hopefully beyond. They would need Fred to handle the dogs.

By April 29 Fred had regained his strength, and Lockwood decided it was time to move. They loaded the *Antoinette* with rations for twenty-five days and forged ahead. Brainard, also suffering snow blindness, reported that he "stumbled about all day like a blind man." The snow condition became crusty, such that the dogs and sled stayed on top, but the men broke through to their thighs with nearly every step, making walking slow and exhausting. After each long day's march, the men would make camp, pitch a tent in the howling wind, and then, after jumping up and down and swinging their arms for circulation, they'd try to heat food. It was difficult and sometimes impossible in the cold and windy conditions. Said Brainard, "[Our] stew, which should have been warm, was full of ice, some pieces as large as walnuts." At times they were reduced to eating a cold stew of lime juice and pemmican.

The dogs were also becoming hungry and wild: "They gnawed at everything like ravenous wolves," said Brainard. One night they broke into the tent and stole pemmican. Another time they sneaked in and stole a hare that Fred had shot. Outside the tent they yelped and snarled, fighting over the spoils.

As the small team neared Cape May, Eskimo Fred became extremely animated, pointing off into the distance and trying to describe something to Brainard. Lockwood checked it out, and it turned out to be an immense tidal crack running in the direction of distant Beaumont Island. Lockwood halted there at the open water to take measurements, interested in the depth of the sea floor. They fastened a five-pound lead to nearly 450 feet of narrow-gauge cod line and lowered it but did not hit bottom. According to Brainard, they added "two hundred and forty feet of sealskin lashings . . . then 140 feet of rope without touching bottom and then our lines were exhausted." At last they added Fred's dog whip, but with all 840 feet of line, they never hit bottom.

On the evening of May 4, 1882, Cape Britannia rose through a thick fog, the headland now just a few hours beyond them. When they reached the base of the cape, they unfurled an American flag at what was then the northern most known point of North Greenland. Beaumont had spotted it from Cape May back in 1876, but had made it no farther, his hungry and scurvy-suffering men unable to progress another step. As Brainard proudly planted the wooden flagpole and secured it with heavy stones, he said: "The British have seen Cape Britannia, but we are the first to set foot on it."

That evening Lockwood and Brainard began to ascend the steep southwestern tip of Cape Britannia. They were stopped by a number of sheer cliffs but worked around these and finally found a steep and stony ravine leading toward the summit. Carefully they picked their way upward until they stood atop the 2,700-foot-high cliff, a scabby headland affording them an incredible view no man had ever before seen. Brainard stood, mesmerized by the multiple fiords below and by a massive cape rising in the great distance:

> As far as we could see into the interior was a succession of lofty mountain peaks, some towering above our position on Britannia. They are not arranged in the form of a chain but are quite disorderly. A great depth of snow covered their summits and an occasional glacier of moderate dimensions struggled toward the sea from out of the chaotic mass.

Strong winds began to blow, biting at their faces and obscuring their vision with drifting snow, so they quickly built a large cairn and left a record of their visit, then descended to camp back down at the base of the mountain, where they slumped, spent.

The next morning, to lighten their load they cached everything that wasn't essential for survival and packed what they'd need to strike along the coast and go as far as they humanly could, bringing rations that might last two weeks. They moved along the ice foot for a few miles until the great mounds along the shore—looking as if giant waves had crashed and frozen there—forced them to move out onto the floe. As they traveled, they were terrified "to hear a grinding noise which could be none other than ice in motion." Now the danger of falling through a tidal crack was very real, so they moved slowly and with great care, Fred spying ahead for open water that would either consume them or at the very least thwart their advance.

For the next week they deliberately picked their way along the shoreline, usually traveling ten to fifteen hours a day and eating only once every fifteen hours to conserve rations. Brainard wore out a pair of boots that he'd been walking in for thirty-three consecutive days; luckily they'd all brought spares. They crossed three large fiords and wound circuitously around the dangerous tidal fracture, which varied in width from one to a few hundred yards. This crack was caused by the near-constant movement of the polar ice pack. The rift extended from Cape May to Beaumont Island and from headland to headland as far as they could see, with gentle curves snaking southward across the fiords. Whenever the men and dogs were driven from a floe to the headland, they were forced to cross the rift where it was narrow enough.

On May 13, 1882, they reached the cape they'd seen from atop Cape Britannia, which was now some ninety miles behind them. "From here," said Brainard, "our intricate windings among the hummocks led us across the tidal crack several times. Every crossing was dangerous, the rotten ice swaying under the dogs and sledge."

On Sunday, May 14, they reached the north end of what they now knew was an island, not an inland cape. They named the pyramid-shaped mass Lockwood Island. Ascending to its highest promontory, nearly three thousand feet, they cast their gaze northward still:

About eight miles north, a point of land similar to the one on which we stand, is visible. . . . Another point about fifteen miles projects farther north still. Looking past these two points, we see a low, blue line stretching away northward. We cannot pronounce it land because of the hazy atmosphere, but that is our impression. . . . The character of the interior is . . . a confused mass of snow-capped peaks and the country badly broken up by fiords. To the north the Polar Ocean, a vast expanse of snow and broken ice, lies before us. Our vision is unbroken for about sixty miles and within it no sign of land.

A storm was blowing in, and they were almost out of food. It was time to take their measurements and retreat. They determined, after checking, double-checking, and even triple-checking, that they were at 83°24′, the nearest man had ever been to the North Pole and a full four miles beyond Markham's record. They once again brandished Henrietta's special American flag. Brainard, nearly delirious with fatigue and hunger, was giddy: "We unfurled the glorious Stars and Stripes to the exhilarating northern breezes with an exultation impossible to describe. . . . We have reached a higher latitude than ever before reached by mortal man, and on a land farther north than was supposed by many to exist."

For three centuries England had possessed the honors of Farthest North. Now the Americans had it. Fog began to engulf the men, so they took one last look to the north, then in all directions from "the farthest," and descended back to the base of the mountainous island.

About thirty feet above the ice foot of Lockwood Island, they built a large, conspicuous cairn, some six feet high and the same in width at the base. Inside the cairn they placed a written record of their journey, which included a list of some of the specimens they had discovered nearby: "Several snow buntings were seen . . . numerous tracks of foxes, lemmings, hare, ptarmigan." They also saw signs of bears and musk-oxen. Lockwood assessed their stores: They needed to head out, lest they have to sacrifice and eat one or two of their dogs. So Fred readied the team, and Lockwood collected a few last specimens—mainly plants, saxifrages, grasses, and poppies—while Brainard scrawled a message on the flat face of the cliffside. He carved the motto for his favorite beer, which he always noticed advertised everywhere back home: "Plantation Bitters—Started Trade in 1860 with Ten Dollars!" Then Fred snapped his whip, the dogs yanked forward in their harnesses, and the explorers struck out toward Fort Conger.

Lockwood, Brainard, and Eskimo Fred return from Farthest North. *(Library of Congress)*

6

The *Neptune*

Lockwood, Brainard, and Eskimo Fred were beyond exhausted when they straggled into Fort Conger on June 1, 1882. All three were suffering from snow blindness, but they managed to squint and smile and raise their arms above their heads in exaltation when they were greeted by Commander Greely and the cheers of their comrades. Now everyone knew they had done it.

Only after they'd been properly fed, bathed, and given liberal quantities of rum did the facts and figures of their achievement begin to sink in. They'd been gone for sixty days and, sleeping in an army tent and sharing a three-man buffalo-hide sleeping bag, had traveled nearly a thousand miles, extending the known coast of Greenland by one hundred miles. They'd made forty-six marches—an average of about twenty miles per march—in temperatures that averaged below zero and once dropped to –49°. Greely praised the men for their "remarkable energy, courage, and perseverance," and added to his official report: "This sledge trip must stand as one of the greatest in Arctic history, considering not only the high latitude and the low mean temperature in which it was made, but also the length of the journey and the results."

The triumphant team recovered their strength and eyesight quickly, helped by the comfort of the longhouse and the warming temperatures of the season.

Around Fort Conger signs of Arctic spring were everywhere. The sloping valleys and lower hillsides bloomed with purple saxifrage, sorrel, and scurvy grass. Willows blossomed along the stream banks. Around the bay, especially where the creeks and streams plunged into it, numerous sea- and shorebirds began to congregate again. The men saw gorgeous long-tailed skuas, gulls, and dovekies, as well as large, resplendent king eider ducks, with their flashy, multicolored heads—bluish-gray, with green cheeks—and knobby, yellow-red beaks. Herds of musk-oxen roamed the valleys too, and the hunters pursued them with much success.

Lockwood and Brainard spent time recording the events and particulars of their record-breaking journey, with Lockwood drawing a number of excellent and highly detailed maps of the regions they'd discovered and explored. Greely, too, compiled records and documents of their stay to date, intending to send the drafted documents back on the resupply ship when it arrived. All the men spent evenings writing letters to their families and loved ones, correspondence they would send back on the relief ship. Everyone was anxious for its arrival, excitedly anticipating the letters they would receive with news from home.

The members of the camp settled back into their routine duties and responsibilities. The weather warmed each day, filling the air and ground with new life: Gaudy butterflies alit on bright yellow poppies, and bumblebees buzzed and swarmed about everywhere. Greely wanted to take advantage of the fair weather and long days, so he put the sledges away for the season and organized a number of foot excursions, with a goal of exploring and mapping the lands to the west, hoping to go much farther than he'd been able to the previous autumn. Until now, not much more than the eastern coastline of Grinnell Land had been charted, and Greely planned to add considerably to the geographic record.

Greely also intended to see what he might learn about—or possibly contribute to—the long-standing perplexity that had vexed Arctic explorers and taken many of their lives: the Northwest Passage, which remained undiscovered. So, with a small team that included Sergeant Linn, Private Biederbick, Corporal Salor, and Private Whisler, "Greely struck out overland to find out

whether the bays and fiords cut deep enough inland to join and form a continuous water passage connecting with the Western Ocean, as explorers of that
period called the uncertain limits of the Arctic Ocean."*

The country they traversed was rugged and steep, with no trails other than
occasional valley paths worn by musk-oxen. Bushwhacking over sharp rocks,
traveling 352 miles in just over two weeks, they discovered numerous large lakes
and sprawling valleys and climbed to the summits of a number of high mountains, all of which they named either for themselves or after famous figures of
exploration—though most of these names would later be changed. One of the
peaks, Mount Arthur, Greely summited alone. The climb was so difficult that
Greely had to send Sergeant Linn back, too exhausted to continue. There was
soft deep snow on the ascent, and for the last nine hundred feet Greely was
reduced to crawling on his hands and knees, his boots soaked and feet freezing. To force himself to keep going, he would throw his eyeglasses five or six
feet ahead up the mountain, so he would have to ascend to retrieve them. At
the summit Greely stood 4,200 feet above sea level. He believed it to be the
highest peak in Grinnell Land.†

"There was no doubt of my being on the crest of Grinnell Land," he wrote
in his journal, "where the far side drained to the western Polar Sea." Below him
the country sprawled for miles and miles, with various lower peaks, mountain
ranges, deep ravines, lakes, and long, sinuous valleys. The country was immense,
with Lake Hazen more than forty miles long. He was gazing down on the world's
largest high Arctic lake.

Of great interest to Greely and his men were the remains of two ancient
Inuit houses, which they explored and even excavated. One house had two fire-
places, what appeared to be a food storage room, and a large main room nearly

---

* The long-sought Northwest Passage (or NWP) was the sea route from the Pacific Ocean through the
Arctic Ocean, along the northern coast of North America via waterways through the Canadian Arctic
Archipelago. The centuries-long search took countless lives. The first complete passage was made by the
Norwegian explorer Roald Amundsen in 1903–6.

† Greely was incorrect. This honor belongs to Barbeau Peak, which is 8,583 feet above sea level. But
Greely had almost certainly climbed the highest mountain in Grinnell Land to date, as Barbeau Peak would
not be climbed until 1967.

twenty feet in length. The sides of the house were constructed of low sod-earth walls, lined with thin slate stone. Inside there were also large flat slabs of slate that were likely used as benches and beds.

The careful excavations of the two houses uncovered about forty artifacts, mostly pieces of wood and worked bone, as well as narwhal horns, arrowheads, skinning knives, sledge runners, and bears' teeth. The bone articles were mostly made of whalebone, walrus, and narwhal. Among the relics were a few hair combs. "It appears evident," Greely recorded, "that these Eskimo had dogs, sledges, arrows, and skinning knives, and fed on musk-oxen, seals, hares, and occasionally fish." Greely pondered the toughness of these ancient hunters, imagining their ingenuity, craftiness, and adaptability in this unforgiving place.

The journey back to Fort Conger—a slog of about 170 miles—proved exhausting. When they struggled into the fort on July 10, Sergeant Linn's feet were so deeply blistered and his ankles so swollen that his feet took more than a month to heal. Greely's toes had worn through his sealskin boots and were bleeding badly. Neither Linn nor Greely was able to do anything more than limp around the house and rest for days after their return, but Greely felt their sufferings had been quite worth it, pleased to have discovered nearly five thousand square miles of new lands.

∽∾∽

During Greely's absence the ice in the harbor had broken up sufficiently for Lockwood to fire up the steam launch *Lady Greely* and test it. He, Brainard, and some of the other men took turns tooling around Discovery Harbor, navigating a lead of open water about a mile wide. The steam launch performed well, and after Greely recovered his strength, he engaged it in a number of voyages through the summer. On one of these a near calamity occurred when Sgt. William Cross, the designated engineer of the vessel, got so drunk that he fell into the water and would certainly have drowned had the attentive Brainard not reached down and hauled him back into the boat.

Greely accosted Cross and physically tried to shake him sober, and once ashore the grim man tried to hide from his commander inside the supply tent.

This was the first serious breach of discipline since Lieutenant Kislingbury's insubordination, and it gave Greely cause for concern. He remarked: "I learned from Lieutenant Lockwood that he [Cross] had stolen a portion of the alcohol which was sent with the launch for fuel. . . . He evidentially avails himself of every opportunity to purloin and conceal a portion of the fuel alcohol sent out with parties." Greely now knew he had a full-fledged drunk on his hands, but there wasn't much that he could do, as Cross was the only trained engineer.

Among the critical jobs during the summer were hunting, skinning, and preserving game to put up for the coming winter. Brainard was in charge of recording and cataloging the harvest, and by midsummer they'd shot some fifty musk-oxen, which dressed out to about 250 pounds of fresh meat per animal. During this time Private Long impressed the commander with his hunting skills. On one trip Long struck out alone and was gone for twenty-two hours. Worried, Greely sent search teams out after him, and they met him on his return. He explained that he'd been stalking a large herd of musk-oxen; with fourteen rounds he'd killed eight and had been delayed in skinning them.

Looming over everyone's thoughts was the anticipation of the relief ship's arrival bearing letters, packages, and newspapers from the United States. It became a daily ritual—particularly for Lockwood and Brainard, who'd bonded during their attainment of Farthest North—to ascend Cairn Hill and peer out into the channel, assessing the condition of the ice and speculating on when the ship might arrive. Brainard jotted in his journal in July: "The entire surface of the ice was covered with a network of small lanes, constantly shifting. A few weeks more of thawing and a boat may possibly have a clear path." Near the end of the month Rice and Ellis climbed to the top of Cairn Hill and saw "a vast expanse of open water, as far as the eye can reach, with only an occasional detached piece of floe." Rice concluded that it was "a golden opportunity for a vessel to enter Lady Franklin Bay."

⌒⌒⌒

As the men stared longingly toward the south, the steam whaler *Neptune* finally departed St. John's, Newfoundland, on July 8, 1882, dreadfully late in the short season to be making a run for the Far North. Gen. William Babcock

Hazen was the chief signal officer in charge of organizing the resupply ship, and because the previous year's passage of the *Proteus* had gone so fast and without incident, he had not been overly concerned about an early start. But 1881, it turned out, had been one of the mildest summers on record, the lack of ice extremely unusual. Compounding the delay was Secretary of War Robert Todd Lincoln, who had never been supportive of Arctic exploration, believing such expeditions to be a frivolous waste of money. He had been against the Greely Expedition from the very beginning. Hazen had reminded Lincoln in May that Greely required resupply by August, but Lincoln claimed ignorance, stating: "I know of no such understanding." When Hazen pressed Lincoln again, and harder, the secretary of war reluctantly acted, sending Hazen's appeal directly to President Chester Alan Arthur. After weeks of bureaucratic wrangling, meetings, and paperwork, Congress signed off on the charter of the St. John's whaler *Neptune*.

Hazen put his former secretary, William M. Beebe, in charge of organizing the resupply mission. Team members included eight soldiers who needed to be ready to replace any men who might have been injured or become ill (or whom Greely deemed no longer worthy, as was the case with Kislingbury), a ship's commander, and a surgeon. In St. John's, Beebe had arranged for eight tons of provisions, with plenty of supplies and food, including tons of meat (enough for fifty men for two months), plus much more Arctic gear. They procured more heavy canvas army tents designed to pitch on snow or ice, and the governor of North Greenland committed to supplying "fifty pairs of sealskin pants and boots, plus sleeping bags lined with dog fur." They also brought on board five dog teams and five sledges, complete with leather harnesses for dogs and men.

Beebe's orders were clear: "You are to proceed to Lady Franklin Bay in Grinnell Land and there report to Lieutenant Greely for further instructions." Then, when the ship and conditions were ready, and Greely deemed fit, the *Neptune* would return with dispatches, reports, and any cargo Greely desired sent back. But should Beebe and the *Neptune* fail to reach Fort Conger, he was to "establish depots at points designated A & B in Greely's memorandum of instructions—Cape Hawks on the Ellesmere side, and Littleton Island off the Greenland shore." After successfully caching these stores of provisions and gear,

Beebe was to leave a record for Greely at Cape Sabine, explaining what he'd done and the situation as it then stood.

By the time the *Neptune* finally left St. John's, Beebe was worried. They were sailing five weeks after their originally hoped-for departure date, and Greely and his men were a full fourteen hundred miles to the north. On this very day Lockwood and Brainard were standing sentinel atop Cairn Hill, gazing south, hoping and waiting.

Beebe was no sailor, and shortly after leaving port, with the ship buffeted by a heavy gale and pelting rains, he grew seasick, vomiting so violently that he wished he were dead. "I did not care whether we floated or sank," he moaned. But the ship was in good hands. The chief mate, James Norman, had been the ice pilot last year on the *Proteus*, and he knew the waters and the vessel well. He assured Beebe that the *Neptune* was worthy and should make quick time, noting that it had a brand-new boiler, had fast top-end speed, and was a powerful icebreaker.

But Norman's predictions were challenged when they reached Disko Island and encountered thick ice, slowing them to a crawl of just a few knots per hour. The *Neptune* broke ice well enough, and Norman navigated through the growing pack until they reached Melville Bay, where the pack thickened considerably. They came in sight of Cape York on July 25, but the weather worsened, and driving rain and sleet turned to snow, obscuring navigator Norman's vision. They drifted aimlessly for three days until the weather improved and they could again advance to just past Littleton Island. There Beebe joined Norman on deck, and what he saw made his heart sink: "An unbroken ice barrier 12 to 20 feet thick extending across the head of Smith Sound." The wall of ice spread from Ross Bay on the west to Cape Inglefield on the east. Norman tried to find various entrances or leads in the pack, but eventually was forced to turn southward, where they found somewhat suitable anchor at Pandora Harbor.

But the weather now hammered them with southwesterly gales, and they rode at anchor for a full week, the storm's force twice shearing the ship's hawser rope. They also lost an anchor. On August 7 the storm abated enough for them to creep north once more, heading for Cape Hawks some twelve miles away, where Beebe was, according to Greely's instructions, supposed to deposit a whaleboat. There the pack began to close in ominously around them, bergs and weirdly formed floes two stories high pressing up against the ship's railings. The ice encasing the ship here was fortunately "broken up and soft, and the pressure of the heavy floes, grinding it to powder, made a cushion underneath and about the hull, which, while it raised the ship several feet, protected her from severe pressure."*

Though the ice did not crush the ship, the pressure and difficulty in moving through the ice forced it to burst her boiler and spring a leak that had to be repaired. They retreated to Payer Harbor, on the Ellesmere side of the Smith Sound between Cape Sabine and Brevoort Island. Beebe knew of the English cache of the Nares Expedition made here in 1875, on the long tidal peninsula, and he wanted to check out its condition. Some of it was in fairly good shape still, but some packages were broken or frail, so Beebe rebuilt, repackaged, and secured the cache, but inexplicably, he landed none of the considerable provisions he had aboard at this site. He did mark the site conspicuously with a pair of oars, securing them upright and shoring them up with stones. He also buried a note recounting their difficulties but assuring Greely of his intentions to "land supplies and a whaleboat as far north as possible."

This would prove to be difficult indeed, for extreme weather bore down on them, sealing off leads and driving the *Neptune* to seek shelter once again back at Pandora Harbor. The hills behind the harbor were now snow covered, and Beebe noticed with concern that all the ducks and shorebirds had disappeared, indicating the looming arrival of an early winter.

It was now August 25, and Beebe understood that time was running out. The sledges and dog teams had been brought along for the eventual contingency of landing stores, but the constant grinding and compressing of the pack had thrown up huge, mountainous rises, making such a landing impractical. As well, Beebe and Norman concurred, the whole of the pack appeared to be drifting southward, and Beebe feared that "he might be cut off from the

---

* This phenomenon of a ship being raised up by the ice was studied with great interest by Norwegian explorer Fridtjof Nansen, who would use the knowledge gained in his construction of his special ship *Fram*.

positions in Smith Sound at which as a last resort he was to make deposits," so
he hurried there.

They would travel no farther north than Cape Sabine, some 250 miles south
of Fort Conger. Beebe hurriedly deposited a paltry 250 rations (only enough to
feed Greely's twenty-five-man group for ten days or so), a small bundle of birch
wood, and a whaleboat in a well-sheltered spot; they covered these with tarpaulins. He also built a large, prominent cairn nearby, providing the exact bear-
ings of the small cache. Then he hastily scribbled a message:

*Whaleboat and cache just above high-water mark N by W magnetic. Cannot
by any possibility get further northward now. If we cannot get further or return here (for we cannot hold on here now on account of ice) will leave other
whale boat on this shore—if possible at Brevoort Island or in sight, marking
spot with tripod.*

Beebe then ordered the *Neptune* back across the sound to Littleton Island,
and although there were small groups of Etah hunters and sealers on the shore
whom he feared would pilfer the stores he landed, he now had no choice. He
anchored at the north end of the island and dropped off another 250 rations,
covering these also with a tarpaulin and securing it down with heavy rocks.
Then he wrote another note to Commander Greely: "I cannot express my regret at the failure of all my efforts to reach you or to carry out fully your instructions." He concluded by promising to "earnestly urge that next year's relief
ship leave St. John's as early as mid-June." They then hurried back across Smith
Sound and left another whaleboat at Cape Isabella, with a last note suggesting
that Greely might be able to use it to get across to Littleton Island, which was
inhabited at least part of the year.

The *Neptune*'s boiler began to leak again, and on September 5, 1882, after
forty days of steaming back and forth trying to find a way through the Smith
Sound and any opening into the Kane Basin, the *Neptune* turned south for
home. It still carried two thousand rations, nearly all the supplies and food
intended to be delivered to Fort Conger, enough to feed Greely and his men
for three to four months.

7

Winter of Discontent

B ack at Fort Conger, the daily vigil to the top of Cairn Hill was reduced to every other day, and then even less than that. By the end of August the harbor was almost entirely clogged with pack ice, and Greely decided it was time to haul the *Lady Greely*, as well as the whaleboat *Valorous*, ashore near Dutch Island for the winter. He sent Lockwood, with Frederick standing in as engineer for Cross—who was still out of the commander's good graces—to undertake the duty. Lockwood returned to report that the boats appeared secure.

The next morning Greely visited Dutch Island to inspect the boats, and it was a good thing he did. Rising tides had drawn the *Lady Greely* seaward, and its stern was a few inches under water. It was in danger of sinking. Greely hurried back to the station and yelled for a party of men and ropes, and after hours of bailing, the men undertook the arduous task of dragging the heavy launch as far up on shore as possible, the haul ropes biting into their shoulders as they heaved. It was difficult to find solid moorings or tie-offs on the ice foot, but they did the best they could, and from then on Greely ordered that the *Lady Greely* be visited and inspected frequently. He knew they could not afford to lose it, as it would be needed for a retreat late next summer should a relief vessel again fail to reach them.

As far as food, Greely was not yet overly concerned, for they were provisioned well enough—especially with the thirteen thousand pounds gross weight of musk-oxen they'd acquired. But he did order some food restrictions as a precaution: "We must live much more simply than in the past year," he told the men. As commander, he had to anticipate the future. This included not only food, but also putting many of the scientific records of last year in order. On September 2, as Beebe and the *Neptune* were making their final effort to penetrate the ice near Cape Sabine, Greely wrote in his journal: "Having given up the ship, I commenced today putting our scientific reports in such condition that they can be readily transported in case of necessity next year." Although he'd been studying the Arctic for more than a decade, Greely now had firsthand understanding of the fickle nature of polar ice, and knew that there could be no guarantee of relief.

As the days once again grew shorter, Greely ordered the overhaul and improvement of heating arrangements around the house. They would insulate areas that had been drafty and extend last year's ice walls all the way to the roofline. They also built a large porch to add more storage room to the building. The object was to keep the men busy and also to ensure, as Greely put it, "dryer, warmer, and more comfortable quarters even than we had during the preceding year." To guard against scurvy, the cooks placed the wooden lime juice kegs in ceiling lofts, where the accumulating warm air would prevent them from freezing. Men filled all the coal bins to full capacity. Private Bender, a tinsmith by trade and an "ingenious tinkerer," fixed everything that he found broken, even fashioning replacements for smashed lamp chimneys from empty bottles. This earned him the nickname "Mr. Fixit."

But despite the continued work, the looming winter ahead cast a gloom over the men, and morale was slumping. Wrote Brainard: "Everything is going ahead for the winter and spring in the same manner as last year, only we have not quite the same enthusiasm. Darkness is becoming noticeable. Lamps are lighted every evening now at eight o'clock and very soon they will be going all day." Lockwood stopped publishing the *Arctic Moon*; no one seemed to have the enthusiasm for it any longer. Since the light wasn't good enough for taking photographs, Sergeant Rice spent his days studying his law books and reading French, taking periodic breaks four times daily to record the tides.

In early October bear tracks were reported in the vicinity of the main house, and wolves could be heard howling quite near. Everyone clearly recalled the savage wolf attacks of last winter, and Greely certainly wanted no repeat, so he initiated an order prohibiting enlisted men from wandering more than five hundred yards beyond the station. The men, who already felt cooped up and were becoming testy, found this order overly strict, yet they grudgingly obeyed. Even the officers—to whom the restriction did not apply—thought that it was excessive and contributed to the men's discontent. Because they were hunters (and technically not in the army), Jens and Eskimo Fred continued hunting wherever they wanted, each bringing in the occasional seal.

The men tried their best to buck up and show some cheer. They celebrated Private Frederick's birthday with the standard issue of rum, and the evening grew a bit rowdy, with Private Schneider pulling out his violin and leading the men in song. Brainard laughed as the men sang "Over the Garden Wall," noting that "the summer has not altered Schneider's violin repertoire!" One of the few tolerable musicians among them, Schneider nevertheless knew only one song.

For his part, Greely tried to integrate with the men, spending some of his time in their quarters to play games of checkers, chess, and whist, as well as to break up his time with Kislingbury and Pavy, with whom he lived in such close proximity. And he continued to oversee the scientific observations, which continued daily.

At the end of October, Pavy persuaded Greely to let him take Brainard and Jens with dogs on a ten-day sledge journey south down the coast of Grinnell Land with the faint hope of finding either caches deposited, or perhaps a ship— though the latter was almost impossible unless it had become icebound. Reluctant at first, Greely decided to allow it, if for no other reason than to give them a break from the monotony. The trip proved arduous. Brainard noted that the light, which had allowed fast sledging early, "waned and then disappeared entirely" by the time they reached Bellot Island, and in these conditions "all outlines and shadows of the hummocky ice [were] lost," causing the sledge to slam into large ice blocks and even walls of blown frozen snow. Brainard was forced to forge out front on foot, identifying the tough terrain and calling out to Pavy and Jens to avoid their crashing the sledge.

They made it as far as south as Carl Ritter Bay, but shore ice blocked further passage. They scoured the shoreline and scanned the horizon for hours looking for signs, but found nothing, "neither a record nor a cairn." The one thing they did see was a white light near the horizon on the underside of clouds hovering low over the Kennedy Channel. They were witnessing "ice blink," a reflection of light, a flashing glare over an ice field, that was used by the Inuit people to help them navigate. Seeing nothing more, they left a record of their own beneath a cairn and returned to Fort Conger after only eight days, cold and exhausted.

Some of the men's general doldrums were temporarily relieved by a series of magnificent auroral events that outdid even those of the previous year. Around mid-November, coinciding precisely with the departure of the sun, the men began seeing the first of these, when Sergeant Ralston held the others rapt at breakfast as he told them what he'd witnessed the previous night while taking readings. He said a brilliant meteor had blazed across the sky, leaving a trail of bright red light that hung in the air for five or six minutes.

For the next week or so the light shows became more and more intense, and appeared so close that they might touch them. Astronomer Edward Israel exclaimed: "By heavens, I thought that aurora was going to strike me in the face!" He also noted that taking observations was greatly hindered by the strong magnetic disturbances and anomalies. He said that at the observation shack the magnetic needle was "violently agitated for three days, revealing extraordinary disturbance." On account of these disturbances, he began taking magnetometer readings every five minutes.

The daily celestial events were so vivid, in fact, that many of the men, for want of much else to do, tried to capture these images in their journals. Brainard wrote: "We observed a brilliant auroral arch of light yellow hue in the northern sky.... It changed to red, with a tinge of blue at the outer edges.... After a few vivid flashes and changes, it disappeared and then a bright streamer shot up from the western sky." Another streamer he described as resembling "spasmodic puffs of smoke rising from the stack of a working locomotive . . . remaining for several minutes and glowing with an intense brilliancy," which then "assumed the appearance of a spiral coil, contorting itself into inconceivable forms."

These spectacular light and star shows motivated Greely to take up evening lectures once more, and astronomy was the natural topic. He invited Israel to give a talk as well, and the men much enjoyed his style. Sergeant Rice, who had been attempting to photograph the phenomena for days, said: "Israel favored us with an excellent lecture on the solar system. . . . It was decidedly the most interesting of the series delivered to us."

The second Thanksgiving at Fort Conger was not as festive as the first, despite Greely's efforts. He gave what he hoped would be a rousing speech, offering thanks for their health, their success in scientific endeavors, and their attainment of Farthest North, after which, as Brainard put it, "an excellent dinner was served to vary the tedium." But with food rations somewhat restricted, the meal of roast musk-ox could in no way rival the elaborate fare—the oyster soup, salmon, ham, ducks, lobster salad—they had enjoyed the year before. Some of the men did venture out into the gloriously full moon for a shooting contest at fifty yards (won by Private Henry), but this event paled by comparison with the previous year's competition festival, which had included races on foot, snowshoes, and sledge. The evening concluded with rum punch, after which the usually upbeat Brainard noted without much enthusiasm: "The party seemed to derive some exhilaration from song."

Similarly, Christmas lacked the joy and gaiety of the 1881 festivities. Rice noted that the holiday "brings with it but little of that joyousness that is supposed to attend the season. Enthusiasm is not so great as last year." Private Long, still the primary cook, tried to lighten the mood. He emerged with dinner for the enlisted men appearing like a clown, his flaming red hair dusted in white flour. Greely, too, tried to make the best of it, handing out some gifts left over from last year as well as some of the remaining English plum pudding Mrs. Greely had sent with them, followed by cigars.

On New Year's Eve, Eskimo Fred attempted to cheer up the group. According to Brainard, he was "the star of the evening. For the first time he revealed his sense of humor. He danced a horn pipe solo, the memory of which will always cause me to chuckle." But even with that performance, the mood

remained somber, and Brainard later groused: "The festive days in this country do not bring us enjoyment. The enthusiasm of the party for these occasions
has diminished . . . and a celebration, no matter how we strive to make it
otherwise, becomes nothing more than a mockery."

For his part, Lieutenant Kislingbury was particularly melancholy. He was
supposed to have been home by now, having taken the ship south and been
reunited with his boys for the holidays. He remained a man disbarred, a man
without a position, a man Greely viewed as an unwanted houseguest and extra
mouth to feed. Though living within a few feet of each other, the two men barely
spoke. He had acquitted himself well enough, and Greely valued his skill as a
hunter and thus remained at least civil, but so few words passed between the
two that Kislingbury had taken to spending more and more time playing cards
with the enlisted men, games like casino and whist. After a time Greely learned
that Kislingbury was playing poker for money with them, and the commander
would have no gambling. Greely ordered Brainard to inform the enlisted men
that he'd tolerate no betting games with Kislingbury. Kislingbury fumed silently, but there was not much he could do about it.

Seeds of discord had also surfaced between Greely and Doctor Pavy. From
the beginning Greely had been put off by Pavy's moodiness and haughtiness.
Pavy believed he knew more about polar exploration than Greely and often
made remarks to that effect, sometimes intentionally within earshot of Greely.
While the commander valued Pavy's skills as a surgeon, Greely had lived a rigid
and structured life for decades in the military, and he did not approve of what
he called Pavy's "Bohemian life." Greely grew tired of the man's complaining,
too. He'd griped that the medical stores were insufficient, "scanty . . . and ill-
chosen"—a direct slight at Greely. Pavy also pointed out—on numerous
occasions—that should the party have to retreat by boat in the event of no relief, they were entirely ill-equipped to do so, as virtually none of the expedition
members—including Greely—had nautical experience. On this score Greely
had to admit that Pavy was right, but it did no one any good to harp on it, and
the Frenchman's constant complaining rankled the commander.

Early in 1883, sensing a pall of uneasiness about the fort, Greely loosened
the restrictions he'd imposed, issuing new orders. Now the enlisted men were

allowed to travel up to three-quarters of a mile from the station with permission: "Signal Corps members could travel two miles after reporting to the observer on duty. Members of the working party could walk two miles beyond the station, with the permission of the Orderly Sergeant. To go beyond that limit required Greely's permission." The new orders got more men out and about daily, which helped morale, as did the knowledge—confirmed by Israel—that the sun would return on February 27, one day earlier than the year before.

Also, as ordered, Greely continued to send officers to check on the condition of the *Lady Greely*, which they'd toiled so hard to secure for the winter. On January 8, Lieutenant Lockwood took a small group to Dutch Island and found the launch sheathed in ice. They spent many difficult hours chipping away at the ice to expose its hull. The pressure had caved in one side, ripped a brace from its fastening, and damaged the rudder post.

Lockwood returned to report the news, and the next day Pavy went with Cross to survey the damage. Cross's assessment was discouraging: He reported that performing such repairs as necessary to make it seaworthy would be nearly impossible, certainly in the teeth of an Arctic winter, in the dark, with the craft icebound two miles from Fort Conger. This news concerned Greely greatly, for he knew they'd desperately need the *Lady Greely* to be operational should a ship once more fail to reach them. He ordered Cross to set to work on it the moment weather permitted.

The second "long night" gave Greely ample time to contemplate the very real possibility of a contingency retreat on their own, with or without the *Lady Greely*. In early February he dispatched Sergeant Brainard and Fred with a dog sledge team to begin work smoothing out an "ice road" so they could establish a depot of provisions to the south at Cape Baird, where Brainard had been the previous autumn with Pavy and Jens. Greely thought it prudent to cache considerable gear, food, and fuel there—and as farther south as possible—in the event of their forced retreat. They'd need to have everything with them, in their boats, on their backs, and in sledges, to support a journey south to the preplanned relief depots, which lay 250 miles below them.

Simultaneously Greely began planning spring sledging expeditions, including further exploration of the North Greenland coast, with an eye toward possibly bettering Lockwood's record of Farthest North, hopefully to the eighty-fourth parallel. Greely ordered Lockwood to begin preparations and preliminary fieldwork come March, fortifying the existing depots, and to prepare all the sledges, gear, and equipment that would be needed for the final push, as before. Pavy, now often contrary and irascible, reacted strongly against this decision by Greely, going so far as to write the commander a letter "which recommended the abandonment of all work of exploration." His stated reason was that such exploration and work might weaken the men and imperil a forced retreat, which he pessimistically now deemed inevitable. But Greely was convinced it was petty jealousy on the part of the Frenchman, who'd failed in his own attempt at the record and was not to be part of the mission. The lead team would again be Lockwood, Brainard, and Eskimo Fred, who'd served so ably before and already knew the route.

Greely responded forcefully, pointing out that the doctor's own weekly medical reports showed the men to be in excellent health, better even than they'd been the first winter. He expressed pride in the fact that no other expedition in history had successfully spent two winters at such a high latitude, and yet they were all doing well. He penned his own official reply, stating, among other things, that their purpose was in part to increase "our knowledge of the Arctic regions," and that as long as he was in command, that goal was exactly what he intended to pursue. He added, with a barb that had a hint of personal pride to it, that to fail in this endeavor he would consider both "dishonorable and unmanly." That ended the discussion.

Doctor Pavy, moody and petulant, read Greely's letter and fumed. After brooding over it for a time, he hatched a scheme: He would take Private Whisler, who was as strong as a musk-ox, steal one of the sledges and the best dog team, and, along with George Rice—who would photographically document the expedition—strike north of Cape Joseph Henry, snatching the record from Lockwood. Pavy excitedly, even maniacally, proposed the idea to Whisler, who flatly refused. Pavy grew incensed, and when he started yelling at Whisler, the dutiful military man drew and leveled his pistol at Pavy to show there would be no more talk of it. Without really knowing the full implications, Pvt. William Whisler had just stopped a mutiny.

Fort Conger in winter with ice block insulation. *(G. W. Rice, photographer / Library of Congress)*

8

"I Am *Not* a Lady Franklin"

When the *Neptune* failed to reach Fort Conger, General Hazen of the Signal Corps had the unfortunate duty of informing Henrietta Greely of the news. She was in San Diego with her two daughters and her family in September 1882 when she received the first curt telegraph message stating: "Failed to reach Lady Franklin Bay. Vessel returned safely. Hazen." Initially distraught, Henrietta was a woman of formidable constitution, and she quickly turned her emotions toward resolve and positive action.

She was born Henrietta Nesmith in Switzerland; she and her family lived in Texas and briefly in Mexico before her father, Thomas Nesmith, settled his wife, three sons, and one daughter in San Diego. Moneyed and industrious, Nesmith soon became a bank president and director of the Texas and Pacific Railway Company. Henrietta—nicknamed "Rettie" by her family—had spent most of her life in San Diego, and after her mother died, as the only daughter she took over most of the household duties as well as the care of her frail and aging father. In late 1877 she met an upright, polite, and serious military man named Adolphus "Dolph" Greely. He was the head of the San Diego Signal Corps Office, in charge of installing a telegraph line from San Diego all the way to Santa Fe, New Mexico. She was impressed if not bowled over, and the two began a courtship.

Greely took her on picnics and out to dinners, and though he'd been attracted to many women before, Henrietta's elegance and intelligence mesmerized him. He described her as "very tall, five feet nine inches . . . a commanding figure . . . black hair, dark eyes. Unusually graceful, considering her height." He admired her bearing, her wit, and her erudition. She was very well read and well mannered, and he respected her strong will and fiery independence. Adolphus Greely was not usually a man given to spontaneity, but he proposed to her in November, shortly after meeting her.

Henrietta was a contemplative person. She also had plenty of suitors, so she needed to know a bit more about this Adolphus Greely. There was also the matter of their very different lives: She was the daughter of a prominent San Diego banker; he was an army man frequently posted to remote locales. When he told her of his ambitious plans to participate in an Arctic expedition, which would be gone for two years, she replied, "I am *not* a Lady Franklin." She had no desire to become the widow of a famous explorer. Greely was scheduled to return to Washington soon, after his work on the San Diego–to–Santa Fe line was in order, and she suggested that they spend some time apart and that he should show his seriousness and "woo her by letter."

As it turned out, Greely was quite handy with a pen. He assuaged some of her initial fears of this impending Arctic endeavor by assuring her that unlike other such journeys, their party would have a comfortable dwelling, with modern appliances, a kitchen with coal-burning stoves, and would be visited annually by resupply steamships. He also told her that he never approached a job or mission half-cocked, saying: "Did I not believe the plan a feasible one, and that I am quite certain of returning to your arms safe and sound I should not desire to lead it." He concluded, with similar confidence: "Could any such trial ever come to you from the expedition as came into Lady Franklin's life I would never go. Doubt as to my fate cannot exist and we cannot be abandoned nor cut off for ships are to visit from year to year." He was persuasive. She believed him and had fallen in love with him. They married in San Diego in June of 1878 at the Nesmith family home, moved to Washington shortly thereafter, and within three years, by the eve of Greely's departure for the North, Henrietta had borne two daughters, Antoinette and Adola.

Now the feisty Henrietta Nesmith Greely still had no intention of becoming "a Lady Franklin." After hearing the news of the *Neptune*'s failure to reach her husband and his men, Henrietta initiated frequent correspondence with General Hazen. He quickly realized she was an impressive and industrious woman, one with deep financial and political connections stemming from her father's business relationships, and also a voracious reader who had, at Greely's urging, studied a great deal of Arctic exploration literature. It turned out that she knew as much about the high northern regions as—and in many cases more than—the politicians in Washington who had sent her husband there in the first place. Hazen subsequently wrote more detailed letters to Henrietta, explaining that she need not be overly worried, as Greely had plenty of coal for heat and cooking via the natural seam on Grinnell Land, food for at least two years, and plenty of musk-oxen, seals, and other game.

But she *was* worried, especially since recent dreadful newspaper reports of the fate of De Long and the *Jeannette* had sparked national concern and morbid fascination. It had been learned that the *Jeannette* had been crushed by the ice in late 1881, some three hundred miles north of the Siberian coast. The crew had retreated by boats and sledges toward the Lena River delta, but the boats had become separated in a gale. There were sensational stories by survivors of horrific suffering from exposure and death by starvation. Of the thirty-three-member crew, only Chief Engineer George Melville and twelve others had survived in a whaleboat. It was a major national story, and a few of the relatives "of some who had died in Siberia demanded a congressional investigation."

Henrietta was committed to doing something and would not sit idly by. She wrote to Hazen, pointing out—quite rightly—that the *Neptune*'s failure was at least in part due to its late departure, and prompted him to make sure that as soon as humanly possible, relief efforts for the next year be initiated. She fully understood the glacial sluggishness of Washington bureaucracy, especially under Secretary of War Robert Todd Lincoln, who had absolutely no appetite for polar exploration—he was in fact downright opposed to it.

In addition to corresponding with General Hazen, Henrietta also began writing to Lt. James Lockwood's father, Gen. Henry Hayes Lockwood, a Civil War veteran and noted military tactics expert. He was influential in Washington, and Henrietta figured he might be able to help get the subsequent relief effort moving. Henrietta also entered into an exchange with Lieutenant Lockwood's mother, with whom she empathized. Mrs. Lockwood was deeply concerned about her son's safety and could perhaps be another ally and confidante.

Henrietta and General Lockwood pushed and prodded, and by November 1, 1882, General Hazen submitted to Secretary of War Lincoln a plan for a relief expedition to depart St. John's for Discovery Bay by June 15 the following summer.

Now it was imperative to find the right ships and the right men to captain them.

9

Farthest West

S pring was upon the men of the Greely Expedition, and at Fort Conger the first rays of sun brought optimism and enthusiasm to the station. Brainard, who was usually less florid in his journal writings, was so inspired as to wax poetic:

> *The sun, as scheduled, showed itself today, throwing a flood of golden light over Discovery Harbor. Like last year the disc was much distorted, but nevertheless welcome. More beautiful by far was the coloring of the sky. Blue tints merged with delicate greens and above all rich carmine predominated, although partially concealed by fleecy cirrus clouds floating along in a lazy procession.*

It had indeed been a long winter.

Greely already had Farthest North in the bag, but he was an ambitious man, and his faith in Lockwood and Brainard was immense. He had also learned enough from the previous year's spring sledging to understand that peril lurked everywhere: in the diabolically low temperatures and threat of exposure, in the fickle nature of the ice, in equipment failure. During the initial reconnaissance trip to Greenland, a ferocious gale had lifted a fully loaded sledge into the air and slammed it down onto Sergeant Ralston's head, a steel runner scalping him to the skull. Private Whisler, complaining of chest pains, had crossed Robeson Channel and returned to Fort Conger coughing and spitting blood from pneumonia. Most perilous of all, of course, was the ever-shifting, labyrinthine, and unpredictable ice pack, which, if weak or unstable, could swallow men, boats, sledges, and dogs in an instant. Experience had taught him that Arctic travel was generally unsafe past June 1.

Knowing this, Greely carefully worded his orders and instructions to Lockwood, his second in command:

> *While reposing great confidence in your judgment and discretion, I cannot refrain from cautioning you against more risks than can be avoided. The dangers attendant on your trip are obvious and serious. If at any time you think you cannot go beyond your farthest of 1882; if the polar pack shows signs of disintegration; if you are personally incapacitated for rapid travel; if any member of your party is badly injured; you will return immediately to the station [and] be at Polaris Boat Camp no later than May 31st.*

On March 27 Lockwood, Brainard, Eskimo Fred, and their dog team headed north. They hoped for a new record, the eighty-fourth parallel, and perhaps as well to crest the top of Greenland and determine whether it was indeed an island.* They progressed with remarkable speed across the Robeson Channel and reached the Black Horn Cliffs—nearly one hundred miles from Fort Conger—in just six days. The trip had taken them twenty-two days the prior year. But the ice this year was weak. Some of the dogs broke through on one occasion, and at the base of the Black Horn Cliffs, which they had hoped to travel around, the ice was so young and breakable that even a small stone, when dropped on it, broke right through into the icy water below. They saw, to their dismay, a continuous lane of open water along the shore at the base of the cliffs.

---

* At this point no one knew. And no one would know with certainty until five years later, in 1888, when the Norwegian explorer Fridtjof Nansen—on skis and pulling sledges—made the first crossing of Greenland to finally prove it was an island.

Brainard reconnoitered inland and found "the face of a sloping glacier," and he and Lockwood took turns cutting steps in the ice until Lockwood finally climbed to the thirteen-hundred-foot summit of the cliffs to assess their options: There weren't any. Lockwood spotted open lanes of water running in all directions, with one clearly defined lead shooting northwest toward Cape Joseph Henry. What Lockwood witnessed next was most impressive—and daunting:

The entire polar pack suddenly set off to the northward. The pack was separated from the shore east and west, as far as the eye could reach, by open water perfectly free from ice and from two hundred yards to a half mile wide. In the direction of Lincoln Bay, it expanded into a broad sea from three to five miles wide.

Lockwood descended. It would be impossible to get a dog team up and over the glacier. Beyond the cliffs to the east was an impassable chain of high mountains. In order to follow Greely's explicit commands, Lockwood and Brainard had no choice but to turn back. There would be no new record, but the men had learned a great deal. Rather than its being one continuous sheet of solid ice, Brainard concluded: "There is not a doubt in my mind that the ice is broken repeatedly during the winter and the polar pack is in constant motion." Even more important, he reasoned that "the severity of the winter can be no criterion as to the condition of the ice." As they headed for home Brainard was disappointed but appreciative. "We realize now," he said, "how fortunate we were last year to have reached our 'Farthest'; even more so, to have been able to return without incident."

Although Commander Greely was surprised by their sudden return after just two weeks, he was glad to see they were in good health. He was also impressed by their speed and efficiency. Lockwood wanted to resupply quickly and make another northward attempt by an alternate route, and Greely considered the option, but in the end decided not to allow it, given the condition of the ice and the uncertainty of the arrival of a relief vessel. He could not afford to have two of his best men, plus a dog team, gone for what might be six to eight weeks.

As both a compromise and a reward, Greely sent the same team of Lockwood, Brainard, and Eskimo Fred, with Corporal Elison in support, to attempt a crossing of Grinnell Land to the west, following the Archer Fiord, and hopefully all the way to the "Western Ocean" (now known to be the Arctic Ocean). Just as with Greenland, no one had yet proved whether this great landmass (Ellesmere Island) was indeed an island. They struck southwest on April 26, 1883, and eventually made it past Mount Arthur, which Greely had summited the previous year. Traveling as many as forty miles a day, they encountered numerous glaciers. One of these they described as being of "colossal proportions," and they sketched it in great detail. Mountainous impenetrable terrain thrust upward from the bottoms of valleys and lakes, and the going became extremely difficult. The dogs limped, their feet bleeding even through their protective hide booties. Brainard noted the past geological violence that must have been wrought on this extreme place: "During some mighty convulsions of nature this place has been sadly defaced. The ground is strewn with rocks and the general aspect forbidding to both man and beast."

By mid-May, after nearly two weeks of constant marches, light snow became more severe, slowing their progress. They ascended to nearly three thousand feet and below could see a truly massive waterway they greatly wanted to reach. What they could see of it stretched at least, by their estimation, eighty miles westward. Picking through a treacherous descent, lowering the sledge with ropes, they descended a few thousand feet and made camp in the shadow of a giant glacier. Brainard was awed by the glacier's "picturesque grottoes and ice caverns. . . . One had icicles hanging over the entrance like the bars of a prison window." They had reached the edge of the great waterway they'd seen from above, and while Lockwood paused to sketch the magnificent glacier, Brainard went to the water's edge to observe it. He was certain they'd reached the Western Ocean. After watching the tidal action, Brainard was nearly convinced, and he knelt to taste the water: It was salty!

Brainard excitedly called for Lockwood and Fred to come taste it as well. They confirmed the presence of salt, but Lockwood cautioned that nearby salt springs could also account for the taste. They now faced a conundrum: The men wanted to continue west to prove their discovery categorically, but they were very low on food and in the midst of a raging snowstorm. They were more than two hundred miles west of Fort Conger, and they made a choice: In order to study tidal activity confirming that this waterway was connected to the ocean, they fasted for nineteen hours to save food before going on one last reconnaissance to record the ebb and flow of the water. The storm abated slightly, and they managed to scramble twenty-six miles down the fiord, making "Farthest West" on May 14, 80°48′5″N; longitude 78°26′W. They named this magnificent find the Greely Fiord.* That done, Lockwood and Brainard turned for home.

They had five days' rations for an estimated six days' travel if all went well. It didn't. They were forced to cut down to half rations. Deep wet snow met them after their ascent back to the top of the Grinnell Land Divide. Lockwood and Brainard strapped on snowshoes, but still they sometimes sank to the waist. En route they ran out of dog food and sacrificed one of the weaker dogs, shooting one named Button and feeding it to the other dogs. Fred sliced off the bottom of his sealskin sleeping bag and tossed scraps to the team as well. Some days later, their best dog—Disko King—gave out and died. Just after midnight on May 26 the men and dogs, wan and haggard, stumbled into Fort Conger. They'd been gone thirty-one days and had traveled 437 miles. It was the first known crossing of Grinnell Land.

Greely was moved by the men's determination and grit. He read their maps and extensive charting of interior Grinnell Land with great fascination, amazed to learn that a large portion of the land was covered by a giant icecap (later named the Agassiz Glacier†). He was also intrigued by Brainard's numerous fossil finds—coral, wood, marine animals—and the branch of a petrified tree they'd found at the summit of a mountain more than 2,200 feet high. Brainard told Greely of an entire fossil forest along the shores of the Archer Fiord, one "more extensive than any discovered in these latitudes." Despite the loss of two excellent and dependable dogs, by any measure the journey had been a resounding success.

---

* This body of water, still named Greely Fiord today, connects with the Nansen Sound and does indeed extend all the way to the Arctic Ocean. The men were right in their assessment that this was connected to what was then called the "Western Ocean."

† Named to honor Louis Rodolphe Agassiz (born May 28, 1807, Motier, Switzerland—died December 14, 1873, Cambridge, Massachusetts), the Swiss-American naturalist, botanist, and geologist who conducted landmark work on glacial activity.

As pleased as Greely was with the impressive team of Lockwood, Brainard, and Fred, he remained equally disgruntled with Kislingbury and Pavy—who seemed to have banded together, and who were now making life difficult for the commander at Fort Conger. Greely often saw the two men together, frequently speaking in hushed tones, especially when within his earshot. Greely's winter-frayed nerves were such that he imagined all sorts of plans the two might be hatching.

Kislingbury had suggested—on multiple occasions beginning in mid-March—that Greely should send a group of men south all the way to Littleton Island, in hopes of leaving a message there for any relief ship that might come, or possibly to wait there for their arrival and then guide the vessel on to Fort Conger. Greely dismissed this notion outright as a ludicrous scheme, and he had no intention of following Kislingbury's suggestion in the matter, even after repeated entreaties.

Even more problematic was Pavy, whose medical reports were now consistently late and sloppily executed. The doctor was supposed to have compiled an entire summary medical report of the previous year, and when he finally did furnish one, Greely found it to be shoddy and unprofessional.

On May 1, just days after Lockwood and Brainard had departed for the interior, Greely ordered Pavy to complete a comprehensive report—by the end of the month—of the expedition's natural history findings, including a complete description of all the specimens collected to date, with notes of exactly where and when they'd been found. Additionally, Greely directed Pavy to provide him with "six complete sets of botanical specimens so arranged that they could be securely stored and transported."

Greely continued to oversee all scientific matters around the fort. He sent Brainard to continue tidal readings and to collect fossil specimens along the nearby cliffs; Elison was to prepare and preserve an entire musk-ox hide. Greely himself, working through early June, remained busy observing, collecting, and categorizing blooming flowers, of which he discovered nine separate varieties. Greely also forbade the men from shooting any birds such as "knots, turnstones, or snow bunting" within a two-mile radius of the fort so he could collect some of their eggs as specimens.

When Pavy finally submitted his required natural history report and collection of specimens, Greely was appalled: The entire collection was disorganized. Pavy had mixed Inuit artifacts together with animal fossils and shells; preserved ermines and foxes were in the same box with some unidentified birds; other birds, also either poorly marked or unidentified, were wrapped in wax paper and stuffed in boxes; insects, now covered in thick dust, had been hastily pinned to corks and tossed into matchboxes. Various animal hides—which were supposed by now to be tanned, labeled, and packed for transport—were still drying on the roof of the house. Greely had Lockwood inspect the report and specimens, and Lockwood confirmed what Greely saw: "I can best state," said Lockwood, "there was no complete itemized list [of specimens]. . . . It was difficult to know what was of the collection and what was not."

Disgusted by Pavy's performance, on the first of June Greely took the ever-dependable Lieutenant Lockwood aside and told him he would be replacing Pavy. By written order Lockwood would relieve the doctor of all duties, reports, and specimens related to the collections. Even though he was no naturalist, Lockwood worked a minimum of six hours a day for the entire month of June to reorder Pavy's slipshod work.

The hunters continued to seek game, the observers kept making and recording scientific observations, and even earlier than they had the year before, the men ascended Cairn Hill every single day to scour the horizon—with field glasses and telescopes—for any sign of a ship.

10

The *Proteus* and the *Yantic*

B ack home, four thousand miles south in the direction the men of the Greely
Expedition were looking, two ships were in fact heading their way—but
they weren't together yet, and they were late.

Henrietta Greely's pressure, along with that of General Lockwood, had
made a difference, but it had been difficult and time-consuming. Secretary of
War Lincoln had been in no great hurry to speed things along. The entire Arctic enterprise remained to him a tedious waste of government funds, a frivolity.
General Hazen, at Henrietta's continued urgings, had written Lincoln the previous fall reminding him of the necessity of relieving Greely and his men, offering specific suggestions. Hazen reiterated that the ship or ships should depart
St. John's no later than June 15, 1883. He also suggested that the men should
be "trained and have experience in rowing and managing boats, and in the use
of boat compasses." Ideally these men should be "familiar with boats and their
management in all conditions."

Lincoln agreed in concept, at least as it pertained to sending trained nautical men, but he wrote back saying: "It seems that it would be much more desirable to endeavor to procure from the Navy the persons who are needed for
this relief party." Hazen was quick to reply that changing departments from

the army to the navy would be akin to "swapping horses while crossing the stream, and when in the middle of the stream." Such back-and-forth continued for months.

Lincoln had other reasons for finding this entire affair distasteful. The national press continued to write about the failure of the *Neptune,* which weighed on his decisions. Even worse, there was an ongoing and embarrassing scandal involving Capt. Henry Howgate, the former property and disbursement officer of the Signal Corps and the man who initially got Greely interested in the Lady Franklin Bay Expedition. Howgate had conceptualized building prefabricated dwellings and colonizing the far Arctic north at or near Lady Franklin Bay. His plan had been to post fifty or so men there, reinforcing them with local Greenlanders if they could hire some, and send annual resupply ships. Howgate even garnered initial support from the media mogul James Gordon Bennett, the publisher of *The New York Herald,* who went on to sponsor the fateful voyage of the USS *Jeannette*. But the first ship Howgate sent up to Greenland—the *Gulnare*—was ultimately deemed unsuited to Arctic travel, and it broke down at Disko Island, effectively ending Howgate's dream of year-round colonization. Dr. Octave Pavy had been on the *Gulnare* to serve as the colony's naturalist, and before that damaged ship limped southward back home, Pavy stepped onto the Greenland shore and eventually into Greely's life.

But there was an even bigger mess regarding Howgate. As disbursement officer, he'd been embezzling funds for over a decade, to a total of two hundred thousand dollars. General Hazen had discovered this and ordered his arrest, but Howgate had absconded. He was tracked down in Michigan and was returned to Washington, where he was placed under arrest, "charged with embezzlement and fraud, and confined to jail . . . to await trial." While out on bail, Howgate fled once again, and was now a wanted fugitive. Lincoln fumed, bringing to bear his full powers as secretary of war by hiring the Pinkerton National Detective Agency—which had notoriously chased after outlaws Jesse James and the Wild Bunch, including Butch Cassidy and the Sundance Kid—to find him.

So the Lady Franklin Bay Expedition continued to be a thorn in Lincoln's side. Fortunately for Henrietta's cause, Secretary of the Navy William E. Chandler responded to the call for help by offering to send the naval vessel *Yantic* as a support ship. This seemed to appease Lincoln's concerns, and a plan was put into motion. But all the back-and-forth bureaucratic wrangling had taken a great deal of time. It wasn't until March 3, 1883, that an official act was signed ordering a mission to find and bring home Greely, all his men, and all the scientific instruments and data. The original plan had been to keep the station operational through 1884 via resupply ships, but with the *Neptune* debacle, things had changed: Lincoln was scuttling the expedition.

Prompted by Henrietta Greely and General Lockwood, General Hazen agreed that the *Proteus*—which had so ably and swiftly carried Greely north in 1881—was the best ship for the rescue job. In late May 1883, while far to the north Lieutenant Lockwood and Sergeant Brainard were returning from their journey to "Farthest West," Hazen shipped out for Newfoundland aboard the *Yantic* to inspect the *Proteus* personally and ensure that it was fit for service. Before he left Hazen wrote Henrietta that the man he'd chosen to lead this expedition was the one for the job, ensuring her that he was "confident everything will go right." The man in question was thirty-year-old Lt. Ernest A. Garlington, the son of a South Carolina plantation owner. He'd graduated from West Point and accompanied the noted Seventh Cavalry as an Indian fighter, including chasing the Nez Percé and Chief Joseph all the way through Montana and into Canada. He hurried from his post in the Dakota Territory to head the rescue mission.

The *Yantic*, a 179-foot-long wooden-hulled gunboat with a large crew of 134 men, sailed under the authority of forty-year-old Cdr. Frank Wildes, an able Bostonian seaman. The *Yantic* was well built, and in preparation for this journey had been retrofitted for Arctic travel: "Her battery and ammunition were removed to allow the stowage of additional coal," and an extra sheathing of oak plank was added at the bow, but "she was in no sense a vessel fitted for ice navigation." Its job was to serve as a "tender," a kind of support or relief ship should the *Proteus* run into any trouble. Commander Wildes had been instructed to accompany the *Proteus* as far as any pack ice allowed, but the *Yantic* should under no circumstances enter the ice.

There were delays in leaving New York due to repair of the *Yantic*'s three-year-old leaky and finnicky boilers. Thick fog en route to Newfoundland also hindered progress, so it was not until June 21 that the *Yantic* finally steamed into port at St. John's, where the *Proteus* awaited. This was already a week later than the mission was supposed to have departed for the north.

One useful development was that on the way north, Lieutenant Garlington had met and been impressed by navy lieutenant John C. Colwell. Although the thirty-two-year-old Colwell was posted on the *Yantic*, Garlington believed that having an experienced naval man on the *Proteus* made good sense, so he quickly sent a telegram to General Hazen requesting that Colwell be allowed to accompany him on the *Proteus*. Secretary Lincoln agreed and signed the order transferring Colwell "to report to Lieutenant Garlington for duty, as a member of his party."

Once in St. John's, Garlington boarded the *Proteus* and greeted Capt. Richard Pike, the experienced ice navigator who'd previously transported Greely and his men successfully through the treacherous gauntlet of Melville Bay, the Kane Basin, and the Kennedy Channel. Garlington was glad to meet the fifty-year-old master mariner and hearty Newfoundlander, and his son, who would serve as first mate. Garlington, with oversight by naval officers and Captain Pike, inspected the two-hundred-foot-long steamship. As an army man fresh off a horse in the Dakota badlands, Garlington didn't find the description of its construction particularly meaningful, but he learned that it was "built of oak, with a sheathing of ironwood from above the water-line to below the turn of the bilge, and her prow was armed with iron." With a ship this sturdy, and an experienced mariner who'd made numerous sealing voyages to the Labrador coast, Garlington had every confidence in his success.

The crew was another matter. This late in the season, many of the best and most experienced local sailors had already signed on with codfishing ships. Captain Pike explained this to Garlington, adding that these fifteen men were "not as good a crew as in the year before. . . . You can never expect to get the same sort of men always." Pike's assessment was confirmed when Garlington inspected their loading of the sealer, which was haphazard and sloppy, certainly not up to military standards. But they needed to ship out. Garlington set the best of his own twenty-two men to the task of repacking, but there wasn't time to completely reorganize everything.

Garlington and Wildes had discussed the relief plan in detail on their way to St. John's, but they went over it again in the last days leading up to departure; they wanted to have it right. One challenge—and this Wildes understood and pointed out more than once—was that once sailing, the ships were supposed to remain in close proximity as long as possible. This would be difficult, as the *Proteus* had a top speed of nine knots, the *Yantic* only seven; also, the *Yantic* consumed much more coal—it would likely need to take on more at Disko Island. There was another matter; Wildes was by order "in support" of Garlington and the *Proteus.* He was to "co-operate cordially with Lieutenant Garlington, affording him all the assistance in his power. He was not, however, to assume any direction of the expedition."

The plan stipulated that the *Yantic* head to Disko Island under sail in order to save coal, and once there, switch to steam power as it pressed north to Upernavik. Wildes was instructed to deposit cairns with messages at the following locations: Cape York, the Cary Islands (southeast side), Pandora Harbor, and Littleton Island (if it was still accessible). The base for the operation would be Pandora Harbor, where the *Yantic* would remain until August 25, awaiting the *Proteus.* The *Proteus* would steam as fast as possible for Discovery Harbor and Fort Conger. Hazen's orders on this were explicit: "Nothing in the northward movement must be allowed to retard progress of the *Proteus.* It is of utmost importance that she take advantage of every lead to get to Lady Franklin Bay." The orders added—and Garlington paused at these words— "Should *Proteus* be lost, push a boat or party south to *Yantic.*" Privately Hazen told Garlington that given the difficulties and uncertainties in these waters, he should let his own judgment govern him "on the spot."

There were further contingencies. If ice prevented the *Proteus* from making the passage north—as it had the *Neptune*—"she should leave small depots similar to those of the year before, at points intermediate between depots already established on the coast of Grinnell Land, thus completing the series of way-stations in case of a retreat by boat." If that occurred, instead of departing south, the relief party was supposed to build a house and relief station near Littleton Island at Lifeboat Cove, using precut lumber they'd brought along. They had coal, wood, and alcohol fuel, and plenty of provisions for the winter.

Once established there, they could send out teams with dogs and sledges in late fall or early winter and bring Greely and his men to the relief station. Other men from this station were to "keep their telescope on Cape Sabine and the land northward," looking for any signs of Greely. Greely's original plans, written at Fort Conger just before the *Proteus* departed in 1881, stated clearly: "No deviation from these instructions should be permitted."

There now remained only enough time to do a final inspection of the ships, and to deal with any last-minute correspondence prior to departure. Garlington reread a letter from Mrs. Greely, perhaps to shore up his courage: "I hear such praise bestowed upon you," she wrote, "that I feel the relief of my husband's party in very earnest hands." The letter moved him, prompting him to respond:

> *You may rest assured, Madame, that every effort possible will be made to reach Fort Conger with the Proteus and enable Mr. Greely to come out this season. Capt. Pike has a very favorable view of the probability of reaching Lady Franklin Bay with his ship. . . . If the ship does not get through to him, I most assuredly will by means of sledges. You may feel perfectly secure that if it be within the reach of possibility he will have relief. . . . I sincerely trust that you will have the happiness of seeing Mr. Greely back and safe and well before the coming of another winter—*
>
> *Ernest A. Garlington*

Just before boarding, Lieutenant Colwell dashed a quick letter off to his mother, assuring her there were "enough clothes for a small army—there isn't much chance for me to get cold." He signed off with excitement and enthusiasm, saying: "We sail in about half an hour. . . . I have always wanted to make a trip to the Arctic regions and couldn't possibly go under more comfortable and favorable circumstances. It suits me exactly." Colwell's boundless enthusiasm underscored his naïveté regarding the conditions he would soon encounter.

The two ships departed St. John's under crystalline blue skies at four o'clock on June 29—the *Proteus* under steam and the *Yantic* under sail. The

Proteus clung close to shore, and the *Yantic*, buttressed by an offshore breeze, coursed eastward, skirting the Labrador ice. Within three hours, the two ships were separated.

They were also two weeks behind schedule.

Captain Pike steered his ship hard north, making fine time and arriving in Godhavn on July 6. While at anchor, Garlington rearranged some of the shoddily packed stores and ordered the coal bunkers filled to brimming. While in the holds he realized they were lacking in Arctic clothing, so he negotiated with local Greenlanders to acquire sealskin garments, as well as two Inuit sledge drivers and dogs. He also awaited the Greenland ship inspector, who didn't show up until the twelfth. The *Yantic* arrived the same day, and Wildes explained that it had lost a main topsail in a heavy gale, and worse, its boilers were failing. It would need four to five days—maybe as long as a week—for repairs, and to take on tons more coal, which the ship was burning through rapidly.

Garlington could not afford to wait, but bad weather pinned him down until July 16, when Pike was finally able to stoke the *Proteus*'s fires and head out of port toward the Smith Sound. Commander Wildes would follow with the *Yantic* as soon as possible, hoping to get to Littleton Island at least. Only a couple of hours out of Disko Island, Pike ran the sealer aground, foundering on a shoal. Running full steam ahead, then all engines astern, back and forth, Pike managed to free the ship, but the mishap gave Garlington pause. Entering Melville Bay, they encountered their first real ice, which was loosely formed, thin, and rotten. Pike plowed right through, and they moved well until the nineteenth, when they rammed straight into pack ice. The force of the collision knocked Garlington from his bunk, and when he gathered himself enough to stand, he "peered through the porthole" and saw nothing but ice.

Garlington hurried above, where he found Captain Pike flustered and Lieutenant Colwell taking readings. Colwell took Garlington aside and whispered that the only explanation was that Captain Pike had made a serious navigational blunder—he had driven them off course and "directly into the land ice."

Colwell climbed into the crow's nest and scanned everywhere for leads, barking out directions to the first mate, who relayed them to Pike. They retreated south, then cut west, the ice growing denser the farther they went into Melville Bay. For two days they picked their way through until finally Colwell spotted Cape York and they eased around the headland through loosening pack. By midday on the twenty-first, they spotted some open water and steamed ahead, and by midafternoon they'd reached the Cary Islands, still some 125 miles from Smith Sound. Garlington sent a small party ashore to inspect the Nares cache—the same one Greely had visited on his way up in 1881. Most of the food stores (eighteen hundred rations) were still in decent condition, as was the boat left there. They also discovered Lockwood's record from 1881 in a cairn, and they took time to copy it, leaving their own message for Wildes. The waters seemed to be clearing. Garlington, growing more optimistic, wrote: "Will steer for . . . Littleton. All well and in excellent spirits."

By the next day they'd progressed around Cape Alexander and entered Pandora Harbor.

Garlington deposited a second message for Wildes, stating that they'd encountered no ice since the Cary Islands, and, looking north from the crow's nest with "the aid of a powerful telescope," no ice had been spotted and the weather was perfect. As long as these clear conditions prevailed, Garlington intended to press north, and he sent Pike right by Littleton Island and swung east toward the Grinnell Land side. As they eased past, they could see the large pile of coal Beebe had left the previous year in the *Neptune.*

By midafternoon the next day, the twenty-second, Garlington called Pike to anchor at Payer Harbor, just off Cape Sabine. He personally went ashore with some men in a rowboat to inspect the provisions Beebe had deposited last year. It took them some time to find the cache, which "was in good condition, except the boat, which bore marks of the claws of bears." They secured this cache well with tarpaulins, setting aright the wooden tripod, which had fallen over. Just nearby, at an island called Stalknecht, they found yet another Nares cache, and Garlington did a quick assessment and considered landing some of his 250 rations. But given that there were already two caches here that Greely knew about from the Nares logs, he decided to press on, remembering his orders to speed to Lady Franklin Bay as quickly as possible. He'd already stopped twice.

Garlington reboarded the ship—they'd been at anchor three hours. There was some confusion as to the state of the waters ahead. Garlington had used his spyglass from a promontory on Stalknecht Island and seen open water ahead. Two other men said that the tides had been shifting and that the sound looked ice-clogged to the north. Anxious to follow his orders, Garlington hurried to Captain Pike's quarters, roused him from a nap, and urged him to depart as soon as possible.

Pike suspected that it was just a shift in the tides and argued that it would be better to wait—even a few days—for any large floes to clear the narrows. But Garlington was persistent, and the longer they waited, the more animated he became. After a couple of hours of disagreement, Pike reluctantly complied. At 8:00 p.m. Colwell and Pike's son ascended the crow's nest to look for open lanes, and Captain Pike, still grumbling and cursing in his heavy Newfoundland accent, called for full steam.

They moved well through the evening and into the night, bashing larger and larger chunks of ice that bobbed and roiled in the Buchanan Strait. Here the great masses of ice that formed in the north were pushed and pulled back and forth by strong tidal currents, and the shifting tides sent huge bergs smashing into one another in violent collisions. Pike nosed for Cape Albert, a craggy headland some twenty to thirty miles beyond, barely discernible in the late light. Near midnight the loose pack started to bind and the lanes to constrict. Colwell and the first mate saw a possible lead between two larger floes, and Pike rammed hard, blasting the floes apart, the ship's ironclad prow bashing and cleaving the ice into shards. All through the night, using this icebreaking technique, the *Proteus* plowed north. The men spotted a long lane of open water that extended "as far as the eye could reach, along the coast." Pike sped for it.

By early morning, however, that long lane of clear water was being steadily filled by boundless floes blowing down the Smith Sound, and the Kane Basin was amassing into a dense, ominous pack, enclosing from every direction. Pike steered south, still looking for a way through, but within four miles of Cape Albert—and just four hundred yards short of open water—the ice floes converged and closed off all leads. By early afternoon the *Proteus* ground to a halt, surrounded and pincered on all sides by giant walls of ice. The ship shuddered at the pressure as the ice walls climbed up its rails, and then there came a macabre groaning sound, a long almost wailing creak, as its thick oak and double-cedar timbers strained and moaned.

Proteus nipped in the ice. *(Courtesy of National Archives and Records Administration [NARA])*

11

Vigil

The constant scanning for a ship had become a vigil. And not only on Cairn Hill; there were plenty of other elevated promontories and bluffs in the vicinity to climb and stare keenly out to sea. Near the end of June Sergeant Brainard took to scaling the summit of the cliffs near Cape Craycroft some miles down the southern coast, gaining enough elevation to get a clear view down the Kennedy Channel. Of their summer watch Brainard remarked:

> *We cannot keep our eyes from wandering hopefully toward the south.*
>
> *Practically all our scientific work is complete until we leave Fort Conger within a month or six weeks. . . . We have little to do except observe the channel, either for a boat or for the opportune moment when our little band must strike out independently to the south. If no vessel arrives, it is our only alternative.*

In fact it was not their only alternative. They could stay. Some, like Pavy and Kislingbury, had even proposed it to Greely. At Fort Conger they had enough provisions, if well rationed, to last another year. But Greely would not even entertain the notion of remaining, since that option was nowhere in the original plans and orders, which stated that if no ship showed they were to leave by September 1. His contingency plans, which he'd sent with the *Proteus* when it sailed away in August 1881, were clear. But having studied the moods and behaviors of Arctic ice for two years, Greely felt that September 1 was too late for safe passage through the Kennedy Channel and beyond in the repaired *Lady Greely* and their two other boats. He set August 9 as their departure date.

There was plenty of packing to do, and items needed to be organized in two ways: one set for if a ship came, and the other much more streamlined should they need to carry it all with them in boats and on sledges. They'd be limited by the amount of weight each man would be allowed to carry. Lockwood, with assistance from Sergeant Linn, set to arranging and packing the specimens for transportation home. Lockwood had done a commendable job organizing and recataloging everything after taking over for Pavy. For his part, the proud—some even said arrogant—doctor had not taken well to being replaced, becoming even more sullen and aloof than usual.

Greely spent much time compiling his official writings, orders, and documents, sealing them neatly in waterproofed containers for retreat, should that prove necessary. The crate weighed fifty pounds. He dispatched men to place depots at various points south to serve them in the event of an exodus: at Cape Baird, twelve miles away; and on the south side of the Archer Fiord. Private Frederick had proved himself to be a highly skilled cobbler, using untanned sealskin (for better waterproof qualities) that Jens and Eskimo Fred called *ugsuk*. Since no ship had yet come and the men had all worn out their original boots long ago, Frederick remained busy all summer, making multiple pairs for each man.

Sergeant Cross and a few assistants had managed to repair the damage the ice had wrought on the *Lady Greely* last winter. At low tide they hauled it from its ice-foot mooring and fastened it to a large floeberg that was frozen to the sea bottom just off Dutch Island. Brainard filled "twenty-seven sacks of finely screened coal" brought from the coal seam and readied them for portage. Cross, who had not been seen drinking since his near disaster falling off the launch into the bay, also oversaw the repair of the whaleboat, named *Narwhal*, fitting it out and improving its oarlocks and bench seats. At Dutch Island harbor he also fine-tuned the sturdy jolly boat *Valorous*, which the English had left at Cape Hawks, and which Greely had procured on his way north two years earlier. Well built, it remained in remarkably sound condition given that it had sat idle for six years in the harsh Arctic weather. They had named it for the one of Nares's ships, the *Valorous*, to which it had originally belonged.

What little work the men had was halted on July 4 to celebrate Independence Day. It wasn't nearly as festive as the previous year's—which had included baseball, footraces, a wheelbarrow race, and a shooting match. Said Brainard: "We no longer have the imagination necessary to provide entertainment for these holiday occasions." They made something of an attempt, unfurling an American flag. "Lieutenant Kislingbury," Brainard added, "caused a little excitement when he presented the only cigars remaining in Grinnell Land to be contended for in a shooting match." Ellis was the victor, and to him went the smokable spoils. They did play a baseball game, with Sergeant Gardiner and Kislingbury serving as captains and picking teams. Fred and Jens played too, causing the Americans a great deal of hilarity during the long, high-scoring contest, won 32–31 by Gardiner's team.

But these amusing diversions soon gave way to deep and dangerous tensions.

Greely was consumed by the two possibilities he faced: relief or retreat. He'd been simultaneously preparing for both. To make matters worse, his rheumatism, which Doctor Pavy had diagnosed and which had ailed him since late the previous summer, was once again flaring up. His right knee grew bulbous and swollen, and his limbs throbbed with pain. Though he did not complain about it, the men could see him hobbling about with a walking stick he used as a crutch.

Near the end of the month Pavy informed Greely that he had decided not to renew his annual contract outlining his official duties and obligations to the U.S. Army. His contract was set to expire on July 20. He'd renewed willingly the year before, but now, under the circumstances, feeling slighted by his removal as naturalist, he said he wouldn't. Greely knew full well that despite his many shortcomings, Pavy was an excellent physician, and whether he liked it or not, his medical skills were required, especially should no relief arrive. Greely immediately drafted an official letter to the man, stating unequivocally: "Ship or no ship, you joined this expedition under a moral obligation to serve during its continuance . . . and that the Surgeon General never would have sanctioned your contract had he surmised even the possibility of your quitting, under any circumstances, a command situated without the confines of the outside world."

As a concession, Pavy said that he would continue to serve in his medical capacity, since he felt a moral obligation to the men. But then Greely ordered Pavy to turn over his diary. This should have come as no surprise—back in 1881, each member of the expedition had been informed in writing that the official journals presented to them must be turned in to Greely when requested. Private letters they could keep. Pavy balked at this order, puffing furiously on his pipe, then stating: "I have furnished you with all my personal views and official opinions by reports, when desired." He then said unequivocally that his diary was of no "official value . . . a mere record of events, hypothesis, and reminiscences, for only the use of my family."

Greely was in no mood to argue. He'd threatened execution by firearm for disobeying orders before, and he'd do it again. But he waited a moment, gathering himself. They were seated in the officers' quarters, and Greely glared at Pavy across his desk, his revolver at his side.

"Turn in your journal or consider yourself under arrest." Pavy stood up and loomed over Greely menacingly. Greely, jaw clenched, called out for Brainard, who arrived to hear Pavy say: "I do not consider myself in service, and I do not accept the arrest." Greely called for guards. Pavy assessed the situation. He had no desire to be imprisoned in some outbuilding, so he blurted out: "I accept the arrest physically but not morally." He would turn in his journal, but under moral protest. Still, he had initially disobeyed a direct order, and Greely duly noted this in his report of July 19. But Greely understood that for practical purposes, physically imprisoning Pavy made no sense, and at worst it could undermine morale among the men, who were already on tenterhooks, uncertain of their fate. Instead he had Brainard inform all the men that Pavy would "remain an officer of this expedition until tried by court-martial on our return to the United States." That settled, Greely took to his bunk, where he mostly remained for the next forty-eight hours, his rheumatism keeping him bed-bound until he recovered enough to limp around again.

For the next few days, high northerly winds blew each morning. Men returning from Cairn Hill reported "lanes of open water south of Cape Lieber and extending across to the Greenland coast," which offered some hope to everyone. But Brainard made his own sorties later in the afternoon and found the pack ice solid. It was never the same. The pack was ever-changing—a living, moving, unpredictable force of nature that could not be trusted.

಄ಾ಄

Sgt. George Rice, the photographer, had remained busy all summer making images, using the small darkroom Greely had ordered built for him last year when the astronomical observatory, which he'd originally used, became too cluttered. As the summer wore on Rice also had the task of selecting and securing the best forty-eight negatives for a potential retreat. Greely had made clear the importance of protecting the photographic documentation of this expedition. Rice chose images that chronicled most aspects of their time here: the building of Fort Conger; the *Proteus* at anchor in Discovery Bay; the Eskimo with their dogs and sledges, as well as skinning seals and musk-oxen; the Eskimo relics Brainard had discovered. He also included images that illustrated the stunning landscapes: glaciers slowly gouging out great valleys in this hard and unforgiving place; immense skylines of craggy mountains; and of course, the ever-present ice, which enthralled Rice's eye and imagination with its subtlety, nuance, delicacy, and danger. All of these Greely packaged, together with the men's private diaries, in sealed, watertight boxes.

Brainard was put in charge of packing up tools they might need for repairing boats and sledges, plus others: shovels and picks, axes and hatchets and saws. All the sledging gear, as well as extra runners, was laid by and made ready.

After religious services on Sunday, July 22, Brainard went for some exercise and to collect wildflowers along the banks of Cascade Ravine. He made a leisurely climb to a thousand feet and, to his great excitement, saw a "long, irregular lane of water near the middle of Lady Franklin Bay." He hurried back down to the fort to report the news to his commander. In the meantime Cross had returned from Dutch Island, where he'd been checking on the boats, and he'd witnessed a similar opening, "a disruption of the ice in Lady Franklin Bay two thirds of the distance across Cape Baird." Not long afterward Kislingbury and Jens, holding their own daily vigils, came to the same conclusion. They'd been at St. Patrick Bay, and found it completely ice-free. The ice in Hall Basin was loosely broken up as far as ten miles out. All of this boded well indeed, and word went around the camp that conditions were looking favorable for a ship to make it through.

These developments, Brainard remarked wryly, "made us all a little happier and more hopeful that we will get out of the Arctic alive."

12

Nipped

Pike knew the sickening sound of ice against wood. He'd heard it before, but in his nine years as skipper of the stalwart *Proteus*, he'd always managed somehow to avert disaster. Now, at three in the afternoon on July 23, 1883, he ran from the pilothouse to the gunwale and witnessed what he most feared: ice floes as high as seven feet climbing nearly to the rails.

Garlington and Colwell also heard the sound of splintering wood, and they convened on deck to assess the damage. The ship lurched and shuddered beneath their feet as the ice crushed ever inward. Pike yelled out to them that the ice was tearing apart the starboard main rail beside the engine and boiler room. They'd better hurry and begin unloading everything they could.

Colwell bellowed that he would start off-loading the whaleboats. Garlington took three men and sprinted to the main hold—barking orders to get everything marked for Greely and bring it to the top decks. He sent a couple of men to the forepeak, where much of the Greely relief materials were stowed, and then he and a handful of others climbed down into the midship hold where their own supplies and provisions were supposed to be. But the poor initial organization by Pike's men slowed their sorting. After an hour of frantic work, men colliding with one another in the narrow hatchways, Garlington felt another jolt. The entire ship heaved and convulsed. Colwell yelled down that the bulwarks had given out, and ice had pierced the hull near the starboard coal bunker. Icy water flooded into the hold.

Pike directed his men as best he could, but they hardly paid attention and mostly focused on gathering their personal gear. Some of them appeared to be drunk, having gotten into the rum stores. Garlington climbed back topside to see Colwell struggling with one of the whaleboats, trying to free rope knots from the davits. He also saw that most of Pike's men had abandoned their posts and were pilfering the Greely stores and stuffing food into their own duffels. Unimaginable forces of ice now ripped at the hull from all sides, slicing into the ironclad prow with the ease of a can opener. Deck plates popped like corks; the top deck's planking bowed and buckled. Garlington called to begin throwing everything overboard and onto the ice.

As men tossed crates, bags, and boxes, one of the whaleboats was close to being crushed, so Garlington grabbed some of his men and a couple of Pike's. They managed to chip it free with picks and lower it to the ice sheet below. Another vicious shift of the ice impaled and shredded the *Proteus*'s hull, and water now poured in from all sides. Pike screamed above the wind to abandon ship, and his men hurriedly scaled the sides and were on the ice. Colwell and Garlington continued to sort what they could, but by now the tossing of gear and food was frenzied and indiscriminate. Some crates shattered on impact; some fell into the water that was roiling at the hull's sides. Twenty-two wild Greenlandic sled dogs tore around the collapsing deck, yelping and whining, and men hurled them overboard too, one at a time, watching them hit and skid—some severely injured from the fall—then run away or limp about, yipping. Garlington managed to save his own dog, Rover.

By early evening—after a few hours of confusion—all the men but Lieutenant Colwell were down on various ice floes some distance from the ship, some sitting on piles of strewn gear. One of Garlington's sergeants—a Signal Corps observer named William Lamar—readied a camera and began taking photographs. Colwell was the last to abandon the *Proteus*, and he, along with Garlington, dragged supplies as far away from the ship as he could. Water now rushed into it with the sound of a raging river, and the men backed away from the foundering steamer and watched as it filled and lowered, sinking fast. Water cascaded over the top decks, and its smokestack sputtered and belched into the air a great billow of steam that vanished in the wind. Finally all that remained above the ice line were the three masts, and then, like a mirage, they too were gone. The *Proteus* was gone.

Thirty-seven men and Rover were now stranded on the ice. Only four hours had elapsed from the moment the *Proteus* was first beset until it had gone under, taking with it nearly all the provisions destined for the men of the Lady Franklin Bay Expedition. This included not only food, but also clothing and correspondence from home in the form of letters and newspapers. Also lost was all the presawed lumber Garlington needed for building the planned winter shelter at Littleton Island, as well as all the coal and fuel, and all the sledges.

Not surprisingly the men had acted like the two entirely separate units they were—and now Garlington and his men stood on a floe across from Pike and his, separated by a lane of open water. What few sled dogs were left whined and pawed at food containers; others yipped far off in the distance. Colwell and Garlington assessed their predicament and understood how perilous it was. They needed to get ashore in the five boats they'd managed to salvage—three that had originally been on the *Proteus*, and the two additional whaleboats that Garlington had fortunately brought along.

It took some time, a few hours using boats, but eventually all the men were assembled together on the same floe. Of Garlington's men, only Colwell was really a mariner, but Pike—still traumatized by having just watched the ship he'd captained for almost a decade sink—agreed to distribute some of his seamen to aid their efforts. He knew they'd all need to work together to survive. Colwell volunteered to take four of Pike's men and as many provisions as they could load into one of the whaleboats and row south to the nearest visible land, a point they could just make out in the distance.

Pike's men, untrustworthy as they were, could row well, and even in the heavily burdened boat they made landfall in just under an hour. There, at a point three or four miles west of Cape Sabine, they established a cache of some five hundred rations including canned goods, bacon, hard bread, lemons, tea, tobacco, and a few sleeping bags. It was a fairly random assortment, and there had been no time to properly think through and organize things. It amounted to about three weeks' worth of rations should Greely manage to make it there. Colwell covered the scanty pile with a canvas tent fly, using rocks to secure it, then headed back toward Garlington, Pike, and the others. They nicknamed the place "wreck-cache camp."

It was around two in the morning when Colwell reunited with the men on the floe. By good fortune, the tides were carrying them toward land, so they all agreed it was best to load every boat and strike for land at once. Garlington went this time, allowing Colwell and Pike's men to rest while Colwell further inventoried and sorted stores. Soon after leaving, Garlington's boat began to swamp, its drain plug knocked loose. They nearly overturned in the quickening tides as only two of his men—excluding him—could row with any skill. Someone managed to force the plug back in, and they bailed out the boat, but by then shifting ice was cutting off their leads. They rowed with great difficulty until they found their way through the maze and landed near Cape Sabine.

Colwell got as much of the remaining supplies as he could—and all the men—onto the other boat. With little room, he was forced to leave at least a boatload of stores on the floe. With eighteen men, rowing the dinghy was laborious, and the small craft sprung a leak, but a tough sergeant named Kinney plugged it with his thumb for four hours as they wound through the closing leads. When the last boat landed and was hauled up, the men all slumped on the rocky shoreline, exhausted from nearly twenty-four hours of continuous work. A dense fog settled on them, and they could dimly see the large floe they'd been on drifting away, carrying with it a ton or so of food, clothing, tents, sleeping bags, and Arctic outerwear of sealskin and fur, all of which had been for Greely.

Rain began to fall on the men huddled on the rocky, uncomfortable spit off Cape Sabine. Some slithered into sleeping bags; others splayed fully clothed on the ground, pelted with sleet. Garlington took stock of the stores, counting forty days' rations. After setting up a few tents, Garlington suggested everyone rest. Colwell agreed. For what would come next, they were going to need it.

The next day, July 25, Garlington crossed over to Brevoort Island and did the tough duty of leaving the grim news for Greely—who was more than 200 miles to the north. Garlington took his time and explained his own plight, how the *Proteus* had become nipped, then crushed by ice, and then sunk: "She stood the enormous pressure nobly for a time," he wrote, "but had to finally succumb to the measureless force." He recorded detailed descriptions of the 500 rations—plus bread, tea, and sleeping bags—three miles from Cape Sabine, as well as the 250 deposited by the *Neptune* in 1882. He also described the location of the small Nares cache at Stalknecht Island, and a "cache of clothing [buffalo overcoats, fur caps and gloves, uniform clothing, Arctic overshoes, and underwear] on the point of Cape Sabine, opposite Brevoort island in the 'jamb' of the rock, covered with rubber blankets." He added: "There is a cache of two hundred and fifty rations on the northern point of Littleton Island, and a boat at Cape Isabella."

Those were the facts. Now came the hard part. It was as if he were writing the last part as much to Henrietta Greely as to her husband, the commander: "It is not within my power to express one tithe of my sorrow and regret at this fatal blow to my efforts to reach Lieutenant Greely. I will leave for the eastern shore just as soon as possible and endeavor to open communications."

Back at Cape Sabine, Garlington told Colwell and Pike his plan. Their own best hope—and what he concluded was now the best hope for Greely—was to find Wildes and the *Yantic*. That way they might have some choices for Greely. The *Proteus* disaster had considerably altered their options for helping Greely. One was to maintain a small relief party at Littleton Island in keeping with the original plan—though that had been complicated by the loss of all the building equipment, sledges, and dogs. Another was to somehow get another ship to Greely—maybe the Swedish steamer *Sofia* they'd heard in Upernavik might be cruising these waters in August; or possibly a sealer from St. John's. But first and foremost, Garlington knew, they had their own problems to deal with. They were themselves shipwrecked, and must somehow reconnect with the *Yantic*, and then decide upon their next actions. Right now they must cross the Smith Sound to Littleton Island, the highest point the *Yantic* had been ordered to travel. If it had not made it that far (and based on the ice they'd recently encountered, and the fate of their own ship, he seriously doubted it could have), they would proceed south, hoping to make contact with it per the original directive: "Should *Proteus* be lost, push a boat or party south to *Yantic*." But where, Garlington could only wonder and speculate, was the *Yantic*?

On the evening of July 25, they loaded the boats—three lifeboats, two naval whaleboats, and a dinghy in tow—and began rowing across the narrow, turbulent sound in a driving rain that turned to sleet. The plan was to stay together as best they could, with Garlington, Colwell, and his twelve men in the navy boats, and Pike's twenty-two in the lifeboats. But with poor visibility in the foggy sleet storm, coupled with swirling currents, the two groups were soon separated. Garlington was deeply aware of the dangers the sound presented; just two days before, the ice had snapped like kindling and then engulfed a two-hundred-foot-long, 467-ton steamer, and now they bobbed like driftwood in the freezing, ice-filled water. But somehow with Colwell leading the way, the Americans made the twenty-some miles to Lifeboat Cove, where they set up camp in a growing snowstorm and hunkered down for the night.

The next morning dawned clear, and Garlington rowed on to nearby Littleton Island, where he left a message—as much for Wildes as for Greely—with word of the lost *Proteus* and the safe condition of the relief party. He included a vague plan that he was "making for the south to communicate with the *Yantic*." Then they continued on to Pandora Harbor, six miles below Littleton Island, where they were glad to reunite with Pike and his crew in the evening. There was no sign of the *Yantic*. Garlington, Colwell, and Pike agreed that their best chance of encountering Wildes was to row south, stopping at the originally agreed-upon spots of communication, or Arctic "post offices" as they were commonly called: Pandora Harbor (their current location), Hakluyt or Southeast Cary Island, and Cape York. Their hope was to meet the *Yantic* as it came north, and Garlington would leave notes of his progress and whereabouts at all these locations. If they somehow missed each other—which seemed unlikely but possible—Garlington's messages would clarify his position, and the *Yantic* could alter its course accordingly. Under steam, it would have no trouble, in theory, catching up with men in rowboats.

At this point Garlington requested that Pike allow the boatswain of the *Proteus* to be transferred to his whaleboat, since only two of his own men had ever rowed a boat. Pike consented, and moving together, the flotilla of five craft made Northumberland Island on the evening of July 29, after three days of hard rowing and eating rations on the move. Strong easterly winds pinned them there for a day while they scoured the coastline for any news or sign of the *Yantic*, finding none. They embarked again, making twenty tough miles before foul weather—and the very real chance of being swamped—forced their return to the Greenland shore.

On July 31, 1883, the shipwrecked boats landed seven miles north of Cape Parry and were held there for two days, slammed by a strong easterly gale. They had no way of knowing that on this very day, as they struggled to set up tents and cook food in the howling wind, Cdr. Frank Wildes, the *Yantic,* and his crew, five hundred miles to the south, were just leaving Upernavik. They'd spent a week tending to the *Yantic*'s boilers and taking on coal, then had been fogged in for two days before it was finally able to depart. It had yet even to cross Melville Bay, but now, at last, it was under way, steaming steadily north.

⌒⌒⌒

During their two days stuck near Cape Parry, Garlington and Colwell discussed their situation. The Cary Islands were close—some twenty miles away offshore to the west—and they were the next of the preordained post offices. Colwell assessed the winds, waves, and prevailing conditions, and told Garlington that he thought going there "would be extremely hazardous with our heavily laden boats in rough seas." Garlington hemmed and pondered. The Cary Islands were part of the plan laid forth at St. John's between himself and Commander Wildes. But to go they risked the very real chance of being swamped and drowned. He decided to heed the advice of Lieutenant Colwell—an experienced seaman. They would await calmer weather, then skip the Carys and strike straight for Cape York, the last of the preplanned stops.

On August 2, under light winds and clear skies, Garlington's and Pike's crews pulled the oars hard, staying close to the shore for safety. By 9:30 p.m. they reached and landed on Saunders Island. There they rested for their push on to Cape York.

Dense fog descended over the bay. Meanwhile, a fifteen-mile swath of shore ice had caused Wildes to bypass Cape York and head straight for the Cary Islands. Later that night, while most of Garlington's and Pike's men slept in wind-whipped tents, the *Yantic* passed quietly by them some fifteen miles offshore, just missing the shipwrecked crew. When Wildes landed at the Cary Islands as agreed late on the night of August 2, he went ashore and found Garlington's previous note dated July 21, but no further word. With deep and bitter irony that would have far-reaching implications for Greely, had the weather been better and Garlington been able to make the Cary Islands, his crew would undoubtedly have met the *Yantic* that very day, August 2. As it was, Wildes would continue north, as planned.

The next morning Garlington and his group rose and began rowing for Cape York, heading due south. The winds had died, but they struggled hard, having to steer around floating rafts of displaced shore ice. By late that same day Wildes could make out Littleton Island in the distance. There, he hoped, would be some word from Garlington and the *Proteus*.

But the *Proteus* was at the bottom of the ocean, and Garlington, the relief mission leader, and Pike, the ship's master and commander, were twenty miles south of them, heaving and straining at the oars, heading in the opposite direction.

Proteus sinking. *(Courtesy of National Archives at College Park)*

13

Farewell to Fort Conger

Will we ever again reach the land of our nativity?
—*David L. Brainard, August 10, 1883*

G reely sat at his desk on August 2, finalizing reports and writing correspondence. Periodically he picked up a photograph of Henrietta and held
it, adjusting his spectacles and gazing at her image. He longed for word from
her and missed her more than he could say—but somehow, he knew no ship
was coming. He folded up the flag she'd sewn, which Lockwood and Brainard
had flown at "the Farthest," and packed it away.

He'd made his final decision—setting August 8 as their day of departure
from Fort Conger, weather permitting. He'd have some of the men begin ferrying gear to the boats at Dutch Island beginning August 7, and once everything was loaded, they'd launch the moment the bay and channel conditions
became favorable.

But there remained a lot to do, and much still to record and organize. Weight
was going to be an issue. They could take only absolute essentials. Next to him

sat three large tin boxes that would carry the most important records of their time here. One box contained all his originals—field journals and reports—as well as his personal diaries up until the current day. He'd be in charge of this precious box. A second box contained the originals of all the meteorological, magnetic, geographical, and natural history observations they had recorded. A third box, whose care he'd entrusted to the dependable Lieutenant Lockwood, contained copies of everything in case Greely's box should be lost; in it were also detailed descriptions of the plants they'd collected, and records of the pendulum transits. All told, the three boxes weighed fifty pounds. Private Schneider had served ably as his clerk in the laborious effort of transcribing duplicates of all the records and reports, which Greely felt crucial to have in the event of some disaster. The originals and copies would be transported in separate craft.

He paused to read over his summary of their accomplishments, pride welling inside a man who typically tried to hold his emotions in check. There was much to be proud of. After more than seven hundred days at Fort Conger, 268 of them—almost nine full months—"marked by the total absence of the sun," the general health of the expedition party was extraordinary, "despite their arduous labors for two years amid unequaled cold and darkness." They'd suffered not a single case of scurvy—due almost certainly to the lemon-juice-infused pemmican they'd consumed religiously. Among the men there had been some injuries and near disasters: attack by wolves, tent fires, a fractured shoulder, a broken leg, sprained ankles, frostbite, lacerations, and abdominal ailments. Doctor Pavy had pulled a few painful rotted teeth. But under the most severe conditions imaginable, not a man had lost limb or life. It was a remarkable achievement.

Greely pored over the field achievements, proud of his men. Lockwood and Brainard had won the prize of Farthest North, which England had held for three centuries. This was news he very much looked forward to reporting to the world the moment he had the chance! That intrepid pair had also crossed Grinnell Land far to the west, reaching a fiord they believed led to the polar ocean. Grinnell Land's coastline and interior had been "surveyed, its physical geography determined, and the contours of its northern half fixed with considerable certainty." On Greenland, more than one hundred miles of new coast-line "never before trodden by the foot of man" had been discovered and explored, adding much to the geographical record.

Greely stopped, adjusting his paper and rereading the next part. He knew it was right, but it was so impressive as to bear reading again: "On two hundred and sixty-two days, one or more sledge parties had been absent in the field, on journeys entailing from two to sixty days' absence, and some three thousand miles had been traveled." During all this time and all these many miles, his men had impressively performed their scientific work every single day without fail, making and recording, on average, five hundred daily observations. Greely thought of the great man, Karl Weyprecht, who'd conceived of the International Polar Year, and wished he were still alive—he would have dearly loved to present his findings to him personally.

Of his own command of the expedition, Greely could also be quite satis-fied. Other than the disbarring and disgruntlement of Lieutenant Kislingbury, and Dr. Octave Pavy's resignation and arrest, the management of the expedi-tion had gone very well. He'd demoted David Linn from sergeant to private in October of 1882 for using disrespectful language directly to his commander, but later reappointed him sergeant. Sgt. William Cross was clearly a drunkard, but since the incident when he had fallen out of the launch into the bay, he seemed to have curtailed his consumption. For the most part the men had fol-lowed orders and done their jobs. Their work had been organized and efficient. There'd been some petty arguments, some grumbling, but that was to be ex-pected when men endured months on end of darkness and monotony, cooped up in tight quarters.

The important Peirce pendulum, though heavy, was a delicate instrument, so it was placed in a wooden box and then soldered into a tin case that was placed tightly into another wooden box, all to buffer it from damage. Once packaged, it weighed more than one hundred pounds. With this taken care of, Greely boxed up most of his personal articles, and looked over his own kit, which lay on his bunk. It wasn't much: one suit of long underwear, a thick woolen blanket, three pairs of stockings, and a sealskin pullover. Officers would be allowed to take sixteen pounds, enlisted men just eight. He had already given the general order that by August 8, all men should be ready to depart at an hour's notice.

Greely went outside to oversee the rest of what they would leave behind. Still using a walking stick, he limped about, surveying the packing and storing. He felt it important to secure everything should they need to return here for any reason. The three tons of remaining coal was bagged, covered, and placed beneath the porches for protection. In preparation for departure, they'd eaten most of the flour, milk, butter, sugar, and vegetables, and the rest of the food—tea, coffee, hard bread, and salted meats—they packed, sealed, and stored inside the kitchen area. Greely estimated it to be about enough food "for a scant year's army rations, not enough for an Arctic ration": In the extremes of the Arctic, a man burned many more calories against the cold.

They would also have to leave behind most of the sealskin coats, nearly a dozen musical instruments, heavy fossil collections, and many boxes of plant specimens. There was only so much room in the boats, and Greely knew it was certain they'd have to do much dragging and portaging.

For the next few days all they could do at Fort Conger was watch the water and wait. On August 7 Brainard returned to report that the conditions in the Kennedy Channel were as "ice-bound as if we were in the midst of the Arctic winter—with the disadvantage that the ice was not sufficiently firm for an overland retreat." But high southerly winds blew for the next twenty-four hours, driving ice out enough to clear what looked to be a number of navigable lanes to the south. The water also looked open between Dutch Island and the south shore of the Archer Fiord. By the morning of the ninth, Greely ordered the exodus. It was time to abandon Fort Conger. Everyone except Brainard, Long, and Israel was ordered to load into the boats at Dutch Harbor. The last scientific reading was recorded at 1:00 p.m., and then the commander sent word to stoke the boiler fires in the *Lady Greely* and prepare to set out.

Brainard and Long did a walk-through of the fort where they'd spent the last two years of their lives. As they moved through the rooms, they remembered the multicourse holiday meals, evenings playing music and laughing and drinking rum punch, and they knew that where they were heading, such luxuries would no longer be possible. Long grabbed some of the dinner he'd been preparing and left everything else as it was. Silverware, still dirty, sat in the sink; there hadn't been time to finish washing up. Brainard noted: "Our beds remained just as they were when we crawled out in the morning." The stove fire still burned. Brainard was the last man to vacate the station. He nailed the door shut.

There was the matter of the dogs. It would be impossible to take twenty-one grown dogs and two puppies along; the boats were going to be overloaded as it was. The men—and especially Schneider, who had borne most of the dog-training detail—had grown fond of these faithful work animals. He'd spent countless hours nurturing many of them as pups, feeding them, and taking care of them when they were injured or sick. Now many of them ran in circles around the fort, confused, and a number of them had followed the men down the shore toward Dutch Island, barking excitedly.

Brainard, Israel, and Long followed Greely's orders and opened and over-turned numerous barrels of food—enough, he figured, to sustain the canines for several months. The dogs had been invaluable and would be needed should the men be forced to return. Brainard dumped out a barrel of hard bread, ten barrels of seal blubber and seafood, and a half dozen barrels of pork and beef each. With that Brainard, Long, and Israel turned their backs to the fort and trod down the shore toward the boats.

They arrived to find Greely and Lockwood directing the final loading of the vessels. Brainard noticed that his commander wore "his sabre and a revolver, as well as his shoulder knots and helmet cord." It seemed a little incongruous, as if he were dressed for battle, and in a way he was. Certainly he was leading men into harm's way. Where they were headed, Cape Sabine, was nearly 250 miles to the south, and they'd be traveling in small boats into waters so violent, dangerous, and unpredictable that they'd prevented powerful steamships from reaching them for two consecutive years. It also dawned on Brainard that Greely wore his military dress as a show of authority. Lockwood wore a revolver as well. Brainard approached Rice and wondered aloud: "Will we ever again reach the land of our nativity?"

The little flotilla numbered four boats and a dinghy, plus the Greenland-ers' sealskin kayak. Greely, Lockwood, and Kislingbury climbed aboard the twenty-eight-foot-long *Lady Greely*, which Lockwood was to captain. Well built, double-cedar-planked and oak-framed, with a seven-and-a-half-foot beam, it bore a total of nine men. Its three keels could potentially be used as runners should the men be forced to drag it across ice—though at ten tons empty, this might prove impossible. And it wasn't empty—it carried a load of five thousand pounds of coal (in thirty-nine bags), gear, and men, drawing five feet of water. Cross was down with the steam engine in the cockpit, covered by a roof of canvas, with Shorty Frederick serving as fireman. The small two-person dinghy or "Whitehall boat" alternately rode on or was towed by the *Lady Greely*. The original plan was to use the *Lady Greely*, with its powerful steam engine, like a tugboat to tow all the other boats when feasible, but those in tow could quickly disengage and row independently if conditions dictated.

Brainard was assigned command of the English boat *Valorous*. Rice, who'd grown up on Cape Breton in Nova Scotia and had spent some time around boats, took charge of the whaleboat *Narwhal*, in which Pavy rode as well. En route, at Cape Baird, they'd retrieve the English iceboat *Beaumont,* which was to be skippered by Sergeant Connell.

Aboard these craft they carried forty days' worth of full rations—and had another twenty days' worth cached at southerly points between Capes Baird and Collinson. They also had weaponry and munitions in the form of four rifles with a thousand cartridges, plus two shotguns with nearly a thousand shells. With luck, as they traveled, they'd be able to bag game to supplement their rations.

Greely looked back at Fort Conger. A thin wisp of smoke rose from the chimney, dissipating in the cold Arctic air. He gazed for a time at the numerous landmarks he and the men had come to know so very well: Cairn Hill, of course, rising just before the fort, site of so many hopeful vigils; the Hogback and Broken Highlands, knuckled crags to the west, thrusting to three thousand feet. A few of the dogs that had followed them to Dutch Island raced along the bank, yelping. Greely turned and surveyed Discovery Harbor. The short, direct exit to the east was choked by heavy ice, but the western passage, between Bellot Island and Sun Cape, looked clear enough. He swung his arm in that direction and called: "Move out, men!"

The steam engine chugged and sputtered, towing the small fleet slowly behind as they distanced themselves from the shore. Greely stood at the bow, scanning the harbor for sharp-edged ice. As they moved out, a man spotted one of the dogs tearing down the shoreline, yipping hysterically. It sprinted onto the ice foot and leaped into the icy water, swimming furiously after them. Private Schneider, who'd named all of the dogs and knew them by their markings, said flatly: "I think it's Flipper." Most of the men in the trailing boats now looked back, watching the dog. Flipper was young, born just last year. Schneider kept watching; surely, the dog would give up and turn around soon. Greely remained at the bow, pointing, yelling out, and directing the helmsman through a few small floes. They were puffing rhythmically, picking up speed and moving well.

By now most of the men craned their necks around to watch the dog. He was beginning to labor, paddling frantically as the distance between him and the boats grew. His whitish head bobbed at the surface, his paws thrashing, until some seconds later his head dipped below the surface like a seal's. Everyone stared silently at the flat, black surface of the water until someone finally spoke: "He's gone." Schneider kept staring at the water in their wake for a long time. He was the last to turn away.

∞

Movement was slow, but they made it out of the harbor and around the point of Cape Baird, which was dotted with stunning blue-white bergs lining the banks. Wind whipped from the northeast, blowing heavy floes southward against the shore. They landed in the late evening to take on cache stored there, then moved on. Near midnight heavy floes cut off open water, and they sought safe harbor. Looking out into the Kennedy Channel, Greely could hardly believe what he saw. A gigantic paleocrystic floe—at least ten-year-old pressure-formed ice—floated past, carried southward by wind and current. It was stupendous. In their two years up here none of them had ever witnessed anything like it. Climbing ashore to gain some elevation, the men figured it to be several miles wide. They watched and waited for it to pass—which took nine hours—as they estimated it to be solid ice floe a full fifteen miles long. Its immensity and power awed the men into dumbstruck silence.

The next few days confirmed that their retreat would be challenging. Early on August 10, the giant floeberg having finally passed, they took off again, weaving through fast-moving ice in dense fog with a few close calls. Once they came to a large, low-lying floe and then realized that ice from the other side was closing in on them. They hurried to haul all the smaller boats ashore, but the *Lady Greely* was too heavy, so all they could do was stand there shivering in the hard-falling wet snow and watch as the ice surrounded it, raising it above the waterline. "She was caught between two floes and severely nipped," said Brainard. "We expected the sides of the *Lady Greely* to succumb to the enormous pressure, but she bore the strain bravely and, in a few moments, settled quietly down in the water."

With that disaster averted by sheer luck, they waited for open water, then dragged the boats and gear off the floeberg and back into the water and headed out again, into the swirling snow and settling fog. They made Cape Craycroft, and Greely sent two men in the small Whitehall boat to pick up a barrel of bread and one hundred pounds of meat they'd cached there in the spring for this purpose.

The fog lifted for a time, and the sun came out. The Kennedy Channel here, all the way to Greenland, looked ice free. For a time the visibility was good enough for Greely to make out Bessels Fiord, "a long narrow opening with its cliffs striped with the great inland ice cap." But the weather and visibility were ever-changing; the fog grew so thick they had to throttle down to half speed. Greely recalled that Sir John Franklin had written that fog was among the chief dangers of ice navigation, and he fully understood that claim now. His spectacles frequently fogged so much as to render him nearly blind, and he'd hurriedly wipe the lenses with a cloth, but the clarity would not last long. His poor vision frustrated him, and he barked orders to the men, becoming more and more agitated. He yelled for men to have the foghorns ready, either to alert a ship they spotted or to communicate among one another, though at this point they still remained tethered together.

Greely was clearly out of his element at sea, and it was starting to show. He'd commanded men on horseback on the Great Plains, and the last few years at Fort Conger had a semblance of normal army command. But now, for the first time in his life, by necessity he was a naval commander in charge of five craft, with a daunting 250-mile voyage ahead. He fully understood the risks to him and his men out here. At every moment pressure mounted on him to make the right decision for the sake of all their lives. When Sergeant Brainard had asked him a question about launching procedure, he'd snapped, swearing at his trusted aide in front of the whole company. Said Brainard, with apparent understatement: "He became much excited and used language toward me which my conduct did not deserve. We were all surprised by his extensive vocabulary and the fluent and forceful manner in which he delivered himself." After his outburst Greely seemed to catch himself, and he calmed down quickly as the men murmured among themselves.

Early on the morning of the twelfth, the party awoke, having camped up above a section of the ice foot worn by weather into a small cove. They moored the steam launch, and it floated in the cove; the other boats were hauled up onto the ice foot. Greely looked down and could see that Sergeant Cross had allowed the *Lady Greely* to become grounded. Greely was livid. More than once he'd warned Cross to avoid grounding at all costs The craft was so heavy and cumbersome it was a tremendous burden to move, wasting energy and valuable time and imperiling all of them. They did not have the luxury to simply wait for the tide to rise again. Every day was crucial; if they arrived near Cape Sabine before September 15, a relief ship could still be in the vicinity, waiting for them. They had just over a month to make the 250 miles, and now here they were—grounded.

Greely shouted down at Cross, who was asleep near the engine, under the canvas cover. "God damn your soul!" Greely boomed. "Come out where I can see you when I want you!" It took a few minutes, but eventually the crusty, heavy-bearded engineer staggered out into the cockpit, holding himself upright by the railing. Greely moved quickly down to him. Cross smelled of liquor. He'd been sucking down fuel alcohol while the others slept. When Greely berated him, Cross mumbled some excuse and became belligerent, swearing blasphemously at his commander.

Greely laid his hand on his revolver and stared straight through the man. "Shut up or I'll put a bullet through you," he thundered. By now everyone was up and watching. The men were just as angry as Greely. Their most experienced engineer—in fact the only officially trained one—was putting them all in danger. For the next few hours they cursed him alternately aloud and to themselves as they were forced to heave the *Lady Greely* off the shoal and back out into the water. It was now clear to everyone they'd need to keep an eye on all forms of alcohol, including the fuel. Greely ordered Shorty Frederick, who'd worked the launch a number of times on trial runs in Discovery Harbor, to replace the engineer until Cross had sobered up.

The next day they encountered a formation that was at once sublimely beautiful and terrifying. Near Carl Ritter Bay—about eighty miles from Fort Conger—their passage was halted by what Greely described as "an unbroken pack of immense paleocrystic floes of great thickness. A mile from shore an enormous floeberg, which reached some sixty feet above the water, had grounded, and from this to the shore extended a single unbroken floe." Snow began to fall hard, pelting the men's faces, and the wind picked up. Greely thought it wise to find shelter and plan what to do next.

There was nowhere ideal to camp, but they found a suitable spot to bring the small boats up onto the ice foot, and they hunkered beneath overhanging rock outcroppings. They used the small boat's sails to cover the food stores, and as makeshift tents. Lieutenant Kislingbury had spotted five narwhals earlier, and he hunted the shoreline for a time, coming back with a young seal. The men were famished from their labors, and Brainard commented: "I never remember eating a more delicious meal." For the first time since leaving Fort Conger, to warm their spirits, Greely issued an allowance of rum to everyone—except Cross.

By morning the entire camp was covered with a thin layer of snow and ice, and the men were sopping wet and miserable. A warm breakfast, with hot coffee, helped somewhat. Greely sent Lockwood and Jens to a cliff he could see some two miles southward to reconnoiter. Lockwood returned to report seeing nothing but ice—with no way through. He also offered the opinion that the great pack beyond had not broken up during the summer. This would explain why no relief ship had reached them.

Lockwood's news was indeed discouraging. With a change in tide, Greely called on Brainard to examine the giant floeberg as closely as possible to see if there was any way to navigate around it. Brainard returned sometime later to say that while there was no way around it, there might just be a way through it. A second reconnaissance revealed something wondrous: They discovered a narrow passageway, some twelve to fifteen feet wide, that had formed when the floeberg had slammed into the shore and grounded. It had split and separated, and there appeared to be a channel or chasm leading through what were now two halves. They could see a band of light through the other side, maybe a few hundred yards away. But now Greely faced a difficult decision. Just a few days ago he'd seen a berg fifteen miles long drifting past. If an ice mass of considerable size struck while they were midway through—or even if the fickle currents shifted—they'd all assuredly be crushed to death.

Greely conferred with Lockwood and Brainard, and they decided to risk it. Everything was readied, the towlines were tightened, and the *Lady Greely* chugged forward, huffing thick black plumes of smoke that curled behind them. As they neared the chasm entrance, Greely raised his hand to slow, and he considered his decision one more time. "All right," he said after a long silence. "Take her through." The instant they entered, the men could feel the temperature drop. Everyone went dead silent, reverent as if in prayer. The opaque blue-green walls of ice on either side of them soared skyward over sixty feet. Waves broke against the launch's bow as the *Lady Greely* steamed slowly through, and it grew colder still as they went on. They gazed in awe at the crystalline structure of the walls, Arctic ice formed by a thousand years and immense pressure. At last they could see the light of the exit as if it were coming from the end of a tunnel, and they emerged from the inside of the gigantic berg.

Greely could finally exhale. Of the ice canyon he wrote: "I recall no other weird mass which so impressed me with the grandeur and scope of nature's forces and works," adding that "the narrow cleft . . . afforded perhaps the most wonderful passage ever traversed by any voyagers."

The awe of this glorious passage was short-lived. Within a few hours winds rose, and heavy snows pelted down on them. Waves slammed into the boats, drenching the men. They had to use the sails to carefully cover the bread. They were reduced to a pace of just two miles a day, and the *Lady Greely*'s engine seemed to be acting up, coughing and sputtering. Brainard was sent to the engine room and found that Cross again "had been tampering with the fuel alcohol . . . and was very much intoxicated." Greely ordered Cross instantly to Rice's boat, replaced him again with Shorty, and ordered him "not to enter the launch again except by special authority." When Shorty went in and checked the engine situation, he reported that had Cross remained down there neglecting the boiler a few minutes longer, it would likely have exploded.

By August 15 they were forced ashore once again to take shelter. Temperatures fell to –20° and ice was closing in around them. There was fear among the men—voiced for the group by Doctor Pavy and Lieutenant Kislingbury—of becoming entrapped in the ice. Even with the cache they'd picked up near Carl Ritter Bay, they were down to only about forty days' rations.

Brainard volunteered to foray down the coast with a small party to see whether a relief vessel had made it as far as Cape Lawrence (some fifty miles south), but Greely would not allow the party to be separated at this time. Instead they sheltered in the lee of a grounded berg, the *Lady Greely* anchored there, the men soaked and shuddering with cold. Greely took Brainard aside and wondered aloud whether it might make more sense, and improve progress, for them to ditch the *Lady Greely*. They could then haul the smaller boats, sledges, and stores up onto a large ice floe and float on it south down the strait. They would likely reach either Cape Sabine or Littleton Island this way. Brainard found his idea "certainly a most extraordinary one."

It was not the first time Greely had suggested it. He'd actually mentioned it already two or three times to the officers, noting that had they done it earlier, they would no doubt already be south of Cape Lawrence by now. Brainard personally thought their best course of action would be to return to Fort Conger using the steam launch—that might still be possible. They had food and shelter there, and game for another month. Without question, they could easily survive the winter. Continuing on into the unknown was foolhardy. They had no idea whether a ship, or enough stores, even awaited them at all. If none did,

Brainard wondered: "What would we shivering wretches do on arrival at the beginning of winter with nothing to subsist on?" But Brainard kept these thoughts to himself and the privacy of his journal. Lockwood seemed the only one who generally supported the idea of boarding an iceberg or floe; at least he did not dismiss the notion outright.

Almost everyone else—and certainly Pavy and Kislingbury—thought the idea of committing to the fate of a floe was insane. On the night of the fifteenth, anchored to an offshore floe, the commander took his place near the engine of the *Lady Greely*, curling into any warmth he could find. The others were variously in the tethered boats, sodden and dank in their sealskin clothes, wriggling inside frozen buffalo-hide sleeping bags. In the whaleboat *Valorous*, Brainard tried in vain to get some sleep. As the berg shifted and groaned and waves sloshed against the boats, Brainard could hear the whispers of Doctor Pavy, Lieutenant Kislingbury, and Sergeant Rice. They talked for a long time, and the conversation appeared animated—a few times one hushed another, apparently concerned about being overheard.

Sometime later, in the nether hours of the night, Pavy, Kislingbury, and Rice quietly called over to Brainard to join them on the *Narwhal.* They wished to speak with him. He rose, stepping onto the boat and adjusting his collar against the driving snow. In hushed tones, taking turns, the three men presented to Brainard "a most extraordinary proposition." It went like this: If Commander Greely persisted with the notion of boarding and drifting on an iceberg, Doctor Pavy, as the expedition's physician, would declare him insane and mentally unfit to lead. Command would then fall to Lieutenant Kislingbury, second-highest-ranking among them, who had already agreed to lead everyone back to Fort Conger. If Brainard would go along with them, they could perhaps persuade Lockwood to join the takeover. If Lockwood refused, they'd simply place him under arrest. Rice finally appealed to Brainard, saying that the plot hinged on him. If Brainard would simply agree, "then all the men would go along. . . . It was the only means of saving the party."

Brainard turned toward the *Lady Greely*, now nearly icebound, where the commander slept comfortably next to the smoldering coal of the steam engine.

Through the low light of the midnight sun he could see the tops of all the mountains in the distance toward which they were heading, already covered with snow. What few plants and shrubs he could see on the hillsides were encased in hoarfrost. Would he, they were asking him point-blank, be the deciding vote in a mutiny?

14

A Game of Cat and Mouse

The *Yantic* sat at anchor at Littleton Island on the afternoon of August 3, 1883. There Commander Wildes read the report from the cairn and learned of the fate of the *Proteus*. He was heartened to know that all hands had survived the sinking, but he was now doubly worried: Very little had been left for Greely and his men, and there were now also the shipwrecked men of Garlington and Pike to consider. Their location was unknown. Wildes's instructions had been explicit—he was to sail no farther north than Littleton Island. His duty, as a naval officer and as head of the "tender," was to the men of the *Proteus*. Reluctantly he turned the *Yantic* south, bearing in its hold "7000 pounds of bread, seven tons of salt beef, pork, and other preserved meats, plus large supplies of other foods." None was left for Greely.

Wildes halted at nearby Pandora Harbor, where he read more records left by Garlington and Pike, and these at least gave further detailed information, stating that the party had between them forty days' rations and intended to "go south, keeping close into shore as possible, and calling at Cary Islands, to Cape York, or until I meet some vessel. Hope to meet U.S.S. *Yantic* or the Swedish steamer *Sofia*, which should be about Cape York."

Wildes's course of action now appeared quite clear. He must pursue the

Garlington-Pike flotilla southward, calling at all the prearranged stations. Surely, under steam he should have no difficulty catching them. Wildes placed a worthy seaman in the crow's nest and ordered him to be on the lookout for any signs of men, boats, cairns, or camps. Wildes next crossed the wind-washed sound to Cary Island, arriving in a stiffening gale around midnight. He fired a gunshot to no reply, and a visit to the island revealed no messages or sign of Garlington having been there. Wildes grew somewhat worried by finding nothing, as Garlington had explicitly included Cary Island in his message at Pandora Harbor. The seas were rough enough that it was possible the boats had all been lost, but Wildes put that thought from his mind and continued on. He backtracked to Hakluyt Island, then over to Cape Parry, scanning the shorelines carefully. Nothing. Wildes ordered that they steam for Cape York, remaining as close to land as shore ice would allow. The weather began to turn foul.

On August 5 the *Yantic* made a point some five miles northwest of Saunders Island, where Garlington had been just two days before. Garlington was in fact at this precise moment near Cape Atholl, just twenty miles south, a mere four hours' steaming for the *Yantic*. But the weather was deteriorating, bringing low-hanging fog and thickening ice. On August 6 Wildes anchored off Northumberland Island, where some of his men discovered empty cans, strewn matches, and bootprints along the beach. It was Garlington's camp of just two days before. Wildes decided to remain there for a few days—at least until the treacherous pack loosened or moved offshore so that he could safely continue south. He intended to then make for Cape York, the last of the agreed-upon stations.

Captain Wildes drew in close to a mainland cape on August 9, but found much ice extending a great distance offshore. It seemed to be closing in hourly from every direction, and visibility had deteriorated. Cape York lay forty miles to the south, but Wildes had another problem—his coal was running low. By the next day conditions had not improved, and a strong southerly gale was blowing in. He made the decision to steam directly for Upernavik, skipping Cape York entirely—he wasn't sure whether he'd even be able to get there anyway, so dense was the shore ice. At Upernavik he would wait for Garlington and Pike as long as possible. Under full steam Wildes and the *Yantic* passed by Cape

York some forty miles offshore in Melville Bay. At that very moment Garlington and Pike had arrived at Cape York and were conversing with Etah natives, asking whether they'd seen a ship—either the *Yantic* or the *Sofia*. They had not. Lieutenant Colwell sat on a rock in a driving snowstorm, peering at solid ice extending far out to sea. It was the second time the *Yantic* had sailed right past the shipwrecked men.

∽∾∽

Garlington, Colwell, and Pike had worked desperately to reach Cape York. The men's hands were blistered raw, and they'd been eating only in the moving, open boats, blasted by alternating rain and snow, which had now kept up for five consecutive days. By August 16, exhausted, hungry, and freezing, they were just east of Cape York. Garlington could now only make suppositions about the whereabouts of the *Yantic*. He figured, based on the condition of the ice in Melville Bay, that it had made it no farther than Upernavik, and that it most likely would be there—but for how long? Garlington conferred with Colwell and Pike. The consensus was that they absolutely must catch up with the *Yantic*. But what was the best way to achieve this?

Staying together was proving too slow, so they formulated a daring plan: They would strip bare and lighten Lieutenant Colwell's boat as much as possible, and he would try to speed across Melville Bay and, if he could, attempt to shoot directly for Godhavn, Disko Island. Garlington and Pike would hug as close to the Greenland coast as they could, stopping at sheltered bays and inlets wherever they could find safe moorage. When Garlington, Pike, and his men made it to Upernavik, if the *Yantic* was there, they'd climb aboard and continue south to pick up Colwell and his men. If the *Yantic* was not there, they would wait there for either a ship or some word from Colwell. Garlington and Pike, if necessary, could spend the winter at Upernavik among the native Greenlanders. Colwell was also prepared to winter at Godhavn, should he make it there and find that the *Yantic* had already departed for home. The plan was risky, but they agreed it was their best chance.

Colwell's small crew included two civilians, a Greenlander, and three soldiers. On August 16 the weather finally allowed departure, and the two groups separated as planned. Lt. John Colwell bore south-southeast, aiming straight for Upernavik. Dense pack ice extended to the northeast, and he tried to navigate along its edge, but strong winds whipped into a steady gale, and driving rain now turned to snow. In the pounding surf three of his men vomited overboard, writhing with seasickness, and the Greenlander could not understand English enough to take directions, so Colwell was effectively left with a crew of two. He was blown off course time and again.

After a night of continuous rowing the winds died, but heavy snow continued to slam them. Colwell handed the tiller over to one of the men whose seasickness had subsided. Burning alcohol in a tin can, he warmed up some tea and canned meat, the first thing they'd eaten in more than twelve hours. The food and tea revived the men somewhat. Colwell ordered his men to shake out the reef "and set the mainsail, making an easterly course on wind" into rough seas. Around noon the wind blew hard once more, forcing Colwell to take in the mainsail. Freezing waves lashed at them, and Colwell squinted through blinding snow at a tiny island he could barely make out ahead to the northeast. In the driving whiteout, they missed the island by about a mile. Colwell spotted a large floeberg in the distance and made for it. When they arrived at three o'clock that afternoon, he had a man secure the whaleboat to the berg with a grapnel hook, and they tried to rest and warm up. All around them great bergs crashed into one another, rupturing and calving into the sea, drenching the men with frigid spray.

The storm raged for the next nine hours, filling the bottom of the boat with snow. Colwell had the oarsman stand with an ax ready to sever the bowline every time the berg broke or disintegrated so they would not be crushed and sunk by falling ice. Four times they had to cut away and cast off for a safer place. Just after midnight Colwell lit the alcohol stove and heated some bacon and tea, then passed out whiskey to the men. They'd been moving on and off the floes for fourteen hours, often at the oars and always at the ready, periodically stuffing soaked hardtack into their mouths for sustenance. By 5:00 a.m. on August 18, near Thom Island the clouds began to break up, then lift, and the winds subsided considerably. Great bergs and floes were packing together and chasing them from the north, pushed by wind and current. Colwell and his men strained hard at the oars until that afternoon; then a steady northeast wind allowed him to sail the remainder of the day, and they could alternately get some rest and even fitful sleep by trading off manning the sail and the tiller.

That evening the winds and sea became so rough that Colwell was forced to take in sail and row all night, pulling toward the east until morning. Morning met them with raging winds and seas, waves crashing over the bow nearly swamping them. Colwell was forced to retreat to a small rocky island they'd passed some hours before. After windmilling his arms to get some blood flow and warmth, he lit the alcohol fire and cooked a hot breakfast for his men. Fed, and having drunk some hot tea, everyone rooted into the frozen ground of the spare isle, passing out from sheer exhaustion.

On August 19, as the wind had fallen and the skies cleared, Colwell revived the men around noon. It was time to make an all-out run for Upernavik, Greenland. For the next three days and nights, alternating between sailing and rowing through a moving maze of floebergs and lump ice, Colwell pressed on continuously, keeping the Greenland coast in his sights as best he could. Near evening on the twenty-second, Colwell, his vision blurred from sleep deprivation, stared at the hazy coast and reckoned they had made Upernavik, but a thick fog enveloped them and forced them to make landfall. Exploring the shoreline, one of his men discovered a barrel, which suggested they might be near civilization. They broke the barrel into pieces and made a warming fire, cooking what food they had left.

After a few hours' rest the fog had lifted slightly, and Colwell loaded and launched again. Some hours later he sighted a wooden structure—a storehouse—and he realized he'd reached the northernmost end of Upernavik. The men, reinvigorated, pulled hard around the island and they landed at 5:00 a.m. on August 23. The island was quiet, and Colwell sent the Greenlander to scout for help. Colwell then took out his pistol and fired gunshots to alert anyone of his arrival. In a few minutes the Greenlander returned, excitedly nodding that yes, yes, this was Upernavik. The settlement itself was just a bit farther along.

Around a point, Colwell and six ragged men stepped from the battered open whaleboat and onto shore. There the governor of Upernavik welcomed them, telling them they'd have everything they would need for their comfort and succor. He also told them that the *Yantic* had departed for Disko Island just nine hours before their arrival: They'd missed the *Yantic* once again.

As Colwell and his men ate and changed into dry clothes, he learned that Wildes and the *Yantic* had arrived at Upernavik on August 12 and remained for ten days, waiting for them. But Wildes had begun to worry about the onset of winter, and after consulting with the governor, decided to take on fifty tons of coal and move south to Disko Island. He left a letter for Garlington and Colwell, stating that he would remain there taking on coal no later than September 15, when he would sail the *Yantic* south to St. John's.

Colwell's seven-day crossing of Melville Bay with six men in an open whaleboat has been called "a journey which takes a place among the best work done by Arctic explorers." The exhausting five-hundred-plus-mile voyage remains one of the most astonishing feats of courage, endurance, and navigational skill in the history of the Arctic. But Colwell wasn't finished. He now knew that in order to save Garlington, Pike, and their crew of thirty-five—whose whereabouts and condition were currently unknown—he had to catch the *Yantic* before it left Disko, which was 230 miles south.

Colwell immediately began to ready his waterlogged and leaky whaleboat for departure, but the good governor of Upernavik intervened, offering his own personal launch, which was decidedly more seaworthy. At 3:00 p.m. on August 23, the same day they'd landed, Colwell and his men rowed away from the Danish settlement of Upernavik to the cheers of the whole town, accompanied by a cannon salute. In excellent weather they alternately rowed and sailed when they could, not stopping for the first forty-eight hours. They made land briefly at the settlement of Proven to take on food and fresh water, and then they plowed ahead. Finally, after seven and a half days of almost constant rowing, on August 31 they passed through the Waigat Strait and arrived at the southeast tip of Disko Island, their arms and shoulders burning, their hands blistered and bleeding.

Colwell sent a soldier to scramble up a cliff, so he could look down on Godhavn Harbor, and to his great relief, the man returned to report that there the *Yantic* sat at anchor. In less than an hour Colwell was aboard the *Yantic*, excitedly telling Wildes the details of his thirty-nine-day, eight-hundred-mile saga since the sinking of the *Proteus*. But there was still no time to lose; now they must sail the *Yantic* back north to rescue Garlington, Pike, and the rest of the boat parties. So that very evening the *Yantic* sped north.

It made good time, and in three days, on September 2, Wildes, Colwell, and the *Yantic*'s crew were jubilant to find Garlington, Pike, and the remainder of the boat party at Upernavik, where they'd arrived just the day after Colwell had departed in the governor's launch. Hugging the coast, Garlington and Pike's journey had been much smoother and safer than the tumultuous and torturous Melville Bay saga. After six weeks, numerous near rendezvous, much hardship, and many close calls, the parties of the *Proteus* and the tender *Yantic* were all reunited, without the loss of a single life. It was remarkable.

But now Garlington, Wildes, and Colwell convened in the warmth of the captain's cabin to ponder the most pressing question: What about Greely?

The relief vessel *Yantic. (Courtesy of Naval History and Heritage Command)*

15

Adrift

We have crossed the Rubicon.
—*David L. Brainard, August 21, 1883*

In the middle of the night on August 15, with Greely sleeping next to the boiler of the *Lady Greely*, Sgt. David L. Brainard stood shivering in the *Narwhal*, stunned by what was being asked of him by Pavy, Kislingbury, and Rice. Brainard exhaled plumes of steam as he contemplated their mutinous plot. It was true that Brainard had misgivings about boarding a floe and leaving their fate to the winds and the currents. He had said before that Greely's "scheme sounds like madness," and he had more than once thought a retreat to Fort Conger the most sensible course, though he'd kept this to himself. It was also true that Greely had, of late, seemed agitated. He'd blown up at Brainard for no good reason. Such behavior was disconcerting but not unexpected—everyone was under incredible stress. Another thing Brainard had noticed, and which had also been observed by Rice, was that Greely really could not see very well. His poor vision hindered him in finding reliable leads through the labyrinth of ice. But this last was easily remedied. Someone more nautically experienced, and with better vision, like Rice, could become ice pilot.

Yet none of this added up to his commanding officer being "mentally unfit to lead." Much was going through Brainard's mind as he stood quietly in the wind and snow, with the others awaiting his response. He suspiciously eyed Kislingbury, who'd been disgruntled from the start of the expedition, and whom he trusted no farther than he could spit. At any rate, Kislingbury had been disbarred, and any logical replacement of Greely—should that be necessary as a result of his becoming incapacitated or killed—naturally fell to Lieutenant Lockwood. Brainard was an army man through and through; he'd enlisted five years ago at age nineteen and had served steadily in the cavalry out West. He'd obeyed every order he had ever been given, and he'd served admirably in the Nez Percé and Bannock Wars under the celebrated Col. Nelson Appleton Miles. Sergeant Brainard was not the kind of man to take part in a mutiny. He looked directly at the trio of conspirators—Pavy, Kislingbury, and Rice—his eyes deadly serious. He told them flatly that he "declined to take part in any such plan." It was a terrible, treasonous idea. He would hear no more of it.

But their situation remained less than ideal. For five days they'd been ice-locked, making no further progress. Men and boats were dusted with three inches of new snow. On the evening of August 18 a small lead opened, and they fired up the *Lady Greely* and it towed the flotilla southward. During this short run Greely stood on the bow, squinting with his poor vision in the low light. As he leaned forward, his sealskin boots slipped on the snow-covered wood and he fell overboard. Lockwood and Kislingbury acted quickly, heaving Greely back on board. It was a very close call.

While Greely got dry and warm, they made a solid four-hour run and reached a small bay short of Cape Lawrence in the middle of the night. But no sooner had they arrived than suddenly, a tidal shift shut their lead, and Brainard saw ice come "charging down on our frail boats with the speed of a race horse." He had never seen ice move so fast. Greely ordered full steam, and they barely made it out of the little bay before it was engulfed by shearing ice that would have torn their wooden craft to shards.

The fast-moving ice and ever-changing leads forced them to constantly crisscross and meander, rarely moving in a straight line and often backtracking. By the time they made it to Rawlings Bay on August 20, they were less than half-way to Cape Sabine, with some 150 miles still ahead of them and winter closing in fast. And that wasn't the only ominous news: Private Frederick, who'd taken over as engineer for the drunken Cross, reported that the engine of the *Lady Greely* was overburdened and struggling, and he lacked the proper tools and equipment to make repairs. While Frederick tinkered with the engine as best he could, Greely sent Brainard and Eskimo Fred ashore to gain some elevation and scan the Smith Sound. Said Brainard: "We set out trudging wearily along through the deep snow and over broken rocks, the sharp edges cutting our boots."

The two reached Cape Lawrence around three in the morning and studied the Smith Sound. The thick pack stretched across the entire Kennedy Channel, according to Brainard, "unbroken and impenetrable. . . . With heavy hearts we turned back." Greely wanted to see for himself, and at Cape Lawrence he ascended a hill to some two hundred feet to scout. He detected large, wide leads to the southeast and due south, and he concluded: "Ice conditions cannot be foretold for any length of time, but depend almost entirely, at this season of the year, on the action of the wind and tides." In the few hours between Brainard's report and what Greely saw, the character of the sound had completely changed.

Greely then saw "an immense paleocrystic floe of many miles extent moving out of the bay, leaving clear water behind it." It wasn't quite as large as the fifteen-mile-long one they'd seen before, but close. Greely hurried back to the boats to try to take advantage of the clear water behind the giant berg, but arrived to find the *Lady Greely* once again grounded. Despite the efforts of the entire party pulling on ropes, they couldn't budge the heavy launch and were forced to wait five hours for the rising tide to lift it. They had lost their chance at that open water. All they could do now was huddle and shiver on the boats and watch the bergs rumble by. They were weirdly beautiful and menacing, some of them fifty feet high and shaped like pyramids, some wind-worn into knuckled fists, and others long and flat as barges. The noise of their creaking and groaning was constant, as was the wail of the wind. Kislingbury remarked: "The whole strait is one moving mass of ice, frightful to look at."

For the next few days the expedition made slow progress south. They subsisted on one pound of bread and the same of meat each day, supplemented with a few ounces of potatoes and beans. They stuffed dried fruit into their mouths as they could. Whenever Jens or Eskimo Fred shot and procured a seal, every ounce was used, and most men had come to relish drinking the blood—warm if possible—which tasted like raw eggs. Some, like Cross, preferred to chew the liver raw.

To save fuel they cooked with barrels taken from the caches along the way, and wood they'd brought along from Fort Conger, but they were running low. On August 21 they came above Cape Wilkes and were driven by winds and tide into an unsafe harbor, but they got through to find better anchorage to the south. Here Greely ordered that they use axes and sledgehammers to dismantle and break up the small Whitehall boat, which had been leaking for days and become too heavy to drag along. They stacked the wood in the other boats, storing it for fuel.

When the last of the Whitehall wood had been loaded, Sergeant Jewell noticed the pack moving offshore and spotted a good lead, with water opening up to the south. Greely called for them to move out, but they had barely gone a half mile when the tide and wind shifted and drove the boats shoreward, grinding them all against the ice foot. Greely, with Lockwood and Kislingbury, toiled to keep the *Lady Greely* from running aground. The hull scraped against the frozen shore but withstood the impact, though the smokestack was damaged by bashing against overhanging ice. Brainard, Rice, and Connell, in charge of the other boats, did well to keep the harm to a minimum, cutting the towlines and rowing into protected inlets, the men helping to haul the craft ashore. Rice's whaleboat took the brunt of the damage during this frightening event. Brainard betrayed some fear as he assessed their situation: "We have crossed the Rubicon and to turn back now is out of the question. We *must* advance although I am fearful it will result in another Franklin disaster."

The next day they landed at Cape Collinson, and Greely sent Brainard and Jewell ashore to collect stores cached by Nares in 1875. Unfortunately the cache had been ravaged by polar bears and foxes—there were tracks in the thin layer of fresh snow. All the bread, sugar, and tobacco that had been there previously were gone, and the rum keg's bung was bitten off and all the rum was gone. They were able to retrieve "two hundred and forty rations of meat, salt, pepper, onion powder, and fuel, and one hundred and twenty rations of bread."

The men were soaked alternately by rain and wet snow in temperatures that were now consistently below freezing. Sleep was nearly impossible, and the men grew irritable. The normally cheerful Brainard recorded on the twenty-third: "I have never spent a more disagreeable night. Snow, mixed with rain, fell all night saturating our clothing, sleeping bags, and other property." Schneider, who'd been serving as cook in extremely difficult conditions, and doing double duty as Greely's secretary in charge of taking notes from dictation, asked to be relieved of cook duty. When Greely refused, Schneider flew into a tantrum, screaming at his commander and then breaking down and weeping. Greely felt for Schneider, with whom he'd spent countless hours making copies of their records back at Fort Conger. He could see that the private's nerves were beyond frayed. He agreed to let Lockwood take over the cooking until Schneider felt better and could resume.

On the evening of August 25, with dense fog closing down on them, Greely watched the ice carefully. He worried that encroaching ice was about to pen them in, so he called for all hands to move, and quickly: "With great difficulty, we bored our way through the moving pack and reached Hayes Point." The fog grew dangerously thick and drove them ashore once more, and while Lockwood prepared food for the men, Greely ascertained open water to the south. When the fog rose, he ordered another move, and they snaked around "immense grounded floebergs and reached good water."

After three hours of moving through relatively safe and open waters, Greely drew the launch up to a high, grounded floeberg and, using a pickax, climbed to its summit to survey. He concluded that the pack was open enough for a large steam vessel but unsafe for their lighter craft, so there they waited to get some rest. Before Greely turned in, he sent Jewell and two men to a high cape, from which they could see into a bay and perhaps locate a ship.

At 2:30 a.m. the watch sergeant awakened Greely to report open ice, and Greely called for everyone to move. They picked up Jewell and the reconnaissance team along the way. Jewell said that fog prevented him from seeing all

the way to Cape Hawks, so he could not confirm or deny the presence of a relief ship. In case a ship was in the vicinity, Greely asked Schneider, who seemed
to be coming around to his former self, to stand in the bow of the *Valorous* and
blow a foghorn every two minutes. They heard no reply except the cacopho-
nous grinding and popping of the ice pack. They made a lengthy detour around
some large floes and arrived at Cape Hawks at about two o'clock on the afternoon of August 26, after twelve consecutive hours of steaming and rowing.

Greely had Sergeant Rice stop at nearby Washington Irving Island, where
he was to inspect a cairn and also climb to the summit and evaluate the conditions south. Rice returned with unfortunate news: The cairn had not been visited since they'd passed through themselves on the *Proteus* in 1881. No other
records had been left there. The paltry English cache he retrieved consisted of
moldy bread, 168 pounds of dried potatoes, one keg of pickled onions, and six
gallons of rum. There was also some stearine* cooking fuel. But most troubling
to Greely was what Rice had seen from the summit: "The ice to the southward
as far as the eye could reach . . . is now in such a state that any well-provided
vessel could easily run through it." There was plenty of open water.

So why was there no ship?

Greely knew now that their state was ominous. He observed: "We are in a
critical position, not knowing what to depend upon. Since no vessel has reached
this point in 1882 or 1883, up to this time, we must all feel an uncertainty as to
the hope for our relief being at Lifeboat Cove [at Littleton Island]." Brainard
agreed: "I do not believe that a relief vessel has been able to approach this far
north since the *Proteus* made the trip with our party. Perhaps, even now, the
ship we await is lost in Melville Bay, or in the pack." Brainard's intuition, though
he could not know it, was correct. The *Proteus* lay at the bottom of the sound
just fifty miles away.

But neither Greely nor his men gave up hope. His men were hearty. With
all their zigzagging, they'd made more than three hundred miles through nearly
constant ice "of such size and danger," he noted, "as must be seen to be appreciated." They would not give up. It was still possible that the relief vessels had

---

* The crude commercial form of stearic acid, used primarily in the manufacture of candles.

made it to either Littleton or the Cary Islands, or even Cape Sabine, whose bluffs they could now see whenever the fog lifted. He reasoned that to make it to any of these, they'd need a confluence of factors and luck: temperatures warm enough to prevent new ice from forming, and gales strong enough to keep the floes moving and create navigable leads. There was the risk of being trapped in the ice, but that was a risk Greely now believed they must take. If trapped, they could use sledges to pull their food and gear on top of the ice. They were low on coal, so Greely had men break up the barrels and casks from the English cache and store the wood for fuel enough to reach either Cape Sabine or Littleton Island, whichever the winds and waters permitted.

Late on the afternoon of the twenty-sixth, Greely, after consulting with Lieutenant Lockwood, called George Rice onto the *Lady Greely*. By now Rice had proved himself the best ice pilot among them, and he'd shown tremendous good humor under all circumstances. On a few occasions early in their retreat he'd slipped from his position in the bow and fallen overboard. Each time he'd been dragged back aboard, and quickly stripped himself to the skin and put on dry clothes. On one occasion he joked that he'd had more baths than all of them put together. Kislingbury called Rice "the most indispensable man we have." Greely instructed Rice to take over for him as ice navigator and make an all-out run for Bache Island, and then, if conditions allowed, to press on to Cape Sabine. They would no longer hug the shoreline but take the shortcut into open water. If they could just break through a mile of pack ice to the open water, they could likely make Cape Sabine in a day.

They steamed away from the coast, bearing offshore, all eyes firmly fixed on the bluffs ahead. But within just a few hours, the opposite of what they'd hoped for occurred. Temperatures plunged to 18°, and new ice started forming fast around them. About seventeen miles from Bache Island, ice locked tight around the *Lady Greely* as the commander ordered Rice to secure the launch to a small floe and directed the other officers to prepare the smaller boats to be hauled up onto the ice if necessary. By early morning the boats were firmly frozen in place. Said Brainard: "We are beset. The ice pack completely encloses us." Greely had the men erect a wooden lookout tripod that allowed them to climb up to fifteen feet and survey their situation, and what they saw nearly devastated them: Just one mile ahead, the waters to Cape Sabine were wide open.

The reality of their situation drove Brainard to conclude: "I do not think that ever before did an exploring party meet with as many adversities as we have on this retreat." He immediately suggested to Greely a reduction in rations. There was simply no telling how long they'd be imprisoned by the ice, and though the sighting of a few narwhals gave them hope, there was no guarantee of effectively landing one even if they shot it, so large and cumbersome were they in the water. Greely decided against reducing rations—he did not want to lower morale among the men, and he also reasoned they were going to need their full strength for the exertions ahead.

Edward Israel now busied himself taking meridian observations to determine their location, and after two days they'd moved a mere one and a half miles south, which was disturbingly slow but at least in the right direction. Temperatures dropped yet lower. Under crisp, clear skies they could survey their desperate and desolate surroundings: To the west, on the Grinnell Land side of the lower Kane Basin, were rugged, rocky cliff lines, and beyond those, the snowcapped Victoria and Albert Mountains soared high above. All the boats and men and gear were crusted with a thin layer of frost. Greely took Brainard aside, and they carefully inventoried their stores. They had about 1,250 pounds of various meats, including pemmican, bacon, and beef, plus 1,100 pounds of hardtack. They determined they had food for fifty days, coffee and tea for forty, but agreed that if necessary the provisions could be made to last sixty days.

For the next few days all the men could do was try to stay warm. The temperature plunged to 11°, and according to Brainard: "No polar party has ever recorded a temperature so low in August." Sergeants took turns climbing up on the tripod on watch, but there was nothing to see in the distance but vastness—water and ice and rock. Their drift was at first gradual, almost imperceptible. But constant was the awful groaning and creaking and splitting of the ice pack, a sound so eerily hideous that it had come to be known by Arctic explorers as "the Devil's Symphony." The sound of ice grinding against ice, shearing and shrieking, was an omnipresent reminder of their unimaginable frailness in this vast and dangerous place. They were marooned, adrift on an island of ice that moved with the vicissitudes of temperature and tides, currents and winds.

Early on the afternoon of September 1, Brainard yelled out for everyone to get ready, to prepare for impact. "The northern ice pack came charging down on our unprotected floe," he said, "breaking like sticks the ice which offered opposition, and heaping it in great, quivering groaning masses about us." The enormous pressure of the pack striking them from the north tore huge rifts and clefts in the floe they were camped on. Everyone scrambled madly, hauling up the lighter whaleboats as ice rent and fractured beneath them. Chunks and rubble from the colliding floe broke around the men, some of the pieces the size of the boats themselves, large enough to crush the men. Those not dodging slabs of ice watched in awe as the ten-thousand-pound *Lady Greely*, pinched by untold pressure, rose upward entirely from the water as easily as a seed squeezed between thumb and finger. All stared agape, expecting it to splinter like kindling. But according to Brainard: "She did not succumb completely as we had expected but rose grandly as the pressure increased and stood high above the water in a cradle formed by the grinding ice." It remained aloft for four hours until the tide shifted, the pressure released, and it eased back down into the water.

The commander ordered the contents emptied and brought onto the floe and secured. The next day, September 2, Greely spoke with Brainard, Lockwood, and Israel, who was busy taking readings. Flood tides had reversed their course, taking them two miles north in the last four hours, away from their destination. But they had a much more immediate problem: The floe they rode upon was young ice—only a single season's worth of growth—and its soft underbelly was being pulverized beneath them by the immeasurable pressure of the older, harder, northern pack.

The grinding ice pack. *(Courtesy of Naval History and Heritage Command)*

16

Forsaken

Garlington and Wildes, dry, warm, and well fed aboard the *Yantic* in Upernavik, contemplated their options. They could surmise that if Greely followed his own orders—which was likely—he would be somewhere along the Grinnell Land coast, moving south by sea or land. But anything beyond that was pure speculation. Given the ordeal that Garlington and Colwell and Pike's men had just endured, they had some sense of the trials that Greely and the men of the Lady Franklin Bay Expedition were likely experiencing. Garlington considered a number of possibilities. The orders from the U.S. Navy regarding the *Yantic* were explicit—"Under no circumstances will you proceed beyond Littleton Island, Smith Sound, and you are not to enter the ice pack, nor to place your ship in a position to prevent your return this season." The *Yantic* was well made, but they all knew that it was unsuited for ice, its sheathing "not calculated to resist pressure in the ice-pack but . . . merely to prevent sharp ice from cutting her sides." Garlington had witnessed firsthand what the ice had done to the *Proteus*, which *was* built for ice.

Winter was setting in early. The option of building a winter station at Littleton Island was no longer viable, since the precut lumber for a dwelling now lay at the bottom of the Kane Basin. Commander Wildes thought that the season was already too far advanced, and they should immediately steam for St. John's—once back in Newfoundland, perhaps there might still be time to engage a sealing vessel and small crew to steam north to try to help Greely. Garlington concurred. Capt. Richard Pike's opinion was neither sought nor offered. He seemed happy just to be alive. So without further discussion, all the men from the *Proteus* boarded the *Yantic* and steamed away on September 2, leaving Greely and his "expeditionary force" standing atop a fractured and crumbling iceberg. Garlington and Wildes now had to admit that so far, the relief and resupply efforts for Greely had both been abysmal failures. As they headed for Newfoundland, they contemplated this tragic set of facts: "From July 1882 to August 1883, not less than 50,000 rations were taken in the steamers *Neptune*, *Yantic*, and *Proteus* up to or beyond Littleton Island, and of that number only about 1,000 were left in that vicinity, the remainder being returned to the United States or sunk with the *Proteus*."

The *Yantic* made good time and arrived in St. John's Harbor on September 13. During the voyage Garlington had had plenty of time to consider the wording of the telegram he dreaded sending. But with a belly full of knots, he dutifully telegraphed the following, which he said was "the saddest duty which I have ever been called upon to perform":

ST. JOHN'S, N. F., SEPT. 13. 1883.

TO CHIEF SIGNAL OFFICER, U.S.A., WASHINGTON:

IT IS MY PAINFUL DUTY TO REPORT TOTAL FAILURE OF THE EXPEDITION. THE *PROTEUS* WAS CRUSHED IN PACK IN LATITUDE 78.52, LONGITUDE 74.25, AND SUNK ON THE AFTERNOON OF THE 23D JULY. MY PARTY AND CREW OF SHIP ALL SAVED. MADE MY WAY ACROSS SMITH SOUND AND ALONG EASTERN SHORE TO CAPE YORK; THENCE ACROSS MELVILLE BAY TO UPERNAVIK, ARRIVING THERE ON 24TH AUG. THE *YANTIC* REACHED UPERNAVIK 2D SEPT. AND LEFT SAME DAY, BRINGING ENTIRE PARTY HERE TO-DAY.

ALL WELL. E.A. GARLINGTON

"All well" considerably overstated things, at least where Lieutenant Greely and his men were concerned. The man who received Garlington's initial cable was Capt. Samuel M. Mills, who was serving as acting chief signal officer. General Hazen, the official CSO and the most ardent supporter and friend of the expedition, was unfortunately far from Washington, D.C., out West in the Washington Territory, inspecting some of the very telegraph lines and signal posts that Greely had personally installed. Mills also immediately telegraphed Hazen the terrible news. In the War Department D.C. office at the time, and assisting Captain Mills, was Louis V. Caziarc, a longtime friend of the Greely family. Mills and Caziarc sat stunned reading Garlington's report, noting its conspicuous omission of anything related to the Greely party. They quickly wired back to Garlington: "Received news of *Yantic*'s arrival. Did you place any stores for Greely? How much, and where? Can anything more be done this year?—Caziarc, Mills."

As they anxiously awaited a reply, Cdr. Frank Wildes was simultaneously writing a telegram to his superior, Secretary of the Navy William Chandler. Wildes conveyed the following:

STEAMER *PROTEUS* WAS CRUSHED IN ICE SIX MILES NORTH OF CAPE SABINE, JULY 23 . . . RETREATED SOUTH IN SIX BOATS . . . SUFFERING MUCH HARDSHIP IN MELVILLE BAY . . . *YANTIC* REACHED LITTLETON ISLAND WITHOUT MUCH DIFFICULTY . . . IMMEDIATELY PROCEEDED SOUTHWARD; SEARCHED COAST AND ISLANDS THOROUGHLY . . . ICE PACK THEN CLOSED IN AND COULD NEITHER GET AROUND NOR THROUGH AND WAS OBLIGED TO RETREAT.

    FRANK WILDES

The Departments of War and the Navy shared offices in a building on Pennsylvania Avenue, just west of the White House, so it was a tense and frantic day of activity in the building as news traveled back and forth from the capital to Newfoundland. Assistants hustled from office to office with papers, alerting superiors and officials to the developments. Secretary of War Lincoln learned of the situation via an Associated Press dispatch—and therefore so did the rest of the United States, including Henrietta Greely. At 2:00 p.m. on September 13, Samuel Mills sent a telegram to Commander Greely's wife in San Diego:

THE FOLLOWING HAS JUST BEEN RECEIVED BY ASSOCIATED PRESS:
ST. JOHN'S, NEWFOUNDLAND, SEPT. 13, 11:15 A.M. THE UNITED STATES GREELY
RELIEF STEAMSHIP *YANTIC* HAS JUST ANCHORED HERE. HER TIDINGS ARE
LAMENTABLE. NO WORD HAS BEEN RECEIVED FROM GREELY OR ANY OF HIS
PARTY . . . WILL SEND FURTHER PARTICULARS WHEN RECEIVED.

    MILLS

The message was difficult for Henrietta to process. As she nervously awaited these "further particulars," news reporters from around the capital flocked to the offices of the Navy and War Departments, clamoring for answers and information and scribbling shorthand in their notebooks. For many hours and into the next days, there was frenzy, blame, and a litany of unanswered questions regarding Greely's fate as telegrams kept firing over land and sea. At 3:00 p.m. on Friday, September 14, a telegram finally arrived from Garlington answering Mills and Caziarc's question about stores delivered and Greely's situation:

TO CHIEF SIGNAL OFFICER, WASHINGTON—
NO STORES LANDED BEFORE SINKING OF SHIP. ABOUT FIVE HUNDRED
RATIONS FROM THESE SAVED, CACHED AT CAPE SABINE; ALSO, LARGE CACHE
OF CLOTHING. BY THE TIME SUITABLE VESSELS COULD BE PROCURED,
FILLED, PROVISIONED, ETC., IT WOULD BE TOO LATE IN SEASON TO ACCOM-
PLISH ANYTHING THIS YEAR.

    E.A. GARLINGTON

It was unclear why Garlington waited an entire day to convey this information, and in that time, the story had spread around the world and the press was feverish. Headlines ran in newspapers from Newfoundland to New York to London: "LOSS OF PROTEUS—GREELY MAY ESCAPE"; "STILL HOPE FOR GREELY." Some, sensational and sparked by rumors, certainly gave Henrietta cause for deep concern: "GREELY'S MURDER REPORTED—SAID TO HAVE BEEN SLAIN BY MUTINOUS CREW."

In San Diego, Henrietta—who was recovering from a serious illness—read this news with a mixture of anguish and disbelief. Given the deep disappointment of the *Neptune*'s failure last year, she had good reason to fear for her husband's life. Yet Henrietta tried to remain calm and levelheaded. She'd read reams of sensational reporting concerning the USS *Jeannette* disaster, much of it inaccurate, and knew that her best sources for correct information resided in the words of her friend Louis Caziarc and acting CSO Mills. She remained unconvinced that nothing could be done this year, and sent Mills an urgent appeal from the telegraph office: "Will not the government send out at once another expedition to meet Greely party if on reaching Littleton Island the latter find nothing there and attempt to work south?"

Acting CSO Mills would answer Henrietta's entreaty in due course, but at the frenetic offices of the War and Navy Departments, there was plenty of juggling to do and higher authorities to answer to over the weekend. No official decisions had yet been finalized. Secretaries Lincoln and Chandler privately discussed what options remained, including launching an immediate relief effort from St. John's. After last year's *Neptune* debacle, they were feeling pressure from an international press that wanted answers to many questions, the most glaring among them: Why had no stores been landed? Millions of deeply concerned Americans demanded to know what their government planned to do about Greely and his stranded men. The failure to help the men of the Lady Franklin Bay Expedition—now renamed the Greely Expedition in the national press—had become the biggest, most-talked-about story since the assassination of President Garfield in 1881.

Together Lincoln and Mills drafted a telegram to Garlington and Wildes, demanding an immediate response:

WASHINGTON, SEPT 14, 1883

TO LIEUT. E.A. GARLINGTON, ST. JOHN'S, N.F:

SECRETARIES OF WAR AND NAVY CONCUR IN ASKING FULL REPLIES FROM YOURSELF AND COMMANDER WILDES SEPARATELY OR JOINTLY. WHY WERE THERE NO STORES LANDED LITTLETON ISLAND ON YOUR WAY NORTH? DID *YANTIC* LEAVE ANY STORES ANYWHERE AFTER LEAVING YOUR DISASTER?

IS THE FOLLOWING PROJECT FEASIBLE: THAT A STEAM SEALER BE

CHARTERED TO TAKE YOUR PARTY NORTHWARD PROVISIONED FOR CREW,

PASSENGERS, AND TWENTY ADDITIONAL MEN, FOR ONE YEAR, TO BE

PURCHASED AT ST. JOHN'S AND ELSEWHERE EN ROUTE. OUTFIT COMPLETED,

ALL DISPATCH AND STEAM TO UPERNAVIK, THENCE TO NORTHERNMOST

ATTAINABLE HARBOR WEST COAST GREENLAND, OR TO LITTLETON FOR

WINTER QUARTERS. TO PICK UP DOGS, SLEDS, AND NATIVE DRIVERS IN

GREENLAND, AND LEAD SMALL PARTY AND AS MUCH SUPPLIES AS POSSIBLE

TO LITTLETON ISLAND, OR TO MEET GREELY IF LITTLETON ISLAND IS

ATTAINED. MILLS, ACTING CHIEF SIGNAL OFFICER

Garlington and Wildes conferred with locals at St. John's and learned that there were in fact three or four worthy sealing vessels available, anchored there with coal on board, ready to depart. One of these, given enough money, might still be hired out. But after the difficulties they'd experienced with Captain Pike's unruly and unprofessional Newfoundland crews, they had serious reservations about this approach. Wildes pointed out that the crew of the *Proteus* had "behaved shamefully." Garlington agreed with that assessment, but he remained open to an attempt to return north, though he was not optimistic about their chances of success. On the morning of the fifteenth, Garlington replied to his superiors, first explaining that "stores were not left at Littleton Island because it was not in my program to do so."

This was technically a reasonable excuse, though to the U.S. government and many Americans, an unconvincing one. Though he'd been given the latitude of "his own judgment on the spot," he'd chosen to "follow as nearly as possible the plan laid down in the letter of Lieutenant Greely, which had been written from Fort Conger."* As to an immediate relief journey north, Garlington wrote that "there is a bare chance of success, and if my recommendations

---

* Garlington at this moment made no mention of a supplemental memorandum of "additional instructions," handwritten by Caziarc prior to the departure of the *Proteus*, that suggested landing all stores at Littleton Island on the way north. The memo appeared to Garlington to be an idea or suggestion rather than part of his official orders, and he therefore opted to follow the signed official documents that he believed superseded this "supplemental memorandum." The entire *Proteus* disaster, including a lengthy discussion of this memo, was dealt with in an official Court of Inquiry, where it was found that Garlington had technically followed orders. General Hazen, as it turned out, bore most of the blame.

are approved I am ready and anxious to make the effort." His plan was for the U.S. government to buy one of the Newfoundland sealers and assemble a crew from volunteers of the *Yantic* and the American warship *Powhatan*, also moored at St. John's. He proposed that the able—even heroic—Lt. John Colwell command the ship but stipulated it must be an entirely American operation. He believed "the ship must be under U.S. laws and subject to military discipline. I believe nothing can be done with foreign civilian officers and crew." Pike's drunken, pilfering crew had convinced him of this last provision. Finally Garlington expressed his doubts and the need for expediency: "The ultimate result of any undertaking to go north at this time is extremely problematical; chances against its success, owing to the dark nights now begun in those regions making ice navigation extremely critical work. . . . If anything is to be done it must be done at once."

Wildes was in general agreement with Garlington, though he struck a much more negative tone in his own accompanying telegram addressed to Secretary of the Navy Chandler:

TO CHARTER ANOTHER FOREIGN SHIP WITH FOREIGN CREW FOR THIS DUTY TO GO NORTH AT THIS LATE SEASON WOULD SIMPLY INVITE FRESH DISASTER . . . SHIP MUST BE AMERICAN MANNED AND OFFICERED BY NAVY AND THOROUGHLY EQUIPPED. UNLESS WINTER QUARTERS CAN BE REACHED THE ATTEMPT WOULD BE USELESS. THIS CANNOT BE DONE. MELVILLE BAY WILL BE IMPASSABLE BY OCTOBER FIRST AT LATEST. SHIP CANNOT WINTER AT UPERNAVIK AND CANNOT SLEDGE NORTH FROM THERE.

While Secretaries Lincoln and Chandler contemplated this correspondence, others offered their opinions. General Hazen, who had been communicating daily with Mills at the Signal Corps office in D.C. from various outposts in the Washington Territory—including Port Townsend, Neah Bay, and New Tacoma—sent a series of six telegrams imploring immediate action and expressing that no cost should be spared: "Get a capable man with money as high up in Greenland as possible to send sledge parties with native food and clothing under pay and bounties to meet Greely," he wrote, adding: "Do all in your power to prevent delay. . . . What I want done requires no preparation. Time is more valuable than all else." Had Hazen been in the capital, he would certainly have been in a better position to personally lobby his case to the ultimate decision makers, the secretaries of war and the navy, and even the president of the United States. As it was, no one was really listening to him. At any rate Hazen knew full well that movement within and between D.C.'s bureaucratic departments required more than impassioned pleas or the snap of fingers: It was slow, cumbersome, and involved congressional approval or executive orders, all of which took time.

A number of Arctic veterans, notably Chief Engineer George Melville of the navy, also weighed in. Melville had been one of the thirteen survivors of the tragic and still-controversial USS *Jeannette* disaster. He submitted a bold plan involving taking the *Yantic* as far north as possible, perhaps to Upernavik, and then traveling via sledge the rest of the way to Littleton Island—where he believed Greely would be by now. (Greely was in fact less than thirty miles away from there, across the Smith Sound.) But his unsolicited proposal was not seriously considered. Behind closed doors, Secretaries Lincoln and Chandler, and President Arthur, contemplated the matter, listening to the advice and counsel of other Arctic experts. They could only speculate on Greely's whereabouts or movements. Some argued that he would follow his own orders and would be retreating south; others speculated that he would have either returned to or chosen to remain at Fort Conger, where he was known to have a year's supply of food.

Henrietta spent a fretful weekend reading the newspapers and continuing to push the Signal Office for action: "Can not a steamer, if started immediately with stores, reach Upernavik or Godhavn and winter, sending sledging parties north?" she asked. In her possession were detailed maps of previous expeditions she'd studied with her husband. She knew the rugged coastlines of Greenland and Grinnell Land as well as or better than many of the men contemplating her husband's fate. She spent most of her time going back and forth from her home to the San Diego telegraph office. She sent one telegram to General Lockwood, who remained her ally and whose son's life also hung in the balance. Lockwood's connections to the military were deep and influential, so she appealed directly to him: "Can you expedite the sending of a relief vessel to winter at Upernavik, sending sledging parties?" She expressed that before he'd left, Lieutenant Greely had told her he had "complete faith in the government's care of its own expedition." Now she was calling that faith into question.

On Monday morning, September 17, Captain Mills answered Henrietta's desperate entreaties, providing her with at least a glimmer of hope. He explained that General Lockwood had been urging Secretary of War Lincoln to send an expedition, and: "Consultation resumed this morning. Will advise you of decision." There remained nothing more for her to do but wait for the decision from Washington.

She did not have to wait long. The next day Mills had the painful task of sending Henrietta the following telegram:

THE SECRETARIES OF WAR AND NAVY HAVE CAREFULLY CONSIDERED WITH KINDLY DISPOSITION AND INDIFFERENT TO EXPENSE THE FEASIBILITY OF SENDING ANOTHER VESSEL THIS YEAR. LIEUT. GARLINGTON AND COM-MANDER WILDES HAVE MADE FULL TELEGRAPHIC REPORT BUT THE SECRE-TARIES CONCUR IN THE BELIEF THAT NOTHING FURTHER CAN BE DONE THIS YEAR. EVERY EFFORT WILL BE MADE IN THE SPRING AND SUMMER OF NEXT YEAR TO REACH THE PARTY AT THE EARLIEST POSSIBLE MOMENT.

She was bereft. Both General Hazen and General Lockwood, when they heard the official decision, tried to console her. Hazen was livid, but he was too far away to do anything more. Lockwood had his own son's life to consider, but he took time to write Henrietta, explaining his efforts to organize a rescue as well as the thinking behind the final decision. The outcome was the considered belief that "the relief party sent out would be put in greater peril than those whom they were sent to retrieve." General Lockwood said that the secretaries of war and the navy had consulted personally with President Arthur, who listened carefully to the expert opinions of Arctic specialists, and the conclusion was reached that relief should not be mounted until next spring. General Lockwood assured her that Secretary Lincoln had considered the matter carefully and described Greely's predicament as "by no means hopeless."

Neither was Henrietta hopeless. She would accept this setback for the moment, still determined to use all her connections and resources to ensure that help be sent for her Dolph and his men as soon as humanly possible. But she felt betrayed and felt that her husband had also been betrayed. As calmly as she could under the nerve-racking circumstances, she composed a letter to her friend Caziarc and his boss, Mills, at the Signal Office. She would put her faith not in Washington, but in her husband: "I have great faith," she wrote, "in Mr. Greely's ability to cope with the situation. He has a clear head and great energy and perseverance, as you probably know, and if any man could escape the dangers that beset his party, I believe that he will, with God's help."

17

❧

An "Irrepressible Little Band"
of Men

The rumbling caused by the pressure from the northern pack had subsided by the afternoon of September 3, but after the tumultuous night hoisting thousands of pounds of boats and gear up and onto the disintegrating floe, all the men were shaken. Israel reported a lowering barometer reading, but by his calculations at least they were now drifting slowly back to the south. Gear, crates, and equipment lay in scattered heaps, and some of the men huddled under boat sails for shelter. Others had slid into their frozen buffalo-hide sleeping bags and sought cover in the whaleboats. Everyone was doing his best to stay warm.

By early evening Greely overheard Kislingbury talking to the enlisted men, telling them that they could not remain like this—they needed to do *something*. Kislingbury doubted Greely's leadership and was trying to convince them that their best chance now was to wait for the first lead to open, put the whaleboats in the water, and row immediately for shore. Greely strode over and intervened, calling Kislingbury aside and reprimanding him, saying that such open criticism "was un-officer-like" and would cause discord. Kislingbury made a feeble attempt to explain himself. Short of an apology, he said simply that he hadn't meant to undermine the commander or speak poorly of him.

Greely could not abide any breakdown in order and discipline. He summoned Brainard, Pavy, Rice, and Lockwood over and moved them all into the *Lady Greely*, well out of earshot of the enlisted men. The commander requested that Lockwood record a meeting in shorthand. Greely started by praising Sergeant Rice on his recent excellent ice navigation, conceding that he himself lacked the required skill and admitting he had "the disadvantage of poor eyesight." He formally assigned the ice-piloting duties to Rice. Because he was their leader, all the men's lives relied on his decision making, and he confessed: "I am not infallible." He expressed the importance of "hearty and united action" among them. He wanted to hear everyone's honest opinion on how next to proceed and agreed to listen to all of their ideas in turn "as to what would be the wisest measure to pursue." It was a significant shift, especially for the rigid Greely, signaling a softening toward more democratic leadership.

Greely firmly believed that "a party, with provisions, and probably a ship, were at Lifeboat Cove" next to Littleton Island. How to get there was another matter. He went on to say that as far as provisions near Cape Sabine, he doubted that there would be any "beyond the 240 rations known to be at Payer Harbor." If true, this was a sobering prospect.

Greely then paused, tilting his gaze directly toward Kislingbury. He valued his opinion, saying: "You are next in seniority." Everyone seemed a bit surprised, given the long-embattled relationship between the two, and considering that at Fort Conger, Greely had disbarred him. Kislingbury, appreciative and emboldened, seized the opportunity. He recommended abandoning the *Lady Greely* and the *Valorous*, and that with sledges and the remaining boats, they should immediately travel from floe to floe, dragging and portaging their five thousand pounds of equipment, gear, and food directly back toward land.

There was some silence and stirring. Spindrift filtered through gaps in the *Lady Greely*'s turtleback covering. Greely turned to Pavy, asking for the doctor's thoughts. Pavy agreed with Kislingbury generally, though he said they'd best wait a day, then abandon all but one boat. He believed they could make four miles a day, landing at Cape Sabine within a month. Then it was Lockwood's turn. He looked up from his note taking and said that while it would be "desirable to get to shore as quickly as possible," it would be better to wait at least "a day or two . . . leaving circumstances to shape our course." He was "unwilling to recommend any change in plans for the present, as waiting on the drift could do no harm."

Brainard, who along with Lockwood had spent more time in the field than any of them, worried that the unstable condition of the new ice, and the "unsettled state of the pack"—coupled with their heavy loads—made it inadvisable and unsafe to move "until the floe had cemented sufficiently for traveling over it." This might take until the end of the month. Rice agreed with Brainard and preferred waiting. They had plenty of food for now, and should any leads or lanes open, they could load up the whaleboats and the steam launch and "go farther in a few hours than they could drag equipment in days."

Greely had been listening carefully to each man, considering their ideas. He weighed them for a time, then said that he thought they should remain on the floe, constantly monitoring the movement of the current. Leaving the floe they were on now was too dangerous because "constant changes were occurring in the pack," and it was not consolidated. Also, immediate action would further exhaust and dispirit the enlisted men. If open water should appear in a favorable direction, they could take to the boats. They had rations of meat, potatoes, and bread, and enough cooking fuel, to last them until at least November 1. The meeting concluded with consensus on Greely's decision: They'd stay where they were either until navigable lanes opened, or the ice more fully cemented for safe travel. Such open diplomacy was new, and the general mood of the officers improved.

Now they needed shelter. The handy and reliable Private Frederick organized the construction of a large tepee. Combining the sails from the *Lady Greely* and a few of the other boats, and by lashing together oars and masts for a center pole, Frederick's "Indian-style" dwelling measured just over fifty feet in circumference and could house between sixteen and eighteen men. Rice suggested that any remaining sails and large canvas tarpaulins be stretched over the *Beaumont*, which could hold nine men and accommodate any who became sick or weak and needed extra shelter. Rice also came up with the idea of tearing the seats out of the *Lady Greely* and fashioning them into two sledges they could use in conjunction with the large English sledge they had brought along. Elison and Cross worked on the sledges, cleverly fashioning the seats from the launch and the *Valorous* into runners and using barrel staves as cross-ties. The runners were "shod with iron bands from the boiler" of the *Lady Greely.* The sledges would be crucial for transporting their heavy burden of boats, equipment, and food over ice. So that they might be more easily spotted, Brainard took an American flag, tied it to a long pole, and erected the pole securely at the summit of their current floe.

For the next few days Greely and his men adjusted to life on the floe. Those devoted to cooking also melted fresh snow and newer top ice for drinking water, coffee, and tea. The giant floe to the north, which had recurrently been bashing and grinding away at their smaller ice raft, moved away a safe distance, and Greely sent Lockwood, Connell, and Eskimo Fred to it to reconnoiter. They spotted several favorable leads opening up, and that evening the tepee was dismantled and packed, and all the boats were put into the water. They fired up the *Lady Greely* and proceeded hopefully but made it only a mile before the lane closed in and they were forced once again to haul up and seek safety, this time onto a tiny exposed berg just two hundred yards square, which felt vulnerable and precarious. However, this small ice platform was moving very fast, and in forty-eight hours Israel reported that they'd traveled seven miles south.

The skies cleared, and they could see Cape Sabine, now less than thirty miles distant, and farther southeast across the Kane Basin, Littleton Island. Despite their recent hardships, the men grew giddy, some laughing, others breaking into song that echoed over their tiny ice raft. Brainard remarked that when they were first beset by the pack, he thought "there would be lamentations without end," but to his surprise the men showed good-natured cheer. Greely also admired their attitudes: "It is strange how indifferent we become to dangers and perils that . . . hourly beset us, which, stirring and exciting at first, now seem ordinary and a matter of course."

Spotting game animals also raised spirits. Jens saw a few seals and slid into his kayak to go after the closest one, but after a short chase it got away. Long, also one of the best hunters, managed to bag a seal, which was immediately skinned and butchered. Most of the men now relished the taste of warm seal blood; the meat, mixed with bacon, provided two full meals for the entire party. Sergeant Connell saw a large walrus in a nearby pool and quickly grabbed a rifle and fired a volley of shots, with Brainard looking on, amazed that "the bullets glanced from [its] skull as if fired against a rock." Christiansen and Kislingbury also shot at the animal, to no effect. Its hard skull and dense body fat made it very difficult to kill.

On September 8, their thirteenth day marooned in the ice pack, the temperature dropped to zero, the winds settled, and the skies were clear and cobalt blue. The giant floe that had consistently threatened them from the north continued to bear down on them, once again coming hazardously close. Brainard remarked that the mass was "likely to prove treacherous." They'd made another six miles south in the last twenty-four hours, and had come ever nearer to land, perhaps as close as three or four miles on the Grinnell Land side.

With the plummeting temperatures—which were highly unusual for this early in September—Greely worried that the ice continuing to cement all around them would soon end any hope of boat travel. Also, it was discovered that the *Lady Greely*'s propeller had been shorn off. On the other hand, the low temperatures might make sledge travel feasible, though risky. He ordered Brainard to oversee construction of the sledges as soon as possible and to prepare everything for departure. Brainard was also instructed to take Eskimo Fred on reconnaissance for a navigable "sledge road through the broken surface of the pack, toward land and liberty." Brainard agreed. He expected it to be "dangerous duty," but had traveled "Farthest North" with the Greenlander and remarked that "the presence of the faithful Fred gives one a feeling of security."

The following day Greely convened the officers—and Sergeants Rice and Brainard—for another meeting, wishing them all to remain included in any plan and to hear their opinions. He outlined his proposal: to abandon the *Lady Greely* and the *Valorous*, and forge ahead with the recently constructed sledges and the large English sledge, along with two of the remaining boats. "As soon as we are close enough to land, I plan to send an officer and two men on ahead to Brevoort Island [just off Cape Sabine]. If we learn that there are any boats there, as there should be, we could drop our own boats and make faster time." Dragging the boats and nearly five thousand pounds of gear with haul ropes—backtracking two or three times to inch forward their load—he figured they could progress maybe two miles a day. Once within striking distance, his idea was to drop everything except food rations, cooking gear, and sleeping bags, and then "move as rapidly as possible to Cape Sabine."

Greely wanted to know what the others thought of his plan. His new diplomatic approach seemed to have had a positive effect on his officers, as well as on Kislingbury and Pavy. Kislingbury agreed completely, suggesting that they should make sure to "take along parts from other guns in order to replace any broken parts which may occur." As one of the most proficient hunters and the best-trained marksman, Kislingbury knew the importance of being able to procure game. He added that it would be crucial not to overwork the men in the first couple of days, for they would need everyone's full strength. All the others were in complete agreement. Pavy recommended only that they leave behind one very heavy keg of lime juice, which Greely thought a good idea.

Greely had an additional thought: He reminded the men that the relief ships had been instructed to depart the vicinity of Smith Sound no later than September 15, now just six days away. It would be impossible for the entire party to move fast enough to make it to them in time. Greely said he would personally trek ahead, along with one willing man, and rush across the moving pack for help. "Such an attempt," said Greely, "while involving possible death . . . might save the party from great future suffering and perhaps death." Brainard immediately threw up his hand and volunteered to go along. The officers unanimously objected to the idea, calling it too dangerous. They did not want their commander in such jeopardy. Others courageously said they should go instead, but Greely wouldn't allow it; it was him and one other, or no one. So that plan was scuttled. At the close of the meeting Greely declared that as they moved forward, he would always be the last man off any floe until they reached safe land. Everyone understood this was an act of bravery, because the last man off always ran the highest risk of being stranded by the sudden movement of a floe. They all nodded, silently appreciating his mettle.

After days of being mostly idle, it was good to be hard at work again, and there was much to do. Snow began to fall heavily. They pulled the gallant *Lady Greely*, respectfully named for the commander's wife, as far onto the floe as they could manage, securing it with chains and an anchor. Some men began stripping it completely, prying off boards they'd use for protection beneath their sleeping bags inside the tepee. Others stripped down the *Valorous* and hung a signal flag from it. Greely, fighting freezing ink, wrote a record of their retreat and destination, to be left in each of these boats, should they somehow be discovered by relief efforts.

Snow fell hard and steadily all day, delaying departure. Men tried to keep busy and fight off the bitter cold by lashing down and organizing gear. When everything appeared secured and ready, Greely called all the men together: There was one last thing to consider. The Peirce pendulum weighed one hundred pounds, and he was willing to leave it behind if they wished to; they had more than enough to carry, and it would be an extra burden. But everyone understood its importance in making further observations, and it served as a symbol of the scientific work they'd been engaged in for two years. To a man, and to their great credit, "Not one would hear of abandoning the pendulum." Greely felt a surge of pride as he looked upon his "irrepressible little band." Lesser men, he reflected, placed in such terrible conditions, might have "lost their spirits, and even all interest in efforts to save their lives." But so far nothing, not "the increasing cold, the monotony and confinement to a narrow compass of ice . . . the grave uncertainty of their future, had the power to dishearten or discourage them, nor quench their exuberant spirits."

It was Sunday evening, and snow swirled around the men and boats. There was no time for reading Psalms as Greely had done nearly every Sabbath since their arrival at Fort Conger. But, as he and the men stared out at the endless frozen sea, he paused to offer a few "words of praise to the Almighty . . . with renewed faith in Divine Providence, with no repining over past sufferings, but with the determination to do our best and utmost on the morrow."

18

Labyrinth of Ice

On the afternoon of September 10, 1883, one month after saying farewell to the comforts of Fort Conger, Greely and his men bade good-bye to the *Lady Greely*, the *Valorous*, and their inhospitable little ice sheet. Brainard, as agreed, went ahead to find a route, and after about a mile, returned to help with the first load in light snow. Greely knew of the brutal undertaking before them, having recently reread Nares's expedition notes, which warned: "When a navigable boat is added to a sledge, the difficulty of the journey increases enormously." They would progress one load at a time, returning again and again for more. In the initial load they piled the iceboat *Beaumont* and six hundred pounds of supplies onto what they named "the twelve-man sledge," with Greely and a crew of a dozen men straining at the drag ropes. According to Brainard: "Following came the two smaller sledges, one carrying about two thousand pounds and the other sixteen hundred." Both of the small sledges broke down after just a few minutes; one was abandoned, the other repaired.

They plowed through foot-deep snow concealing hummocky "rubble ice," and were forced around small bergs, rarely traveling in a straight line. Brainard toiled greatly, running ahead to seek safe passage, then hustling back to the party, where "each load had to be advanced alternately with all hands in the drag ropes." Heaving sluggishly forward, the ropes cutting into their shoulders, the crew pulled the burden into the evening, and after five arduous hours, they slumped exhausted to the ice amid their haul. They had moved everything less than two miles, though counting the back-and-forth, some men had journeyed three times that. Greely ordered the tepee set up, then issued rum and praise for all: "Everyone pulled with great energy," he said, "and the heavy work, coming after long inaction, taxed everyone's strength to the utmost. For myself, I am thoroughly worn out physically, not to mention mental anxiety as to both present and future." Greely, Pavy, Lockwood, and nine others slept in the tepee; the rest of the men climbed into boats, seeking refuge from the wind and snow beneath snapping sailcloth and tarps.

At daybreak snow continued to fall, so Greely told the men to remain resting in their sleeping bags until the weather improved. A few hours later the skies cleared enough for them to see little Cocked Hat Island not far in the distance, and they struck out for it. Brainard led out first to seek routes, taking along Jens, who carefully poked at the ice with his harpoon, constantly checking its condition: Falling through anywhere could be deadly. After six strenuous trips in the drag ropes, the group had advanced only one mile. They halted to cook a meat stew and to melt ice for tea and coffee. Greely sent Brainard and Pavy onto a large grounded iceberg some two miles away to gauge their options. They saw Cape Sabine clearly about ten miles away, "across a great expanse of new ice." While they stood gazing, a group of walruses burst their heads through the ice from beneath, convincing Brainard that the young, slushy ice was unquestionably not safe to bear their sledges.

Brainard reported to Greely: "Our outlook is dismal," he said. "The party could never reach land over this ice." Greely cleaned frost from his spectacles and contemplated. He asked Brainard to gather the officers. They had some important decisions to make, and he wanted their input. Once they were convened, he reminded them that the coming "spring tides" in a few days made their next moves crucial. The tides might dislodge the ice enough to allow boat travel and a desperate row for land; but depending on where they were at the time, and the direction of the winds, they could as easily be blown far out to sea. Greely then listened to the officers. Brainard, Pavy, and Kislingbury thought they should move near the edge of their current floe—which might take two days of strenuous work. Then, from the edge, they could await the impact of the tides and act accordingly. Lockwood preferred a move eastward, where they could avoid this young ice and hopefully find some that was firmer. They could camp there and send out small parties to seek better routes. Sergeant Rice believed there might be better ice to the west.

Greely reiterated that they had "only forty days' rations, and time just now was important, as darkness was fast approaching." He felt sure that a series of floes extended south a number of miles in the direction they wished to go, and this was the route he favored. Since there was no consensus, Greely decided on a compromise: The next day he would send out two small groups, one led by Kislingbury and the other by Pavy, to do further reconnaissance, after which he would make a decision.

Just after noon on September 12, both parties returned with their news. Kislingbury found that the southwest route was unfavorable. Pavy and Rice were slightly more encouraging; the southeast course was "practicable but difficult." That was enough for Greely, and he called for the men to get ready to move. As the men broke down the tepee and packed their gear, Brainard and Rice—with support from the other officers—strongly urged Greely that they should abandon the whaleboat *Narwhal*; it was breaking down the large sledge, which they desperately needed. Greely instantly agreed with his officers, who seemed pleased with his recent newfound compliance. Brainard had someone hoist a flag on its mast while Greely wrote a record, which he stashed in the boat, tucking it beneath the cleats. Then he turned his back on yet another of their watercraft and trudged onward.

They moved faster with their lighter load, passing over recent bear tracks, as well as disconcerting "walrus-holes in the young ice." Jens continued ahead with Brainard, probing with his harpoon for dangerous weak spots. They happened onto a stretch of windblown, smoother ice and made excellent time, prompting Greely to give praise where it was due: "Our progress showed the decided advantage of detailing Brainard to select the route." Making multiple trips back and forth, they came to the edge of the floe, beyond which was a dicey channel of open water. Brainard eyed the watery rift, remarking that "the wide crack at the edge of the floe does not argue well for tomorrow." As it was late in the day, Greely decided they would camp there. He sent a group back for another load and set men to cooking. They used up the last of their sugar in coffee and tea, and Greely continued rewarding his men with rum after each day's labor. He ordered a night guard, owing to the numerous bear tracks they'd seen throughout the day.

The next day was clear and beautiful, low light shimmering on the pack. Cocked Hat, just north of Cape Sabine, appeared alluringly close, and men made friendly wagers as to its distance. The more pessimistic said ten miles, the optimists four, with Greely splitting the difference at eight. As the group moved out, Brainard and Jens returned from their foray to say they'd seen numerous walruses poking their heads through, and that the "new ice was thin and dangerous." Despite these warnings both Pavy and Bender broke through, but others quickly hauled them out. Neither man experienced frostbite.

After another day of slow but steady progress toward land, Greely felt a rising wind and consulted with Israel, who had been taking readings at the conclusion of each day's march. Unfortunately it didn't take an astronomer to realize what was happening: A gale was blowing offshore from the southwest, and the floe they were camped on had begun drifting perceptibly to the north-northeast. Men started tying down anything loose as the winds increased. It took hours to erect the tepee, the great sail threatening to fly away. Men sought refuge where they could, but few managed to sleep, as everywhere ice split and thundered. Even the stalwart Brainard was alarmed: "The roar of the moving and grinding pack . . . is something so terrible that even the bravest cannot be unconcerned. . . . Dark, portentous clouds hang over the horizon to remind us that our floe is not connected with the land but drifting helplessly in the Kane Sea." Greely lamented their bad luck as well: "We are losing all the ground gained; we go back as far as we advance . . . driven farther north in three hours than we had travelled southward in as many days."

The storm raged all night. Inside the tepee tempers raged, too. Pavy snapped at Greely in front of the enlisted men, saying he'd favored staying at Fort Conger from the start, and that had Greely only listened, they'd all be safe, warm, and well fed now. Greely yelled back that no such discussion had ever occurred (he was unaware of Pavy's previous conspiracy), and that at any rate remaining at Fort Conger past September 1 would have been in "direct disobedience of orders." Pavy angrily barked that Greely wasn't pushing the men hard enough, and with that, he stormed out of the tent. Greely told Lockwood to immediately record "every word that had passed," calling Doctor Pavy's behavior "insubordinate and mutinous."

When they all awoke the next morning, tempers had cooled, but overnight they'd lost five full days' worth of muscle-aching, shoulder-searing toil. Despondent, Kislingbury declared: "We are completely at the mercy of the wind now and God alone knows what is in store for us." Later in the day Israel, with Rice, took another set of coordinates and handed them to Greely and Brainard. It was highly discouraging. They were now well north of where the *Lady Greely* had been abandoned. Brainard was dismayed by the turn of events: "We continue northward, drifting in the sea on a piece of ice of uncertain texture. We do not know what to expect of the Polar Pack. Too much pressure will shatter the floeberg and too little will leave us open to the danger of drifting into collision with an iceberg." Greely told Israel that from now on, he should report the coordinates to him alone, lest the others become dispirited.

But there was no way to hide the fact that their floe was now revolving counterclockwise, spinning like a saucer. It spun 180 degrees in just twenty-four hours. They were now in the middle of the sound, both coasts clearly visible but neither reachable. Greely called another meeting. Brainard had taken inventory, and with the two seals the Greenlanders had just shot—each weighing about 150 pounds—they had forty days' full rations. Pavy alone maintained that they should depart at once over the broken pack for Cape Sabine, though it now lay nineteen miles south. The others preferred waiting out the tides, which should subside in the next two days. It was decided they would stay where they were for now. Once more Greely offered to ditch the pendulum. And once more the men were unanimous in agreeing to carry it.

Their erratic rotating drift continued for the next few days. At one point, land appeared near. Water lanes had opened up, and using the boat, they made a desperate effort for land. They "crossed five lanes by boat . . . which involved constant change from sledge to boat and consequent separation of the party. . . . There was constant danger of floes splitting and drifting away with parts of gear and even men stranded on them." Sergeant Rice broke through the ice and was completely submerged, but Greely was there to drag him out, and he instantly had Rice strip to avoid freezing. Greely removed his own clothes and gave them to Rice, both struggling into layers of semidry clothes as others arrived to help. Early darkness was becoming a problem, with men tripping and falling from the poor light as well as exhaustion. The darkness was also making it difficult for them to estimate distance to land accurately. By the end of the day they'd been constantly working for thirteen hours. Everyone crumpled on the ice at the edge of a floe, too tired to erect the tepee, and most of them just sprawled shivering on the bare ice.

They awoke to find that winds had driven them a great distance into the middle of the Kane Basin, maybe twenty miles from land. It was hard to know exactly, with winds too strong to allow Israel to take readings. Their sleeping bags were all covered with snowdrift and, according to Brainard, frozen "spray from the huge waves which broke against the southern edge of the floe." They spent the day in their bags, Greely directing the cooks to issue the men pemmican and water where they lay. There was nothing to be done, said Brainard, but "listen to the roar of the waves and meditate on our helplessness."

That evening Greely, by now unnerved and even becoming desperate, called yet another six-man council. He wanted to ditch everything except twenty days' rations, the records, their sleeping bags, and some extra clothes and strike for the Greenland shore, about twenty miles east. He reasoned that they'd seen no ships at Cape Sabine, and that Greenland "was the only place they could be certain of relief," and with their reduced load they could travel much faster. None of the others agreed. Lockwood, a daring man who usually supported Greely, said they should stay where they were. Brainard and Rice were noncommittal, but later that night Brainard wrote in his journal that he thought the idea "Madness!" Respecting his officers' opinions, Greely agreed to wait until the next day, but barring significantly changed conditions, they'd then carry out his orders and start for Greenland.

The weather the next day made the decision for them. Clouds, fog, and snow rolled in, making movement out of the question; they had no way even to determine their position. So they waited. By great good fortune, that afternoon Eskimo Fred shot a very large bladder-nose seal, which was a rare and treasured find in those waters. It measured eight and a half feet long and weighed 650 pounds. Men, now growing hungrier by the day, took turns lapping the warm blood spouting from the bullet holes. The tepee was set up, and they ate inside, nourished by the protein-rich seal meat mixed with corned beef. Greely praised Eskimo Fred profusely for the excellent kill, giving him extra rum, and the Greenlander danced about, "whistling by blowing across the top of the empty cartridge shell" that had taken the animal.

Foul weather kept up for many days, snow soaking everyone to the skin. Rice and a number of the other men had been sleeping out on the ice since they'd abandoned the whaleboat, and Greely offered to trade with Rice and let him in the tepee, but Rice declined. Instead Rice, the industrious and multitalented man from Cape Breton, rallied some men and built a "snow house," a sort of igloo with ice-block walls and a sail-and-tarp roof that at least protected them from wind and snow. Men tried to stay busy as best they could. Schneider, using some of the treated leather and sealskin from Fort Conger, worked at sewing reinforced uppers and soles for their boots, which were wearing thin. During the long days the Greenlanders kept hunting, and Jens proudly brought in three harbor seals.

As they floated through frozen mist and fog, one day Private Bender yelled that he spotted the abandoned whaleboat, its signal flag flapping, a mile or two southwest. The party stirred with excitement. Greely sent Brainard and seven others to try to retrieve it—they might still use it—but the group could only get within a few hundred yards of it before they were halted by a breakable, slushy water lane.

Doctor Pavy attended to the growing number of sick and injured men. He'd brought crates of medicine and medical equipment from Fort Conger and treated various conditions: dysentery—which he suspected was from eating seal blubber—frostbite, fever, cut fingers, headaches. In the event they reached navigable open water, Greely experimented by loading all twenty-five men into their boat, and found that though cramped, it held them all and still had the capacity for nearly one thousand pounds of baggage. But this would be safe only over calm, smooth water. Rough seas would likely sink them.

The whaleboat appeared again, and Greely thought it worth another try to go after it. Brainard, Lockwood, Jens, and Bender went for it and got close enough that they could just see its outline and flag, but they soon heard Bender's voice calling out, and turned to see him waving his arms frantically. Something wasn't right. The others hurried back toward him to discover the narrow gap they'd previously crossed now "rapidly widening. The ice bent, crumbled, and broke beneath their feet with that dismal groaning sound." The three sprinted and leaped to the other side, skidding over the ice and barely making it to safety. The whaleboat disappeared, and had they not made the jump, they would have disappeared with it.

Back on their own floe, the situation was equally terrifying. They returned to find the floe caught in the wild tidal turbulence of the Smith Sound, with a furious storm whipping up. As Brainard had earlier feared, a colossal paleocrystic floe was careening into them from the north, chewing apart their lesser island. Dark waves broke onto its edges, and everyone heard a horrendous cracking sound. Men crawled out of the igloo, dragging their frost-laden sleeping bags and duffels. Just as the last man exited, the rupture widened and "swallowed up a portion of the abandoned house."

As others frantically rolled up the tepee, another fissure formed beneath their feet. The corner where they'd been camping fractured off, and they floated away on a "small bit of the original floe," only a couple of acres square. Men burrowed behind wind-formed hillocks to escape the howl as temperatures reached zero. Brainard described the slab of ice they were now on as a mere "raft," and they spent "a wild and awful night in the driving storm, with dark water foaming about us." Freezing spray drenched those near the edge. Most of them were resigned to being engulfed by the waves.

They were now hurtling southward at a startling speed, first passing Brevoort Island, then Cape Sabine. Greely and Brainard agreed that they could not remain there much longer. At 5:00 a.m. on September 27, Greely rallied everyone: They must leave at the first beams of daylight. Their tiny chunk of berg, though forty to fifty feet thick, was being "crumbled like chalk under the tremendous pressure of the surrounding floes." The wind screamed at more than fifty miles per hour, so there was no possibility to pitch the tepee or to light stoves for food or water. Greely knew that if the tempest carried them through the Smith Sound narrows and into the wider, yawning chasm of Baffin Bay, they would all die.

By dawn on the twenty-eighth the winds had mercifully stopped, and the storm subsided. Men wriggled from their iron-hard buffalo bags to look around. Blocks and shards of ice and rubble lay heaped around them. Brainard took stock and noted that fortunately, their "floe had lodged against a grounded iceberg" and had kept them from being thrust through to Baffin Bay. Sergeant Rice was up and busy, as always. He had found a water channel leading to a bigger floe. He and Brainard consulted with Greely, and all agreed this was their chance to go. Greely put Rice in charge of the boat, ordering him to ferry small loads due west. In rough seas, moving as fast as they could because their lives depended on it, by day's end the team had transported everything across to a safer, mile-wide floe. Spent, freezing, and famished, they tried to sleep. Few could doze, despite their exhaustion, knowing they'd been close to land before, then blown back out to sea.

Greely awoke Brainard at 4:30 a.m. on the twenty-ninth, urging him to find any route to land. He rousted the cooks to prepare a meal; the men desperately needed sustenance. Brainard returned a few hours later with glad news: Land was just four miles away, and the route was decent, with solid ice and some navigable water to cross. They left at once, slogging over hard, weather-gouged ice, then using the boat for water passage, alternately dragging and ferrying their load. When Greely felt confident that landfall was assured, he sent the Greenlanders to hunt. They'd seen many walruses during the day, as well as some eider ducks, and Greely wanted to miss no opportunity to acquire food. The rest continued to struggle, sometimes dragging the twelve-man sledge over rock and ice, and then, when they reached water, pulling hard at the oars of their two remaining boats.

At 5:20 p.m. on September 29, Lieutenant Lockwood and the first group stumbled ashore at the mouth of the Baird Inlet, near a prominent, cone-shaped knob of rock. It was a boulder-strewn, granitic shoreline mostly devoid of ice.

Greely, as had become his practice, came with the final load an hour later and was the last man to set foot on land. A few of the men weakly lofted their arms and shouted a hoarse cheer for everyone's safe landing. Cross, whose frostbite had all day prevented him from tugging at the drag ropes, had landed with the first load and was more celebratory than the others. He'd broken into the rum and was already drunk and tripping over snow-covered stones by the time Commander Greely strode aground.

But for the moment Greely didn't care. There was too much to be proud of and thankful for. Since August 9—nearly seven weeks ago—they'd traveled for fifty-one days over nearly five hundred miles by boat, sledge, and iceberg. His men had acquitted themselves commendably, exhibiting grace and courage under heinous circumstances. Not a man had been lost, and the party still bore with them all their scientific records and instruments, including the pendulum. Against those odds, there was cause for celebration. He named their landing place Eskimo Point for the rock remains of ancient Eskimo huts they found there. As the tattered and frost-caked assemblage unpacked the last of the baggage, a pair of ravens, black and ominous as the Arctic waters, hovered overhead. The superstitious among the group eyed them warily, believing them birds of bad omen.

Greely cared little about that either. What concerned him was that the men of the Lady Franklin Bay Expedition were, by his calculations, at least twenty to thirty miles south of Cape Sabine, they were running out of food, and within two weeks, the Long Night would descend on them and it would be dark for the next four months.

19

Eskimo Point

With everyone safely ashore on the rocky, barren coastline on the Elles-mere side of the Smith Sound, Greely took stock. Combing the area for flat ground and protection from the elements, the men discovered more rem-nants of what had once been permanent native habitation—ancient founda-tions and walls of granite houses and scattered nearby the bleach-white bones of a large whale, a long narwhal horn, and "a toggle of walrus ivory for dog traces." That families had once carved life from this unforgiving place gave the men a faint beam of hope in the dying sunlight.

Finding food and suitable shelter was now of paramount importance. Con-sulting with Brainard, Greely calculated rations for only thirty-five days. Brainard thought that these might be extended to fifty days of reduced rations but added: "The suffering will be extreme in this low temperature where a man requires from two to three times the normal diet." Having learned the effec-tiveness of democratic counsel during the retreat from Fort Conger, Greely gathered the officers and men and asked their opinion—he wanted consensus: Should they maintain full rations while building shelter, or immediately reduce them? Everyone except Doctor Pavy—who protested on medical grounds—agreed they should cut rations to twelve ounces of meat per man (either seal, corned beef, or pemmican), two and a half ounces of potatoes, six ounces of hardtack, and one ounce of beef extract. Brainard was put in charge of distributing the food, and the resourceful Private Bender made him a crude set of scales from scrap metals for the purpose of evenly weighing out rations.

Greely sent Corporal Salor and Jens to scout the shoreline and promontories on the south of Ross Bay, in the hope that a cache might have been deposited there. The commander reasoned that had a ship been unable to make it all the way to Cape Sabine, perhaps it had left some food here. It was wishful thinking but worth investigating. Greely then issued orders for Lieutenant Lockwood to repair and ready the twelve-man sledge for a journey to Cape Sabine, which he was to commence the next day.

Salor and Jens returned in late afternoon to say that a large lane of water had prevented them from traveling far along the shore—open water stopped their progress—and once they'd been stranded on a moving pack, forcing them to leap back to solid ice. It was a very close call. But scanning the cliffs, they'd seen no cairn or any sign of visitation along the cape. Salor did present to Greely some clams, mussels, and a sea cucumber, saying that at least there was evidence of sea life that they might be able to cook and eat. Greely knew that soon winter would set in hard and freeze over the coastline, so feeding twenty-five men on shellfish would hardly be viable, but he didn't mention that reality to Salor or the others.

Given the dangerous traveling conditions reported by Salor, Greely scuttled the plan to send out Lockwood and the twelve-man sledge and considered other options. Sergeant Rice had an idea: He and Jens could take food for four days and a large one-man sleeping bag they'd share, and traveling light and fast, would go on foot, overland across a large glacier, to Cape Sabine. Greely had come to trust Rice's skills and judgment, so he agreed, immediately writing detailed records of his expedition's trials to date and their location, which Rice was to deposit at a cairn at Cape Sabine. Rice's central duty, of course, was to determine whether any U.S. relief ships had ever made it there and possibly left food. He would depart first thing the next morning. Next was the immediate need for shelter. Greely entrusted Lockwood and Brainard with finding a suitable protected location, and they set off in search of one.

Greely wanted to get a better look at their surroundings, so he went alone and climbed through huge crags and boulders to the summit of the knobby promontory beneath which they were camped. Ascending to nearly one thousand feet, he stood and surveyed the scene. The day was so clear he could see more than fifty miles down the coast, but even more alluring to him was the landscape directly across the Smith Sound. Just twenty-three miles distant, due east, he could make out a tiny dimple that was Lifeboat Cove, as well as the summit of Littleton Island. Had one of the relief vessels established a winter quarter there? If so, they'd have food enough for all. Even if they had not, Greely knew there were permanent Etah Eskimo settlements in the area whose people would take his men in, and house and feed them.

It appeared so tantalizingly, temptingly close. But as Greely contemplated the safety, warmth, and comfort they'd find there, he also knew the perils of those ice-laden waters. Currents churned viciously through the channel, running five to eight miles a day to the south. Powerful tides rose and fell ten to twelve feet every six hours, "disrupting and twisting the pack in all directions." He and his men had just narrowly escaped the crushing pack and gale-force winds with their lives, and he knew that under the best of circumstances, they could progress no more than two miles a day, over uncemented slush-ice that could not bear the weight of a sledge and hardly that of a man. Perhaps, when and if the sound became completely frozen, they might try. But for now, to attempt crossing was outright suicide, and he would not subject his men to it.

When Greely returned from the summit, Lockwood and Brainard told him they'd found a decent location for winter quarters, slightly protected by a high glacier wall. Greely set the men, except the hunters, to work in teams of three, building three separate stone huts under the direction of Brainard, Kislingbury, and himself. Using what few tools they had—picks, shovels, and axes—they dug into snow-covered ground and frozen hillsides. Some used their bare hands—their mittens being too cumbersome—prying out large stones from the ancient Eskimo settlement and carrying these to the site.

Greely worked day after day right next to his men, his fingers and knuckles, along with everyone else's, becoming "bruised, bleeding, and swollen." Sergeant Gardiner had split open a finger during their retreat, and it had become so infected that, despite Pavy's treatment, he feared he might lose it. Greely gave Gardiner his personal sleeping bag and his place in the tepee as a break from the hut building, which took most of four days in temperatures plunging to near zero. The light also continued to fade, with Israel unable to take readings even at noon.

While the men worked on the huts, Eskimo Fred, Kislingbury, and Private Long hunted constantly. One day Long shot a walrus, but it slipped beneath the surface before he could secure it with a harpoon. The sight of walruses gave everyone hope. If they could manage to harvest a few of these enormous animals, they would likely be able to survive the winter. But privately Eskimo Fred confided in Brainard, telling him that most of them—as well as most of the seals—had by now left the small pool near their camp and sought the open water. Another day Eskimo Fred bagged a seal, and someone else shot a lone ptarmigan, but it was clear to all that they were going to need much more game if they hoped to supplement their dwindling food supplies. Everyone anxiously awaited word from Rice and Jens.

The backbreaking stone-hut building continued, and everyone was feeling the effects of the hard labor. Their clothes were tattered, their footgear shredded. Greely's back was so strained that he hunched, bent over at the waist, unable to stand upright. "The work has taxed to the utmost limit my physical powers, already worn by mental anxiety and responsibility," he said. The long days, bitter cold, weak tea, and monotonous food—all accompanied by the interminable grinding roar of the pack—was taxing a number of the others as well. One evening Lieutenant Lockwood confidentially informed Greely that Corporal Elison had been complaining aloud and directly criticizing his commander in terms "which might easily be described as mutinous." Greely had no choice but to give Corporal Elison a serious tongue-lashing in front of all the other enlisted men. He simply could have no insubordination. Elison at first tried to lay the blame on Lieutenant Kislingbury, whom he said had put him up to it, then stammered weakly that he was merely voicing all of the men's concerns. Greely held up his hand to say that the matter was closed—he would hear no more about it.

The huts were constructed according to the wishes of the men in each squad.

Greely's team chose to build an icehouse first, then erect a stone one inside, providing some insulation. It measured eight by eighteen feet and would have a canvas roof. The two other parties did the reverse, constructing the granite structures first and afterward surrounding them with ice blocks and compacted snow. Greely could see that the men were all on edge, and he wanted no further disagreements, so when it came time to distribute materials for the final outfitting of the makeshift houses, he offered to do so by lot, with his own group getting last choice. He had Kislingbury and a few others make three separate piles of useful items—poles, canvas, and even the small iceboat *Beaumont*, along with its oars and rudder—for even distribution. Brainard's party won the whaleboat, which they used as their roof—with the strict provision by Greely that the boat be used in a way that did no damage to it, as they might require it for future service.

As the items were being distributed, Edward Israel wrongly accused Brainard of taking the finest materials for his house. Greely firmly reprimanded him, saying that Brainard would never do such a thing. Greely attributed Israel's indiscretion to his being "the youngest and weakest of the party . . . and growing out of hard work, insufficient food, and severe exposure." Greely told Brainard not to worry—he had the utmost belief in his "fairness, equity, and impartiality." Brainard thanked his commander and told him that he was certain that Israel had been prompted by "the fault-finding of Connell," who, dating back to their last days at Fort Conger, had become a constant complainer and instigator of discord among the men.

Greely gathered the men and lambasted a few of them by name, including Connell and Salor, whom he accused of fomenting disunity. He demoted Connell from sergeant to private. Connell snapped: "I don't care a God damn about it!" Then he turned his back on his commander, muttering more profanities as he stormed off. Greely later took Lockwood aside and had him record that when they arrived back in the United States, he would levy charges of mutiny against Kislingbury, Pavy, and Connell. Lockwood did his duty and took down the dictation in shorthand, but he was distressed as well, exhausted from carrying heavy stones and sleeping on cold hard ground. He wrote in his private journal: "This is a miserable existence, only preferable to death. Get little sleep day or night on account of hard sleeping bag and cold."

On October 7 they'd been ashore just over a week. All were now housed in either the tepee or the finished huts. For bedding men had painstakingly tugged moss and lichens from beneath snowdrifts and crevices between rocks in the hillsides, and they lined the floors four inches deep with the plants. They also "chinked" spaces between the granite walls with moss to cut the wind and add insulation. That evening Greely sat in his house wondering and worrying about Rice and Jens. He'd hoped they would have been back by now. Perhaps they had merely been slowed by the recent bad weather. At any rate, just after departing, Rice had sent a note back with Ellis and Whisler, who'd assisted with their packs for the first few miles of their journey, then returned to camp. Greely held the message in his swollen, scabby hand: "Don't worry about me if I'm not back until October 9," it said. "The journey should take about four days each way." Still, it was hard not to imagine the worst—that Rice and Jens had been swallowed by the ice.

During those short, brutal days Greely also dreamed of home. October 7 was Henrietta's birthday, and he leaned back against the hard rock wall and closed his eyes and imagined her at home, worried sick about him. He imagined his daughters playing in the warm sitting room of his father-in-law's sunny San Diego home. He took out his journal and wrote: "Mrs. Greely's birthday; a sorry day for her and a hard day for me, to reflect on the position of my wife and children should this expedition perish as did Franklin's. However, I hope in faith that we shall succeed in returning. We will at least place our records here where our work will live after us." Then he poured a half gill of rum he'd saved for the occasion and drank to her health.

While Greely reflected on home and grew melancholy, Israel approached him privately and apologized for his unnecessary and false accusations against Brainard. Greely had personally recruited the young astronomer, whom he regarded in an almost paternal way. He found his apology "touching . . . and very affecting."

The hunters continued to be confounded by ill luck. One day Long and

Eskimo Fred shot another walrus on a small floe, but it managed to roll over and slide into the water, where it vanished, leaving only a long slick of blood on the ice. Later Eskimo Fred shot a pair of seals, but both of these also sank as he slid into his kayak to retrieve them. Said Brainard: "It is heart-rending to see this food, which is our very life, disappear before our eyes." To improve their chances for snagging the seals and walruses before they slipped away, Bender fabricated another harpoon using the spear tip from Greely's dress sword.

By October 9 everyone was anxious about Rice and Jens. Greely sent Whisler and Ellis over the top of the glacier to look for them but found no sign. Greely, too, forayed to the glacier to look and stood for a long time watching slabs thirty feet high calving into the sound with a booming splash. He returned to the huts and sent Kislingbury back up the glacier to keep watch. It was Lieutenant Lockwood's thirty-first birthday, but there was hardly enough rum to pass around in celebration. Late in the afternoon Kislingbury came running into camp to report he'd seen two figures approaching from the north. Greely ceased collecting moss and hurried out to greet the pair, and others roused as well, eager for any news.

Rice and Jens arrived back at Eskimo Point looking haggard from their ten-day journey, but they were wearing brand-new army-issue boots and fresh new sealskin outer garments they'd discovered at a cache. All of the expeditionary force huddled around now, excited by the prospects. Breathing hard through his cracked lips, his scraggly beard crusted with hoarfrost, Rice addressed his commander, pulling packets of papers from his pack and handing them over. They contained Garlington's lengthy letter from July 1883, and Beebe's scribbled notes from the year before. Rice said they contained "both good and bad news."

As Greely carefully read the document, Rice gave the good news first: All told, there were about thirteen hundred rations in the vicinity of Cape Sabine. And during his journey there and back, Rice had established a feasible sledging route they could use to get there. Between deep breaths, he also reported an unlikely but happy discovery—the whaleboat they'd abandoned during the retreat had drifted to Payer Harbor and lodged in ice between Brevoort Island and Cape Sabine. It remained in excellent condition.

At that Greely had all the men gather in one of the stone houses—he wanted to get Rice and Jens out of the elements. With trembling, puffy hands, Greely read the bad news aloud to the men. His voice was coarse and scratchy and hard to hear, but most caught the salient points in Garlington's letter, dated July 24, 1883, from Cape Sabine: Their own trusty steamer *Proteus* had been "nipped" by ice on the afternoon of the twenty-third while attempting to reach Lady Franklin Bay. "She stood the enormous pressure nobly for a time," the note said, "but had to finally succumb to this measureless force." The biggest blow to the men came with the words: "The time from her being beset to going down was so short that few provisions were saved." The message then listed those provisions—"500 rations of bread, sleeping bags, tea, and a lot of canned goods" three miles from Cape Sabine tucked under a steep cliff.

Everyone listened intently as Greely read on. Some 240 rations had been left by a Major Beebe of the Signal Corps in 1882. He'd been aboard the *Neptune*, which had apparently—the details were sketchy—been turned back by ice. They'd left a boat as well, and it was in decent condition though its bottom had been clawed by bears trying to get at the food. Beebe and the *Neptune* had left another 250 rations or so across the sound at Littleton Island, which did them no good at this point. The letters stated that a whaleboat had been cached on the Ellesmere side, just south of where they now stood, at Cape Isabella. Finally Greely read that the USS *Yantic* (presumably a support vessel) had been headed to Littleton Island but had orders not to enter the ice pack. A Swedish steamer was also said to be heading toward Cape York, and Garlington wrote that he would attempt to communicate with one or both of those vessels immediately. Garlington closed by saying: "Everything within the power of man will be done to rescue the brave men at Fort Conger from their perilous position," adding finally: "It is not within my power to express one tithe of my sorrow and regret at this fatal blow to my efforts to reach Lieutenant Greely."

Greely folded and tucked away the papers. The men shuffled back outside into the wind with mixed emotions. The news revitalized the spirits of many. Some were so hopeful they even convinced themselves that more caches might be found—near the whaleboat at Cape Isabella, perhaps. Sergeant Ralston, one of the main meteorologists, was nearly giddy. "Glorious news!" he exclaimed in his journal. "About 1200 rations at Sabine, which we think will carry us safely through the winter. . . . Two vessels outside ice looking for us." Others harbored optimism that maybe Garlington and Pike's men had successfully met the *Yantic* or this Swedish ship and had either set up winter quarters across the sound, or at least left significant stores there. Kislingbury was of this mind, believing that "Garlington must have met the *Yantic* and told her captain to leave all available supplies if he got the ship that far north." Garlington was Kislingbury's friend, and he had tremendous faith in him, convinced that he was just twenty-three miles away right now, and that "he will remain until we can cross. God bless my friend Garlington for his efforts, and also our government! Poor fellow. His suffering and anguish must have been great indeed . . . but I firmly believe he is now at Littleton Island."

Others, including Brainard—who was in charge of the commissary—saw their situation quite differently. He fully understood that the total of rations, somewhere between one thousand and thirteen hundred—it was hard to know exactly because Garlington had not had time to classify them specifically— would never be enough to get them through the winter. "The finding of these records," he lamented, "has dissipated all the daydreams of rescue which we have been fostering and brought us face to face with our situation as it really is. It could hardly be much worse." Lockwood concurred, saying: "Our situation is certainly alarming in the extreme."

Greely sat for a long time processing the news. He was momentarily heartened by cryptic lines directed to him, including "Your friends are all well," which he took to mean that his wife and children were fine. He let good feelings wash over him for a time, but those were soon replaced by reality: The total of their food, if severely rationed down to one-quarter of normal, might possibly last until April, but the means to cook were now also an issue, and he worried: "Our fuel is so scanty that we are in danger of perishing for want of that alone." He went outside and looked at the huts that they'd worked so hard to build. Men were bent at the waist or on their hands and knees nearby, pulling more moss from the ground to use as padding against the sharp rocks on which they slept. He shared no such rosy fantasies about their fate, envisioning ahead of them "a winter of starvation, suffering, and probably death for some."

But Greely would do everything in *his* power to keep these men alive. He contemplated a boat journey south—using the whaleboat and dinghy they'd brought ashore, their abandoned whaleboat that had turned up at Payer Harbor, and the reported boat at Cape Isabella. With these it was theoretically possible to try the crushing waters of Baffin Bay and a dash for the Cary Islands. But with only a week or so left of reasonable light, and no certainty of stores there, Greely dismissed this notion immediately. Most of the food and supplies they needed were at Cape Sabine, but it would weigh too much to bring back to Eskimo Point. The only reasonable course of action began to settle in his mind.

Now, as he looked around at the stark scree slopes, the crumbling glacier, the raging, erupting pack, he knew what he must do. He would share the plan with the men, but he had already made his decision. They would leave their just-finished huts behind and strike for Cape Sabine. It was twenty miles north, and there was no shelter there, but if rescue were to come, as Garlington had promised, it was there that it would do so. It was their only hope for survival.

Kayak used by Eskimo Fred and Jens to hunt seals. *(Courtesy of Naval History and Heritage Command)*

20

∽

Camp Clay

They awoke the next day to heavy snow, wind, and such low light that Greely thought it ill-advised to depart. Instead most remained in their bags, resting for the labors ahead. Brainard and a few others loaded the sledge, ready to depart when the weather allowed. Pavy attended to split fingers, blistered feet, and stomach ailments. George Rice told Greely again of his recent journey and detailed what he'd found. For one thing, he'd determined that Cape Sabine was indeed not a cape at all, but an island, separated from the mainland by a narrow strait that Greely immediately named Rice Strait for the intrepid explorer's discovery. Greely also read with great interest from the *Official Army Register* Rice had found among the cache; it contained news of the completion of the Northern and Texas Pacific Railways, and hopeful news about President Garfield's condition since being shot; it appeared that he might recover.

When Greely finished reading the news from back home, Rice volunteered to go ten miles south to Cape Isabella. There he would try to locate the English cache of 144 pounds of canned meat said to have been left there by Nares during his expedition of 1875–76. Rice could also see whether the whaleboat referenced in Garlington's letter was there and usable, and determine if the *Yantic* might, by some miracle, have made it through the maze of ice after the sinking of the *Proteus*, and left food for them on the cape. Greely did not have high hopes for the mission and thought it hazardous, but finally consented, telling Rice that if he rested the remainder of the day, he could leave first thing in the morning with Eskimo Fred, as Jens appeared fatigued from the previous journey.

At 5:30 a.m. on October 11, Rice and Fred left on foot, with light packs and a sleeping bag, heading south for Cape Isabella. The temperature had dipped to −4°. Since Rice knew the way to Cape Sabine, he'd meet everyone there after a thorough search—and a total journey of more than forty miles. The first sledge party departed north for Cape Sabine within the hour, with twelve men in the drag ropes. Greely estimated that it would take five to seven days and at least two trips, traveling back and forth a little over twenty miles, to transfer everything of necessity to their permanent winter encampment. Greely went along, helping in the drag ropes for the first few miles, then returning to Eskimo Point to decide what they should leave behind—it would be too difficult to take everything.

The initial sledging party returned around three that afternoon, having portaged the first big load as far as Ross Bay. Upon their arrival back at Eskimo Point, someone noticed that Cross, who'd stayed behind, was stumbling around the huts, tripping over rocks, and caterwauling, drunk on fuel alcohol once again. Greely was livid, as were the rest of the men. They desperately needed every ounce of alcohol they had for cooking and melting water to drink: Fuel meant life. Greely and Brainard discussed the violation, and Brainard—along with others—felt that "violent measures could be resorted to," which was a suggestion that he should be executed for his repeated transgressions. Greely scowled at Cross, saying: "What can be done with such a man?" But Greely just levied another firm reprimand at the drunkard, and Brainard simply conceded that such a drastic measure would be too extreme, as no one "wished to bring disgrace to the expedition at this late date."

Workable daylight now totaled only about six hours, and the men rose each morning at first light, pulling in shifts all day over rock, snow, and uneven ice. Traveling with their heads bowed to the wind and cold, they could progress about one mile per hour. After another full day of hauling, in which they moved everything about six miles, the men were exhausted. Greely could barely stand, and many of the others were just as weakened. Greely decided that they'd have to leave behind the iceboat *Beaumont*, which rested atop Brainard's hut as a roof. It was simply too heavy to manage. They left the oars with it. Given the hard workload, Doctor Pavy and Lieutenant Kislingbury argued for full rations. After some discussion Greely compromised and agreed to a slight increase.

On the morning of October 13 Pavy and Kislingbury came to Greely again, this time urging him strongly to leave everything they could not carry in one load. They wanted to leave behind the heavy crates of scientific instruments, boxes of records, everything not directly essential to their survival. The men, they contended, were simply too tired to drag it all. Greely flatly declined this suggestion. He said that while he knew it would be difficult, he was simply unwilling to leave behind the instruments and records of all the work they'd accomplished. He wanted everything but the *Beaumont* with them at Cape Sabine. So they stripped the rock huts of all the canvas, sails, and poles they'd used for roofs, packed the remaining tools, fuel containers, and cookstoves onto two sledges, and left Eskimo Point for good, reaching the edge of Ross Bay and setting up camp after seven grueling hours. That night the temperature fell to –16°, and the wind howled as they set their frozen bags on the hard ground, completely exposed.

Now they had to cross Ross Bay and Rice Strait to their final destination. They began to encounter thin ice that sagged and cracked beneath their weight. Moving slowly and carefully, keeping the sledges a distance apart to lessen their weight, they passed large, imposing bergs, some towering thirty feet above them. As they crept around one such mass, they heard a shrieking rupture and watched the ice heave and split just ten feet in front of them as a mass cleaved. Brainard watched in terrified awe as "the ice was torn asunder as with an invisible hand. A huge block of ice, detached from the base of a berg close by, shot up, protruding many feet in the air and throwing fragments of ice in every direction."

In the mornings, to preserve fuel they ate raw dog pemmican. Private Henry sat on the ground, complaining of a frostbitten foot and gnawing hungrily at the ends of some raw seal intestines from a kill a day or two before. Others were frostbitten, too. Greely knew they needed to get to the caches, inspect them carefully, and then build a shelter as soon as possible. He took Jens and Gardiner, whose infected finger still plagued him, and went ahead to visit

Garlington's *Proteus* "wreck cache" and also to find a suitable location for their winter quarters. Lockwood and Brainard were to lead the rest of the party and proceed as carefully as possible, always cautious of any weak ice.

He reached the wreck cache in a couple of hours and was disheartened to find that there were only one hundred rations of meat and not the five hundred that Garlington's missive had led him to hope for. He decided he'd wait to go through the entire lot with Brainard when he arrived, and moved on to the *Neptune* cache. It was encased by wind-hardened snowdrift, and Greely had no shovel with him, so that too would have to be inspected and categorized later.

After exploring the entire coastline around Cape Sabine, Greely chose to make their quarters on a fairly level lowland spit in close proximity to the wreck cache and an inland, glacial-fed freshwater lake. The spot, located on the northeastern shore of the island, was only slightly sheltered by a low, one-hundred-foot-high ridge that edged the shoreline. They were on an island about eight miles long and four miles wide, with numerous other islands off their shore. The Buchanan Strait ran to the northwest, separating them from Bache Island. Three miles west, down the strait in that direction, was Cocked Hat Island; to the east, and just off the curved easternmost point of Cape Sabine, sat tiny Brevoort and Stalknecht Islands and Payer Harbor. From the low hillside west of the campsite, Greely and the men could ascend and gaze across Smith Sound, whose opposite shore was visible under clear skies.

By late afternoon Lockwood and Brainard arrived. A broken sledge runner had delayed them, and they'd had to leave behind a heavy load of gear that Brainard promised to retrieve soon. Not long afterward the entire party was excited to see Rice and Fred coming up the spit, returning from Cape Isabella. Shrugging out of his pack, Rice told Greely that he'd found the 144 pounds of canned meat left by Nares at the peak of a one-thousand-foot hill, but as they had no sledge, they were unable to bring it with them. He'd further secured it and knew its location. Though Rice and Eskimo Fred had searched the shoreline carefully, they'd been unable to locate the whaleboat Garlington had mentioned. Some of the men groaned with displeasure, having convinced themselves that more food would have been left for them at Cape Isabella.

With everyone now together at their new campsite, Greely and Brainard sorted through the *Proteus* wreck cache. It was paltry at best, containing five hundred pounds of bread, assorted canned vegetables, lemons boxed and wrapped in newspaper, and some raisins, but only one hundred pounds of meat. There were also sundry items: clothing, looking-glasses, and twenty pounds of Bull Durham smoking tobacco and ten pounds of plug chew. Brainard handed out tobacco to the men who used it; the others took raisins. Private Henry remarked that they just stood and "gazed upon the box of Durham tobacco and wished it was meat."

Greely had no time to bewail the disappointing cache; there was too much to do. For now they would forget about the Cape Isabella cache and focus their efforts on compiling all nearby stores, including Beebe's *Neptune* cache and whaleboat, clothing, and tents at Payer Harbor, and all the provisions abandoned by Brainard the day before when the sledge broke. And they must immediately start building a new shelter. There was plenty of rock here for building walls, and many wind-formed snowdrifts from which they could hack out ice blocks. By Israel's calculations, what little sunlight they had would disappear by October 25, only nine days away. "And in that time," said Greely, "an immense amount of work must be done by the half-frozen, half-starved party."

After consulting with officers and men about the design, Greely oversaw the construction of the rectangular dwelling, which would be twenty-five feet long by eighteen feet wide, with walls four feet tall and two feet thick. They laid the cornerstones, then—using axes and picks and a few shovels—scraped a level floor and covered it with a layer of loose glacial gravel and sand. This would provide some buffer against the cold, hard ground, and perhaps keep their sleeping bags relatively dry. The inner walls would be stone, the outer walls compacted snow and ice. Some men hauled stones from nearby, others cut ice blocks from the glacier and drifts, and working in subzero temperatures, they erected the walls within a few days. For ceiling rafters they tied oars and long poles together with rope, and with these, rigged five sturdy beams atop the walls.

Next they hauled up their whaleboat from Payer Harbor, and using the strength of nearly every man, set it upside down across the rafters, over which they stretched canvas sails, the tepee materials, and extra tarpaulins for the roof, lashing these down tight. In the center of the squat hut, Private Bender placed a cookstove—made out of a cylinder of sheet iron—and erected the stovepipe chimney, which he'd fashioned from empty tin cans, up through a hole he had cut in the bottom of the boat for this purpose. One end of the hut served as the entryway; it was left open but covered by thick canvas for a door. Next to the entryway, using stones, blocks of snow, and the remaining tent materials, they constructed a storage shed for supplies and food, the latter of which would have to be guarded against stealthy foxes.

All suffered during the building of the shelter. Both of Cross's feet were now frostbitten; Long developed chest pains; and Biederbick complained of sore and inflamed joints and limbs. Working on the hut walls, Greely was struck in the face by an ax-handle when he got too close to Whisler, who was hacking out an ice block. But together they'd finished the quarters and moved in by the evening of October 19. Sleeping bags were tucked one next to the other, heads facing the walls, providing a narrow aisle for them to shuffle in and out, either by crawling or scuffling on their knees. The only place inside where a man could almost stand upright was next to the chimney where it exited through the belly of the whaleboat. From the centermost beam Israel hung the barometer and a seal-blubber lamp, which flickered and smoked as it burned. When the taller men sat upright against the walls, their heads brushed against the canvas ceiling.

The close proximity of the men, with their three-man buffalo-hide bags touching one another, provided needed body heat; it was now down to –13° outside. Greely had the cooks make hot chocolate and coffee, a welcome indulgence, but each man was allotted only one small serving. A severe storm had driven everyone inside, including the hunters Kislingbury and Eskimo Fred, who to everyone's joy had recently killed a fox. The low-lying hut was considerably better than sleeping outside, which they'd done every night since leaving Eskimo Point, but Greely noted that "we are so huddled and crowded together that the confinement is almost unbearable."

After being hut-bound by poor weather for two days, Greely finally decided that since only five days of light remained, he would send Lockwood and Rice, and a dozen others with sledges, to bring in all the remaining supplies left by

Nares, Beebe, and Garlington. Lockwood would be accompanied by Long and the two Greenlanders, who would camp in a tent at Rice Strait and hunt until the daylight died, then return. The rest of the men, including Greely, remained busy hauling in more sand and gravel for the floor and shoring up the hut walls with more snow and ice. Late that afternoon Lockwood came back, having left the sledge and its load a couple of miles from camp. They were simply too weary to drag it all the way back and would get it tomorrow.

The next morning there occurred an unusual and unexpected development. While unpacking lemons from the wreck cache, Brainard noticed they'd been wrapped in newspapers. Each man had been issued a lemon, and Brainard carefully removed the pieces of newspaper and laid them out to dry, then pieced them together. Greely held some of these up to the feeble light of the seal-blubber lamp, and squinting through his spectacles, he shook his head and began to read aloud to the men. The paper, from September 1881, reported that President Garfield had died seventy-nine days after being shot, from infection (septicemia) and pneumonia. The men now knew that Chester Arthur was their president. The scraps of paper also revealed that the entire cabinet, except Robert Todd Lincoln, had changed. Greely and his men all hoped—indeed they had to believe—that Lincoln would not forget about them. It was astonishingly unlikely, but they'd learned about the fate of their president from a packaged lemon, wrapped in newspaper, salvaged from a sinking ship.

Greely mused for some time about Garfield's death. He had known the man personally, and it was under his governance and aegis that the Lady Franklin Bay Expedition had been approved. Their last meeting had taken place in the East Room of the White House, where Garfield had held a small gathering to wish the explorer well and talk privately about the Arctic endeavor. "Under your leadership," Garfield had said, "I am confident that the work will be a success. The honor of our nation will be maintained in this scientific contest with other civilized nations." Greely felt a twinge of sadness, followed by a wave of responsibility, reminded as he was of the importance of their mission and his duty as its commander.

Greely wanted all available supplies brought in now. He accompanied a few men to the nearby *Neptune* cache, which was just a mile away to the southeast.

They could sledge only part of the way, "as no ice-foot yet formed along the rough, rocky coast." They broke through a number of times, sinking to their knees in icy water, but managed to get everything back. Greely and a few of the others suffered minor frostbite, needing to change hurriedly into drier footgear inside the hut.

Rice and three men went on foot once more to the *Proteus* cache, with orders to "bring up as much of the clothing as possible by packs." While rummaging through the cache and sorting clothing, Rice came across a brass ship's lantern wrapped in newspaper. A headline caught his eye: it was an article concerning the Lady Franklin Bay Expedition! Rice carefully tucked the paper away and brought it, along with folded stacks of clothing and blankets, back to the hut.

Greely and the others waited anxiously as Rice slowly dried the paper by the cookstove, then began to read aloud, pausing now and then to blow the pages dry. The article was a letter to the editor, appearing in the *Louisville Courier-Journal*, and written, amazingly, by someone they knew—Henry Clay. Clay had been, along with Doctor Pavy, on the original failed Howgate Expedition, and had joined the *Proteus* on its way up to Lady Franklin Bay. But his and Pavy's personalities had clashed, and since Greely needed a doctor, he'd sent Clay back to the United States on the *Proteus*. Because of his personal connection to the expedition, Clay had kept a keen interest. His three-column letter was dated May 13, 1883; it was but five months old. Written before the departure of the *Proteus* and *Yantic*, Clay's words spoke volumes. He attacked the government's relief efforts, rightly arguing that it was flawed to assume they could easily hire Etah Eskimo and dogs to sledge along the Greenland coast, and at any rate, Greely and his men would be across the Smith Sound at Cape Sabine, with no guarantee of their ability to traverse the hazardous ice at that time.

The men leaned forward, hushed and transfixed as Rice read on:

> *They cannot return to Fort Conger, and there will be no shelter for them at Cape Sabine. The cache of 240 rations, if it can be found, will prolong their misery for a few days. When that is exhausted, they will be past all earthly*

succor. Like poor De Long, they will then lie down on the cold ground, under the quiet stars, to die.

With this news Greely now knew that De Long had perished. And at least he knew, with some consolation, that he had a strong supporter back home in Henry Clay. In appreciation Greely named their winter quarters Camp Clay. The news from home caused everyone to think about their loved ones, who would now at the very least be worried beyond measure and at worst think them lost. Greely thought of the long-suffering Emma De Long, whose letter to her husband he still had packed among his possessions, to be delivered by hand had Greely found him. What grief she must have endured during that long, silent absence. Then the commander reflected on Henrietta and the girls. He knew in his heart that his "Rettie" would not give up on him, and that gave him solace as he closed his eyes and dreamed of home.

Lieutenant Lockwood was particularly struck by Henry Clay's letter, and—trying to at least retain a sense of humor under the circumstances—wrote in his journal: "We all think Clay's letter is most prophetic, except, of course, our lying down under the quiet stars to die."

Thereafter, anything wrapped in newspaper was treated as a kind of treasure, and men took turns reading by the dim lamplight. One night, while reading the *Army Register* once more, someone blurted out that 2nd Lt. James Lockwood had been promoted to first lieutenant! Given his stalwart service during the expedition, he certainly deserved it. He would soon have an opportunity to sign his name with his new rank. On Rice's return from the wreck cache the previous day, he had observed firm ice consolidating on the shore as a result of the consistently low temperature. He thought it might allow safe travel, and perhaps they could make it as far as the Nares cache. Greely deemed it sensible, and he sent Lockwood and eleven men to go after as much of it as they could carry. They were already on reduced rations, but Greely estimated that even with the limitations, the food would hold out only until March 10 of the following year.

Before they left, Greely took Lockwood aside and entrusted him with a special mission. Lockwood nodded, and led eleven men out of the hut and toward

Payer Harbor. Once there, at the south side of the harbor, Lockwood ordered some of the men to begin packing up the contents of the cache, while he and a few others, burdened by heavy crates and a sextant box, ascended to a high promontory at the summit of Stalknecht Island. They built a large cairn at the island's summit, piling rocks high and erecting the tall Peirce pendulum at its apex, thrust skyward like a flagpole, so that it stood sentinel over the harbor below. Greely had ordered it positioned "so that no one visiting the harbor can miss seeing it." Buried within the cairn, Lockwood left the following message:

> *October 23, 1883. This cairn contains the original records of the Lady Frank-lin Bay Expedition, the private journal of Lieutenant Lockwood, and a set of photographic negatives. The party is permanently encamped at a point mid-way between Cape Sabine and Cocked Hat Island. All well.*
>
> *James B. Lockwood, 1ˢᵗ Lieutenant, 23d Infantry*

With his first mission as First Lieutenant Lockwood completed, he and the men loaded up the Nares cache and headed back toward Camp Clay. The journey there and back took them ten hours.

While they were slogging back along the shoreline and dealing with a broken sledge, Greely was in the hut, leaning against the wall and writing in his journal, explaining his rationale for the cache: "I know that point will certainly be visited, and that possibly our present camp might be missed by a relief expedition, and all the records lost if left here. I am determined that our work shall not perish with us."

Peirce pendulum and rescue cairn containing First Lieutenant Lockwood's letter. *(Courtesy of Naval History and Heritage Command)*

21

Henrietta's Powers of Persuasion

Lt. Ernest Garlington's arrival back in Washington was not a pleasant one. He'd made it to New York on the *Yantic* and proceeded by train to the nation's capital, arriving on October 1, 1883, just two days after Greely and his men had straggled ashore at Eskimo Point. As Garlington settled back into his office, amid a blackening news storm about his decisions, his first official duty was to draft a formal report to General Hazen, chief signal officer. Despite the fact that the decision to delay any rescue attempts for Greely and his men until next year had already been made by Secretaries Lincoln and Chandler and President Arthur, the press had not let it go, and as Garlington wrote his report, he could not escape the growing national outcry and criticism that he was receiving on a daily basis.

In his report he tried to focus on the bare facts of what had happened and how he had reacted under the extreme circumstances, but there was no way of ignoring the public shame he was enduring, as well as calls for his court-martial. Sensational accounts continued to haunt Garlington, as well as Henrietta Greely. One story came from crew members of the Swedish steamer *Sofia*, which had been in the region of Upernavik, Greenland, while Garlington was attempting to relieve Greely. The story alleged that while the *Sofia* was at anchor along the coast, the two Greenlanders, Eskimo Fred and Jens, had visited the crew and "had told them that the doctor of the party [Pavy] at Lady Franklin Bay had been killed, his arms and legs cut off."

Despite there being no corroboration for such tales, that didn't stop newspapers, ravenous for salacious stories, from publishing them. Some reporters even went so far—when they learned that his husky, Rover, had been with him and survived the *Proteus* wreck—as to question Garlington about whether Rover had consumed food meant for Greely and his men. "No," Garlington replied, insulted. "Rover's presence had not denied a scrap of nourishment" to the Greely party. In his report Garlington could only say: "I am confident that all sensational stories which have been recently published are without foundation in fact." Garlington added that such stories, in addition to creating a national hysteria, had done "manifest injury" to his character and reputation. Garlington sent his final report to General Hazen on October 2, 1883; it would be forwarded on to and read by Secretary Lincoln two weeks later, and Garlington knew that would not be the end of it.

∽∼∽

Back at her father's home in San Diego, Henrietta continued her own campaign. Though busy caring for her elderly and now-failing father, and attending to her young girls, Antoinette and Adola, Henrietta wrote constantly to General Hazen and others, expressing as diplomatically as she possibly could that haggling over what had already happened in the past seemed much less important than figuring out what should be done in the future. Her friend and ally Hazen was at last back in the capital, and she wrote imploringly to him: "I do not feel that much is to be gained by looking into the failure of the expedition this year. It seems to me the important thing is to bend every energy toward preparing a fitting plan to rescue the party at the earliest moment next year."

Henrietta also took time to visit personally with an old family friend, the influential publisher Douglas Gunn of the *San Diego Union*. Gunn had bought the paper in 1871 and was politically shrewd, with an eye on public office. Henrietta had met Gunn even before she'd met her Dolph; they'd attended a few dances and dinners together; their families were close, and she trusted him and trusted his judgment. When she suggested that she might herself go to Washington to try to push along a relief effort, he countered that the power of the press could get more done, and that her efforts should be directed there, using all of her considerable contacts across the country. He offered to help her any way he could, saying: "You don't have to go to Washington. . . . We can get the Washington papers and every newspaper in the nation working for us." Henrietta thought this sensible. Her time would be better spent using her pen and her voice. Gunn suggested that she contact all of her closest and most powerful friends and enlist their support, adding: "And I will work from here to arouse every newspaper in the country to demand that your husband and his men be rescued."

During her brief time in Washington, Henrietta had struck up a close friendship with General Hazen's wife, Millie. Millie Hazen was deeply connected in both political and journalism circles, and as such had access to many influential men. She happened to be the daughter of Washington McLean, a powerful business- and newspaperman who had owned *The Cincinnati Enquirer* until 1881, when he sold it to his son, her brother, John McLean. The father-and-son McLeans later went on to acquire *The Washington Post*. When Henrietta wrote asking for support, Millie was enthusiastic, saying that she would encourage her father and brother to lobby her cause through their newspaper outlets. As to her innumerable contacts in national politics, she would need to prod them with discretion, given her husband General Hazen's high profile in the matter. Henrietta was grateful for Millie's assistance, and could at least feel hopeful that she'd begun a quiet groundswell to help her husband and his men. She was ever mindful that most of the men of the expedition also had families who were as heartsick as she was, and they would do the same if they had the means. This thought sustained her and kept her vigilant.

Since the failure of the first relief of the *Neptune*, under Private Beebe, Henrietta had been corresponding frequently with Dolph's mother, Frances, in Newburyport, Massachusetts. "Mother Greely" (as she signed her letters) was attentive to Henrietta's pains and worries, and she honestly expressed her own: "I am glad to know that you are so hopeful about Adolphus's ability to winter in the arctic regions," she wrote her dear "daughter Rettie," whom she had never met in person. "I hope God will protect them and that they will come home all right. . . . What worries me most is that Adolphus has left the station and is now suffering with cold and perhaps sickness and hunger. 'Tis dreadful to think of." Mother Greely closed one letter with poignant words:

> *I have seen two or three pieces in the papers about you. They say that you are a beautiful woman, and I know you are as good as you are beautiful. I am glad to hear that the babys is so well. I wish I could see them, the Dear Darlings, Adolphs babys. 'Twas a dredful thing to leve you and go to that dredful place.*
>
> *I hope you will come East in the spring. I think you could do a grate deal about getting up the next expedition. But if we should be disappointed again I dare not think of the result. . . . Rettie I want you to know if anything happens . . . everything belongs to you and the babys. Please write me soon.*
>
> *Mother F.D. Greely*
>
> *P.S. I have saved all the papers and laid them aside for Adolph, if he ever comes home again to read.*

One article, published in both *The New York Times* and *The* [Washington] *Evening Star*, caught the attention of everyone involved with the Lady Franklin Bay Expedition. It concerned Pvt. William Beebe of the *Neptune*. On returning from the Arctic without provisioning Greely, he had taken his failure hard and fallen into a depression, spending his evenings in some of Washington's many drinking establishments. He wished to redeem himself, and both wanted and expected to be involved in the second relief. But Washington circles were small and rumor filled, and stories of Beebe's excessive drinking filtered their way to the Signal Corps Office. Hazen certainly heard them, and when it came time to outfit another trip to Lady Franklin Bay, Beebe was excluded, leaving him at home alone—he had no wife or children.

A couple of months after the *Proteus* and *Yantic* embarked without him, Beebe was spotted at the National Hotel in Washington, reported to look like "a man who had been drinking hard." The next day Beebe was found dead in his house, the cause of death suicide by laudanum. One of the articles attributed his suicide to his health and mind being "impaired by the hardships he was exposed to" in failing to relieve the Greely Expedition.

Henrietta would have fretted over the news of such a tragedy, directly connected as it was to her husband's expedition. It also starkly underscored the hardships Dolph and his men must necessarily be enduring at that very moment, in October 1883. By the end of the month she learned—somewhat to her dismay—that there would be a presidential court of inquiry into the *Proteus* disaster. It was reasonable, she thought, to determine everything that had gone wrong, and perhaps avoid such mistakes in the future. But to her mind, time was essential and precious, and it would make more sense for the government to focus attention on what to do next. Even more troubling was that Henrietta learned through some of her channels in Washington of a comment attributed to Secretary Lincoln, who had been unsupportive from the beginning and now, given two consecutive public failures, was becoming privately downright hostile toward future efforts. Of the Greely Expedition, Lincoln was reported to have quipped: "I do not see any use in throwing away any more money on dead men."

If this appalling attitude prevailed in Washington, Henrietta knew that nothing would be done in time. Tremendous effort was required, and she steeled herself to action. She determined to appeal to her twin brothers, Loring and Otto Nesmith, for help. Otto was a well-connected Boston lawyer, and she would ask him to persuade his editor friends in the city to raise awareness of her husband's plight. She would write everyone she knew who wielded power, every senator and congressman she could reach—even President Arthur himself—and urge them to do what was right. She would remind them that the men of the Lady Franklin Bay Expedition were serving their country, and their country owed a service to them. Indeed, it was a moral obligation. Henrietta vowed to use all her powers of persuasion, bolstered by the power of the press and the will of the people, to do their duty and save her husband and his men.

22

Darkness Descends

During those last days of October 1883, as Henrietta busied herself in warm and sunny San Diego writing letters and sending telegrams across the country, Commander Greely was also writing, making journal entries. On October 26 he wrote: "Our last day of sunlight for one hundred and ten long days, and how to pass this coming Arctic night is a question I cannot answer." By now, with great difficulty owing to severe cold and breaking sledges, all the local caches had been brought in. Fuel was running short, and the cooks were using alternating sources for the stove—splinters of barrel staves, wood ripped from the washed-up whaleboat, seal blubber, stearine, alcohol—even rope and boat lines. The cooks—usually Shorty Frederick and Private Biederbick—bent over and blew the fire to warm drinking water and mixed-meat stews, acrid smoke searing their eyes and choking them as the others ducked into their bags to evade the smoke.

Flaring auroral streamers were beginning to slash across the sky, signaling the onset of winter, but the men were no longer enthralled by them as they had been at Fort Conger. The little freshwater pond near their camp had frozen solid, making drinking water available only at mealtimes twice a day. The men grew agonizingly thirsty. Greely detailed a few of the strongest to begin hacking a deep hole through the ice in the pond to get water, an arduous job. After bringing in one of the last various caches, Brainard found a barrel of dog biscuits—one hundred pounds of dry cakes that were a mix of grains, vegetables, and beef—but most of them were "thoroughly rotten and covered with a green mold." The bitter irony of this canine food cache was not lost on the men, as they no longer had dogs. Perhaps the foxes would like them. Greely told Brainard to dispose of them and warn the men against eating them lest they become sick, but when Brainard tossed them on the ground, "the half-famished men sprang to them as wild animals would." They ate every ounce of the biscuits.

On one of the final days of October, Eskimo Fred shot a seal that dressed out to about seventy-five pounds, and Bender, remarkably, killed a blue fox with his bare hands, pounding it with his fists while the slinking creature had its head stuck in an empty meat tin. But even with these supplemental meats, Greely knew it was time to further reduce rations. He brought the men together to discuss the idea, by now comfortable in inviting their opinions; it was crucial that they come to a group decision on important matters such as this. His new approach was to give his proposal first, and afterward listen to everyone's thoughts, and then try to reach a consensus. Greely suggested that starting November 1, they should cut down to four ounces of vegetables, four ounces of meat, and six ounces of hardtack, which would potentially last until March 1 and leave them ten days' rations to attempt crossing Smith Sound. He prayed it would be completely frozen by then.

After a reasoned and calm discussion, once again Greely's proposal was agreed to almost unanimously, with the exception of Doctor Pavy, who believed that such a reduction would dangerously diminish their strength and possibly result in scurvy. In the end Pavy was overridden by the group, and they all consented to the lowest ration levels, which could be increased if necessary, and potentially supplemented with game—though successful kills were becoming rare. The hunters agreed to remain afield, hoping for something large, either a bear or a walrus. Greely expressed his appreciation for the backing of his men, saying: "While this should ordinarily be expected from a party under military discipline, yet, under the present circumstances, where moral influences alone have sway, and where so great hardships and privations have already been experienced, I cannot but be gratified by this general expression of confidence in my judgment and discretion."

Despite these privations—they were now to live on fifteen ounces of food per day, while at Fort Conger they'd had seventy—the men maintained fairly high spirits, at least outwardly. Sorting through the caches, Brainard found bundles of additional clothing, which he distributed. He also discovered heavy woolen blankets, buffalo coats, and a few rolled mattress pads. Brainard passed these out as equitably as possible, with Greely's orders to give preference to the sick and injured. The entire party voted that their leader receive one of the mattresses, but Greely handed it over to Sergeant Gardiner, who was still feverish, suffering from the lingering infection in his hand.

There remained the matter of the 144 pounds of English beef at Cape Isabella. Rice knew precisely where it was, and although the Long Night was now once again upon them, Greely made the tough decision to send a party for it, despite it being forty miles south, and the temperatures now consistently well below zero. "It would give nearly an ounce of meat to each man daily," said Greely, "which, in the coming winter, could mean life or death." Sgt. George Rice once again volunteered to lead a dangerous mission. His proven hardiness and knowledge of the route made him the natural choice. Accompanying him would be Shorty Frederick, Pvt. David Linn, and Cpl. Joseph Elison.

They planned to travel light and fast, with just a four-man sledge, a canvas tent fly, a four-man buffalo-hide bag, a pot and cooking stove, and a rifle. Brainard distributed provisions for eight days, with five ounces of alcohol fuel to cook their eight ounces of meat per man per day, and an equal ration of bread. For clothing they were equipped, according to Brainard, with the best that the humble party could offer, "for every member of the party has denied himself some article of clothing which will add to their warmth and comfort." On November 2, under low-lying snow clouds, a light northwest wind, and with the temperature at –10°, the four courageous men left Camp Clay and trudged south for the planned eighty-mile round-trip journey. Those feeling strong enough crawled out of the hut quarters and stood to see them off with a hearty cheer.

⌒⌒⌒

At Camp Clay, Doctor Pavy was busy tending to a growing number of injured and infirm men. Bringing in all the caches and the remainder of the whaleboat for wood fuel had taken a severe toll on a number of the party. Commander Greely and Private Henry were recovering from frostbite; Connell and Schneider were suffering from moderate dysentery; and Sergeant Israel sprawled in his bag from general exhaustion. Greely remarked proudly that the young Israel bore his pains stoically, uttering not a single complaint. Kislingbury had returned bearing one of the last loads and mentioned internal discomfort, and when Pavy examined him, the sharp, shooting pains caused Kislingbury to faint twice. Pavy worried that an organ rupture—perhaps a spleen or appendix— might prove fatal. For the next few days Kislingbury required constant aid from others in order to walk or move about, but he gradually improved.

With Kislingbury recovering and the primary hunters much fatigued, Brainard, Bender, Schneider, and Ralston took turns hunting, and their fresh legs and eyes were successful: each man shot and killed a fox. Long later dragged in a harbor seal weighing close to 150 pounds, lifting everyone's spirits. All this meat was added to the larder and contributed to extra rations each week. The industrious Bender, using sheet-metal scavenged from the whaleboat bow, and tin cans, improved the chimney stovepipe to reduce the smoke; he also fabricated two small, efficient cookstoves that burned less fuel. Long returned one day from hunting to report the tracks of two large bears in the vicinity, raising the party's enthusiasm for a short time. A bear kill would be something to celebrate.

The strongest of the men continued improving the insulation of the hut walls with snow blocks, but the work was slow and debilitating even for them. Some resorted to desperate measures to supplement their fare. First Lieutenant Lockwood admitted in his journal that he was reduced one morning to "scraping like a dog in the place where the moldy dog biscuits were emptied. Found a few crumbs of small pieces and ate them mold and all." He began to fantasize daily about the food he would eat at home, concocting elaborate and delicious dishes in his mind—roast suckling pig, smoked goose—which he would record in detail in his journal.

In the first days after Rice and his team had left, Brainard began to notice that someone, or perhaps more than one person, had been pilfering food from the temporary snow-block storeroom. Brainard reported this to Greely, who ordered hurried construction on a more permanent storeroom with a thick tarpaulin roof and a door, fashioned from some wood saved for this purpose. Fortunately he'd brought along a lock and key from Fort Conger, with which he hoped to better guard the food. But until it was finished, incidents continued: Schneider stole rum, becoming drunk quickly on his empty stomach. Greely berated him publicly, shaming the man. An open can of milk was found in the storehouse a day or so later, tucked behind a small snow block, its tin lid cut open with someone's knife. The can remained full, as if the perpetrator had feared being caught and left in a hurry. Next to the can was a broken-off knife blade. After some questioning, Henry admitted that the knife was his, but he claimed that Private Schneider had borrowed it. Neither Greely nor Brainard could determine who was telling the truth. Inside the hut that night, Greely forbade anyone other than the designated commissary sergeant from entering the storehouse. These food-pilfering developments deeply concerned him; he was now worried that their hunger might drive the men to anarchy.

⌒⌒⌒

Out on the sledge trail, moving south toward Cape Isabella, Rice and his small team initially made good progress. Moving over wind-ridged snow and ice for two days, they reached Eskimo Point and sheltered one night in the huts they had built there, then pushed on toward Cape Isabella, rough ice eventually slowing them so that after many hours they were almost crazy with thirst. Elison and Linn, against Rice's warnings, scooped their mittens into the soft snow and stuffed it into their mouths. This gave fleeting relief for their thirst but dangerously lowered their body temperature and frosted their hands. On the fourth day out, they left behind everything but the sledge and reached the foot of Cape Isabella. Climbing upward without the sledge, bringing bags and packs, they scrambled up the slick, ice-hardened rock knoll to the summit, where they un-earthed the undisturbed boxes of meat. Before descending, they took time to stare out to sea. The sky, said Frederick,

> was clear, the moon bright, and to the southward, we saw open water as far as the eye could reach. Waves with white caps came rolling in to the very cape. Even at this season a vessel could have navigated without difficulty. Could we have embarked at this point, I have no doubt but we all would have reached our homes in safety.

They did not linger at the summit. The temperature was down to –30°, so they descended, strapped the meat boxes to the sledge, and began the long, cold slog back, trekking for fourteen hours on no food and merely a cup of tea. By the time they reached their tent fly and four-man sleeping bag, Elison's face, hands, and feet were severely frostbitten. Said Frederick: "I placed one of Elison's hands between my thighs and Rice took the other, and in this way, we drew the frost from his frozen limbs." As his hands thawed and blood flow returned, the pain overtook him, and Elison wailed all night in anguish.

The next morning, November 8, they warmed some food and tea and went on. The snow became soft and deep, and they labored, sometimes breaking through up to their knees. Elison's feet had never thawed and had become "stiff as cord wood." Unable to feel his feet, he began to stumble and stagger. By the next day, just short of Eskimo Point, Elison could no longer walk on his own. At times Frederick slung Elison's arm over his shoulder and led him forward; at other times he hoisted the man onto his back and carried him. Eventually Rice had to choose between the meat and Elison's life. Without hesitating, he pitched the boxes of meat from the sledge, and they loaded Elison onto it. Then Rice thrust the Springfield rifle butt-first into the snow to mark the meat's location, so they could eventually recover it, and he, Frederick, and Linn took to the haul ropes.

They reached the abandoned stone huts at Eskimo Point after ten hours and hurried Elison inside. Rice ripped wood from the iceboat *Beaumont* and built a fire, and they stripped Elison of his clothes to dry them, now violently rubbing his legs, which were white-hard to his knees. As the fire warmed Elison's extremities, there came the blood-flow pain, and he yowled in agony. "His sufferings were such," said Frederick, "that it was enough to bring the strongest to tears."

They left for Camp Clay early on the tenth, with Elison now attempting to walk ahead with Linn supporting him, but almost immediately his legs froze again, and he buckled and fell, his face completely white, his eyelids sealed shut. "It seemed that every moment the frost was striking deeper into the poor man's flesh," said Frederick. "No person can imagine how he suffered." They could not haul Elison and the gear up a steep hill between Baird Inlet and Ross Bay, and after a futile attempt to start a fire, during which he froze his hands, Rice decided he must go alone the last fifteen miles to Camp Clay to get help. Frederick and Linn put Elison in the four-man bag, then slid inside with him as Rice crunched away from them, the sound of his boots soon swallowed by the expanse.

Gnawing continually on a chunk of frozen meat as he went, Rice shuffled along over mounded, crumbled ice through glowing moonlight, unsure whether the auroral flares that exploded in the sky like fireworks were real or hallucinations. Driving himself forward into a biting north wind hour after hour and mile after mile, near midnight he finally reeled his way to the canvas door of Camp Clay and fell to his hands and knees. Hearing something, Greely knee-walked his way to the entrance and pulled aside the flap.

Rice's frozen lips could barely crack open, but he managed to cry out: "Elison is dying!"

23

"Son of a Gun"

Rice's face was so ice caked that Greely barely recognized him. He called for men to help drag Rice inside, then plied him with warm tea and brandy and listened carefully as he relayed the dire situation. Elison was in terrible condition; when Rice had left him—he had no idea how long ago—he was in the sleeping bag between Frederick and Linn, who were trying to keep him alive. His hands and feet were all frozen solid, he said. They were with the sledge, twenty-five miles away at Ross Bay the last time he had seen them, but they may have tried to keep moving forward.

Greely sent Brainard and Eskimo Fred in an advance rescue party, giving them brandy and food for the three men stranded at Ross Bay. Lockwood, Doctor Pavy, and four others who felt strong enough to go—Jens, Schneider, Ellis, and Jewell—would follow behind two hours later. Brainard and Fred stumbled along through the darkness, tripping and falling over snow-covered mounds, the ice crackling underfoot. About noon, after seven hard hours in a gale, they reached the three men, who lay on the ground, ice cocooned inside the block-hard sleeping bag.

Biting gusts covered them all with drifts, and with great difficulty Brainard managed to build a small fire and heat food and drink. He gave them brandy and spoon-fed them warm meat stew. As the men roused, Linn began babbling incoherently, crying out to be released from the bag. Brainard stood over the men's heads; Elison's nose and cheeks were chalk-white in the muted moon-glow. Brainard leaned forward—Elison was trying to say something. The man rasped out, his voice pleading: "Kill me. Please kill me."

Frederick and Linn had kept Elison alive with their body heat, but the bag was hard as iron around them, and they had remained in that position for un-told hours, unable even to roll over. Frederick and Linn said they weren't sure they'd be able to walk, as their feet had become frostbitten too. Brainard gave them more stew and brandy, and they revived slightly. Linn, who Frederick said had been incoherent for hours, kept struggling to free himself from the frozen bag, but Brainard told him firmly to stay inside or he would likely die. Frederick mumbled that if he could stand, he might possibly be able to make it back to Camp Clay under his own power, but he doubted whether he and Linn had the strength to help haul Elison. Given the situation, Brainard decided he must start back with Eskimo Fred and meet Lockwood and the others and tell them to hurry; they would need all hands on the drag ropes. As Brainard turned his back to the men, he could hear Elison's faint plea again: "Oh, will you kill me? Please."

At Rice Strait, under a strengthening storm, Brainard met the larger relief party along the sledge track. Lockwood, Pavy, and the others had struggled for twelve hours to get there, and they all camped and rested. They woke at 4:30 a.m., ate a paltry breakfast, and started back for their compatriots Elison, Linn, and Frederick. Brainard got there first and found them all "still frozen and shivering in the bag." He told them that the others were coming to help. The wind was too strong for Brainard to light an alcohol lamp, but using some wood he had brought along from the iceboat at Eskimo Point, he succeeded in starting a fire, though he damaged his fingers, "which were alternately burned and frosted." Once again he spoon-fed them hot meat stew.

An hour or two later they heard voices drawing near. When the relief party arrived, they used knives to cut the three men out of the frozen bag. It smelled strongly of urine. The men had been frozen inside it for almost twenty-four hours. Working quickly, the rescuers slid Elison into a one-man dog-skin sleeping bag, then wrapped him in heavy canvas for added warmth. Frederick and Linn at first tottered feebly, leaning on others, but after moving around to get some circulation back, they were eventually able to stand on their own, and then began trudging forward together toward Camp Clay. Brainard helped Lockwood and Pavy load Elison onto the sledge, and they all took turns pulling him and talking to him, trying to bolster his spirits. Fighting through biting winds all day, with the temperature near –20°, they made it back to Rice Strait, where they stopped to rest for a few hours. With numb hands they struggled to set up the tent, and eventually succeeded, sliding the delirious Elison inside the shelter.

At eight o'clock they struck the tent and started again, pulling Elison, their "half-conscious burden," behind them and trying to avoid knolls and bumps that would cause him pain. When they reached Rice Strait, they now believed they would make it; they were within a few miles of Camp Clay. Throughout the ordeal Brainard had been moving almost continuously for twenty hours, traveling nearly fifty miles, and his stalwart will had nearly been shattered. But in the last hours of the rescue journey, the skies cleared, and Sergeant Brainard was overcome by the stark, surreal power and beauty of this place:

> The wind died away and the moon rose and shed soft light over the barren ice-fields, making the night one of the most attractive that I have ever known. The ice-bound coast with the chaotic masses of pulverized bergs at its borders, and the weird scene of desolation spreading about us on every side, were never so apparent as now. A feeling of awe seemed to take possession of the party and we moved forward slowly and in silence.

Reaching Camp Clay four hours later, at 2:00 a.m. on November 13, 1883, Brainard, Lockwood, and the rest of the rescuers were greeted with loud cheers from the men who had come out of the hut to huddle in the –35° temperature. Frederick and Linn had made it safely back many hours before. Under Doctor Pavy's direction, they hurried the miserable Elison inside, and with the assistance of Biederbick, Pavy stripped him of his clothes. Elison had been outside, except for a few hours in a stone hut at Eskimo Point, for eleven days.

Pavy examined Elison and concluded that amputation of some of his limbs was indicated, but lacking a sterile environment and a proper surgical setting with clean dressing cloths, such a procedure would likely prove fatal. Still, Elison was in critical condition. All they could do for now was wrap him in layers of thick woolen blankets and thaw him out. They cut open a sheepskin sleeping bag, fanned it wide open, slid him inside, and laid him on a mattress. Then Pavy and Biederbick alternated in twelve-hour shifts night and day, gradually raising the temperature of his limbs by swabbing them in cloths soaked in first cold, then warmer water. As they continued to change dressings, the color of Elison's limbs turned bruised blue. For many days they attended to him like this, spoon-feeding him what little he would eat at mealtimes, and when necessary, holding a tin can for him to urinate in. Noted Brainard with humble admiration: "Never did rough-bearded men express more sympathy or tenderness for a crippled comrade." Elison rarely complained, and after a time, he stopped asking to die.

The others in the rescue party had also suffered. Once back in the hut, most of them, according to Private Henry, "sank exhausted upon their damp bags and lay like logs for a considerable length of time; nor were any of them fit or able to stir for about a week." Fortunately their frostbite was minor and quickly improved. Brainard, hardier than most, was back at work two days later shoring up the walls of the commissary storehouse in −40° temperature. Greely wanted to help, but the men wouldn't allow it. They agreed unanimously that his mental capacities as their leader were most important at the moment.

There remained work to be done, but a diminishing number of able bodies to do it. Rice and Brainard stayed active. Brainard finished the commissary storehouse, complete with the wooden door, lock, and key Greely had ordered installed. Only the keyholder would be allowed inside, and Greely chose his most trusted men for the duty. Together Brainard and Rice also climbed one day to the high cliffs above their encampment, at the far end of the peninsula. There, using an oar, they erected a tall signal pole bearing a flag in the hope that it would be visible to any relief vessels moving along the coast. Greely was dubious, saying: "I have not the faintest expectation of such a party this winter, but some of the rest have, and I am unwilling to depress their spirits by destroying any hopes they may nourish." Other chores included the laborious job of pickaxing a hole in the ice of the lake to fetch fresh water, thus saving the fuel used in melting; emptying the frozen contents of the urinal tub, which sat outside the entryway in the vestibule; and cooking and cleaning dishes.

Long and Jens continued to hunt, with some success. In less than one week in late November, the duo killed six foxes, adding nearly the entire animals to the larder and wasting nothing. Brainard noted that "the intestines, in fact everything but the skin, are used for our stews and eaten without the slightest repugnance." Brainard also made a happy find when he opened the last barrel of dog biscuits and discovered that all but a few pieces were in prime edible condition—with only a few moldy ones, unlike the entirety of the other barrel. He retained his sense of humor, saying: "This is food which any well-bred dog would refuse, but if we had plenty of it, I for one would be happier!"

But conditions inside of the hut remained grim. The temperature within the walls ranged between 15° and 30°, rising above freezing only when the central stove was burning. To stay warm, men would clap their hands together, swing their arms in circles, and, according to Brainard, "knock the feet together in the most frenetic manner to keep them from freezing." By now their sleeping bags had frozen in place to the ground, and, said Brainard: "The hair inside is filled with frost, and the moisture thus produced is absorbed by our garments, which are usually saturated by morning."

Although the bitter cold burned precious calories, on bright, clear days some of the healthier men would ascend the high cliffs along the cape and gaze longingly across the Smith Sound, able to make out the jutting outline of Greenland's coast. They would discuss the conditions of the ice and the skies: Water clouds were a bad sign, indicating open water, which would thwart any attempt to cross. Sustained cold temperatures were most favorable for the pack to solidify and allow safe passage across a firm bridge of ice to their deliverance. Some men stood atop the bluff, imagining not only food and warmth, but the sounds of families—squealing children, happy chatter. They also remembered the "Eskimo belles" they had met along that coast on their way up in 1881, and some of the men imagined their supple and curvaceous female forms.

Greely had little for the men to do, and knowing that the Long Night could depress them and even drive them to madness—he could not forget Jens's sudden departure, on foot, from Fort Conger during their first winter—Greely resurrected his lecture and reading series. "After much thought and some consultation," he said, "I have decided to give a daily lecture of from one to two hours in length, upon the physical geography and the resources of the United States in general; followed later by similar talks on each state and territory in particular." These were to be held from nine to eleven each morning. When Greely announced his first two lectures: "The Physical Geography of the United States, Particularly with Reference to Its Mountain and River Systems," to be followed the next day by "The Grain and Fruit Products of the United States," some of the men privately wondered whether these lectures alone would drive them mad, yet they humored their commander and listened attentively. Lockwood, Henry, and Jewell also helped with nightly readings from books they had brought along from Fort Conger.

As Thanksgiving approached, hut talk invariably turned to food, particularly of their favorite dishes from home. Soon Lockwood was not only recording his imagined meals in his journal, but reading them aloud to the others, including their preparation and where he had consumed them. As the men spooned down their "stewed sealskins and fox intestines, thickened with moldy dog biscuits," Lockwood would regale them with culinary recollections like the following:

> Boston baked beans and brown bread at Godfrey's . . . : Fromage de Brie, Magruder's, New York Ave., Washington . . . : Vienna Coffee House, Broadway and 14th Street, New York, large assortment of cakes, bread and pastry. . . . Omelets at the Vienna Cafe.; prices moderate.

Such recalled delicacies were incongruous with the reality of their greatest actual indulgence, a pudding someone named "Son of a Gun," which consisted of a congealed mixture of hardtack, raisins, seal blubber, and canned milk. This concoction—which, in addition to being relatively tasty, was also filling—became their special Sunday-morning breakfast. Of "Son of a Gun," Brainard said: "All during the entire week, we look forward to this satisfying dish with pleasant expectations." To spice it up, and with Greely's support, the hardtack pudding was made even more flavorful by the addition of lemon peelings.

As the men looked forward to Thanksgiving—on which day they had been assured extra rations—they talked of what schemes they would hatch and businesses they would run once back home. The wistful banter grew animated, almost fun, with men chiming in one after another: "Long said he would set up a restaurant in Ann Arbor, Michigan; Frederick would do the same in Minneapolis, but include a saloon; Jewell would start a grocery store in Kansas." Ralston, somewhat missing the theme, implored any man who wanted "to join him in establishing a colony at Independence, Kansas."

On the evening before Thanksgiving, Lockwood created a newfound diversion. After telling the men of his experiences as a farmer in Annapolis, he first invited all to come to his home and enjoy a fine Thanksgiving with him next year, where they would dine on traditional "roast turkey stuffed with oysters and eaten with cranberries." To return the favor, he asked each man to recite a short bill of fare, which he took down in shorthand. The members were instructed to partake of these with Lockwood once home, or, if not all together, then by themselves, or on their birthdays with their friends and families. Their menus were as follows:

> *Linn wanted a roasted turkey; Ralston, hot hoe-cake; Ellis, spare-rib; Long, pork-chops; Biederbick, old regiment dish called buffers; Connell, Irish stew; Bender, a roasted pig; Snyder, tenderloin-steak; Brainard, peaches and cream; Frederick, black cake and preserves; Salor, veal cutlets; Whistler, flapjacks and molasses; Jewell, roasted oysters on toast; Rice, clam-chowder; Israel, hashed liver; Gardiner, Virginia pone; Ellison, Vienna sausage; Pavy, pâté-de-fois-gras; Henry, Hamburg steak; Kislingbury, hashed turkey, chicken, and veal; Greely, Parker House rolls, coffee, cheese, omelet, rice, and chicken curry.*

Thanksgiving came, and with it the promised extra rations. At breakfast they enjoyed a double-portion of coffee. Late that afternoon, the cooks served a "warm fox stew with bacon, after which rice pudding, chocolate and seven ounces of hard bread were issued to each." The evening culminated in "an extra half gill of rum and a few lemons, under skillful manipulation," which gave the men "the most delicious punch they ever tasted." Lightheaded, even giddy from the punch, the men laughed, sang songs, and told stories until midnight. Said Brainard: "I think with perfect sincerity . . . I may say it has been the most enjoyable day of my life."

The men, as a group, though suffering from persistent hunger, were as contented as they had been in months. When Doctor Pavy suggested that everyone get slightly lower rations for a time in order to supplement Elison's, whose healing required more sustenance, they all agreed. Elison had sacrificed much for the group in trying to retrieve the English beef—in fact, he would likely lose his hands and feet. He had shown tremendous stoicism in bearing his pain and suffering, lately even becoming talkative and cheerful. Such fortitude was, to a man, admired. They had no qualms about giving him a little something extra during his time of need.

This selfless camaraderie, unfortunately, was short-lived. Foul weather, squalid conditions, and unsavory incidents at Camp Clay gave Commander Greely cause for deep concern. In early December strong winds hammered from the west, pounding the hut and blasting snow through cracks, covering Brainard and those near him with nearly a foot of snow. The wind blew so hard that they feared the boat, which served as the roof, would fly off. The roof of the entrance vestibule did blow away, as did stacked wood to be used for fuel. It took the reduced men some days to dig out the entryway and collect the scattered materials. During a lull Brainard and a few others ascended the cliffs and again saw open seas, diminishing their hopes of crossing the Smith Sound.

Discord and grumbling arose. Bender complained that his bedding was not as warm as that given to others. Pavy, Schneider, and Cross accused Frederick, the cook, of giving them lighter stew rations than he gave to Brainard. Greely listened patiently to these complaints and accusations and used diplomacy to quell them. Even worse than these petty grumblings were continued incidents of food theft. One night Greely witnessed Doctor Pavy stealing bread from Elison's bread can. He had been nearby and had no doubt that the theft took place. Now he was suspicious as to whether Pavy had wanted to increase the invalid's rations to supplement his own. After all, Elison's hands were useless and he relied on others—often Pavy—to feed him.

Greely was angry. He told only Lockwood, his second in command, and Brainard, who was in charge of the commissary, asking them to keep an eye on Pavy. "I was shocked," said Greely, "that the surgeon of the expedition should so fail in his duty to the men and his commanding officer, and the discovery gave me great anxiety." But Greely, after considering Pavy's importance from a medical standpoint—they relied on his skills ever more each day—chose to do nothing about this transgression for the moment.

Brainard and Rice continued their work, the pair seemingly tireless. They went out in –20° temperatures and spent hours hacking the waterhole open again, finally reaching fresh water after cutting through four feet of ice. They also spent days reconstructing the vestibule and shoveling the entryway clear. Whenever they paused to rest, they listened with awe to the loud grinding and groaning of the ice pack "crashing against the rocky point of our peninsula and tumbling outside as the currents whirled it swiftly along . . . producing a mournful, rumbling sound which strikes terror in the heart of the listener."

Besides Brainard and Rice, most of the others were too drawn down to work. Schneider and Salor often helped, and Cross volunteered to saw and chop wood for the cooks' mess. He did this work inside, avoiding the harsh elements. The cooks suffered terribly as they had to lean close to the stoves and blow the embers aflame, so they were constantly inhaling smoke and sometimes had to lie down immediately, feeling faint and nauseated. The hunters continued to go out daily, and foxes remained the main game killed. There was some incentive for hunting, since Greely rewarded success. The Greenlanders were given tobacco, and all the hunters—primarily Jens, Fred, Long, and sometimes Brainard—were given the fox livers, hearts, and kidneys to sustain them afield. One day, firing into the darkness, Brainard luckily killed two foxes with one shot, meaning double organ meats for him.

Brainard celebrated his twenty-seventh birthday on December 21, the winter solstice, with an extra half gill of rum. He climbed the bluff behind camp and happily saw no open water in the sound. The Greenlanders told him that the ice conditions appeared to be favorable for traveling soon. Watching the channel that day, Brainard thought of his home and family, musing: "They are probably discussing my fate and perhaps mourn me as lost forever." Lockwood also ascended the hill on the winter solstice, and its signaling of the sun's eventual return caused him to well up with hope: "Thank God, now the glorious sun commences to return, and every day gets lighter and brings him nearer. It is an augury that we shall yet pull through all right."

Yet there were constant reminders of their situation to serve as ballast against such hope. One day Brainard observed Doctor Pavy and Biederbick changing Elison's bandages and was repulsed by what he saw: "His feet are black, shrunken, and lifeless. His ankles are a horrible sight. The flesh has sloughed away leaving the bones devoid of covering." Pavy believed he might yet save his feet, but his assistant, Biederbick, disagreed, telling Lockwood and Greely that "Elison would lose his feet and part of his hands, as the line of demarcation is quite plain, being just below the ankle in the feet, and through the fingers of the hands."

And always their ever-present hunger wore on. Said Lockwood: "Hunger tonight fights hunger tomorrow." Greely worried constantly about the mental state of his men: "The ravenous, irritable condition of the entire party cannot but have the effect of making most men morbid and suspicious." Private Whisler became so short-tempered that he started yelling and cursing for no apparent reason, challenging anyone who dared to come outside and fight him. No one took him up on his offer, and most could not blame his outburst under the trying circumstances. Said Greely: "We are all more or less unreasonable, and I only wonder that we are not insane. All, including myself, are sullen and at times very surly. . . . I wonder if we will survive the horrors of this ice prison."

The hard work with insufficient food was taking a toll even on Brainard, who had been toiling constantly outdoors in multiple roles: as commissary chief, where he stood inside the cold storehouse weighing food with freezing brass scales; ice-hole breaker and water bearer; and hunter, plus helping with anything else that needed to be done. One day while working outside gathering wood, he grew faint, then crumpled to the ground. His companions helped him back inside, and Greely begged him not to overextend himself. Brainard simply replied: "I am very weak, but cannot refrain from working as long as I am able." But privately Brainard, too, was worried. While hand-bathing with wet cloths, he looked at himself in their shared mirror, holding it out and moving it so that he could view his torso and limbs: "It seems incredible," he wrote in his journal, "that my strength has been diminished until it scarcely equals that of a child. Tears spring to my eyes when I look on my emaciated features or feel my shrunken muscles."

As Christmas approached, the men at least had another holiday to anticipate. Some of them, wanting to create some semblance of a feast, began saving portions of their rations—they called this "scanting themselves"—to add to the general meal. Greely also assured the men that extra portions would be added by Brainard. When the day finally came, everyone knew it was also Kislingbury's thirty-sixth birthday, so there was much to celebrate. At dawn the thermometer read –35°, under "brilliant, scintillating skies of the deepest azure." For breakfast they had "a thin pea soup, with seal blubber and a small quantity of preserved potatoes." A little later the cooks surprised the men with two cans of cloudberries, which were tasty and sweet.

For diversion Brainard went to the far end of the peninsula and climbed the bluff to replace the flagpole and signal flag; the oar had snapped off in the recent storm. He returned to report no water clouds visible, which augured well for a February or March crossing. Private Long and Shorty Frederick began cooking in the early afternoon, preparing the dinner. That evening everyone relished the main course: "a seal stew containing seal blubber, preserved potatoes, and bread flavored with pickles and onions." The main course was followed by "Son of a Gun," and afterward, they were each served a small portion of chocolate. The cooks tried to improve upon the Thanksgiving rum punch by adding even more lemon—a quarter lemon per man instead of just peels—and at the end of the meal, everyone felt satisfied, even full.

Once again the rum punch produced euphoric effects, making "the spirits of the party wonderfully joyous and exuberant." Toasts went around, with three cheers—Hip, Hip, Hooray!—given in turn to Commander Greely for his leadership; to Elison for his courage; to the cooks for their creativity; and finally, to Sergeant Rice, whom Greely had chosen to lead a group over to Littleton Island in February. Kislingbury, inspired by the goodwill, produced his tobacco box and rolled a cigarette for all who wanted one.

Late in the evening men broke into song, with tunes like "O Tannenbaum" sung in German and Danish, "Silent Night" rendered in German and in English, their united voices rising out through the canvas roof of the hut and echoing roundly inside the belly of the whaleboat above their heads. Pavy and Rice sang in French; and Eskimo Fred and Jens crooned the Danish national anthem and chanted native folk songs, their voices harmonizing, high and plaintive. Among the men Greely observed "a great deal of kindly feeling and good will, and a desire to heal over any old wounds or uncharitable feeling."

As the seal-blubber lamp spat and flickered into the night, the men felt a restored kinship, a renewed brotherhood.

24

A Four-Man Relief Board

F ar to the south in the United States, efforts to do something for the men of the Lady Franklin Bay Expedition seemed to Henrietta Greely to be merely inching forward, but at least there was movement. The official inquiry into the sinking of the *Proteus* was ongoing in Washington, with lengthy testimonies by the major parties involved, including Garlington, Pike, Colwell, and Wildes. Henrietta rightly surmised that this inquiry's main outcome would be laying blame, and as such would do little for her husband and his men.

The inquiry lasted ten weeks, and its final report was a stupendous 575-page document, detailing with excruciating minutiae every piece of equipment, every board, nail, and food item now resting at the bottom of the Kane Basin. The court found that Lieutenant Garlington had made a number of errors of judgment—particularly in allowing the *Proteus* to become separated from its tender, the *Yantic*—but none of these blunders rose to the level of court-martial-worthy offenses, and he was effectively merely scolded. As for Captain Wildes, it was found to be regrettable that he did not take the time to cache a portion of the *Yantic*'s provisions at or around Littleton Island—even a small portion of the supplies from his hold could have fed Greely and his men, should they have found it, for many months. But in the end he was similarly exonerated.

Somewhat surprisingly, especially since he was not even present on either of the relief ships, the bulk of the criticism and culpability landed on General Hazen. The court felt strongly that his written orders should have dictated more explicitly the importance of leaving stores for Greely on the way up to Lady Franklin Bay, and that certainly under no circumstances should the *Yantic* have been under orders to return to St. John's carrying many thousands of rations earmarked for Greely and his men. Failing to leave food, the court determined, "which was essential—threatens serious danger to the lives of Lieutenant Greely and his command." The court concluded that General Hazen's "instructions to Lieutenant Garlington were insufficient." Hazen was spared a court-martial as well, but the official rebuke, and the public criticism, certainly stung. He was furious. In his mind the man he had chosen for the job, Lieutenant Garlington, had blundered miserably by boarding the *Yantic* and steaming away from Greely and his men. "This is the first time in military history," General Hazen fumed, "that an officer was ever commended for the celerity with which he effected his flight from his post of duty."

Henrietta felt sorry for her friend General Hazen, who she knew had her husband's best interests always in his mind. So she was heartened to learn, shortly thereafter, that on December 17, 1883, President Arthur selected Hazen to lead a four-man board of army and navy officers (two from each branch) to begin plans for a relief effort in the coming year. The board convened three days later in the offices of the Navy Department in Washington, and immediately recommended procuring two full-powered whalers or sealers and "prepar[ing] them for service in the Arctic," and that a U.S. Navy vessel or other suitable ship should act as tender. Over the next month the board carefully considered three main relief proposals, and sought the expertise and opinions of numerous men possessing a wealth of experience in the Arctic regions. Significant among these were Capt. George Tyson of the United States–sponsored *Polaris* expedition of 1871–73; Chief Engineer George Melville and Lt. John Danenhower of the USS *Jeannette;* and Sir George Nares and Captain Markham, who had served on the *Alert* in 1875, who telegraphed their opinions to the relief board from England.

The first proposed plan was put forth by Lieutenant Garlington, who was clearly hoping to redeem himself and make amends for his recent failure. He volunteered to personally command a steamship whaler, to be supported by a navy vessel under Lieutenant Colwell. At the earliest moment in the season, a ship should be sent to land men at Cape York on the Greenland side, and then, if necessary, send out sledge teams. If they found Greely's expedition, they would lead them to Pandora Harbor, where the relief vessel would be at anchor. If Greely was not there, they would continue on to Littleton Island, and then on across to Cape Sabine, establishing depots at each location and searching for messages from Commander Greely detailing his movements and whereabouts.

The second proposal was made by Lt. Cdr. Bowman H. McCalla, a U.S. naval adviser. He was firm in his opinion that the relief should be strictly a navy-run expedition, using two sealers and a U.S. Navy vessel in support as tender. He believed the ships ought to be provisioned for at least a year, bringing along prefabricated lumber for a fort, as well as coal, clothing, and food to support their own crew plus Greely and his men. The first ship should head straight for Littleton Island, looking for Greely, and then continue north if he was not found there, checking the shores up the length of the Smith Sound all the way to Lady Franklin Bay, should ice conditions allow their progress. The second ship would hang back, heading north only as far as the Kane Basin if the lead vessel was sunk or seriously delayed. The tender would go no farther than Littleton Island, awaiting the return of the others.

The third and final plan, proffered by army captain George Davis, was something of a composite of the others. He suggested employing two ships, with the entire command under the navy, comprising men from both the army and the navy. His proposal also called for the inclusion of a medical doctor, which seemed prudent, and at least ten enlisted men per vessel.

While all the formal proposals were being considered, a few additional informal ideas came to the board. Captain Pike's ice navigator, James Norman, mentioned the possible use of so-called sea punts, small, portable boats that could be taken onto the ice pack via sledge. He said they were used by whalers because of the relative ease in hauling them on and off floes and might be useful in moving along the Smith Sound's buckled ice foot and broken shoreline searching for Greely. This novel idea was temporarily considered but ultimately rejected.

George Melville, who had only recently survived the harrowing *Jeannette* disaster and learned a great deal from the experience, was adamant that whatever ships were used, it would be necessary to outfit them specifically for *ramming* ice. To be effective, he believed: "The stem must be protected by a broad guard of iron bolted through, and the bow must be covered with iron plates extending well aft to withstand the heavy shocks in ramming or smashing through floe-ice." Additionally, the wood hulls must be sheathed in extra-hard ironwood "to prevent abrasion from the jagged edge of the pack when forcing through broken floes."

As for procuring the best ships, the board briefly entertained the idea of building brand-new vessels in the United States. After some discussion it was agreed that while such an endeavor might be possible, any building delays would unnecessarily imperil Greely and his men, a risk that could not be taken when departure time was so critical. Rescue ships would best depart no later than May 1, 1884, and to ensure that happened, the more prudent course would be to purchase existing steamers. The board, after hearing expert opinion, determined that "the only vessels in the world" suited for the job were "the sealers and whalers of Dundee and St. John's," displacing from five hundred to six hundred tons. Armed with all this information, the four-man board agreed to make a final recommendation to the Departments of War and the Navy, and the president, in one month.

For his part, however, General Hazen chose to act immediately. Fortunately he found a willing ally in Navy Secretary Chandler, who agreed in December 1883 to begin secret correspondence with noted shipowners in St. John's and in Dundee, Scotland, to get a head start on purchasing appropriate ships. Both Hazen and Chandler knew that any rescue expedition would still need to go through a lengthy appropriations discussion and then garner congressional approval, and they had no intention of sitting on their hands and waiting for that dull process to play out. Within days Chandler had sent letters to the U.S. consul in St. John's and to his most trusted contacts in Scotland. If and when the U.S. government finally acted, as was its duty, Chandler vowed that, by God, he would have ships.

The men charged with rescuing Greely. *Seated left to right:* Secretary of War Honorable Robert T. Lincoln, Commander Winfield S. Schley, USN, Secretary of the Navy Honorable W. E. Chandler. *Standing left to right:* General Hancock and Commodore T. S. Fillebrown, USN. Photo taken on board the relief steamer *Thetis* at the New York Navy Yard. *(Courtesy of Naval History and Heritage Command)*

25

"This Ghostly Procession of Emaciated Men"

The New Year, 1884, opened auspiciously for the men at Camp Clay, the Christmas joy buoying their spirits for nearly a week. Practically everyone stayed awake until midnight on New Year's Eve, wishing one another "Happy New Year." Many talked of home and wondered aloud how their friends and families were spending the evening, what parties they were attending, what elaborate meals they were eating.

On January 1 Brainard reported that "the wound in the sound appears to have frozen over," reviving the party's belief that they might eventually cross. Brainard also told Greely in private that he had accidentally been underestimating the provisions, his scales being less than accurate, so that boded well. And there was the gradual return of the sun to look forward to. But the men's confidence in their survival continued to rise and fall with the tides and the state of the pack ice, and with their own physical and mental states.

For a time, as a diversion from the dark monotony inside the hut, the men began trading their food. Deals were struck—one man's meat for another's bread, a ration of fox stew for another's portion of "Son of a Gun," and for a short time, this market atmosphere produced enthusiasm and levity. Some were even trading their food for tobacco—which was almost all gone—or their dog biscuits for another's rum. But after a short time Greely discouraged the practice, as it was creating unnecessary competitiveness and ill will, and within a week he forbade it entirely, ordering the men to keep and consume their own rations.

Given what Elison had been through, his attitude was remarkably positive, but his fingers and feet continued to blacken and shrivel from necrosis and were nearly falling off. One day Doctor Pavy used a scalpel to snip a tendon from which Elison's left foot was barely hanging, and the entire foot came off without Elison even knowing. Some days later Pavy cut off the other foot too, as well as a number of his fingers. Pavy initially dressed the wounds with petroleum jelly, but that ran out and he improvised by using lard. Biederbick continued to assist Pavy in nursing Elison. They needed more bandages, so Biederbick rummaged through the "wreck cache" and found some clean undergarments, though they were frozen. He thawed them out inside his bag "against his own chest," then tenderly wrapped Elison's stumps. Elison remained oblivious to his loss of limbs, mentioning for the next few weeks that his feet and toes were painful and itchy.

Lockwood, for the first time, began to show outward signs of weakness and confusion. Greely visited him as he lay despondent in his bag, trying to instill some hopefulness in him and entertain him with stories. That seemed to cheer him up temporarily, but Lockwood spoke incessantly of food, and had started to horde portions of his meals for days, saving them up to eat all at once to give himself the illusion of a full belly. Brainard also noticed Lockwood's erratic behavior: "For hours he stares at the lamp and frequently requests that it be kept burning during the night." Biederbick, who slept next to Lockwood, confided in Brainard and Greely that he believed Lockwood was losing his mind. Given this information, Greely had Jewell, who shared a bag with Greely, switch with Lockwood so Greely could more closely monitor his second in command.

Most troubling for the entire party was a growing pattern of food theft. Brainard entered the commissary one morning to find a sizable hole sliced through the canvas, and about a quarter pound of bacon stolen. The thief had attempted to hide the hole with a large block of ice, but it was obvious to Brainard what was going on. A few days later Shorty Frederick told Brainard that "someone had been tampering with the bacon," in the mess inside the hut, and when Brainard inspected the frozen meat he noticed recent knife marks. He weighed the block of bacon and confirmed that another four ounces had been pilfered. It got worse. Brainard next saw that someone had used an ax or a hatchet to hack into one of the barrels of English hardtack, absconding with five pounds. This treasonous behavior had to stop.

Brainard had his suspicions about the identity of the thief, and he consulted with Greely about what to do. At first Greely called a meeting and asked that the guilty party come forward and "confess and repent." Many of the men even offered an ounce a day of their own bread if the thief would admit his wrong-doing and cease immediately for the well-being, and even survival, of the entire party. When this plea was also met with silence, Brainard, with Greely's permission, told all the men that he was immediately rigging a booby trap—a spring-loaded gun—inside the storehouse and that any man who purloined provisions "did so at the risk of his life." Privately Brainard told Greely he hadn't actually set the spring, but perhaps the threat would work as a deterrent. In the meantime they would try to obtain solid evidence before publicly accusing the culprit.

Brainard had been working so hard for so long that Greely offered to increase his bread ration by one ounce a day, but Brainard, although definitely having earned it, and his body requiring it, refused. He told Greely he could not in good conscience take more, "on the grounds of injustice to my comrades." Greely accepted his decision, with the caveat that "he promise to advise me whenever he felt that he could no longer perform his arduous services without it." Greely fully comprehended how important Brainard was to all of their lives.

❧❧❧

From the day they had first landed at Eskimo Point three months before, Sgt. William Cross had never completely recovered. His frostbitten foot—which he had suffered while on the ice floes during their retreat—had turned as black as Elison's. Although he had yet to lose any toes, he struggled to put any weight on it, and the only work he had done at Camp Clay was to cut wood for the stoves. Greely discussed his condition with Pavy, and Pavy's assessment was that the engineer had been spending too much time idle in his sleeping bag, so he ordered Cross outside for exercise and fresh air. Pavy was now performing daily examinations of the men and reporting their various symptoms to Greely. It appeared from the conditions of their mouths that Ellis, Linn, Schneider, and Cross might all be developing scurvy.

Both Greely and Pavy were increasingly concerned about Lieutenant Lockwood, who continued to share a sleeping bag with the commander. Throughout the nights he babbled incessantly about food, narrating his favorite dishes. Greely had to help him when he needed to roll over. For a number of mornings Greely had to prop him up to eat breakfast, and Lockwood complained of double vision. He begged Greely for rum, which Greely refused. In the evenings, after Greely had given his daily talks—on the opening of Indian Territory, or on gold and silver production in the United States—the commander spent hours conversing with Lockwood, attempting to keep him interested and engaged. Lockwood admitted that his depression was in part due to his perpetual fear that open water would keep them from crossing the sound to their salvation. Greely tried to comfort him, but there was only so much he could do. He suggested it might do him good to write to his family.

Life at Camp Clay was worsening for all of them. Seawater had encroached on their waterhole, so they now had to melt ice for fresh water once more, and the evening stews tasted dreadfully salty, increasing their thirst. Greely took to breaking up ice chips and putting them in a rubber bag, then melting it with his body heat to provide fresh drinking water for those suffering the most. With the tobacco nearly gone, men were now smoking a mixture of finely chopped wood and tea leaves, and Eskimo Fred had even resorted to smoking old discarded rags. To save fuel the cooks started burning the soles of army boots from the wreck cache.

On January 17 Sergeant Cross was unable to walk without assistance; he declined precipitately. Pavy determined that his scurvy had progressed, and his condition was critical. That night Cross kept crawling out of his bag and crying out, begging for the return of the sun, babbling about his fortieth birthday the following Sunday, and calling out for his mother. Biederbick filled rubber bottles with hot water and put them in Cross's bag for warmth to try to reduce his intense shivering and shuddering. The next morning Jewell shook Greely awake to say that Cross was unconscious. Pavy tried to revive him with hot soup and brandy, and though he opened his lips and took the fluids, he did not open his eyes. His breathing became hoarse and wheezy through the day, and "at 1:45 PM he breathed his last, passing quietly away."

Doctor Pavy—who in the last few weeks had begun speaking much of the time in his native French, saying it was easier for his mind than using English— examined Cross. Privately he told Greely that the causes of death were un- doubtedly scurvy and starvation, but they agreed to report to the men that his death was the result of "dropsical effusion of the heart"—or excess fluid around the heart—so as not to "excite a feeling of depression among the party." What- ever the official report, every one of the men knew that they were severely mal- nourished.

The death of Sergeant Cross devastated the men of the Lady Franklin Bay Expedition. Certainly the man had had his faults. The chief engineer had re- peatedly stolen alcohol, and his addiction to drink had on numerous occasions threatened all of their lives. And yet he had been one of them, living and work- ing at their sides since their arrival at Fort Conger back in August 1881—more than two and a half years before. That seemed so long, long ago now. He had shared in the triumph of reaching Farthest North, had braved their terrible fifty-one-day retreat down the Ellesmere coast, helping to drag boats and gear across the broken ice floes through the terrifying pack. And now, just a few days before he would have turned forty, Sgt. William Cross was the first of the expedition to succumb to the unforgiving Arctic.

Greely tried to shore up the men with a brief speech honoring Cross, say- ing they all now owed a duty to the living and they must have courage. He told them that Cross's "constitution had been undermined by his early habit and impaired physical condition." The group responded well to Greely's words, and they spent the remainder of the day and all evening reminiscing and giving one another reassurance and support.

The next morning Biederbick and Brainard wrapped Cross's corpse in sewn-together burlap coffee bags and canvas and covered his remains with an American flag. By dim lamplight, with the somber men sitting upright in their sleeping bags, Greely read the Episcopal burial service:

> I am the resurrection and the life, saith the Lord;
> he that believeth in me, though he were dead, yet shall he live;
> and whosoever liveth and believeth in me shall never die. . . .

At noon Commander Greely asked First Lieutenant Lockwood and Lieutenant Kislingbury to assist him with the funeral. They placed Cross's body on the sledge and six of the men—Brainard, Rice, Connell, Israel, Salor, and Whisler—hauled his remains slowly across the edge of the little lake—which Greely named "Cross Lake"—to a ridge at the crest of a hill. Brainard was deeply struck by the scene:

> One cannot conceive of anything more unearthly—more weird and solemn— than this ghostly procession of emaciated men moving slowly and silently away from their wretched ice-prison in the uncertain light of the Arctic night, having in their midst a dead comrade about to be laid away forever in the frozen ground.

The ground was so hard they were able to dig the grave only fifteen inches deep, and as Lockwood said last words over the dead man, Private Biederbick, who had nursed Cross tenderly during his final hours, pawed and dug at the earth with his mittens and spread the gravelly dirt and snow over their fallen companion. They were too short on ammunition to fire a gun salute, so instead, according to Brainard, "carefully arranged a circle of stones about the grave, this being the only attention we could bestow on our comrade." They named the place "Cemetery Ridge."

Soon after the loss of their first member, Greely devoted his attention to the attempt to cross Smith Sound. There was minor discussion about who should accompany Rice on this quest, but the list of men fit enough to attempt it was growing short. It could certainly not be Lockwood, who remained fragile and despondent, his senses wandering and then returning. His enfeebled and emotionally delicate state was difficult for Brainard to bear, as the duo had shared in the glorious adventures of Farthest North and Farthest West. Said Brainard: "His fitful moods almost break my heart. As I watch him, tears gather in my eyes and there is a lump of sorrow which almost bursts my throat. That this should be the strong, daring and enthusiastic Lockwood with whom I went to 'Farthest.' He said to me a few days ago, 'Brainard, I have lost my grip.'"

A day or so later Lockwood crawled over to Greely and whispered that he feared he would not have the strength for any future crossing, and that Greely should leave him behind with some rations—he would only hold up the group. If Rice and Jens found help at Littleton Island, then they could return for him; if they found no relief, he said, then "he must perish in any event." Greely admonished Lockwood for even considering that his commander would leave him behind; he told Lockwood that if they must, they would haul him on a sledge as they would have to do for Elison anyway. Greely then took Brainard aside and confidentially told him that Lockwood's mind and spirit were crumbling, and that, should any disaster befall Greely, it was now evident that Lieutenant Kislingbury would have to succeed him in command.

After considering all his options, Greely selected Jens to accompany Rice, and "the faithful native appeared deeply touched that he should have been selected for this important and hazardous duty." With the team members settled on, Rice began fabricating thicker leggings and footgear by cutting the bottoms of some extra sleeping bags, and others helped make a warmer fur and sealskin suit for him. Frederick and Schneider worked together to get their packs, gear, and cooking equipment in order. Brainard set aside a week's worth of rations for their journey, including pemmican, hardtack, and blubber. Greely ordered an increase in rations for Rice and Jens up until their scheduled departure, now set for February 2. In his journal Commander Greely referred to the mission as "Forlorn Hope."

In the last few days before Rice and Jens were to leave, Greely spent hours writing a record and instructions to be cached at Littleton Island should no one be there, including the most essential provisions they needed if relief ever arrived. Doctor Pavy added his own list of the most crucial medicines and equipment he required immediately. Greely also wrote letters to General Hazen, Garlington, and Henrietta. He recorded that twenty-four of their number remained yet alive, "and though haggard, emaciated, and suffering, we were yet confident and hopeful." A couple of the men handed Rice their wills to take with him, but most of them still held the strong belief that Garlington and immense stores from the *Yantic* were at Littleton Island, though Greely seriously doubted it. He privately believed their best chance was for Rice and Jens to locate Etah natives and bring them back to help them: "Once among these Arctic highlanders our safety would be assured."

On the day before departure Rice handed Lieutenant Kislingbury a note he had scribbled in pencil: "My dear friend Kislingbury," it began. "In the event of this pending journey ending fatally for me, I desire that yourself and Brainard act as my executors, in conjunction with Moses P. Rice [his brother] of Washington, D.C. . . . Of my trinkets I desire that a diamond ring, which will be found among my effects, to be sent to Miss Maud Dunlop of Baddeck, Cape Breton, as a souvenir of a few sunshiny days." Rice instructed that the remainder of his assets and articles be bequeathed to his mother and a Miss Helen Bishop, to the latter of whom he also gave a thousand dollars from his estate, "without condition." He ended the letter by instructing Kislingbury to go carefully through his personal effects, stipulating that "all papers, letters, photos, etc. which from their nature of the rights of others should not be seen by my parents or others, should be at once destroyed."

Greely roused the cooks at 4:45 a.m. on February 2, 1884, to prepare Rice and Jens a hearty meal of roast beef, and he sent Brainard and Eskimo Fred ahead carrying the travelers' fifty-pound packs for a few miles to help them as they set out. Rice and Jens caught up with them soon, and the four men stood together for a few moments, embracing and shaking hands. Said Brainard: "After a tremulous 'God bless you,' we turned away in tears from those brave souls who are daring and enduring so much for us." Brainard stood for a long time, then turned for one last look. Rising above the wind, he could hear the distinct shearing, grating, and moaning of the moving pack. "We waited," he said, "until their receding forms were lost to view in the bewildering confusion of the ice-fields and then slowly retraced our steps to the hut."

26

Henrietta's "Bounty Plan" and a
Gift from the Queen

As Cdr. Adolphus Greely and his men prayed for Rice and Jens's successful navigation to the Greenland side of the Smith Sound, clinging by
sinew and bone to their "Forlorn Hope," a world away and four thousand
miles to the south, significant pressure—spearheaded with considerable
force by Henrietta—was creating impetus for Washington to act, and to do
so immediately. Greely's persistent and dedicated wife wrote to Gen. Henry
Hayes Lockwood, 1st. Lt. James Lockwood's father, imploring him to hand-
deliver her words to President Chester Arthur himself, insisting: "It seems to
me that no expense or pains should be spared this year as it is the last that
can hope to see the party brought home alive." She knew that late relief de-
partures had been part of the previous failures, and would not allow that to
happen again.

General Lockwood had no way of knowing that at this very moment his
son was suffering hallucinations, double vision, and the depths of depression
and starvation, but both he and Henrietta had certainly imagined the worst.
General Lockwood assured Henrietta that he would honor her wishes, and he

personally met with President Arthur. After the meeting he immediately wrote back to Henrietta:

> *I called yesterday on the President and I submitted your views. . . . He requested me to leave your letter that he might refer it to the Secretaries of War & the Navy for mature consideration. He seemed to think that having referred the subject of relief to them, that he could act only through them. He expressed solicitude as to the condition of the party but had no apprehensions as to the effectual relief next summer.*

Henrietta could be pleased that her words were being read and at least considered at the highest levels of government. How much weight they had she could not be sure, but she had no intention of quitting, just as she knew in her heart that somewhere in the dead cold of the Long Night, her Dolph would not quit either.

General Lockwood included in his letter to Henrietta details of another meeting he had had, this one with John G. Walker, chief of the U.S. Navy Bureau of Navigation. Their meeting had gone well, General Lockwood assured Henrietta, and indeed rescue plans were in the works and confidence was growing: "Walker remarked," wrote General Lockwood, that "no naval commander would dare, after all that has been said on the recent failure, to return without having reached in some way the end of his journey."

About a week later, under bright and cloudless San Diego skies, Henrietta opened a note embossed with the official seal of the White House, sent from the "Executive Mansion, Washington." It had been dictated to President Arthur's private secretary, Fred J. Phillips. Henrietta clasped the note and read:

> *The President has received, and read with much interest, your letter. . . . The suggestions that it contains will have very careful consideration, and the President wishes to assure you that nothing which is considered essential to the success of the expedition will be left undone.*

So Henrietta had the ear of the president, and she could feel reasonably confident that her government would send relief. But she would not stop there, and she would leave nothing to chance. She had learned from Dolph during his years preparing for the Arctic that contingency plans were essential, and she devised a clever one of her own. To increase the chances for a successful rescue, Henrietta conceived of the idea to offer a bounty, or reward, to the seasoned commercial sealers or whalers who knew the waters of the Arctic regions better than anyone—they made their livelihoods there. All summer long, she knew from discussions with Dolph and from her own research, they cruised the fiords and the thousands of miles of coastline and inlets while fishing. Surely these civilians' vessels should be included in the hunt for her husband.

It made sense to her that a hefty reward—say to the tune of twenty-five thousand dollars—would provide much incentive for these tough northern seamen to search for her husband's expedition, independent of any official governmental relief. Her idea became known as the Bounty Plan, and she urged Navy Secretary Chandler to present it to Congress for approval.

Henrietta's entreaties to her brother Otto Nesmith in Boston were also paying off. He had contacted numerous friends in the regional and national press, and articles about the imperiled Lady Franklin Bay Expedition were beginning to be published, raising great public awareness and national concern. These came not only from civilians but U.S. military men as well, and among them Civil War veterans and heroes. Henrietta wrote to some of her close cousins, too. One in Atlanta was able to get pieces on her campaign published in *The Atlanta Constitution*; another cousin persuaded Joseph Medill, the editor in chief of the *Chicago Tribune*, to publish stories. Henrietta continued to be supported and encouraged during her quest by her neighbor and ally Douglas Gunn, and as he had promised, articles appeared across the country, including in major newspapers in Denver, New Orleans, and Philadelphia.

Inspired by the articles as well as letters from Henrietta, an old army comrade of Commander Greely, a man who dabbled in poetry, wrote a sonnet that was published in *The Independent*, a widely read journal that frequently published poems by such literary luminaries as Elizabeth Barrett Browning and Harriet Beecher Stowe. Edward Pomeroy's sonnet to his friend Adolphus Greely stirred the hearts of many readers:

Genial companion of my army days
Here sitting in the soft enchanted light
Of home, before my glowing anthracite,
I think of wastes of snow, of ice-closed bays,
Of the near North with its auroral glaze,
Of ghostlike Nature in her gown of white—
Somnambulist that roameth through the night,
With horror fascinating all that gaze.
But more than all besides, I think, dear friend,
Of thee and thy heroic band forlorn,
For whose return so many prayers ascend,
Now waiting for the tardy Arctic morn,
Determined still to battle to the end,
And win "the victory of endurance born."

Henrietta was also thrilled to learn that her call for the Greely rescue cause reached far beyond American shores to the great seafaring nation of Great Britain. Navy Secretary Chandler's secret negotiations to secure ships were yielding results, among them a profoundly humbling offer from the Royal Navy. Chandler's U.S. Navy emissaries had been in contact with Britain, expressing their need for any assistance that might be available from among Her Majesty's formidable fleet. On February 2, 1884—the very day that Rice and Jens struck out across the pack toward Littleton Island—the U.S. Navy received the following correspondence from First Lord of the Admiralty Northbrook, in the name of Queen Victoria:

February 2, 1884.

 Her Majesty's ship Alert might be of use to the United States Government in an expedition to be dispatched in search of the expedition which is missing in the Arctic region. I write a line to say that we have not forgotten the very considerate conduct of the Government of the United States on the occasion of the recovery of the Resolute, and that if you should be instructed to make any suggestions through the usual official channel, that the Alert would be of any use to the United States Government, we shall be happy to ask you to accept her as a present.

Yours very sincerely, Northbrook.

This generous gesture was incredible news indeed. The U.S. Navy, with the deep personal appreciation of the president of the United States, immediately and graciously accepted the offer of the *Alert*. They would be honored to use it. The ship would be employed as the third vessel, primarily as a tender. It was from the *Alert*—a wooden-screw war sloop—that Sir George Strong Nares had made a number of the caches found and used by Greely, so it was appropriate and moving that this venerable ship be used in a rescue expedition. The *Alert* would be made ready for service at Green's Shipyard on the Thames. Nares himself visited the shipyard frequently to offer his advice and expertise on its outfitting. The *Alert* would be in fine shape, the Royal Navy promised, to sail to New York by the end of March, in time to join the relief expedition.

Secretary of the Navy Chandler had also remained relentless in his efforts to purchase the two main rescue ships. Working through his naval attaché at the U.S. embassy in London, he consulted with British Arctic luminaries—including Nares as well as Captains Markham and Beaumont—about the best ships suitable for the duty. After a month of constant negotiations via intercontinental telegrams, Chandler reached an agreement to purchase a ten-year-old steamer called the *Bear*. A sister ship of the sunken *Proteus*, the *Bear* had recently undergone a complete overhaul in Scotland and happened to be sailing for St. John's during the negotiations. Chandler agreed to pay one hundred thousand dollars, provided the ship be delivered in New York.

Secretary Chandler had been operating clandestinely, without the official authority of the U.S. government, though he believed there was such impetus now that his decisions would certainly be supported and given congressional approval—which was currently ongoing. Although Chandler had been careful not to release information about his activities, leaks still occurred, and the press learned that the secretary of the navy was making deals to buy ships without official authorization. One reporter, questioning the legality of Chandler's actions, asked what he would do if Congress thought it was too expensive and failed to adopt a resolution to purchase ships. Quipped Chandler with a wry smile: "I suppose I will become the part owner of a good whaling ship." Ironically, on February 15, two days after Congress's passage of the Relief Expedition Bill that formally allowed its purchase, the *Bear* docked in New York at the Brooklyn Navy Yard, ready for outfitting.

Two days later the *Thetis*—just two years old and considered by the British Arctic experts to be the finest of all the remaining available ships—was purchased from Dundee shipbuilders Stephen & Son for twenty-eight thousand pounds. It underwent inspection and was appropriated by the U.S. Navy on February 25. Four days later, after taking on coal, provisions, and a crew of American sailors gleaned from the European Squadron, it left from the Thameside docks and steamed for New York.

So Secretary Chandler had his ships. Now—even more important—he needed the right man to lead the expedition. Not surprisingly Lieutenant Garlington was eager to go, wanting very much to redeem himself and erase the memory of the doomed *Proteus*. He appealed to Secretary Lincoln, almost pleading: "My reputation as an officer," he said, "will be severely injured, I fear, if I am left out of the undertaking." But it had already been decided by the president that the new rescue mission would be an entirely naval affair, and as an army officer, Garlington would not be going. This kind of work was the domain of men made for the sea. "The work of the relief expedition of 1884," the navy rightly reasoned, "was as purely nautical as any work that was ever entrusted to a seaman; the ultimate question of success or failure depended primarily on seamanship." Secretary Lincoln was inclined to agree, and for his part, he was perfectly happy to have the army done with it. He could not personally, nor could his branch of the military, bear another disastrous failure. It made sense to let Chandler and the navy take over.

While Secretary Chandler had been secretly and shrewdly procuring ships, he had also been privately pondering who should command them. After considering a list of possible candidates, Chandler focused on Winfield Scott Schley, a U.S. Naval Academy graduate and Civil War veteran who had later distinguished himself as a combat leader while on assignment with the Asiatic Station. He had also served in Europe, on Africa's west coast, and in the South

Atlantic as far as Brazil, aboard the USS *Essex*. Now forty-five, Commander Schley had spent the last four years as lighthouse inspector for the Second Naval District, whose headquarters were in Boston. He and his family had settled in Brookline. Schley had certainly followed with interest the initial departure of the Lady Franklin Bay Expedition in 1881, and the two failed attempts in 1882 and 1883 to reach the men. As a lifelong navy man, he had read widely on all manner of nautical voyages and studied the accounts of previous Arctic explorers with fascination, absorbed by the harrowing tales from those vast and rugged regions. The Arctic north remained one of the great nautical challenges for seamen the world over.

Secretary Chandler offered Schley the appointment, counting on his wealth of experience, his organizational skills and attention to detail, and his reputation for being bold and daring. Schley, a stern man of short stature, with a receding hairline and a long, pointy chin patch, accepted the command under the condition that his appointment be kept secret as long as possible; he knew that his wife would be worried sick about such dangerous duty. Chandler consented, waiting until the last week of February to make the announcement official.

Commander Schley had first read about the Lady Franklin Bay Expedition when it had departed back in 1881. He is said to have been at the Charlestown Navy Yard, and on finishing the article, he had quipped to some of his friends: "This means that some Navy officer will have to go up there and bring them back." As fate would have it, the man that the secretary of the navy and the president of the United States wanted for the job was him.

27

The End of the Longest Night

On the day that Rice and Jens struck out across the strait attempting to reach Greenland, Eskimo Fred announced in front of the remaining party inside the hut at Camp Clay that he planned to commit suicide. Brainard attributed this shocking pronouncement to Fred's loneliness and fear that he might never see his friend Jens again. Greely and Pavy recalled both of the Greenlanders' erratic and depressed mental states during that first Long Night of 1881–82, and everyone agreed to keep an eye on Eskimo Fred, making sure he did not have access to any guns for a few days, or walk off on his own. Others were exhibiting concerning symptoms as well. The next night, February 3, "Jewell fell down in a dead faint."

To counteract these degenerations—and partly owing to the cruel fact that with Cross dead, there was one fewer mouth to feed—Greely raised the daily rations slightly, adding a few ounces to warm stews of beef, pemmican, and lime juice. This helped morale and strength, and within a few days, Lieutenant Lockwood, who had also been struggling, made a turn for the better. He rose from his bag and moved about on his own for the first time in weeks, even showing some humor and cheerfulness. Of the food increase, Lockwood said with ironic exaggeration: "This week is to be a feast!" Long bagged a blue fox, and Connell, returning from the bluff behind camp, reported clear skies, a view all the way to Greenland, and an ice bridge as far as he could see. The entire party appeared rejuvenated by the small increase in food.

Unfortunately Rice and Jens surprised everyone by returning to camp after just four days, having been stopped by open water a few miles east of Brevoort Island. They entered the hut shivering, caked with ice, both moderately frostbitten. Outside it was –20°, with winds gusting and snow swirling down in flurries, and both Rice and Jens asked for water. Rice, his voice a harsh whisper, said that the previous night had been agonizing. Jens's fingers had frozen trying to light the field stove to melt water—which he failed to do—and Rice had to thaw Jens's fingers on his bare chest. It was so cold—they believed it got down to –50°—that they were forced out of their bag and had to "run about in the snow to keep from freezing" to death. Rice reported that they had traveled probably fifty miles total, stumbling and tripping through the darkness, traveling south until they were directly parallel with Littleton Island. Through the dim light they could see it perhaps ten miles distant, but open water prevented them from going any farther.

The news was a blow to everyone. Still, Greely told the men that preparations for crossing Smith Sound would continue. If the weather cooperated and remained cold enough, he believed, a solid ice bridge should form by March 1. Greely assigned small teams different jobs to keep them busy and bolster morale. Salor, Ellis, and Schneider sewed mittens and socks; Private Frederick and Jens stitched and reinforced footgear. Brainard inventoried the stores and reported to Greely that they had food enough to last until March 12—"and then have ten days full rations with which to cross to Littleton Island." If crossing should prove impossible, he calculated that they could stretch rations until April 10.

All the men now knew that their fate was in the hands of the ice. Brainard continued his daily strenuous plod up the hill to assess the sound, but by mid-February the ice pack had still not cooperated: "I visited the hill this morning and could hear the crushing of the pack very distinctly. It sounded like thunder and made me tremble. Our lives depend on its quiescent state. . . . Without firm ice for the crossing to Littleton Island slight hopes for life remain to us. . . . We are all dead men in a few weeks more." Lockwood, who had become more lucid in recent days, wrote in his journal: "So here is the upshot of affairs—if our fate is the worst, I do not think we shall disgrace the name of Americans and of soldiers."

It had been six months since they had departed from Fort Conger, and as the men hunkered in their half-frozen sleeping bags, they longed for the warmth and comfort of that well-built and coal-heated shelter. They also constantly craved water. The waterhole had been frozen solid for a month, but none of the men had the strength to hack open a new one, and Greely continued to melt ice in rubber bags against his body and dole out driblets to those most crazed by thirst.

On February 17 Israel calculated that the sun had returned and was hovering at 10 degrees over the horizon, but dark water clouds obscured it from view. None of the men had seen the sun for 115 days, and even the knowledge of its presence improved the mood in camp, with each man hoping to catch a first glimpse of it whenever the clouds parted. Still, despite the return of the sun, the overwhelming boredom, thirst, hunger, and uncertainty about their future had all the men on edge. Pavy and Kislingbury argued so viciously it nearly resulted in a fistfight; and the next day Pavy and Bender had harsh words as well. Greely chose to let these episodes resolve themselves without interfering, reasoning that "bitter talk relieves the mind at times." He would intervene only in official matters.

However, an unofficial matter a few days later did force Greely to intercede. One night he heard a loud ruckus coming from Bender and Schneider's bag, and he crawled over to break it up. After calming them down and speaking with them, he concluded that Bender had made untoward advances toward Schneider: "I reproved both men," he said, "and told them that such a condition of affairs was outrageous and must not occur again; that we were men and not brutes."

Brainard and Rice continued to trudge up the knoll to assess the ice conditions. It was practically all they had to do, and it reminded them of their days climbing to the summit of Cairn Hill near Fort Conger, where they had gazed out to sea, hoping to glimpse a ship on the horizon. Ironically, back then, during the short summers of 1882 and 1883, they had been praying for open water. Now they wished for the exact opposite. But by the end of February 1884, all they saw in the Smith Sound was "a great sea with rafts of ice drifting on the surface." Brainard watched "waves and whitecaps rolling in against the edge of the fast ice with a dismal roar. . . . The roar sounded like the knell of our impending doom." He added: "I think we are doomed to die in this place, but however horrible the end, most of us are prepared to face it like men."

Rice, who had discontinued his journal entries when the winter darkness had descended, resumed his writing on March 1. With their food stores ever dwindling, Rice, as Lockwood often did, began to record elaborate food fantasies, jotting down the delectable meals he would eat if he were at home in Washington, should he ever return there. For breakfast he imagined ordering "scrambled eggs, broiled smoked herring, baked Irish potatoes and butter, Parker House rolls, soft-boiled eggs, and a cup of chocolate; for dinner a half-dozen raw clams, bean soup, roast goose and applesauce, cabbage, bread pudding, sweet potato pie, apples, raisins, nuts, cheese and crackers." In reality, for breakfast that day he spooned down a lukewarm gruel of dog biscuit, dried potatoes, and a few ounces of rice and canned tomatoes. His dinner had been six ounces of hardtack and bacon mixed with the tallow they also used for making candle wax. Outwardly, among the men, Rice constantly maintained an iron-hard exterior and projected an unbreakable will to survive. But privately in his journal he wrote: "I much fear the horrors of our last days here."

On March 8, for the first time since leaving Fort Conger, some of the men decided to have their hair cut. Their hair and beards were wild and scraggly, their faces covered in grime and soot. A little grooming, they reasoned, would do them good. According to Brainard: "Those wishing to be cropped crawled on their hands and knees to the foot of their sleeping bags and held their heads in the alley-way. The tonsorial artist passed along the line armed with a huge pair of shears and devoted about ten seconds to each head. My hair was over six inches long."

Greely continued to consider every available option for obtaining more food. For many weeks Long had been unsuccessful hunting, reporting virtually no game or even tracks in the vicinity of Camp Clay. Rice came to Greely and volunteered to go with Eskimo Fred and try to find the English beef that had been abandoned in order to save Elison's life the previous November. Rice thought he knew where it was, and if the Springfield rifle still stood upright in the snow marking the spot, he believed he could locate it. But Greely thought the journey too difficult just now, Rice still being weak from his recent fifty-mile attempted channel crossing.

Greely had been reading in one of his journals from the Nares expedition of 1875 that the area around Alexandra Harbor to the northwest was rife with game. So as an alternative, he decided to send Long and Eskimo Fred in that direction, where perhaps the lowland valley Nares wrote about would offer winter grazing for herds of reindeer* and musk-oxen. In front of all the men, Greely showed Long a map of what was currently known of Hayes Sound and Alexandra Harbor, and instructed him to find game first and foremost, but also, if he could, to climb to the summit of Mount Carey and survey any new lands they might discover. Even in their desperate plight, Commander Greely strongly remembered the exploratory nature of the Lady Franklin Bay Expedition and made sure to remind his men of their duties, and to impart to them "a keener realization that there is yet a world and something worth striving for." Brainard practically begged to go along as well, but Greely said he needed him at camp.

On the morning of March 11 brilliant sunshine beamed down on the hut at Camp Clay for the first time since mid-October the previous year. Long and Eskimo Fred departed under crystalline skies at 9:00 a.m., provisioned for six days. Brainard said they all knew that this would be "a journey of extraordinary hardship and danger," and some men came outside see them off. Long and Fred turned and bade their friends farewell, according to Brainard, "with the kindest wishes of their grateful companions whose eyes they will perhaps never see again." As they strode north, a raven hovered overhead. The black

---

* Many of the Arctic explorers referred to "reindeer," but the animals they were describing were technically "caribou." Reindeer and caribou actually belong to the same species, *Rangifer tarandus*, but are different subspecies, and there are substantial differences between the two. Caribou—which are found in northern North America and Greenland—are large elklike animals that have never been domesticated, whereas the smaller reindeer occur in Eurasia and were first domesticated around two thousand years ago.

bird was ordinarily viewed as a bad omen, but Brainard said flatly: "We have suffered too long to give way to superstition at this hour."

Long and Fred traveled well the first day over smooth ice in cold, clear weather, dragging behind them the sledge—which they had brought to haul back game. They made camp the first evening and were able to heat a meal for dinner, but when they tried to climb into their sleeping bag it was so frozen they could wriggle in only up to their chests. Lying halfway out of their bags, they found the intense cold too much, so at two in the morning they got out and started traveling again, chewing on raw bacon for energy.

By dawn the next morning they reached Alexandra Harbor, but were disheartened to find no musk-oxen or reindeer in the valley. Long did not even see any tracks. The hoped-for winter pasture was covered with ice and snow. As ordered by Greely, Long left the sledge, and with Fred he ascended Mount Carey and scanned the lands through his field glasses. He observed three distant snowcapped capes never seen before by any Arctic explorer.

They descended to reconnoiter. Long thought they might skirt around and explore the land beyond Mount Carey, but bluffs and cliffs rising two thousand feet from the valley floor prevented further travel to the west. They trudged on for nine hours due north, reaching a high promontory providing clear views to the north and west, but still they saw no game. Reluctantly they turned back, gnawing on pemmican and hardtack as they moved, finally making camp after nearly fourteen hours of continuous walking. They sat on the sledge and were able to make hot tea, but once again when they tried to enter the sleeping bag it was so stiff they could enter only up to their hips. They writhed uncomfortably for hours. Long became stricken by cramps throughout his body.

Fred got out of the bag and warmed a mixture of rum and spirits of ammonia, which alleviated Long's cramps. Fred struggled with the bag and was able to mostly cover Long; then he stayed up all night, alternately walking and running back and forth across the ice field to keep warm. At daybreak Fred roused Long and they moved out. When they finally straggled into Camp Clay they had been traveling for another twelve straight hours. Entering the hut on the night of March 13, both men were exhausted and frostbitten, but otherwise uninjured.

Once he recovered Long showed Greely the maps and described the new lands he had discovered. The commander applauded Long for "extending Hayes Sound at least twenty miles beyond the farthest of our predecessors," and Greely named the westernmost of the capes Cape Francis Long for the intrepid hunter and explorer. By their reckoning, Long and Fred had walked seventy miles in only three days, finding only the tracks of a single fox. The entire party was disappointed that Long had found no game, but they were all glad to have him and Fred back among them.

∾∾∾

The brave men of the Lady Franklin Bay Expedition were now desperately low on food. Supplemented by three ptarmigans Brainard shot, they ate their last meat stew on March 15, adding to the stew the birds' beaks, claws, and entrails. Long, back out hunting again, killed four dovekies weighing about a pound each. With all the remaining provisions—unless the hunting improved—Brainard and Greely figured that they might possibly remain alive until the first of May. A dull fear spread through the camp, and there were hushed, whispered, unsettling conversations deep into the night. Rice mentioned overhearing "an unpleasant discussion," and Private Ellis confided in Rice that he had heard whispers of unthinkable acts. Rice wrote in his journal: "I am much afraid of the demoralization of the party. The conversations and hints show a state of warped imagination which may result in things too bad to contemplate."

Given the circumstances, Rice again asked Greely to allow him to try to bring in the 144 pounds of English beef. Greely said he would consider it, but first wanted to send out more hunting parties closer to their vicinity, as a few seals had been spotted nearby in open water, and it appeared that more birds were returning.

Brainard had no intention of giving up. He remembered that some of the men had netted mussels and clams back at Eskimo Point when they first landed on these shores, and while hunting down at the end of the spit at Cape Sabine, Brainard had seen thousands of tiny crustaceans in the water. They were about the size of a kernel of rice, or as Brainard put it, "the size of a half-grown fly." Known by whalers and sealers as "sand fleas or sea lice," Brainard called them "shrimp," and he proposed rigging a net using a bent iron hoop and some thin cloth to attempt catching some. Greely, impressed by the ingenuity, thought it could not hurt—men could try shrimping while out hunting. Rice liked the idea too, and volunteered to be the first to try out the net.

On his first try Rice netted only a few ounces, and discovered that they were mostly composed of shell—it would take a great deal more of them to feed the men. With help from Brainard, Rice improved one net and built a second. A couple of miles from Camp Clay, just off the ice foot, they baited the nets with dovekie legs and strips of fox and sealskin and sank the nets below the water surface. On his second attempt Rice returned to the hut just after low tide with four pounds of the shrimp. There were great cheers from the men, and Sergeant Linn yelled out the motto of his home state of Kentucky: "United we stand, divided we fall!" The cooks added the shrimp to the stewpots, and, after mixing in seal blubber, they all enjoyed a fishy broth. Inspired by Rice's success, a few of the men pitched in and gave him a scarf, rubber mittens, and a large basket for bringing in his daily catch. Rice was now the main shrimper.

On the morning of March 24 the skies were bright and the temperature, –25°, boded well for ice formation, but by this time Greely had privately given up the idea of crossing the Smith Sound. Even should a solid ice bridge form—which now appeared unlikely—the men, being on such low rations, would not have the strength to make the twenty-five-mile journey. Rice, by now consumed with catching shrimp—he was hauling in seven to ten pounds a day—had left the hut at 3:00 a.m. in order to set the nets at low tide. At breakfast Sergeant Israel began to feel nauseated, which these days was not uncommon for many of the men. Doctor Pavy told him to lie down and that he would feel better shortly. A few seconds later, at the far end of the hut, Biederbick passed out. Israel then swayed for a moment and crumpled to the floor. Greely, himself now woozy, tried to revive Israel, shaking him and slapping him across the face. The commander heard Gardiner crying out: "It is the alcohol, open the door! Open the door!" Someone threw open the canvas door, and all but a few of the men crawled their way outside, most fainting near the entrance.

Brainard got outside quickly, but he stumbled around like a drunk, reeling and falling, getting up, then slamming onto the icy ground again a half dozen times. When Greely exited the hut, he saw Brainard splayed out on the snow, his face "perfectly white," apparently dead. In the confused minutes that followed, almost all of the men lay or knelt on the ground, coughing and wheezing. None had had enough time to dress properly, and all were becoming frostbitten. Gardiner helped Greely, thrusting a pair of mittens onto the commander's stiff hands. One by one men began to revive, including Brainard, who had regained consciousness and was now assisting others.

As men came to and hurried back into the hut, Gardiner explained that the cooks had forgotten to remove the rags they stuffed into the chimney stovepipe at night to retain heat, and potentially lethal fumes had infiltrated the hut. They had all nearly been asphyxiated. By the time everyone had come to and was back inside, most of them had frostbitten hands, faces, and ears. Biederbick and Israel, according to Doctor Pavy, had nearly died, but were regaining consciousness. After everyone settled back in their sleeping bags and warmed up, breakfast was served, but one of the cooks told Greely that during the confusion, a half pound of bacon had gone missing.

When the theft became known, men began cursing in rage. Who would do such a thing? What man would be so heartless as to steal from his starving companions as they lay outside, possibly dying? It could only be someone who had remained inside the hut, and that narrowed the suspects. Some hours later Jens confided to Greely that during the event, he had seen Private Henry stuffing the bacon inside his shirt. Jens also said that Henry had not once moved to help any of the others. Greely eyed Henry for the remainder of the day, and sure enough, as dinner was about to be served, Henry stood up, saying he felt sick to his stomach, and a moment later, Greely and others watched the private vomit into a can. Shorty Frederick snatched the can, inspected it, and found that it contained a large chunk of half-chewed, undigested bacon.

The next day Greely held a formal hearing. Private Henry professed his innocence, saying he'd eaten the bacon at dinner, but Greely and everyone else knew dinner had not been served yet. The man was lying.* Henry's sleeping companions came forward, saying they had seen him repeatedly steal bacon,

---

* What perhaps only Brainard and Greely knew (evidenced by references in Brainard's field notes), was

bread, and rum. Ellis claimed he had witnessed Henry stealing canned food. Connell said that the previous fall he had seen Henry stashing an unopened can of roast beef "before any of the roast beef had been issued." It was unanimously agreed that Henry was guilty, and many argued that he should be hanged on the spot. Others wanted him locked up, but that was impractical, as the only locked room was the food commissary, which obviously defeated the purpose. Greely pondered what to do. He could plainly see that Henry, the biggest man among them to begin with—around two hundred pounds at the start of the expedition—had lost the least amount of weight. No two or even three men could subdue him. Greely silenced the men, calling for order and reminding them that they were all under military command and he was in charge, and that he alone would order "extreme measures when needed." For now Greely relieved Henry of any duty and "prohibited him from leaving his sleeping bag except under supervision."

❧❧❧

April 1884 brought improved hunting and shrimping. Rice was now bringing in twenty to thirty pounds of shrimp a day, and the hunters killed and brought in thirty-three dovekies in one day. Long spotted a seal and a walrus in open water just off the peninsula, which was promising though he did not get close enough for a shot. But the shrimp, while substantially adding to the volume and flavor of the stews, offered scant nutrition, as they were mostly shell. Said Brainard: "The shrimps are of very little benefit. We are all longing for a thick, rich stew of the flesh and blood of a seal to strengthen and restore our reduced and emaciated bodies."

On April 2 Eskimo Fred grew noticeably and uncharacteristically volatile,

---

that Pvt. Charles B. Henry was actually an impostor, a convicted felon living under an alias. His real name was Charles Henry Buck. As a soldier in the Seventh Cavalry, he had been caught forging checks and military orders and been dishonorably discharged, sentenced to a year of hard labor and forfeiture of pay. After he served out his hard labor, Buck had killed a Chinese man in a fight in Deadwood, Dakota Territory, then evaded the law and later joined Greely's former outfit, the Fifth Cavalry, at Fort Sydney, Nebraska, under the name of Charles B. Henry. When a last vacancy opened up in the Lady Franklin Bay Expedition, the commanding officer of the Fifth Cavalry—Capt. George Price, a personal friend of Greely's who incidentally had been a rival suitor for Henrietta Nesmith's affections while the two men were stationed in San Diego in 1877—recommended Henry, and Greely took him on.

angrily demanding that he must have more food, then growing quiet and melancholy, mumbling about his family in Greenland and his home hunting grounds. Greely upped his ration, but the increase did little for him. Greely discussed his condition with Brainard, and they agreed that the recent hunting trip with Long to Alexandra Harbor and the summit of Mount Carey had been too much for him. On the night of April 4 Fred had fits of delirium, rising from his sleeping bag and leaving the hut for a time, then later returning. The next morning he sat up, ate his breakfast, then slumped backward and died.

The loss of Eskimo Fred—Thorlip Frederik Christiansen—hit Lockwood, Brainard, and Jens particularly hard. The tough Greenlander had driven the sledge that took Lockwood and Brainard to their record-setting Farthest North and to Farthest West across Grinnell Land. "He was a good man," said Lockwood, himself now dangerously weak. "I felt a great affection for him and his death brings me great sorrow." Brainard and a few others loaded Eskimo Fred onto the sledge and dragged him up to Cemetery Ridge, where they dug a shallow grave next to that of Sergeant Cross, offered some brief words, fired a gun salute over him, and interred him, Jens sobbing uncontrollably.

It was now clear to Greely that there was no more time to wait: He must send someone on a second "forlorn hope," a desperate effort to get the English beef. Lockwood, Linn, and Jewell, according to Pavy, were all in critical condition. Brainard's assessment of the commissary was grim: They were down to five pounds of meat and three pounds of hardtack. Once again Brainard volunteered to go, but after a lengthy discussion with Rice, Greely made his decision: Rice would take Shorty, since they were the ones who had left the meat and so had the best chance of locating it. Rice had recently taught Corporal Salor how to shrimp, and Brainard was essential at Camp Clay. Rice and Frederick were to depart on the morning of April 6.

To prepare for the journey, Kislingbury, Ellis, Whisler, and Brainard hauled the loaded sledge to the highest point of Cape Sabine so that Rice and Shorty could start on a downhill, at least easing the beginning of their trip. The sledge bore a two-man buffalo sleeping bag, a lamp and cookstove with five daily ounces of fuel alcohol, a rifle, and an ax. For food they carried six days' rations of six ounces of pemmican and six ounces of hardtack per man. For medical emergencies Doctor Pavy packed a small flask of rum and one of spirits of ammonia—which could be drunk or inhaled. Rice bravely assured Greely that he was strong enough for the journey, which would be thirty to forty miles round trip, but privately he wrote in his journal that day: "I am pretty well used up."

That Sunday afternoon, April 6, Sgt. David Linn started begging for water, but before Greely could melt ice against his own chest in a rubber bag, Linn fell unconscious. He died several hours later. Linn had never fully recovered from those horrible nights trapped in the frozen sleeping bag with Elison. It was now late, and most of the men were either too sick or too exhausted to move Linn that evening. They left him where he lay and said a few words over him. They would bury him tomorrow should they have the strength. Brainard spoke of Linn at Fort Conger, remembering him as a "noble, generous-hearted, faithful fellow." Greely spoke with quiet reverence, praising Linn as "a strong, vigorous man of even temper . . . a kind comrade and a faithful soldier whom all liked and respected." Sgt. David Ralston, one of Linn's closest friends, reminded all the men of Linn's motto, which the proud Kentuckian had uttered daily during that longest of Long Nights: "United we stand, divided we fall." Ralston wrote in his journal that night: "Linn quietly passed away without a struggle and gone to his eternal rest. He done his duty manfully in the Arctic. Peace be with him."

Rice wished to get a couple of hours' sleep—or at least rest—before their scheduled 9:00 p.m. departure; they planned to walk through the night. Rice's own sleeping bag was strapped to the sledge on the crest of Cape Sabine some miles away, so with no other place to sleep, he crawled into the three-man bag and curled next to the corpse of his comrade David Linn, with Ralston on the other side of his best friend.

Greely would send Rice and Shorty off in a few hours, and the commander knew he must shore himself up and continue to lead the men by confident example, but he wrote in his journal: "The fates seem against us—an open channel, no game, no food, and apparently no hopes from Littleton Island. We have been lured here to our destruction."

28

Relief Preparations

In Washington, at his desk at the Navy Department offices, Secretary Chandler read over the papers relating to the Greely affair and signed documents. Chandler had his man for the third relief attempt in Cdr. Winfield Scott Schley, and with a few strokes of his pen, he entrusted the career naval officer with making "immediate and full preparation for the performance of your duties." As commander, these duties included examining and equipping the three ships chosen for the mission, and strengthening and outfitting them for perilous Arctic travel. Schley would command the flagship *Thetis*, and he was empowered to select subordinate officers to captain the other two ships, as well as pick their chief engineers and ice navigators.

Schley's orders also required him to research and form a comprehensive understanding of Greely's initial voyage up to Lady Franklin Bay in 1881, as well as read all the official reports and inquiries about the two failed relief attempts in 1882 and 1883. Schley took it upon himself to study widely on the history of Arctic exploration, with a keen focus on the journeys that had been made in the treacherous region he and his men would attempt to penetrate: from St. John's, Newfoundland, north, through the Labrador Sea, the Davis

Strait, Melville Bay, the Smith Sound, the Kane Basin, and finally the Kennedy Channel to Fort Conger at Lady Franklin Bay—should he not find Greely before that.

Never having been to the Arctic, Commander Schley determined to take along a number of men who had sailed there. To accompany him on the *Thetis*, he selected as his navigating officer Lt. Uriel Sebree, who had sailed as far as Littleton Island in the early 1870s in search of the lost *Polaris*, which had been the first United States attempt to reach the North Pole. For his chief engineer he chose the experienced George Melville, and the ice pilot James Norman. The *Bear* would be commanded by Lt. William Emory, and Schley also requested Lt. John C. Colwell, naval hero of the retreat from the sunken *Proteus*. Cdr. George Coffin would captain the *Alert*, on which Schley included two men who had Arctic experience: Lt. (j.g.) Ridgely Hunt had been on an expedition in search of the lost *Jeannette*, and Ens. Albert Ackerman had been a crew member on the previous relief effort aboard the *Yantic*.

Commander Schley organized small, efficient crews. Including officers and men, there would be thirty-seven on the *Thetis*, thirty-four on the *Bear*, and thirty-nine on the *Alert*. The light crews would provide extra room for food and comfort in the event that the ships were forced to winter in the Arctic. The crews were subjected to rigorous medical and dental examination before being signed on. For the danger and importance of the duty, Secretary Chandler allocated an extra ten dollars' pay per month for the duration of the mission, with two months' bonus pay should they successfully return by their scheduled date of September 1, 1884.

Though both the *Thetis* and the *Bear* had been designed to deal with the deadly ice in the treacherous Melville Bay, Schley left nothing to chance. After inspecting both ships carefully, he consulted with Secretary Chandler and others at the Department of the Navy and requested that each ship be better reinforced. His recommendation was granted, and while docked at the Brooklyn Navy Yard, the two vessels underwent considerable overhaul and strengthening. Truss frames and additional supporting beams were added belowdecks. To the forward and aft ends were added watertight bulkheads, and "iron straps were put over the stem and secured with through-bolts to the forward deadwood" for ramming ice. Steam jets were constructed in the holds and coal bunkers of the ships to extinguish fires.

Having thoroughly read the *Proceedings of the "Proteus" Court of Inquiry* and after reviewing the details of the ship's final hours before sinking, Schley had the *Thetis* and *Bear* fitted with "sponsons or filling pieces to close up the space in the angle between the keel and the ship's bottom, so that the thrust of ice forced laterally against the lower part of the hull would be borne on without resistance and all danger of forcing open the bottom planking avoided." The ships received fresh caulking and paint, and all their rigging and sails were either repaired or replaced with new gear.

To accommodate the men in the event of wintering over, the living quarters on both ships were increased in size, providing greater air space, and all the walls and ceilings received thick layers of felt for warmth and to combat moisture from condensation. Both the officers' and men's quarters were heated by coal stoves rather than boiler steam, reducing coal consumption when the ship was not under steam.

Schley had recently discovered that ships powered by Welsh semibituminous coal moved up to 20 percent faster than those burning the anthracite coal the navy normally used, and he ordered two thousand tons from Cardiff, Wales, to be brought over to New York, and five hundred tons to be delivered to Littleton Island.

All three ships would have on board a small steam cutter or whaleboat, which could either be employed as water craft under steam or sail or pulled as sleds across the ice. They were outfitted with tent poles and tan canvas tarps, and in foul weather could be hauled aground or onto the ice for use as shelters. In total the three ships would take food for 115 men to survive for two years. Schley was greatly pleased to find that on its arrival, the *Alert* was in first-rate condition, owing to the pride and excellence of the Royal Navy. Its sails and rigging required minimal alteration, and the addition of berths for the crew.

Commander Schley was known to be a stern, detail-oriented leader with supreme organizational skills. His plan for each ship was scheduled nearly down to the day. Because the *Bear* had arrived first, and its reinforcing and retrofitting would be completed first, Schley ordered that it depart New York on April 25 for

St. John's, where it would take on coal. Captain Emory was to purchase sled dogs and inquire with local whalers and sealers about the season's reported ice conditions to the north, as the sealing season would close near the end of April and all these vessels would be back in port at St. John's. Without delay the *Bear* would then proceed to the Greenland ports of Disko Island and then Upernavik. Schley projected the *Bear*'s arrival there on or before the third week of May.

Under Schley's command, the flagship *Thetis* was scheduled to depart New York no later than May 1, 1884. At St. John's he would rendezvous with the coal ship *Loch Garry* from Wales to take on more of the superior semibituminous coal, procure more dogs, and continue to Upernavik to join the *Bear*, arriving there on or before May 25. Once together, the *Thetis* and the *Bear* would continue on to Littleton Island. The *Loch Garry,* chartered by the U.S. Navy from Wales, was to go as far as Upernavik to await the arrival of the *Alert*, which, having been designated as tender, would be the last to depart, no later than May 10, and bring on board all materials needed to build winter quarters, should they be needed. Schley ordered that if for any reason the *Thetis* failed to arrive at Upernavik, the *Bear* had permission to press northward across the Melville Bay, leaving records of its progress in cairns at Littleton Island. If Greely and his men were found, the *Bear* was to bring them back to Upernavik.

While all the preparations for the convoy's departure were under way, Henrietta Greely's proposed Bounty Plan, urged constantly by General Lockwood, had been taken up by Sen. Joseph Hawley of Connecticut and introduced to the Appropriations Committee. The bill would assure a twenty-five-thousand-dollar reward for any "private seafarers . . . not in the military or naval service of the United States" who either discovered and rescued, or ascertained the fate of, the Lady Franklin Bay Expedition.

Privately neither Secretary Chandler of the navy nor Commander Schley thought that engaging private mercenary vessels was a good idea. For his part, Chandler certainly did not want to see anyone other than the U.S. Navy rescue Greely. Chandler went so far as to write President Arthur opposing the plan, saying that, should private foreign vessels become lost or crushed by the ice in these dangerous seas, the navy would then be compelled to come to their aid, further endangering U.S. servicemen—both officers and crews. Schley was more concerned about logistics and thought a fleet of bounty-hunting New-foundland vessels would just get in his way or even create unnecessary confusion or a further disaster. But ultimately it was not up to Chandler or Schley. President Arthur passed the decision on to Congress, letting them—amid a vitriolic public clamoring for action—decide the bill's fate.

On Good Friday, April 11, after lengthy argument in the Senate, the Bounty Plan was approved, and General Lockwood telegraphed Henrietta the good news. A reward of twenty-five thousand dollars would no doubt pique the interest of plenty of seamen once official word of the signed proclamation reached St. John's. So, in addition to the U.S. Navy's resources, he told her, there would be a flotilla of private mariners searching for her husband and his men.

Once Commander Schley received the news of the passage of the Bounty Bill, he put his personal feelings aside, knowing that there would be a fleet of whalers at St. John's or farther north in the whaling waters, clamoring for the prize. He would deal with that when the time came. For now he concerned himself with all the details and final preparations for departure. Secretary Chandler had empowered Schley with complete command—"full power and responsibility"—of every aspect of the mission. Privately Secretary Chandler expressed his utter confidence in Schley, telling him he felt no apprehension whatsoever about the success of the relief expedition.

As he went over the hundreds of minute details in April 1884, Commander Schley tried to ignore the onslaught of newspaper articles, but it was nearly impossible to do so. There were daily editorials about previous Arctic tragedies and speculation about his own expedition to come. As Schley put it:

> There was little encouragement to be drawn from the popular newspaper utterances; the recollection of all the disasters in the Arctic region, and especially of those which had recently overtaken the brave De Long and his fellows in the Lena Delta, was too fresh in the public mind to permit any great hope of success for this new enterprise.

There remained plenty of dubious reporters who believed it impossible for Greely and his men to have survived this long, and that Schley's mission—no matter how well prepared and provisioned—was "not only fruitless but a fatal errand."

Nevertheless Schley remained confident in his abilities and his chances for success, and he imparted this attitude to the captains of his fleet. He spoke with his captains and officers frequently, reminding them that "the object of the voyage was something above and beyond the ordinary calls of service." They all knew, given the tragedies and failures of the past relief attempts, that the Arctic was a formidable and merciless foe, that they faced certain danger and potential death, and that there was a very real possibility they might be gone for a year or more. If things went wrong, some or all might never see their families and loved ones again. And yet, after consulting with his captains, officers, engineers, and enlisted men and instilling his confidence and bravado in them, Commander Schley concluded that to a man "they evinced a determination to spare no pains, to incur any exposure, to assume any required risk, and to be unflagging in watching for opportunities to gain a mile, a yard, or a foot on the journey toward Greely and his party."

29

Triumph and Tragedy

On the evening of April 6, George Rice crawled from beside his dead companion, David Linn, and shuffled over to Commander Greely's sleeping bag for last instructions. Greely roused, and the two spoke for a few minutes. Rice predicted the trip should take four or five days—two out and two back—with some extra time factored in for searching for the boxes of meat and for weather, as a storm had kicked up and snow was falling steadily. Greely agreed that seemed about right, cautioning him against overexertion, and impressing on him that both Rice and Frederick be honest with the other if they became too exhausted. Greely opted not to give Rice any formal written instructions, trusting Rice as the natural leader of this second "forlorn hope." He offered a firm handshake and said: "Simply go and do the best you can."

Rice and Shorty Frederick dressed in the warmest clothes they had—it was −8°—and made their way to the exit of the hut at Camp Clay. They were thankful that the day before, Brainard, Kislingbury, and Ellis had hauled the sledge to the crest of the island—a journey that had taken the three men four hours to the top, but only an hour and a half to return, so at least the first leg of their trials would be unburdened by the heavy, cumbersome sledge. As they turned to bid their friends farewell, the others hailed their bravery. Said Greely:

"Though our hearts were almost too full for utterance, we managed to send them off with a feeble cheer, that they might know our prayers and Godspeed were with them on their perilous journey."

After they left, Brainard was overcome with gratitude, but he was resolute about what his companions were about to encounter:

Weak and despondent, they go out alone in the bleak wastes of an Arctic desert, taking their lives in their hands, to bring food to their starving companions. Before them lie famine, indescribable cold, torture to their minds and then, perhaps, failure. And in the hut, we must wait for the end of the story.

David Linn, the third of the men to die, was buried at ten o'clock in the morning. Eight men hauled his skeletal body to Cemetery Ridge and laid him next to the graves of Cross and Eskimo Fred. Lieutenant Kislingbury was so weak that he could shovel a grave only six inches deep, so that much of Linn's corpse remained above ground, slowly being covered by a continuous dusting of snow.

For the next two days snow fell constantly, and the winds howled a gale, buffeting the hut with large drifts. The men could only imagine what Rice and Shorty were going through out there without even a tent. Inside the hut men began writing their wills and last letters to their friends and families. Corporal Salor, who had taken over shrimping duties for Rice, returned from outside saying that regrettably, he no longer had the strength to walk to and from the shrimping pools, so Brainard relieved him. He managed to bring in fifteen pounds that day.

Since the deaths of Eskimo Fred and Linn, Lockwood had declined steadily. Greely began issuing him four ounces daily of raw dovekie meat, hoping the rich protein would help, but it had little effect, and Lockwood uttered that "he wished it was over" for him, too. He fell unconscious early on the morning of the ninth, hung on with labored breathing throughout the day, "his mind wandering but never unpleasantly so," and late in the afternoon, with Biederbick by his side, he died. Brainard went over and helped Biederbick straighten Lockwood's limbs and prepare his remains for burial, dressing him in an officer's coat. Said Brainard: "This was the saddest duty I have ever yet been called on to perform."

Like the others, Lockwood was laid to rest on Cemetery Ridge. In eulogizing 1st Lt. James B. Lockwood, Greely spoke of the man who had led the record-setting mission to Farthest North as "a gallant officer, a brave, true and loyal man. . . . He always did his best, and that best will give him a name in Arctic history as long as courage, perseverance, and success shall seem worthy of a man's praise and ambition." Brainard, harder struck than most by the loss because of his many adventures afield with Lockwood, reflected: "He had been my companion during long and eventful excursions, and my feeling toward him was akin to that of a brother."

The death of Lieutenant Lockwood prompted Greely to make a military decision: He called the others in the hut to listen carefully. He was hereby officially reinstating the previously disgraced 2nd Lt. Frederick Kislingbury to command and restoring him to active duty, revoking the written orders of August 1881, when he had disbarred him. Looking directly at the lieutenant, Greely praised Kislingbury for his courage and dedication in their retreat from Fort Conger, for his tenacious work in bringing in all the scattered caches once they had landed at Eskimo Point and made their way to Cape Sabine. He had also distinguished himself as one of their finest hunters. In closing, Commander Greely "expressed a wish that their future discourse might be of the most agreeable nature." Kislingbury accepted his reinstatement, thanking his commander with deep emotion. In the event of Greely's death, command of the expedition would now fall on Kislingbury.

Sgt. Winfield Jewell had been faltering for several days, and Greely, though dangerously weak himself, his "hands shaking as if palsied," began spoon-feeding Jewell four ounces of extra rations a day. He sat with the man day and night, telling him stories of the Civil War and trying to "inspire him with new courage and vigor." Now all he could do was wait to see if the supplemental food would revive him. With the storm outside continuing to howl, all the men's thoughts were with Rice and Shorty, wondering how they could possibly survive, and silently praying for their safe return with 144 pounds of beef.

On the morning of April 11, which dawned bright and clear and −23°, Long and Jens headed out to hunt. They soon spotted a walrus lounging on an ice floe but were unable to get close enough for a shot. Jens slid into his kayak and, with a rifle tucked at his side, began paddling quietly toward the walrus. Long headed down the shoreline and then stepped onto a flat ice floe, hoping to get close enough for a shot as well. Suddenly Long heard a crack like the report of a gun and looked up to see whether Jens had succeeded. But the noise had not been a rifle shot; it was the sound of the floe Long himself was on, cracking beneath his feet and snapping into two halves: Now he stood on a small ice island that was drifting away from shore and into the sound.

Seeing what was happening, Jens abandoned the walrus and paddled furiously to Long, grabbing onto the side of the small berg. Long desperately urged Jens to leave him and paddle out of the rough water back to shore to save himself, but Jens refused, saying flatly in English: "You go, me go too." By great fortune the winds shifted, driving them both back to the fast ice of the shoreline. Long leaped to safety and helped pull Jens and the kayak out of the water. When they looked back, the walrus was gone. They headed back to the hut to get warm, recover, and tell the men the story of their near disaster.

That afternoon Brainard was down at the shrimping grounds. He pulled out one of the nets and dumped about five pounds' worth into his bucket. To keep from freezing, he took the bucket and began to walk up and down the spit, daydreaming about all the food he would prefer to eat rather than sand fleas. As he stood there in thought, he looked up and was startled by "a medium-sized bear about two hundred yards away, approaching at a shambling gait." Brainard moved slowly and quietly to the shrimping ground and picked up his hatchet and spear, wondering for a moment whether he might be able to use these to kill the bear. The absurdity of that plan dawned on him quickly, so instead he took the shrimp bucket and moved away from the bear and as fast as he could toward the hut: He had to alert the others.

By the time he reached Cemetery Ridge he was exhausted and pitched forward onto the ground. He dropped the shrimp bucket and began crawling down the slope toward the hut, hoping the bear had not seen him—and if it had, praying that the hungry bear was not coming after him. Brainard crawled on his hands and knees to the entryway, flung the canvas door open with his head, and panting, yelled out: *"Bear!!!"* Then, halfway inside the hut, he passed out.

∽∽∽

Far to the south of Camp Clay, Rice and Shorty were in the midst of their own ordeal. In the driving snowstorm, they had dragged the sledge slowly, plowing through knee-high drifts for ten hours before pitching camp on the leeward side of a grounded iceberg. Strong winds prevented them from lighting the camp stove for food or water, and they wriggled into the two-man buffalo bag, pinned there by the furious storm for twenty-two hours. When the storm abated, they peeked out to see that they were covered with more than a foot of new snow. They wriggled from the sleeping bag and jumped up and down, swinging their arms to get warm. Too cold to make tea, they pulled the sledge for an hour to produce some body heat. When they finally stopped to make tea, they realized they had gone thirty-six hours without a drink.

Another full day of labored walking at about a mile per hour brought them near Eskimo Point, but they were too tired to continue and found shelter between a large iceberg and the sheer face of a glacier. Early the next morning the skies had cleared, and they made it to the stone huts of Eskimo Point within an hour. They were now roughly six miles from where Rice remembered leaving the English beef. Rice thought that with a reduced load they could make it to the meat and back in one long march, so they left the heavy sleeping bag and tools and departed with a lighter sledgeload.

Their progress was slowed by open tidal pools they had to navigate around, sometimes breaking through thin ice and soaking their boots. Around noon the storm returned, hammering them from the northwest, the blinding snowdrifts creating a whiteout, so they could see barely twenty to thirty feet in front of them. By late afternoon they had struggled to the area where Rice believed the meat to be, and they commenced searching, looking everywhere for signs of old sledge tracks, for the rifle, for the boxes of meat. After a few hours of crisscrossing throughout the area, they had still found nothing. Rice was certain this was the place, and the only explanation was that the ice they had left it on had broken up and moved out into the Baird Inlet, taking the meat with it.

Shorty suggested that they upend the sledge to mark the spot and head back to the huts at Eskimo Point to rest and get warm. They could return to search again the next day. But Rice wanted to keep looking. He spent another hour or so stumbling around until Shorty could see that Rice was in trouble; they desperately needed to get to shelter. Shorty led Rice to an iceberg about a thousand yards away, with Rice tumbling exhausted at its base. Shorty managed to light the cookstove and warm some tea and pemmican. He forced Rice to drink some brandy and spirits of ammonia. This partially resuscitated Rice, and with Shorty's help he stood up, but when he tried to walk he wobbled like a drunk, then collapsed again. Shorty rolled Rice onto the sledge, thinking he might somehow muster the strength to drag him to Eskimo Point.

Rice started reminiscing about home, talking fondly of his friends and relatives, recalling all the delicious meals he could remember. At one point he became lucid enough to give Shorty detailed instructions as to his personal effects, journals, and letters. "We remained there," Frederick later recalled, "on this desolate piece of ice, with the wind blowing a hurricane, for two hours or more, after which time my poor companion lost consciousness." Shorty took off his own fur parka and covered Rice with it to keep him warm, then lay beside him, hugging him. Rice died in Shorty's arms at 7:45 p.m. on April 9. It was a profoundly lonely and frightening moment for Shorty Frederick. He was alone on the ice: "The death of my companion under these circumstances made a deeper impression on my mind than any experience in my whole life."

Frederick considered staying there and perishing alongside Rice. Eskimo Point was six or seven miles away, and he doubted he could make it. But the more he thought about it, he remembered the men at Camp Clay and how they awaited their return. If he did not try to go back, they might send out a search party and die trying to find him and Rice. Bolstered by thoughts of his duty to his country and his comrades, he decided to try to make it back to Eskimo Point. Before leaving, Shorty paused: "I stooped and kissed the remains of my dead companion and left them there for the wild winds of the Arctic to sweep over."

After seven long hours Shorty stumbled into the stone hut at Eskimo Point. The buffalo sleeping bag was frozen so solid and he was so exhausted that at first, he could not even unroll it. He rooted around and found a vial of spirits of ammonia and quickly swallowed it. Invigorated, he managed to unfurl the bag and force his way in, where he stayed until the following morning.

When he awoke he cooked warm food and tea, and felt much improved. But his conscience weighed on him: He could not stand to think of his dear friend Rice disemboweled and chewed on by foxes or bears, so he left the stone hut with an ax and hurried back to Rice's body. It took him a few hours to dig a grave, hacking at the ice and then kneeling to remove the broken pieces by hand. He rolled Rice into it, covered his remains with snow and ice, and turned away to begin the long, slow slog back toward Eskimo Point. If he could make it, he would spend another night there, and then, if he had any strength left, return the next day to Camp Clay.

∞∞∞

Commander Greely and a few others dragged Sergeant Brainard all the way into the hut, where Biederbick poured brandy down his throat and he came to, stammering: "A bear, a bear!" As he regained his senses, the faces of Long and Jens came into focus. "Where?" they wanted to know. They had already donned their outer garments and stood over him. He told them its last location in proximity to the shrimping grounds, and they each grabbed a rifle and hurried from the hut, Lieutenant Kislingbury following after them with the shotgun.

Those left in the hut waited anxiously. Kislingbury sprinted up Cemetery Ridge but grew faint after less than a hundred yards and fell to the ground. As he lay there, he checked his weapon and pockets and realized that, in his excitement, he had forgotten shells. He returned to the hut for ammunition, then slumped to the floor, too tired to go out again.

Long and Jens had reached the peninsula near the shrimping grounds They spotted the animal moving away from them, heading along the ice foot toward open water a few miles distant. Long gave Jens a hand signal that they should split up and try to flank the bear. They moved as fast and as quietly as they could over the rough and undulating ice, hiding behind broken ice boulders whenever the bear stopped to look back. They gained on it but could see it ambling along a strip of shore ice leading to open water. If it plunged into the icy water and swam, their chance would be lost: They needed to get close enough for a shot while it was still on the ice.

Long and Jens were separated by about fifty yards, with Jens slightly ahead. They could see the bear clearly some 250 yards out and knew this was as close as they were going to get. Jens pulled up his rifle, aimed, and fired, hitting the animal in the forepaw. It reared and roared, then limped toward the water. Long was deliberate. He shook off his right-hand glove, pulled his hood back over his head, and dropped to one knee. He shouldered his rifle and exhaled: The bear was now ten yards from open water. Long held his breath, drew a bead, and fired. The bullet struck the animal in the head. The bear splayed out and slid forward a few yards, and when it came to rest, both Jens and Long each fired another shot into its body to ensure the kill, then ran toward to it.

After a few hours—an almost interminable, nerve-racking wait—at about ten that evening the men in the hut heard distant voices from above on the hill. The men sat up in their bags, trying to discern the tone of the voices. Were they exultant or despondent? Finally they heard Long belt out, with levity in his voice: "Make your bets, gentlemen, make your bets!" A minute later Long and Jens flung open the canvas and crawled into the hut, beaming. Jens, who had developed a deep kinship with the disfigured Elison, shuffled over to his side. "You all right now, Elison," the Greenlander said to him, slapping him on the shoulder. "You all right."

Heartened by this good news, Greely put Brainard in charge of bringing in the bear. The commander had him issue three ounces of bacon each to the large party of nine it would take to haul the heavy animal back. They scarfed the bacon happily, and within thirty minutes Brainard had readied a sledge and they set off, with Long leading them the three miles to the location. They arrived at midnight. In the lengthening northern light, they could see the bullet holes in the head, front paw, and body as a light wind swept over the white tufted fur of the magnificent beast. With five men pushing from one side and four pulling from the other, they rolled the bear onto the sledge. A large quantity of blood had flowed from the bullet wounds and seeped into the ice. Brainard chopped at the edges of the stain and loaded the blood-soaked ice onto the sledge, and, working together, they hauled the bear back to Camp Clay. As they pulled the drag ropes with renewed strength, someone noted that it was Good Friday.

At 2:30 a.m. they dragged the bear into the center of the hut to a round of cheers. As Bender and Biederbick began skinning it, bets continued as to the animal's weight. Greely gave the final estimate at four hundred pounds fully dressed. Jens patted the bear on its head, amusing the others by making smacking noises with his mouth and licking his lips. Brainard hustled to get cans and buckets. Every possible part of the animal would be used: "Intestines, lungs, heart, head," even the brain. He tossed the feet, stomach, windpipe, and liver into a bucket to use as shrimp bait. The blood-drenched ice chunks would be melted, and the blood used to thicken their stews. "This fellow," Brainard exclaimed, "is our salvation."

As a reward to the hunters, Greely gave Jens shots of rum and promoted Pvt. Francis Long to sergeant. To celebrate the kill, he called the cooks to prepare a hearty pemmican stew mixed with fresh bear meat, and ordered that raw fat be issued to everyone while they awaited the feast. Some of the men, now believing once again that they might eventually reach their homes and see their families, wiped away tears.

The elation of the successful bear kill was tempered the next morning, however, when Sgt. Winfield Jewell died in the commander's arms. Greely had been attending to him and feeding him for days. He admired and appreciated Jewell's dutiful work, especially back at Fort Conger, where Jewell had painstakingly made scientific observations, contributing to their methodical work of more than five hundred daily scientific readings. Brainard and Biederbick—who continued to take on the difficult duty without being asked to do so—gently closed Jewell's eyes, arranged his bony arms against his sides, and dressed him for burial. At two o'clock that afternoon, they laid him beside the others on Cemetery Ridge.

The next morning Shorty Frederick stumbled into Camp Clay, alone. He was nearly frozen to death, his face chapped white by wind and cold. He told the commander of their failed search for the English beef, of Rice's death, and of his own ordeal. It had taken him three days to return to Camp Clay after burying Rice's body. He had hardly eaten or drunk during that time, having depleted his own rations days before. Shorty produced a few of Rice's personal effects, and he returned Rice's food rations, which he had not thought proper to consume, since he knew the men were starving and he had not brought in the beef. Greely, with great emotion, thanked Shorty for his valiant service, then handed Rice's rations to Brainard to commit back to the commissary larder.

The news of George Rice's death, according to Greely, produced mourning that was "deep and prolonged." One man broke down and wailed, sobbing uncontrollably while the others tried to console him. George Rice had come on the expedition as the photographer, and had made photographs in the harshest of conditions, recording the expedition's exploits and daily lives at and around Fort Conger, near the top of the world, for two full years until their eventual retreat toward Cape Sabine. During the retreat he had distinguished himself as an exceptional ice navigator, his keen vision and astute decision making certainly saving all of their lives on numerous occasions.

On their arrival at Eskimo Point, Rice had volunteered to make the forty-mile round-trip trek to Cape Isabella, bringing the 144 pounds of meat as far as he could, then leaving it behind only in order to save Corporal Elison's life. Recently he had ventured out onto the deadly ice in an attempt to reach Littleton Island. He had given every ounce of his considerable strength, and finally his life, in service to his comrades and his country. Biederbick said a few words for his fallen companion: "My heart bleeds for our so dearly beloved and esteemed friend and comrade." Brainard, choking back tears, called George Rice "the bravest and noblest member of this expedition."

Sometime later, after all the men had spoken of Rice and his heroic sacrifice on their behalf, Greely heard the chirping of a snow bunting coming from the roof of the hut. Others heard it too, and everyone hushed to listen to this harbinger of spring on Easter Sunday. No one spoke a word, and "all noise stopped as if by magic," every one of the men listening breathlessly to the high, lilting whistle of the little songbird until it flitted away on the Arctic wind and was gone.

30

∼∞∼

A Flotilla of Rescue Ships

While Greely and his men clung to life with their four hundred pounds of fresh bear meat, four thousand miles to the south in New York, Cdr. Winfield Scott Schley was finalizing the ships to set sail. Going over the proposed departure dates, Schley realized that the *Bear*, slated first to leave, was to steam away on April 25, which was a Friday. A long-held sailors' superstition cautioned that it was bad luck to commence a voyage on a Friday, so Schley immediately contacted Secretary Chandler and urged that the departure be moved up one day to Thursday, April 24, which was approved.

Commander Schley held his final orders in his weather-worn hands. They were remarkably brief and devoid of detail, given the responsibility they bore:

NAVY DEPARTMENT, WASHINGTON, APRIL 21, 1884.

COMMANDER WINFIELD S. SCHLEY, U.S.N.—

COMMANDING THE GREELY RELIEF EXPEDITION

Sir: The Thetis, Bear, *and* Alert, *the ships of the Greely Relief Expedition of 1884, being ready, you are ordered to take command of them and to proceed to the coast of Greenland, or further north if necessary, and, if possible, to find and rescue, or ascertain the fate of Lieutenant A. W. Greely and his comrades.*

All the officers and men under your command are hereby enjoined to perform any duty on sea or land to which you may order them. No detailed instructions will be given you. Full confidence is felt that you have both the capacity and the courage, guided by discretion, necessary to do all that can be required of you by the Department or the nation for the rescue of our imperiled countrymen.

With earnest wishes and high hopes for your success and safe return, I am, Very respectfully, William E. Chandler, Secretary of the Navy.

By April 23 the *Bear* was ready and lay moored at its pier in the Brooklyn Navy Yard. Its imminent departure was national news, and all through the day visitors numbering in the hundreds were allowed to board the ship and inspect it. Many brought flowers, and the well-wishers—some of whom were family members or friends—wreathed the foredeck with resplendent floral arrangements and colorful bursting bouquets. As the visitors disembarked, enlisted men handed them either a parasol or a white glove—which they were encouraged to smudge against the *Bear*'s brand-new coat of paint as a souvenir.

Around midday on April 24 Lt. William Emory called for the decks to be cleared and the ship's horn blown. A tugboat pulled the *Bear* from its moorings out into the East River, and under steam the ship moved out of New York Harbor: "The wharves on the Brooklyn and New York sides were thronged with cheering crowds of people, while steamers and other ships of the port were dressed with flags and pennants." Calls of "Godspeed!" and "Bon voyage!" rang through the harbor. As the *Bear* passed beneath the newly completed Brooklyn Bridge—its grand suspension spans connecting the boroughs of Brooklyn and Manhattan—the officers and crew, dressed in their navy blues, looked up to see and hear thousands of people waving and cheering, wishing them good luck. The *Bear* appeared glorious on the East River, "her shiny white figure head of a polar bear gleaming beneath her bowsprit."

As the *Bear* passed Governors Island, ships continued to sound their whistles in respectful salute, and a processional convoy accompanied the grand renovated steamer through the Narrows to Sandy Hook, and on out into the windblown and choppy North Atlantic.

One week later, on the afternoon of May 1, Commander Schley boarded the *Thetis*. Before departing, he went to his cabin and sat down to write a letter to Henrietta Greely:

> *You may rely on the expedition to get some news to your husband and I don't think I overstate its purpose when I say it will remain as near to him as practicable until substantial mental and bodily relief has been afforded him and his noble party. Yes, my dear Madam, I leave the dearest home ties in the earnest hope & with the sincerest purpose to return to you the noblest of husbands. May God bless our efforts and help you to be patient in the long hours between our sailing and return.*

Later, reading the letter, Henrietta was encouraged to know that in Winfield Schley, Secretary Chandler had chosen a man of character, deep conviction, and purpose. She willed herself to believe that at long last, her husband's life was in the hands of the very man for the mission.

At 2:30 p.m. on May 1, Commander Schley sailed north with his crew to fanfare equal to that for the *Bear*: "Salutes were fired from the Navy Yard, from Governor's Island, and from Fort Hamilton," with the relief ship *Thetis* "dipping her colors in return." Ens. Charles Harlow, aboard the *Thetis*, said of the moment: "The blasts of whistles and dipping of colors of the vessels we passed testified to the widespread interest all had in the enterprise." At Sandy Hook, Schley swung the *Thetis* to check compass deviation, then advanced out to sea. The *Alert* would follow, departing no later than May 10, bearing building materials required for establishing winter quarters if necessary.

The *Bear* soon encountered rough seas and thick fog traveling north, a heavy gale on the third day out tearing away the bridge, but it landed at St. John's after one week, remaining there for two days. During that time, as it took on coal and men procured lumber to repair the bridge at sea, Lieutenant Emory asked sealers and whalers about the ice conditions in the northern waters, and also ascertained which whaling vessels had heard about the twenty-five-thousand-dollar bounty and planned to go after Greely themselves. The news regarding the ice was good. Strong northeasterly winds had blown for weeks, likely setting the pack in motion and sending it southward earlier than usual for the region.

As for the private bounty hunters in whaling vessels, sure enough, there were nearly a dozen planning to go at least as far as Littleton Island, should the ice allow it. From St. John's, Emory sent Secretary Chandler a telegram addressing his thoughts on these bounty hunters:

THESE STEAM WHALERS ARE ABLY COMMANDED AND ARE EFFICIENTLY FITTED OUT. THEIR MASTERS ARE AMBITIOUS TO SECURE THE GREELY PARTY; AND ALTHOUGH THE REWARD WILL NOT BE A SECONDARY CONSIDERATION, THEY ARE ONE AND ALL DESIROUS OF OBTAINING THE PRESTIGE OF THE RESCUE. FROM INFORMATION THAT I CAN GATHER, IT WOULD SEEM THAT THE WHALESHIP *ARCTIC* WILL BE OUR ONLY DANGEROUS COMPETITOR. SHE IS NOT STRONGER THAN THE *BEAR* OR *THETIS* BUT HAS MORE POWERFUL ENGINES.

I HAVE ARRANGED EVERYTHING AT THIS PLACE TO AVOID ANY DELAY TO THE *THETIS,* AND HAVE LEFT FULL INFORMATION OF EVERY EVENT FOR COMMANDER SCHLEY . . . AND AM LED TO BELIEVE THAT EVEN SHOULD THE SEASON PROVE MOST FAVORABLE, COMMANDER SCHLEY WILL BE ABLE TO REACH UPERNAVIK BEFORE ANY OTHER VESSEL CAN UNDERTAKE OR ATTEMPT THE PASSAGE OF MELVILLE BAY.

With that correspondence, it was clear that the high command of the U.S. Navy was deeply aware of the prestige and honor attendant on finding Greely, and that whatever else anyone wished to call it—a relief mission or a rescue mission—it was also a competition, with the reputation of the navy at stake. Before putting to sea again on May 4, Emory purchased seven trained Greenland sled dogs and eighteen Labrador dogs, which, though less adept at pulling sleds than Greenland dogs, were more manageable and had the advantage of being excellent water dogs, willing and able to swim from floe to floe. On May 4 Emory boarded the *Bear* and left St. John's, planning to rendezvous with Schley and the *Thetis* at Upernavik near the end of the month.

The *Thetis* had seen clear sailing under blue skies and calm seas, but on the third day out the air pump's connecting rod broke. Chief Engineer Melville proved his worth, spending an entire night forging a replacement rod, and they soon got back under way, arriving at St. John's on May 9 under heavy fog, rain, and sleet. Commander Schley was pleased to see the Welsh coal steamer *Loch Garry* already docked in the harbor, as planned. It carried five hundred tons of coal and was to accompany the *Thetis* to Littleton Island. This way all three ships in Schley's flotilla would have ample fuel to do their work. At St. John's, Schley also purchased eighteen more Labrador dogs, reminding his men to exercise great caution around them, as they were "savage and wolfish and if a man falls on the ice they will attack him at once."

Schley purchased two thousand additional pounds of food at St. John's so that his crew could have fresh meat and vegetables "once or twice a week until the region of reindeer or other game was reached." They hung the beef high in the rigging, out of reach of the dogs, where it would freeze and be preserved in the frigid temperatures after a few days' sailing north. Schley earmarked a considerable portion of the beef "exclusively for Lieutenant Greely and his party, for it was recognized from the beginning that when found they would probably be in a destitute condition."

The *Thetis* and its men were in fine shape and ready to depart. To prepare them for the dangers of the ice pack, Schley had his officers—including Lieutenant Colwell, who had experienced the sinking of the *Proteus* and those chaotic last hours—go over procedures for abandoning ship. Each officer and man was issued a personal kit for use should their ship be crushed by ice: "Rubber knapsacks were packed . . . containing a complete shift of underclothing and footgear, a [pad] and pencil for records or notes, and a box of rifle or sporting ammunition," plus extra footgear in the event of many days on the ice. Two months' supplies of provisions were stowed on deck for quick access in case of abandonment: There would be no repeat of the *Proteus*.

Early on the morning of May 12, the *Thetis* and the *Loch Garry* steamed away from St. John's toward Upernavik, Greenland. As soon as they cleared the harbor, they met with high winds and rough seas, and in a short time they vanished into the fog.

The last thing Schley had done before leaving was to inspect the explosives he had brought along. To assist in ramming the ice, and to blow up smaller floes to create leads, he had on board a great many "torpedoes": five-pound explosives of packed gunpowder and gun cotton, contained in tin cylinders, rigged with electric connections and fuses. The plan was to use ice augers to drill holes in the ice ahead of the ships, place the torpedoes, and detonate them. Commander Schley intended, if it came to it, to explode his way to Greely. Reflecting on his prospects, Schley said: "It is doubtful if the *Thetis* and *Bear* could carry enough explosives to blow their way through the pack for the 1,400 miles engaged in their ice battle." But he was going to try.

LEFT: Commander Winfield Scott Schley. *(Courtesy of Naval History and Heritage Command)*

CENTER: Relief vessels and whalers moored to the ice—a flotilla of rescue ships. *(Courtesy of Naval History and Heritage Command)*

BOTTOM: The *Thetis,* the *Bear,* and Dundee whaler racing against time to rescue Greely. *(Courtesy of Naval History and Heritage Command)*

31

~

"To Strive, to Endure, to Live"

The arrival of spring brought continuous sunlight to Camp Clay, which greatly improved the spirits of the men. Near the end of April most of the men spent midday crawling from the squalid hut and basking in the sunshine, letting the warmth wash over their bodies and, eyes closed, pointing their faces toward the sun. Greely even loosened the "arrest" of Private Henry and allowed him outside, too, though Henry was still restricted and ordered not to go beyond the end of the spit. To improve conditions inside the hut, Private Whisler cut a skylight window in the bottom of the boat that served as the roof, allowing beams of light to pour into the hut for the first time in six months.

Making creative use of what food was on hand, the cooks occasionally impressed the men with their originality. On Sunday, April 20, they treated the party to what Brainard called "the event of the entire winter! Trimmings of bear and seal heads, their hearts, lungs, kidneys; and a large quantity of bear blood which we had chopped from the ice. The blood enriched the stew beyond conception, making the gravy thick and delicious and imparting a delicate flavor."

But despite the twenty-four hours of sunlight and the occasional "feast," the hunters had bagged no game since the bear, and what had appeared to them to be an endless bounty of meat was dwindling, and all the men continued to weaken. Lieutenant Kislingbury was slipping away, exhibiting, according to Doctor Pavy, "decided mental derangement." At times he would say that he was ready to go out hunting, but when he tried to rise, he would fall back down and then start babbling like an infant. One day he spoke lovingly and hopefully of the future and being able to see his sons again, then later lay down on the sledge outside and, "weeping like a child," said: "It is hopeless. I cannot fight longer."

Commander Greely developed such pronounced heart palpitations that Doctor Pavy became deeply concerned. After discussing his medical condition with the doctor, Greely penned an official letter making Sergeant Brainard his legal successor and next in command should he die, since Kislingbury lacked the mental or physical capacity to lead. Greely also wrote and gave Brainard "directions for the disposition of his effects in the event of his death."

Brainard kept shrimping, but many of the men no longer had the stomach for the stews of mostly shell, and some were refusing to eat them. Because Brainard was also doing the very difficult work of cutting up the remains of the frozen bear carcass with a saw, Greely ordered that a number of the men take turns shrimping to ease Brainard's workload. Jens maintained a positive attitude and rigged together a makeshift net, using part of a broken old sledge and some cloth, hoping it might help him secure a seal. The last few he had shot had sunk in the water as he had paddled toward them in his kayak. Early in the last week of April, by Brainard's estimate, they had food enough remaining for twenty days. The bounty of the bear had not lasted nearly as long as they had tricked themselves into believing it would.

For Greely it was becoming more and more difficult to maintain order and discipline. For many weeks various members had reported to Greely that they had seen Doctor Pavy stealing bread and meat from Elison, whom Pavy continued to feed personally. Pavy had also been seen drinking Schneider's small allotment of rum. Greely brooded about what to do. Now more than ever they all desperately required Pavy's medical expertise, so the commander refrained from taking any action against him, but privately he worried about utter breakdown in command and even eventual anarchy. On Sunday, April 24, while everyone was asleep in their bags, Private Henry stole a large quantity of cooking alcohol, guzzling enough to become "disgustingly drunk." There was general outrage, and Sergeant Gardiner was so incensed that he crawled toward Henry, threatening hoarsely: "I'll kill him." But he was too weak to even make it over to him. All Greely could do was reinstate Henry's "prisoner" status and give him the menial daily task of emptying the urinal.

Two days later Jens had finished his seal net and was so anxious to try it out he rose with Long at five in the morning. Jens was in excellent spirits, and Greely noted: "For the first time in many weeks he came and shook hands with me before he left, laughing pleasantly." Around noon Jens spotted a large seal sunning on a small drifting ice floe. Jens slipped into his kayak and paddled for it, but he encountered some ice between him and the seal. As Long watched from the shore, Jens climbed out of the boat and onto the ice and then pushed the kayak ahead until he could enter the water again. Suddenly Long could see that the stern of the kayak had started sinking, and Jens was paddling furiously, trying to turn the kayak around and return to the ice. Jens got near the ice, stood up, and leaped, but the edge of the new ice broke off, with Jens desperately trying to pull himself up.

Long sprinted out onto the new ice to within a few feet of Jens, who had ceased flailing and now bobbed facedown in the water. Long broke through near the edge as he reached out, trying to grab hold of Jens, but after a few moments Jens sank beneath the surface and slipped out of view. Long fell through to his waist trying to retrieve the kayak and Springfield rifle, but the kayak soon bubbled under, taking the rifle with it. As the kayak went down, Long could see a tear in its sealskin bottom, and he figured Jens must have torn a hole in it while pushing it across the ice. Long managed to wrest himself up onto solid ice. He backed carefully away from the edge and began a slow, heavy-hearted walk back to Camp Clay.

Long returned to the hut that afternoon bearing the sad news. The loss of Jens Edward was felt by everyone. They had nicknamed him "Little Man" for his diminutive stature, but Greely noted his "great heart, unwavering truthfulness and integrity." Greely had shaken hands with the indefatigable hunter just hours before, and he reminisced with the men for a long time about him, remembering his happy, singsong voice, his constant whistling and laughter. Greely also recalled, with grim irony, that back at Fort Conger, Jens told Greely that his own father had drowned in his kayak while hunting at his home in Greenland. They had all lost a true and faithful friend, as well as their only kayak and the best remaining hunting rifle.

⁓⁓⁓

During the first week of May, Brainard was at the shrimping grounds testing out a new tool he had constructed. He had attached iron barrel hoops onto the end to fashion a sort of rake. Standing near the water's edge at low tide, he reached out and scraped the bottom, dragging in seaweed to supplement the shrimp and what remained of the rations. One day he brought in nearly ten pounds of the kelp. The men liked the chewy saltiness and it added a briny flavor to their broth, but it made them thirsty. Fortunately the warmer spring weather had softened the ice around the hut, and Doctor Pavy had become industrious in chopping it to melt for drinking water. As fuel was running extremely low, men were now collecting tufts of blooming saxifrage to burn, which was working well. Private Henry—who remained considerably stronger than all the others combined, likely a result of having stolen food all winter—made himself useful and gathered large quantities of the saxifrage plants.

On May 3 Greely felt so poorly that he confided to Brainard: "I think I am near my end." Later that day, as Greely sorted through his papers and began writing instructions to Brainard, he heard a commotion and angry voices outside the hut but was too weak to rise and sort out the situation. After a while Bender and Henry entered, with Henry pushing Whisler forward by the collar. Bender reported to Commander Greely that he had just seen Whisler inside the storeroom stealing a large slab of the remaining bacon—the loss of which would have been devastating for the rest, as they were down to just nine days' meat. Whisler admitted the offense but explained that Henry had already broken down the door, and it was open as he was walking by. He said when he saw the bacon sitting there, "he was too ravenous to resist."

Whisler immediately said he would accept any punishment—including death—that Greely and the rest of the party felt appropriate to his crime. But in his defense he pleaded that he was driven by famine and mental weakness, and that "his terrible hunger overcame his principles." Greely accepted his confession, and because it was a first offense, let him off with a stern warning, telling all present: "I believe in his deep repentance."

A few days later a sudden storm blew down on them from the southeast, blasting Cape Sabine with gales and snow for twenty-four hours. Drifting snow completely blocked the entryway, and it took great effort to dig out a clearing. Greely called Brainard to his side and handed him further written instructions in the event of his death. Then, too tired to write any more, he dictated messages to Henrietta Greely and General Hazen, which Brainard wrote down for him.

Later that day, Doctor Pavy became increasingly irritable and erratic. He asked Greely to increase the shrimp rations, which the commander refused to do. Then Pavy began yelling, in English and in French, that Greely had been ignoring his medical reports, and he simply must increase the rations. Greely told him firmly to calm down, as he was inciting the others. But Pavy railed on, animated and appearing violent. Greely told him numerous times to quiet down, until finally he had heard enough and barked back: "If you were not the surgeon of this expedition, I would shoot you!" Private Bender, also now incensed, began screaming at Commander Greely as well. Despite repeated warnings to "shut up," Bender would not. Sensing a mutiny, Greely reached down and grabbed Long's hunting rifle and leveled it—first at Bender and then at Pavy. Brainard moved in quickly and seized the gun from Greely, but kept it pointed at Bender and told him to get in his sleeping bag and be quiet, which Bender did. Pavy calmed down too, and after a tense and nearly fatal few minutes, the dispute was over. But it was clear to everyone that Greely's orders were to be followed, and that he would not hesitate to enforce them.

Despite all their efforts, the party's decline—with the notable exception of Henry—had become widespread. Brainard returned from shrimping one afternoon with blood gushing from his nostrils, with no explanation for the spontaneous hemorrhage. The next day, after climbing to the high bluff to stare longingly at the now ice-free Smith Sound, Brainard was blown to the ground by a gust of wind. Later that afternoon Ellis returned from collecting shrubs and crumpled in the entryway from exhaustion. But the sun returned, and the men once again crawled their way out of the hut and "basked in the sunshine like seals," the warmth providing some small comfort in their suffering.

On May 15 at dinner, the men sat with the last of their provisions, their spoons scraping the bottoms of their metal bowls. The meal was "twelve and a half ounces of bacon and tallow to each man" that they could spread out over two days if they wished. Some sprinkled green saxifrage buds into their stew for flavor. Brainard told everyone that from then on they would be eating only shrimp and kelp unless game could be shot.

A few days later at four in the morning Shorty Frederick burst into the hut and woke everyone up, whispering frantically: "Bear outside!" Private Long got up and hustled outside as fast as he could, with Shorty right behind him. Brainard grabbed the shotgun and followed them, but after an hour's pursuit he turned back, no longer able to keep up. All the men waited silently in the hut, praying for another miracle. Shorty returned at ten, shaking his head. He had never gotten close enough for a shot, but Long had kept going after the bear. While everyone waited for Long, Pvt. William Ellis "quietly breathed his last," but all remained focused on Long and the bear. Said Brainard: "Death in our midst has ceased to rouse our emotions."

An hour later Long entered the hut and slumped down, despondent and trembling with exhaustion. Shorty kept mumbling and berating himself for the lost opportunity. When he had first spotted the bear, it was only a few feet away, but he had been chopping ice to melt, and did not have a gun. There was a long silence among the men, who had dreamed of the dense flavor of fresh bear meat, the smell of fat cooking, the dark blood thickening and enriching their stews. No one said anything, but most knew that might have been their last best chance for survival.

To supplement the saxifrage, Doctor Pavy had also begun using a knife to scrape black lichen from rocks. He called it *tripe des roches*, or "rock tripe," and believed that it, as well as the green buds of the saxifrage, would provide some much-needed nutrients. Greely, now too weak to walk for any extended period, would also scuffle on his hands and knees fifty or sixty yards outside the hut in the sun and gather lichen and saxifrage, adding them to a bucket.

Some of the men decided to erect the party's old tent up on the hill near Cemetery Ridge, on a level spot about three hundred yards from the hut, because the location received constant sunlight, offering warmth as well as some emotional solace. The hut had also begun to leak since they had been stripping the wooden whaleboat roof for fuel, and most of the men were waking up soaked every morning, adding to their wretched state. It took five of the men many hours to set up the tent and haul up a few of the heavy sleeping bags and blankets. It was decided that the weakest of the men would move up into the tent where the warmth might sustain them and make them more comfortable. Sergeant Israel made it halfway from the hut to the tent on his own before needing assistance from others. Elison, with his amputated feet, had to be dragged on a mattress. Greely made it all the way to the tent on his own, but was distraught to discover that in transit he had broken the barometer. He had intended to make observations and take readings until the very end.

Late in the afternoon Sgt. David Ralston, who had been working hard cutting up the wooden sledge to use as fuel, became dizzy and nauseated and returned to the hut. Greely tipped Ralston's head back and poured him some rum, and Ralston felt better for a time. Ralston clutched handfuls of raw saxifrage, stuffing bits into his mouth and chewing on them languorously, humming and singing songs between mouthfuls. By dinner he was semiconscious and too weak to feed himself, and Greely held him in his arms and spoon-fed him from his own rations of shrimp stew, but it was no use. Ralston died before midnight in Greely's arms. Greely read burial rites over his body, "and ordered that he be buried in the ice foot northwest of camp if the party were unable to haul him up to Cemetery Ridge," which was becoming too difficult for even the strongest among them.

Early the next morning, May 24, before breakfast, Brainard and others managed to bury Ralston partway up the hill toward Cemetery Ridge. By noon Greely found Whisler just outside the tent, lying on the ground. He begged the commander's forgiveness for stealing bacon some weeks before, then fell unconscious and died. Once more Greely lowered his head and read the Episcopal service over a dead comrade. Whisler was left where he died until, some days later, a few men managed to bury him under a thin layer of gravel.

On May 27 Sgt. Edward Israel, the expedition's astronomer and the youngest of the group, was unable to rise from his sleeping bag inside the tent. Just three years before, Israel had been a promising astronomer who had recently graduated from the University of Michigan, when one of his professors recommended him to Greely. The commander had long looked upon him in a paternal way. Israel asked for rum, and Greely helped to prop him up and spooned a little rum into his mouth. Between sips Israel spoke quietly of his home and his childhood days, and Greely saw a look of contentment and acceptance in his eyes just before he passed away. He had been universally admired by the entire party, but his death struck Greely the hardest: "His death affected me seriously," said the commander, "as his cheerful and hopeful words during the long months he was my bag companion did much to relieve my overtaxed brain."

In the last week alone, four more of the men had died, bringing the total who had perished to eleven. Fourteen of the once proud and vigorous Lady Franklin Bay Expedition remained, eking out life by eating saxifrage blossoms, seaweed, and shrimp. Commander Greely's trembling hand could barely hold his pen as he scrawled in his journal: "We have done all we can to help ourselves and shall ever struggle on, but it drives me almost insane to face the future. It is not the end that affrights one, but the road to be traveled to reach that goal. To die is easy, very easy; it is only hard to strive, to endure, to live."

Brainard was now cutting strips of sealskin from clothing and boot soles and adding these to the stews to substitute for meat, making a thick, gelatinous gruel. On one of the last days of May 1884, Brainard noticed Private Bender crawling around on a bare slope partway up Cemetery Ridge, just outside the tent, and he staggered over to investigate. As Brainard leaned down, he saw that Bender was picking caterpillars from the ground and popping them in his mouth. He chewed slowly, swallowed, and looked up at Brainard: "This is too much meat to lose," he said, then crawled away, hunting for more.

32

From the Crow's Nest

Commander Schley gripped the rope ladder and climbed the 130 feet toward the crow's nest of the *Thetis*. Biting wind cut through his thick woolen topcoat and blistered his face and ears as he ascended. At the top he pushed upward on the wooden trapdoor, its heavy iron hinges squeaking, and clambered up into the crow's nest, "a large barrel with the upper head knocked out, attached to the mainmast" by stout iron bands. Standing upright, he kicked the trapdoor shut, rested his telescope on the iron edge of the barrel, and fixed his gaze on the ice pack.

It was May 24, 1884, and Schley was ready to commit his ship to the dangerous ice pack of upper Davis Strait, just below Melville Bay. From his vantage point high above the deck, Schley could see ten to fifteen miles ahead, noting that "the ice fields stretched out in a wide panorama, every lead and crack marked out like the lines on a map." He contemplated the best lead to take, his hand holding one of three twine lines connecting to the bellpull, by which he would signal the helmsman. Each line was connected to a different-colored lead cylinder that was plainly visible to the quartermaster—one was green, one red, and one green and red. Ensign Harlow had devised a convenient code of communication that allowed Commander Schley to steer the ship from the crow's nest without yelling from above: "A pull on the green meant 'starboard,' on the red, 'port,' and on the green and red, 'steady.' Two pulls meant 'hard starboard,' or 'hard port,'" as required.

It had taken nearly two weeks to arrive at this point. Working slowly through dense fog and blinding snowstorms, the *Thetis* and the coal freighter *Loch Garry* had arrived at Disko Island on May 12, ten days after leaving St. John's. Foul weather and an ice-choked harbor had pinned them there for two days. Schley had used this time to reacquaint his men with fire drills and maneuvers for abandoning ship, and to take on coal from the *Loch Garry*, which he ordered to remain at Disko Island until the winds and ice conditions improved considerably.

Now Commander Schley stood high above the *Thetis*, surveying the pack and looking for "stringy black lines" suggesting water leads between the ice floes that offered a pathway through the churning labyrinth. Schley also looked hopefully for "water blinks," dark clouds or spots on the horizon "formed by ascending mists which gather in clouds and hang over pools of water." The opposite of these were "ice blinks," flickering bands of light just over the horizon caused by reflection off the ice. Areas around ice blinks he must avoid. After careful consideration Schley made his decision. He rang the signal bell, and the *Thetis* steamed north toward Upernavik.

For the next five days Commander Schley remained almost constantly in the crow's nest, sometimes spending nearly twenty-four hours at a time aloft, drinking only water and eating hardtack and canned meats. Avoiding giant icebergs protruding two hundred feet above the water, he sought every available lead. When these closed off, he reversed and charged full speed ahead, ramming the prow of the ship through the ice, the shock shuddering through the ship's timbers and jolting everyone on board. Sometimes the *Thetis* became nearly nipped, and Schley sent men down onto the ice to bore deep holes with their ice augers, place gunpowder torpedoes, and explode them, allowing the ship to continue ramming its way forward. One morning they were anchored to what Schley believed to be a grounded iceberg, but without warning the berg "pivoted on its center and swung round with the current." The crewmen cast off lines, but the *Thetis* was thrust into the fast-moving current and its bow slammed into the sharp walls of the careening iceberg, "carrying away a small part of her headgear and mutilating the figure-head."

Working constantly in this way, thrusting through and exploding ice pans and floes, by May 29 Schley had successfully guided the *Thetis* into harbor at Upernavik. Schley carefully descended the slippery rope ladder from the crow's nest, the rungs, mast, and rigging all coated with rime. It had been harrowing, and according to Schley, "Poor *Thetis* lost an arm and part of her nose, her dress was considerably torn away, her body was split in two," and when she finally made anchor she was in a "dilapidated state." Schley saw the *Bear* and the bounty-hunting whalers the *Polynia*, the *Tribune*, and the *Nova Zembla* already at harbor. Schley set men to work on repairs of the *Thetis*. Immediately on Schley's arrival, Lieutenant Emory, commanding the *Bear*, boarded the *Thetis* to discuss plans. Emory informed Schley that while ashore at Upernavik, he had heard a rumor that five white men had been seen by native Etah in the vicinity of Cape York, so Schley decided they should depart as soon as the ships were made ready.

From the deck some hours later, Schley watched as five more whalers—the *Arctic*, the *Wolf*, the *Aurora*, the *Cornwallis*, and the *Narwhal*—pulled into harbor. Schley assessed these well-seasoned vessels. He fully understood that the captains of these whaling steamers had much greater experience in these ever-changing, ice-filled waters than he did; he in fact had never been here before. He also knew that the crossing he was about to attempt would be arduous and potentially disastrous. Much later in the season, in 1881 the *Proteus* had made the passage of Melville Bay in a record thirty-six hours. In 1882 the *Neptune* had crossed in eighty hours; and in 1883 Garlington had steered the *Proteus* through in seventy-two hours. But Schley would be probing these waters a month earlier, in June, and it was impossible to predict how long it might take, or whether this early he could make it through at all.

But Schley was bold, proud, and deeply driven to rescue Greely for the pride of the navy and for the glory of his country. His ships were much better reinforced for ramming than were the whalers. He would do whatever he must, "seizing every opening and lead and fighting for every inch of progress." Schley gave Emory orders that they would move north that afternoon, and it was against these eight bounty-hunting whaling vessels that the *Thetis* and the *Bear* "were to contest the honors of the passage of Melville Bay."

∾∾∾

At Camp Clay, on the barren shores of Cape Sabine, Greely and his men clung desperately to life. Sergeant Brainard continued his daily crossings of Cemetery Ridge to the shrimping grounds, passing by the burial mounds of his dead comrades. The winds that scoured the ridge had blown away the thin layer of scree they had managed to dig to cover the dead, and one day Brainard noticed Sergeant Linn's feet "protruding from the gravel heaped over his body," but he had not the strength to cover him with any more.

On June 1, as Brainard staggered up the hill, his eye caught a glint of reflection from the buttons on Lieutenant Lockwood's military coat, noting "the brass buttons worn bright by the flying gravel, protruding through the scant covering of earth." He mused: "At first these dazzling buttons awakened thoughts of those bright days at Fort Conger," but now Brainard simply wondered how long it would be before he would join Lockwood and the others on that awful, wind-shorn slope. When he returned from shrimping with a paltry few pounds for the evening stew, he struck a fire and cut sealskin from boots and clothes and charred these over the dried saxifrage coals. He parceled out the small strips of burned skin and the men chewed greedily on them, relishing the cinder-burned pieces as if they were tender cuts of grilled beef.

A few of the remaining fourteen men had mustered the strength to construct a canvas-covered lean-to next to the tent, so by now all had abandoned the hut completely and slept together in the tent and lean-to on the hill near Cemetery Ridge. They had at first moved up on the hill because the location received more sun. But though no one said it out loud, it also offered closer proximity to the burial ground and greater ease in burying their dead. A sudden storm blew in and dumped a foot of wet snow on the hut and tent. When the skies cleared and the temperatures rose, the snow melted, soaking their bags and wetting the men to the skin.

Through all the wretched hardship, Commander Greely strove to maintain morale and discipline. He ordered Brainard to lock all the shrimp and sealskin in the storehouse and keep a close watch on Private Henry. Also, it had come to Greely's attention that Doctor Pavy had been removing and hoarding quantities of medicine from the stores, and refusing to issue iron, and Dover's Powders—used for fevers—to some of the men. Greely suspected that Pavy was keeping certain medicines—like opium—for himself, and the commander firmly ordered Pavy to return the medicines to their proper place, which the doctor did after a heated argument.

Most of the men had grown to deeply appreciate Commander Greely and his selflessness. When they had begun their retreat from Fort Conger, some had been concerned by his early confusion and indecisiveness directing the boats, as he was not nautically trained. Others had been critical of his harsh, unyielding, and even bullheaded discipline. But as time had gone on, Greely had changed, becoming more democratic and equitable, permitting all the men their say in most major decisions. Biederbick, the hospital steward, had watched Greely closely, noting especially his tender treatment of the dying men. He was impressed and greatly moved by Greely's transformation and by his leadership: "He has shown himself to be a man of more force of character and in every way greater than I believed him to be," Biederbick wrote in his journal, adding: "During the whole winter Lieutenant Greely has done everything for us that one could do to keep us up and alive. I am very sorry not to have sooner found out his full worth."

Greely continued to be attentive to the weakest among them, and on the morning of June 1, he could see that Lieutenant Kislingbury was near his end; he had begun speaking incoherently, then humming a tune and asking for water. Although their relationship had been fraught and contentious, Greely felt a strong connection to the man. Kislingbury had been the only one of the expedition whom the commander had personally known prior to their departure for the Arctic. Greely had supervised Kislingbury in 1875 building telegraph lines across the plains of the Southwest and remembered him during that time as "an active, hardworking officer who had acquired an excellent reputation for frontier and Indian service." Kislingbury had practically begged Greely to allow him to come on the expedition, hoping his time in the Arctic would somehow allow him to escape, or at least salve, his depression and grief after having recently lost two wives and a sister in a span of just three years.

Now Greely went to Kislingbury's bag and spoke quietly with him for a short time, trying to calm him and ease his burden. He praised Kislingbury's excellence as a hunter and for putting the physical needs of others before himself. Sometime later, Kislingbury sat bolt upright, got halfway out of his sleeping bag, and began to sing the Doxology, his voice thin and feeble but the words rising clear and melodious even above the wind billowing the tent: "Praise God, from whom all blessings flow; Praise Him, all creatures here below." The group, recalling how Kislingbury had led them in songs during their joyful first Christmas in the Arctic at Fort Conger, remained silent until he finished singing. Then he leaned back into his bag, fell unconscious, and, observed Brainard, "was soon in the embrace of death." Greely read the burial service over him that afternoon, and they moved him outside the tent, to be buried at Cemetery Ridge the next day. Greely had made his peace with Kislingbury, saying: "We were fully reconciled before his death."

Warming winds and fair weather blew in from the southeast, melting snow on the hillsides so that streams began running down and forming pools near the tent. For the first time in many months, at least they would not have to work for fresh water. But this convenience could hardly reverse the extended malnutrition the men had endured. Nearly all of them now believed they were going to die, and had written their wills. Private Connell asked Commander Greely to promise to send his diary to his former military commander as a token of respect. Gardiner requested that his journal be given to his wife, Minnie, whom he had married just two months before departing for the Arctic. Doctor Pavy, showing intermittent signs of delirium and incoherence, also asked that his writings be delivered to his wife. Pavy had begun prescribing random medicines for the men as well as for himself—which gave both Biederbick and Greely concern. Elison desired that his amputated "arms and legs should go to the Army Medical Museum in the interest of science."

Commander Greely, too, experienced episodes of deep doubt and despair. On June 2 he remembered that it was his daughter Antoinette's birthday. A few days before, Greely had written a letter to Henrietta, conceding: "We but await the grave. . . . Do not wear mourning for me. How happy we were four years ago at the Aberdeen Hotel with Antoinette. God bless her and you and Adola."

Private Henry, much healthier and huskier than the rest, still held out hope, writing in his journal with a clarity and optimism that confirmed he was getting more nourishment than the others. "The majority of us," he wrote, "have given up all hopes of seeing our friends again, but a few still have a chance, after the conclusion of this terrible tragedy, to be welcomed with universal acclamation as worthy frontiersmen . . . men who have made themselves immortal by a splendid victory." The "splendid victory" he referred to was their expedition's collective achievement of Farthest North, something in which they all took great pride.

On June 3, during the middle of the night, Brainard, sleeping next to Corporal Nicholas Salor, woke to hear Salor muttering unintelligibly, then listened to him taking his last few shallow breaths. Brainard roused the others to tell them of Salor's passing but remained next to the corpse of his dead companion. Said Brainard: "I went to sleep with his remains and did not awake until breakfast was announced at 9 AM." They buried Salor down at the shoreline, it being downhill from the tent and easier to manage. "Not feeling strong enough to make a grave for Salor in the gravelly soil on Cemetery Ridge," said Brainard, "we placed his remains where they will be inaccessible to the wild animals—in the tidal crack." The Smith Sound beyond lay calm and devoid of ice, "the surface as smooth as a mirror." "How easily," thought Brainard as he turned away from his dead friend, "we could be reached by a relief vessel."

During the last week Long had remained out hunting, and although he had seen an increase in seabirds, sighting eider ducks and a very large guillemot, he had bagged only two dovekies, which Greely ordered to be divided among the hunters, whose strength was needed if any of the men were to survive. Private Bender—not one of the hunters—was so famished and distraught that he pleaded, with tears streaming down his face, for a morsel of the birds. Greely reluctantly conceded. The warming temperatures brought new green blooms to the hillsides, including "reindeer moss, poppies, saxifrage and grasses" and Brainard paused while returning with five pounds of shrimp to note that "the mosses growing in damp ground are looking quite beautiful."

June 5 dawned clear and warm, and the waters on the sound were once again smooth. Most of the men managed to get outside the tent into the fresh air and forage for plant shoots and buds, which at least improved the taste of the shrimp, seaweed, and sealskin stews. Greely had been informed that Private Henry continued to steal shrimp, and Greely had himself seen Henry skulking about suspiciously, moving with ease back and forth between the abandoned hut—where the storehouse was—and the tent. Brainard reported that he had seen Henry twice take most of the dovekie reserved for him and Long, the shrimper and the hunter. Said Brainard: "He was also detected eating seal skin lashing and seal skin boots from the public stock," adding with grim honesty regarding their plight: "The stealing of old seal skin boots etc. may seem to some a very insignificant affair, but to us such articles mean life."

Greely accosted Henry and asked him if it was true. Was he indeed continuing to steal from the group? Henry boldly admitted to the act, but he looked his commander in the eye and "promised to deal fairly in the future." The commander spoke forcefully to Henry, stating unequivocally that should it happen again, he would take "severe action" and the private "would come to grief."

Greely doubted that Henry would stop his thieving. That night, for the survival of the rest of the party, the commander finally felt compelled to act. He sat in his bag and wrote the following order:

NEAR CAPE SABINE, JUNE 5TH, 1884.

To Sergeants Brainard, Frederick and Long: Private Henry having been repeatedly guilty of stealing the provisions of this party which is now perishing slowly by starvation, has so far been condoned and pardoned. It is, however, imperatively ordered that if this man be detected either eating food of any kind not issued him regularly, or making caches, or appropriating any article of provisions, you will at once shoot him and report the matter to me. Any other course would be a fatal leniency, the man being able to overpower any two of our present force.

A. W. Greely,
Lieutenant Fifth Cavalry, U.S.A. and Assistant
Commanding Lady Franklin Bay Expedition

Henry broke his promise within a day. At breakfast Shorty Frederick thought he saw Henry taking shrimps out of the communal stewpot, but rather than shoot him on the spot inside the tent, he reported it to his commander. Greely surveilled Henry carefully for the rest of the morning, observing him as he twice strode down to the hut, was gone for some time, and then returned. On Henry's second trip back to the tent, Greely confronted him and demanded to know what he had been doing down near the storehouse and hut, and what items he had with him. Henry waited a moment, then boldly admitted that he had taken some sealskin thongs, which were under his coat, and he had also hidden a bundle of sealskin nearby.

Greely dismissed Henry, then turned away in disgust and immediately went to the tent, where, his hands trembling with fury and fatigue, he penned an overriding order, to be carried out immediately:

NEAR CAPE SABINE, JUNE 6TH, 1884.

Sergeants Brainard, Long and Frederick: Notwithstanding promises given by Private C. B. Henry yesterday he has since acknowledged to me having tampered with seal thongs, if not other food at the old camp. This pertinacity and audacity is the destruction of this party if not at once ended. Private Henry will be shot today, all care being taken to prevent his injuring anyone as his physical strength is greater than that of any two men. Decide the manner of death by two ball and one blank cartridge. This order is imperative *and* absolutely necessary *for* any chance of life.

A. W. GREELY,

First Lieutenant Fifth Cavalry, U. S. A., and Assistant, Commanding L. F. B. Expedition

When Brainard returned that afternoon after seven hours of shrimping and raking for seaweed, Greely handed his sergeant the new order. Brainard read it quietly and then passed it to Shorty. Brainard and Shorty left the tent and had a brief, hushed discussion just outside. They then departed in the direction of Sergeant Long's usual return route from hunting. Greely opened the tent flap and watched until he saw Long returning. Long was intercepted by

Brainard and Shorty, and the three of them stood together a few hundred yards away from the tent. For some time Greely watched them as they engaged in what appeared to be an animated discussion, likely about how best to carry out his order. He could not hear them but viewed them intently. After a few minutes the three men split up, two heading down the hill toward the stone hut and storehouse, the other taking a different route, as if to flank them.

At 2:00 p.m. on June 6, two gun shots rang out, their percussive reports echoing off the granite slopes of Cemetery Ridge and heard clearly by Greely and those in the tent. Not long afterward Greely and the men heard the scuff of footfalls nearing, and Sergeants Brainard, Frederick, and Long entered the tent to report that the order had been dutifully carried out and they had left Henry where he lay. Greely called all the men together and had Biederbick read aloud the official order to execute Henry. Brainard reported that "all were unanimous in the opinion that no other course could have been pursued," and Greely corroborated this, saying: "Everyone, without exception, acknowledged that Henry's fate was merited."*

Greely ordered an immediate search of Henry's personal effects and much was discovered, including twelve pounds of sealskin strips, a pair of sealskin boots that Commander Greely had given to Sergeant Long for hunting just two days before, and various scientific instruments that Greely had left behind at Fort Conger. In one of Henry's pockets they found Greely's personal and "valuable silver chronograph."

Later that afternoon a day already marred by dishonor and death got worse. At 5:45 p.m. Pvt. Jacob Bender died suddenly. Doctor Pavy died just fifteen minutes later. Biederbick divulged to Greely that the day before, he had seen Doctor Pavy drinking from bottles in the medicine chest, compelling Greely to conclude that Pavy's death had been "evidently hastened by the narcotics, as by all accounts he had dosed himself continually."

---

* There are various and conflicting versions of the exact process of Private Henry's execution and of the guns used. See Glenn M. Stein, "An Arctic Execution: Private Charles B. Henry of the United States Lady Franklin Bay Expedition, 1881–84," *Arctic* 64, no. 4 (December 2011): 399–412. Of the execution, Brainard said that "the three of us took an oath before the event never to tell on this earth who fired the shots . . . They [Shorty and Long] never told who shot Henry and I never will." (Brainard, *Outpost of the Lost,* 292)

Early the next morning Brainard, Frederick, Biederbick, and Long, who were now doing almost all the work, "dressed the bodies of Dr. Pavy and Bender" and dragged them a short distance from the tent. As always, Greely read the burial service over his fallen men, and said some words. He praised Private Bender's ingenuity and craftsmanship, especially his metalwork, and his ability to fabricate just about anything from "scanty material." Greely lauded Doctor Pavy's great medical skill throughout the expedition, and particularly at Camp Clay, where he exhibited "restless energy" and "physical exertions" on behalf of the party. After the service it was determined that when and if some men had strength enough, Pavy and Bender would be buried either on Cemetery Ridge or down below at the ice foot, with Greely suggesting "probably the latter."

The Lady Franklin Bay Expedition was now down to nine members. Fourteen of their dead lay in various states around Camp Clay, the earliest to perish properly buried and mounded with earth, the more recently deceased only partially covered by coarse gravel and scree, and other corpses deposited between large rocks and ice walls at the tidal crack. The last few lay unburied just near the tent. As the day warmed, flies began hovering in countless numbers around the tent and about the growing number of bodies strewn and heaped nearby, the insects lighting in swarms upon the carnage, both the dead and the nearly dead.

33

A Race against Whalers and Time

Late on the afternoon of May 29, 1884, Cdr. Winfield Schley made way north aboard the *Thetis* out of Upernavik, with the *Bear* following in its wake. Commander Schley was confident and possessed with purpose, but he also knew that he was embarking on an unprecedented endeavor, for no ship had ever successfully crossed the waters of Melville Bay so early in the season.

After four hours of slow steaming, the *Thetis*, the *Bear*, and all eight of the whalers landed at Kingitok, an Eskimo outpost and former Danish trading post, where there were a handful of Eskimo huts and an old abandoned storehouse. Poor ice conditions to the north kept all the ships, the relief vessels and the whalers, at Kingitok for two days. Schley used the time to get to know some of the captains of the famous Scots whalers. He was impressed by these famous "ice kings of the Dundee fleet, with their bronzed faces and their hearty laughs, and their broad Scotch accents." The whaling captains were tough and hardened men, but generous and forthcoming with information about the northern waters they knew so well, and Schley could see that they took "keen enjoyment in their difficult and dangerous work."

After two days of waiting, a squall blew from the southwest and broke up the harbor ice. All the captains stoked their steam engines and headed for leads that began to open to the north and west. The race to rescue Greely was on. But that afternoon, just four hours out, the *Thetis* came to a wall of impassable ice and tied up to wait. Right behind, Lieutenant Emory was guiding the *Bear* through a tight lead close to shore, running between two spire icebergs rising forty feet out of the water. Easing through, Emory and his men felt a massive jolt, and the ship shuddered violently but kept moving. Emory, worried that the *Bear* might be seriously damaged, found safe harbor in the lee of an off-shore island and anchored.

Emory's engineer used their "water telescope," an invention made by whalers, to examine the damage. They lowered the device—a sort of inverted periscope "made of ordinary stove piping, with a glass fitted in the lower end to exclude water"—two or three feet below the surface and, peering into it, could see the ship's hull. Emory was relieved to learn that the damage was not as severe as he had believed. Some sheathing was gone, but they were able to locate a leak that was pouring in at "seven inches per hour," patch it, and move on.

Schley once again climbed up to the crow's nest of the *Thetis*, and when leads opened, he headed for them, with the *Bear* following in his wake. The leads wove and coursed in serpentine pathways, a complex maze of water and ice, islands and icebergs. For the next two days the *Thetis* and the *Bear* plowed slowly north, with the whaling ships close behind, sometimes finding their own leads but often following Schley.

On June 4 Schley had reached the tiny island of Tassuisak, the northern-most Danish settlement. Ice blocked further progress, and Schley anchored here for a few hours until he saw a lead ahead, open for several miles. He cast off lines and pushed full steam, rushing to try to make it through. But soon the lane narrowed, and Schley attempted to ram the point of the ice, "but not having enough room to strike fairly, she glanced off, and was driven into the sharp point of the crack. At that moment, the ice closed, and she was held fast in a nip." The *Bear* was dead astern, and though it was not beset, the lane was too narrow for it to turn around. Schley had men run hawsers from the stern of the *Thetis* to the bow of the *Bear*, and "both vessels reversed their engines and put on a full head of steam, but the *Thetis*, driven into the crack like a wedge between the fibers of a tree, would not budge an inch." Two hawsers, one of six-inch rope and another of three-inch steel, were sheared and then broken attempting to pull the *Thetis* out of the nip.

The situation had now become dangerous, and Schley must certainly have thought about the *Proteus* disaster as ice encroached around the *Thetis* "and crushed up against her side, raising her bow three or four feet." Commander Schley dispatched men down onto the ice ahead of the ship. They bored holes through two layers of ice and planted five gunpowder torpedoes six feet deep at intervals of fifteen feet. On detonation the ice ahead exploded into the air and fractured in lateral cracks, and Schley saw that the torpedoes had created a rift all the way to open water beyond. But still the ship was unable to move.

Schley next exploded a gunpowder torpedo in the ice off the port bow, and "an hour later, five gun cotton and six gun powder torpedoes were exploded off the starboard bow and beam." These blew large holes in the ice, creating new fissures. They also loosened some of the ice directly thrusting against the side of the ship, easing the dangerous, pinching pressure. By good fortune, while Schley was detonating the torpedoes, the moving pack shifted, and the *Thetis* slipped free of the nip. Schley checked for damage to the hull, and finding none, proceeded to reverse and then ram the ice at full speed repeatedly until the ship had successfully bashed its way into "a narrow stream of open water beyond, followed by the *Bear*." It had been a very close call, but for the moment, at least, they were safe and still moving forward.

For the next two days the *Thetis,* the *Bear,* and the eight whalers picked their way northward, contending for position. Sometimes Schley waved the *Bear* on ahead, letting it lead. Just south of the Duck Islands, the far "outpost for advance through the much-dreaded Melville Bay," a series of navigable lanes opened ahead, and the ships broke fast for them under full steam. Schley stood in the crow's nest and marveled at the beauty of the ice gleaming and glittering for miles in every direction. The ships were close enough for the captains to hail one another from their crow's nests as they wove through tortuous water lanes and passed beneath looming icebergs. They reached the Duck Islands on June 7 and anchored there to assess the pack ahead.

Schley sent a man to the summit of the highest hill, and he returned with a grim report: "The vast sea of ice lay unbroken to the north and west, and it

seemed as if it would never break up." Late that evening, fog descended and a
storm blew in, enveloping the *Thetis* and the *Bear* in mist and wet snow. Schley
retired to his cabin to rest. He had been in the freezing crow's next almost constantly for the last two days. Now, though he knew that Commander Greely
must be in terrible condition if he was even alive, all Schley could do was wait.

∽∽∽

On the morning of June 7, after they had consumed a breakfast of a measly few
ounces of shrimp stew, all the men at Camp Clay took to the hillsides to collect
saxifrage, rock lichen, and reindeer moss. Bumblebees buzzed about, signaling the pending arrival of Arctic summer. Brainard gathered all the remaining
sealskin from the abandoned hut and brought it to the tent. Schneider bent to
a low fire, burning the hair off sealskin clothing, which he cut into strips for
the evening meals. Shorty Frederick helped Biederbick to nurse Gardiner and
Schneider, the sickest among them.

That night they ate "a stew composed of a pair of boot soles, a handful of
reindeer moss, and a few rock lichens." The men were now relishing the plant
buds, which they found "sweet and palatable." After dinner Schneider told the
others that in the last few weeks, Henry and Bender had been eating large
amounts of sealskin clothing after everyone else had fallen asleep. They talked
of Henry's thieving, and Greely reminded the men that they must show courage and restraint for the good of the party. He understood as well as any of
them "the great temptation of appropriating a morsel of food to satisfy the terrible and continuous gnawing at our vitals." But they must not succumb to the
temptation.

For the next few days the men continued to forage for food, some stagger-
ing slowly on foot, others dragging themselves on their hands and knees. A few
of them had resorted to eating old ptarmigan droppings, worms, and even, said
Brainard, bits of hardtack found down at the abandoned hut which were "occasionally exposed through the melting snow, and picked from heaps of the
vilest filth and eaten with relish."

Long kept hunting, Brainard continued shrimping, and Frederick did the
cooking. Long and Brainard made a laborious trip down to the winter hut and,

with great difficulty, brought back all the wood they could find there to use for fuel. One day, while out gathering lichens—which the men now nicknamed "Arctic mushrooms"—Biederbick found a small cache of bear meat hidden between some rocks near the tent. Everyone agreed that Henry must have stashed it there. Although there was little of it, they were glad of the find, and they savored the flavor of deep red meat for the first time in many months.

On June 9 the strongest of the men dragged the bodies of Doctor Pavy and Bender—who had been lying unburied just outside the tent for three days—down to the tidal crack. They committed Bender there in the morning, and in the evening, noted Brainard: "Dr. Pavy was plunged into the same crystal grave." Staring out at the open water of the Smith Sound, Brainard reflected on their prospects: "If we are to be saved at all, the vessel which is to find us will have to make haste. Very few days remain to us." Greely spent six hours outside the hut gathering about a quart of rock lichen, and he, too, felt the weight of what was to come: "This constant expectancy of death," he wrote, "at first a sharp, dreadful trial, gradually passed into a vague and deadening feeling, which nevertheless was a terrible mental strain." During the day Long had been fortunate to bag a dovekie on his thirty-second birthday. The dovekie was added to Long and Brainard's stew, and Greely issued Long a spoonful of brandy as a celebratory reward.

On June 12 Brainard discovered a new shrimping ground nearer to the tent, which required less energy to get to and was fairly productive. He managed to bring in two pounds. Before noon Sgt. Hampden Gardiner began babbling dreamily. He crawled partway out of his bag and, holding two pictures in his hands and staring at them, then collapsed to the ground, unconscious. Thinking him dead, the men dragged him outside the tent. Sometime later Gardiner revived, and the men rolled him onto a soft buffalo robe to comfort him. "For hours," remarked Brainard, "he held a portrait of his wife and mother in his hand, gazing fondly on their faces." Finally he whispered quietly: "Mother, wife," and died. "When his spirit had passed into another world," said Brainard, "his skeleton fingers still clutched the pictures of those he had loved." That evening Brainard walked down to a rocky point near the old winter hut and managed to climb to its top, placing a distress flag—a few pieces of tattered undergarments tied to a broken oar—facing the sea, where he hoped it might be seen from some distance.

There was now little else Greely and his men could do but scavenge for food, wait, hope, and pray. Greely stared expectantly at the Smith Sound, for he vaguely remembered that this was around the time that the earliest whalers usually reached the northern waters. On June 13 Greely noted that Biederbick's term of service had expired, and, as the expedition remained a military command, Greely issued him a "written certificate of discharge." The next day Biederbick requested and was reinstated as "a hospital steward of the first class." The dutiful steward continued to dress Elison's wounds every other day, and to assist Schneider, with help from Brainard and Long. Schneider had become too weak even to sit up on his own, so the others propped him up so that he could write in his diary.

The next day Long and Brainard mustered the strength to drag Gardiner down to the tidal crack during a snow squall, "the party not being strong enough to dig a grave or carry him to the ridge through the snow." Brainard noticed that high winds had knocked down his distress flag. That night for dinner Greely took out his knife and sliced off the oil-tanned hide covering of his sleeping bag and distributed it among the men. He also offered up his "sealskin jumper, which had been reserved for shrimp bait." Late in the evening Brainard fought his way through the storm and replaced the distress flag, which might be their salvation.

The long days of continual sunlight were slow and monotonous, the tedium preying on everyone's mind. Long could see numerous walruses and seals swimming in the sound, but could not get close enough for a shot, and even if he could, he had no boat or kayak to try to retrieve one. On the fifteenth Schneider pleaded for Biederbick to issue him opium pills so that he might die immediately, but neither Biederbick nor anyone else would give them to him. Connell suddenly made the outrageous claim that he wished to abandon the rest of the group and go live alone, fending for himself. He became "quite abusive and used profanity" toward Greely. Brainard chastised Connell for being selfish, as did a few of the others, saying that as difficult as things were, they simply must remain united. Greely forgave Connell, reasoning that "all are weak and much discouraged. I do not know how we live, except on our hopes and expectations of a ship."

Having used the last of their English tea, they were now steeping saxifrage buds and leaves in tepid water and trying to drink that as a substitute, but not all could swallow the liquid. When outside, those who could still walk stumbled about like ghouls, sometimes tripping over the barely covered bodies of the dead. Connell, now resigned to staying with the group, remarked that his vision was dimming and blurring. Brainard and Long sliced sealskin covering from their sleeping bags and parceled the strips evenly among the men. Schneider was too weak to cut his strips into bite-size pieces, so Commander Greely did it for him. It was the last of the skin material at Camp Clay that could be eaten. Brainard observed: "The sense of hunger seems to have disappeared. We eat now simply to preserve life."

The conditions inside the tent were fetid and dreadful. None of them had bathed since leaving Fort Conger eleven months before. On the morning of June 18 Schneider "was very weak and out of his head, and later became unconscious." He lay in his bag all day, barely breathing, and died at six o'clock, three years from the day he had signed on with the expedition. Greely read rites and recalled Schneider's excellence in training the dogs at Fort Conger and praised his contributions to the scientific work. Brainard remembered his violin playing. Among Schneider's effects they found a confession, written a few days before he died: "Although I stand accused of doing dishonest things here lately, I herewith, as a dying man, can say that the only dishonest thing which I have done is to have eaten my own seal skin boots and the part of my pants."

There now remained just seven men.

On the morning of June 20 Greely awoke and began fumbling through his box of papers and articles. He realized it was his sixth wedding anniversary. Some days before, he had taken off his ring and tucked it safely among his personal effects while getting his final affairs in order. Though he had little feeling in his worn and swollen hands, he managed to pull out the gold band. Shorty Frederick lay next to him, and Greely said to him: "I am putting my wedding ring back on today. I have the feeling it may bring us good fortune, just as it did to me six years ago."

Frederick rose slowly and with tremendous difficulty, owing to the blasting wind, struggled to light a fire. He eventually managed to cook a lukewarm stew of rock lichens and the last remains of Greely's oil-tanned sealskin sleeping bag cover. Biederbick tethered a spoon to Elison's fingerless right hand, so that he might feed himself should the others perish first. Connell was unable to get out of his bag, saying that his legs were "paralyzed from the knee down."

Long forced himself from the tent, picked up his rifle, and went down to the shore where seabirds had been congregating in increasing numbers. It had been more than a week since he had managed to secure one. Two days before, he had killed two eider ducks and two dovekies and reached out for them with a long pole but had watched hopelessly as the ebbing tide carried them out to sea. Hours later he returned, once again with nothing.

Late the next day the wind knocked down the tent's ridge pole, but no one had the strength to set it right, and by evening Greely, Long, and Brainard were being pressed upon and pinned down by heavy, wet canvas. Writing in his journal by the light of the midnight sun, Brainard spoke with flat resignation for the rest of the group: "We are badly broken down and will all go together. We are calmly awaiting relief or death. One or the other must come soon."

The *Thetis* heading north, stopped by ice. *(Courtesy of Naval History and Heritage Command)*

From Schley's crow's nest, the *Bear* navigating leads through the ice. *(Courtesy of Naval History and Heritage Command)*

34

"Did What I Came to Do"

In the early morning hours of June 18 the *Thetis* and the *Bear* sat four miles off Cape York, still hundreds of miles south of Greely and his six barely surviving men. It had taken Schley twenty days to arrive from Upernavik, slow and challenging and dangerous days probing and butting and exploding his way through the ever-shifting ice pack. Of the eight whaling vessels to have started, only the *Aurora* and the *Wolf* were still in the contest, the others having quit and fallen south.

Schley sent Lieutenant Colwell—who knew the region well from the prior year during his daring boat retreat from the sunken *Proteus*—ashore at Cape York to see what he could learn from the local inhabitants about the rumored "five white men" in the vicinity. Colwell went onto the ice with three men, one of whom was an interpreter. They brought along a small dory and a dog sledge team. Colwell crossed the ice for a few miles by sledge, then launched the dory when they met open water and rowed across to more ice, where Colwell spotted fresh sled tracks and followed them. The tracks led to a native seal fisherman, and after a brief exchange through the interpreter, Colwell learned that no white men had been seen or heard from in over a year. He boarded the *Thetis* and gave Schley the bad news.

Schley ordered Lieutenant Emory to take the *Bear*—the faster of the two ships—toward the southwest, and should he find open water, to continue north to Conical Rock, Saunders Island, and Cape Parry, and to stop at the Cary Islands en route, checking for messages left in cairns. If he could, Emory was to proceed as far as Littleton Island and wait there for the *Thetis.*

Capt. James Fairweather of the whaler *Aurora* boarded the *Thetis* and spoke with Schley. For the last three weeks they had contested the confounding ice together, the whalers sometimes taking the lead, at other times closely following the *Thetis* and the *Bear.* The competition to find Greely had been spirited but also collaborative, with all the boats helping one another in the common cause of threading their way through the labyrinthine pack. During their four days detained at the Duck Islands, Schley had gotten to know the whaling captains well, spending a few evenings drinking "hot Scotch whiskey and beer," and he had come to admire these men deeply.

Captain Fairweather told Schley that the *Aurora* and the *Wolf* were going no farther north—they had risked their vessels long enough and were conceding the contest to the U.S. Navy. Fairweather wished Schley the best of luck in his attempt to rescue Greely, for that was their purpose all along. He thrust his powerful hand out to Schley and smiled warmly, then, in his thick Scots accent, said: "Gude bye, Captain. We may live without *fesh* [fish], but those poor fellows up there must have *breed* [bread]. God bless you! It's no use for us to go further." There would be no bounty, but the brave bounty hunters had helped the *Thetis* and the *Bear* get this far, and their efforts, said Schley, would "never be forgotten." The two men wished each other godspeed, and the *Aurora* and the *Wolf* started south for the whaling waters of Lancaster Sound. Watching them sail away, Schley saw the outline of the *Bear* far in the distance, plumes of black smoke smearing the horizon.

At two o'clock in the afternoon on June 19 the pack loosened, and Schley sped north, skirting Cape York, then ramming through the pack past Cape Dudley Digges. Just off Cape Atholl, the *Thetis* came to a formidable ice barrier, but from the crow's nest Schley spotted open water only five hundred yards beyond. He rang the bell for full steam, and they plowed headlong into a narrow crease in the ice. After making about two ships' lengths in, "she found herself stuck fast like a wedge, helpless," unable to move either forward or backward.

Once more Schley employed torpedoes, this time both of cotton powder and gunpowder. Men augered deep holes ahead of the ship, "and on each side abreast of the foremast, a little abaft of the bluff of the bow . . . and as usual, ten or twelve yards away from her side." The men moved away and ignited the torpedoes, the explosions booming across the ice and sending long fractures ahead of the ship, freeing it from the jam. They plowed through and ran on northward, reaching Saunders Island at 2:30 a.m. on June 20, where they set ice anchors and made fast.

Soon a group of Greenlanders arrived by sledge at the side of the *Thetis*. "They were fine physical specimens," said Schley, "and in their bear-skin suits appeared hardy and robust, with good natured and laughing faces." Using his interpreter again, Schley learned that none in the small village of about fifty had any information about Greely and his men. Schley offered the Greenlanders pork, bread, and "broken oars and pieces of wood to mend their kayaks." He also gave them metal scrap and nails, anything they might find useful.

Colwell disembarked with the interpreter and walked over ice and snow to the village, consisting of ten skin tents and a single stone hut. An elderly man with a wooden leg, apparently the village leader, told Colwell that "earlier in the season, before the ice had broken, a hunting party had gone over the ice, well on towards the Cary Islands, but that no white men had been seen." When Colwell returned with this information, Schley concluded that Greely had not made it this far south. Without delay they continued north.

The *Thetis* steamed for Cape Parry near five o'clock on the morning of June 20. From high in the crow's nest Schley watched walruses basking on the larger ice floes, and "thousands of screaming little auks [guillemots] were found in the wide spaces of open water between the floes, but they were so small as hardly to make it worthwhile to waste ammunition." Schley landed at Cape Parry in the early afternoon, and had men build a cairn on a prominent knoll and leave a record for the other ships, including the *Alert*, marking the spot with a white flag. They eased north through loose pack and icebergs, that evening running very close to Hakluyt Island. Schley scanned with his telescope for any signs of life. Seeing none he pressed on, creeping along "through twenty-four miles of enormous bergs, thickly studded together, often so close to each other than an opening could hardly be discovered until the ship was right upon them."

Some thirty miles north of Hakluyt Island, the *Thetis* reached the fabled North Water, which was nearly free of ice. Peering expectantly through his telescope, Schley's pulse quickened: "There was open water as far as Littleton Island, and for the first time since entering the ice seven hundred miles to the southward, the ship rose slightly to the motion of the swell." Schley called for full steam and raced northward, passing Cape Saumarez, Pandora Harbor, and Foulke Fiord, arriving just off Littleton Island at 2:30 a.m. on June 21. Schley and all hands on deck peered eagerly at the island's shores for any signs of Greely and his men, "but there was no trace of human life about the island." They sailed around to the north side of the island to gain shelter from the strong southwesterly wind and, using ice anchors, made fast to a large offshore grounded berg.

Schley climbed down from the crow's nest and went ashore with landing parties under the command of Lieutenant Colwell, Chief Engineer Melville, and the ice pilot, Norman. They spent the rest of the night and the entire next day spread out in lines, scouring every yard of Littleton Island, but found no sign of Greely. It was obvious to Schley that Greely had not made it this far. By late in the evening Schley ordered all hands back on board the *Thetis*. It was the summer solstice, "with the sun at its farthest point north of the equator," and yet no one could see it through the blinding snowstorm. In fact the winds and snow were so powerful that "it was impossible to see half the ship's length away." Throughout the day Schley had scanned across the waters toward Cape Sabine with his telescope hoping to see something, but it was "shut out from view by the blackness of the Arctic storm."

Schley retired to his cabin to contemplate his options. He was now deeply concerned about the fate of the *Bear*. It had been four days since he had watched it steam away toward the southwest from Cape York. The *Bear* was the faster vessel and should by all rights have arrived first at Littleton Island. Schley could not help fear that the ice-laden sea had proved fatal for it, like the *Proteus*. His thoughts moved back and forth between the *Bear* and Commander Greely. He wondered, if Greely had made it as far as Cape Sabine, why had he not crossed the Smith Sound to Littleton Island? Certainly he could at some point have made the twenty-three miles either by boat or over ice. It was possible that Greely had either remained at Fort Conger or was stranded somewhere south of the fort along the Grinnell Land coast, and that "failing strength, or loss of boats, or some other misadventure had prevented his reaching Smith Sound."

Schley mulled it over throughout the night. He concluded that Greely would not have stayed at Fort Conger. He was a dedicated army officer, and his own orders had stated that should no relief come after the summer of 1883, he would make his way south to Cape Sabine and, if possible, cross over to Littleton Island. Greely, Schley determined, would never contravene his own orders. That settled it. Early the next morning, on June 22, Schley wrote messages and instructions and called for men to deposit them in cairns for Emory and the *Bear,* reporting that he had taken the *Thetis* across to Cape Sabine to search for Greely. If Greely was not there, they would cache four thousand rations in the event of their own potential disaster, and push on north along the Grinnell Land coast, all the way to Fort Conger, searching for Greely.

Before noon the men returned from making the cairns and caching the records and rations, and Schley ordered lines cast off from the iceberg. Within minutes men reported that they had spotted a ship approaching them from the south. Schley stood on the deck and, squinting through the swirling snow, saw a steamship, its bow and rigging encased in rime, plowing through the sound. It was the *Bear.*

Emory anchored the *Bear* "on the port quarter of the flagship" *Thetis* and came aboard. He informed Commander Schley that foul weather and dense fog had pinned him near Cape York for two days. At one point the *Bear* was nearly crushed by ice: "She was just clear of the point of pressure," Emory said. "Had she been but a few yards astern, she might have met the fate of the *Proteus.*" Emory escaped that nip and continued northward but met with days and nights of trials through the ice. He told Schley of nearly disastrous collisions with enormous icebergs, of landing at the Cary Islands and determining that Greely had not been there. Beyond the Cary Islands, motoring before the strong southerly gale, he had encountered no further difficulties and made swift passage to this point.

Commander Schley listened intently, nodded, then told Emory to prepare the *Bear* with sledges, dogs, and landing equipment ready on deck. At 3:00 p.m. they would traverse the Smith Sound and search for Greely at Cape Sabine.

Coursing to the northwest, the two steamships found the strait relatively clear of ice and made passage in four hours. Heavy winds increased as they came to Payer Harbor, and Schley found it frozen over, with no safe place for anchorage. They headed toward the northernmost edge of the ice, and both the *Thetis* and the *Bear* set anchor just off Brevoort Island, two miles south of Cape Sabine. Commander Schley ordered four landing parties off to inspect all the known cache locations in the vicinity, and to search for any signs of Greely.

One group headed for Brevoort Island, a three-mile-long slab of black rock. Another, under Ensign Harlow, went to small, low-lying Stalknecht Island. A third, led by Chief Engineer Melville, proceeded to Payer Harbor with orders to search as far along the rugged coastline as they could go. The last party, using the *Bear*'s steam cutter, nicknamed the "Cub," was directed toward the bare-ridged and glaciated Cape Sabine, seeking Beebe's cache as well as Colwell's "wreck cache" from the *Proteus*. Lieutenant Colwell, having made this cache the previous year, would lead this party, bringing along ice pilots Norman and Ash, plus a coxswain and two men.

Within half an hour, as Colwell was just about to launch the "Cub," Commander Schley heard voices yelling, barely audible above the howling wind. He could not determine from which direction the voices came. He heard more shouting, and then cheering, from the direction of Brevoort Island. Seconds later one of Schley's men said he could make out a flag signaling from Stalknecht Island. Ensign Harlow had discovered the Peirce pendulum that First Lieutenant Lockwood had placed there, jutting prominently from a tall cairn. At the base of the pendulum, below a number of stones, Harlow had also uncovered scientific records and a letter written by Lockwood. Now Schley paid close attention as Harlow signaled by semaphore: "Have found Greely's records."

Schley saw a man sprinting over the ice, coming from Brevoort Island. By the time he arrived and had climbed aboard the *Thetis* he was gasping and could hardly speak. He handed Commander Schley a bundle of papers and managed to blurt out that Greely was at Cape Sabine, and all were well. The package contained six records, one signed by George Rice, the other five signed by Greely. Said Schley: "The excitement of the moment was intense, and it spread with the rapidity of lightning through both the ships." Schley quickly shuffled through the papers, and his own excitement turned to horror when he reached the last of the pages and learned that "the latest date borne by any of them was October 21, 1883." Schley read carefully:

> *My party is now permanently encamped on the west side of a small neck of land which connects the wreck cache cove or bay and the one to its west. Distant about equally from Cape Sabine and Cocked Hat Island. All well.*
>
> *A.W. Greely, First Lieutenant and Commanding*

That had been eight months ago, and at that time Greely's men had but forty days' rations. Schley put the pages away and readied to sail, dreading what he would find at Cape Sabine. A few minutes later another man was seen running across the ice from Stalknecht Island. He boarded the *Thetis* and handed Schley First Lieutenant Lockwood's note of October 23, 1883, confirming the same location Greely had recorded.

Commander Schley wasted no time. It was now 8:00 p.m. on June 22. Colwell remained close by in the "Cub," and Schley ordered him to take his ice pilots Norman and Ash and a small crew to the "wreck cache" immediately. Colwell loaded the little steam cutter with blankets, spirits, pemmican, hardtack, and condensed milk in the event—though Schley now doubted it was possible—that they found anyone alive. Colwell set off, the "Cub" pitching in choppy seas and driving gusts. Schley transferred over to the faster *Bear*, in which he would follow Colwell's course. The *Thetis* would await the return of the remaining search groups. Schley ordered the recall signal to bring everyone in, and the *Thetis* blew three long blasts of its whistle. The *Bear* pulled up its ice anchor and steamed away.

❧❧❧

Greely and the six surviving men lay shivering in the nearly flattened tent. They were barely able to move beneath the weight of the snow-soaked canvas.

They had consumed nothing but a few swigs of water since eating the last of Greely's sleeping bag cover two days before. Brainard attempted to sit up and write in his journal, but he was unable even to hold his pencil, and he slumped back down and lay there, in and out of consciousness. Greely tried to read from his prayerbook, but his eyes could not focus. Connell had not spoken all day, and his face was badly swollen, his eyes glazed and rheumy. Biederbick checked on him now and again to see if he remained alive. Connell's legs were cold and lifeless below the waist, but he still breathed, his exhalations shallow and foul with scurvy. Schneider's corpse lay halfway out of the tent. His head and shoulders, poking from beneath the canvas, were covered with a layer of snow.

Sometime that evening, rising just above the gale, Greely heard a long, moaning wail. He shifted position and craned to listen. The sound seemed familiar, like that of a ship's whistle. Greely asked the others if they had heard it. No one had. Greely badly wanted to believe his ears but feared it might be only "the impression of his disturbed imagination." In a hoarse, weak voice, he asked Brainard and Long if they could possibly make it as far as the ridge to investigate. He himself was too weak to stand, but he wanted to be certain that he wasn't imagining the sound. The two sergeants summoned their strength and crawled from the tent, promising to return as soon as possible with any news.

Brainard and Long moved on their hands and knees toward the ridge. Helping each other up, they managed to stagger forward on foot. When they reached the edge of the ridge they gazed out at the windswept sound and listened to waves washing onto the ice foot below. Dovekies keened eerily, their shrieks mingling with the cry of the high Arctic wind. Through the overcast skies they saw nothing but a few flat pans of ice bobbing in the sea. Long noticed that the distress flag Brainard had erected had blown down, and he said he thought he might be able to go put it back up.

Brainard started toward the dilapidated tent to give Greely the bad news. He was so exhausted that he used the slope of the hill to roll most of the way back down. As he crawled the final yards, he passed some empty cans the men used to carry fresh water from the waterholes. "The wind blew over them, producing a low, mournful sound." Brainard concluded that this was the sound Greely had heard, and he wriggled back into his buffalo bag to die.

✐✐✐

Lieutenant Colwell steamed the "Cub" around the rocky coast of Cape Sabine, scanning the coves, the jutting headlands, and "the line of the ice pack which had ground up the *Proteus*, dimly seen in the mists to the north, across the tossing waters of the Kane Sea" to the north. Colwell recognized the location of the wreck cache but saw nothing there, and kept on, rounding the next point of rock and moving into the cove. Colwell looked up at the ridge, and there, some sixty yards above the ice foot, stood the lone figure of a man. Colwell had the coxswain wave a flag, and the man on the ridge "stooped, picked up a signal flag from the rock, and waved it in reply." They watched as the figure stumbled slowly down the slope toward them, falling twice, then picking himself up and limping until he reached the "Cub" at the shore ice. Colwell jumped off and approached him.

"Who all are left," asked Colwell.

"Seven left," the man said. "As he spoke, his utterance was thick and mumbling, and in his agitation his jaw worked in convulsive twitches." Colwell looked at him and shook his head in aghast amazement: "His cheeks were hollow, his eyes wild, his hair and beard long and matted." His grimy army jacket was torn and ragged. There were holes in the toes and heels of his boots.

"Who are you?" asked Colwell.

"Private Francis Long," the man said. Long lifted his arm in a shaky salute and then pointed, telling Colwell that the others were in a downed tent over the hill.

"Commander Greely?" Colwell asked.

"He's alive," said Long.

Colwell ordered the men in the "Cub" to care for Long and ferry him back to the *Bear*.

Colwell then hurried up the rocky slope after Norman and Ash, who had already started, carrying blankets and food. Above and beyond "was a range of hills rising up eight hundred feet, with a precipitous face, broken in two by a gorge, through which the wind was blowing furiously."

When they arrived at the tent, a man was just crawling out. He teetered as he stood, but he "drew himself up into the position of a soldier and raised his right hand to salute." Colwell reached forward and shook his hand. It was Sergeant Brainard, who had heard running footsteps and realized they could not possibly be Long's. Colwell looked around and saw cans and refuse and empty rifle shells scattered about among scraps of clothing. A man, apparently dead, lay halfway out of the tent bottom. There was commotion from inside the tent, and voices calling out: "Who's there? Who's there?" Norman yelled back: "It's Norman. Norman who was in the *Proteus*!" A weak cheer came from within the tent, and the men were struggling to get out, but the weight of the heavy canvas held them down.

Colwell took out a knife, cut a large slit through the canvas, and peered inside, accosted by vile stench. At Colwell's feet lay a man, his eyes wide and glassy, his mouth agape. Two others, kneeling on the ground next to him, were pouring liquid from a rubber bottle and spooning it into the invalid's mouth. Beyond them Colwell saw "a poor fellow, alive to be sure, but without hands or feet, with a spoon tied to the stump of his right arm." The stony floor beneath them was strewn with torn clothes and a few cans of congealed jelly, the remnants of boiled sealskin. Colwell saw another man moving toward the tent opening on his hands and knees. He was "a dark man with a long, matted beard, in a dirty and tattered dressing gown with a little red skull cap on his head, and brilliant, staring eyes." The man reached Colwell, rose onto his knees, and put on a pair of oval-shaped spectacles.

Colwell leaned down and took the man by the hand, steadying him: "Greely, is that you?"

"Yes," Greely answered. His voice was a thin thread of a whisper, breaking with emotion and stammering as he said, "Yes—seven of us left—here we are, dying like men. Did what I came to do—beat the record." Then he crumpled to the hard ground, too exhausted to say more.

The dilapidated tent at Camp Clay, Cape Sabine, June 22, 1884. *(Courtesy of Naval History and Heritage Command)*

35

"Preserve Tenderly the Remains of the Heroic Dead"

Colwell, Norman, and the other rescuers wiped tears from their eyes and attended to the survivors. Colwell took some hardtack from his pockets and gave pieces to Greely, Elison, Biederbick, Frederick, and Brainard. Connell, who barely had a pulse, was given a few drops of brandy and started reviving. Colwell parceled the food out in small bits to the gaunt men, obeying the ships doctor's instructions not to overfeed them. Using his knife, Colwell scooped servings of pemmican to Greely and his men as they knelt before him, chewing indifferently.

Colwell and Ash righted the tent and wrapped the survivors in thick blankets. They tried to encourage the men with talk of warmth and more food soon, and Colwell told Greely that there were pictures of his wife and children aboard the *Thetis*, and letters from home, and that they were all well. Greely looked up and replied: "It is so kind and thoughtful."

Soon more men from the *Bear* arrived, including the two doctors, and the relievers struck a fire next to the tent. Using a stove that they had brought ashore, they heated condensed milk and beef extract and administered the liquids in small portions every ten minutes for two hours throughout the night. The doctors estimated that had relief not arrived when it did, Connell would have died within minutes, and the rest could not have lasted much more than a day or two.

Ensign Harlow, who had discovered the Peirce pendulum atop Stalknecht Island, trotted up to the scene with a camera and tripod. Assigned as the designated navy photographer, he had for some time imagined recording the historic "Meeting with Greely," but had missed the heartrending first encounter by a half hour. Harlow struggled to set up his equipment, the tripod and camera twice blown over by the blasting wind. He exposed one plate of the emaciated Commander Greely and the others inside the tent; two images of the rescue in progress outside the tent; one of the abandoned winter quarters; and the last plate captured the line of ten graves on Cemetery Ridge. The graves, beginning with that of Sergeant Cross, had at first been made with care, but as the mounds descended the hill, "the later graves showed less and less of preparation, until at the end there was little done besides placing on the body a thin covering of the gravelly dust that formed the only soil about the place and from one or two a hand or foot protruded."

By the morning of June 23 Captains Schley and Emory had come ashore to direct the transport of Greely and his surviving men to the awaiting *Thetis* and *Bear.* Wind and sleet pounded the inhospitable coast of Cape Sabine as the emaciated army men were wrapped in blankets. Brainard, Biederbick, and Frederick asked to walk on their own down to the steam cutters, but when they tried, they were too weak to do so and were secured to the stretchers and carried carefully down to the ice foot.

Commander Greely was the last to leave Camp Clay. Schley told Greely that he had determined that "the bodies of the dead should be brought back with the living to the United States." Greely disagreed, arguing that they should be allowed to "lie where they had died . . . in the ground consecrated by their achievements." But Commander Schley was adamant, countering that the friends and families of the dead deserved the opportunity to pay their last respects, and that "the relief expedition would fail in its duty if it left these explorers in their rude graves at Cape Sabine." Greely at last consented, and he too was placed on a stretcher and portaged, "following the slow procession as it wound its way around the rocks and through the snow-filled hollows to the sea."

The storm raged on, making the short crossing of just a few hundred yards to the ships perilous. Waves crashed over the gunwales, nearly swamping the small boats, but soon the survivors were safely aboard: Lieutenant Greely, Brainard, Biederbick, and Connell on the *Thetis*; and Elison, Frederick, and Long on the *Bear*.

Schley surveyed the chilling scene at Camp Clay with amazement, astonished that they had managed to survive at this place for eight months:

On one side of the slope were the rude graves, and on the other the deserted and roofless hut, with the ice foot below it; while between them was the wrecked tent. . . . Everywhere was the barren rock, except where deep snow lay in the hollows. There was no soil, except the sandy disintegration of the rocks themselves, and but little of that. On the southern slopes, here and there, were little patches of flowering moss, the only vegetation that could find support in this Arctic wilderness.

The remaining work involved collecting all of the property belonging to Greely and his men as well as the exhumation of the dead. Inside the tent every man had prepared a bundled package of articles, addressed to a relative or friend back home. The tent was folded and packed away, along with notebooks, diaries, and guns and ammunition. Emory, Colwell, and Harlow then began the grim work of disinterment. First they drew a diagram of the graves, "numbering each one from the right facing their heads. This precaution was necessary to avoid confusion in identifying the remains." Afterward each of the dead was unburied one by one and the bodies were wrapped in blankets. Colwell and Emory sewed canvas tags to the blankets in the exact order of exhumation. The corpses were then carried down to the shoreline for transport to the ships.

Lieutenant Colwell ventured down to the stone hut and found more piles of rubbish and broken pots and pans. Then, off to the side of the hut, Colwell saw "a dark object outlined by the white snow." On inspection Colwell discovered "the mutilated remains of a man's body." It was the corpse of Private Henry, which had lain unburied in the elements for two weeks and was partially covered with snow, and, they noticed immediately, decapitated. Colwell and another man carried Henry's body* to the awaiting transport boats, and men began loading the eleven corpses.

Schley's men made a brief search of the tidal crack—where Greely had said they had placed the remains of Doctor Pavy, Gardiner, Bender, and Salor—but found nothing. Schley reported: "They were swept away by winds and tides before my arrival. No trace of them could be discovered."

The storm howled violently, and the small transport whaleboats had great difficulty in the pounding whitecapped surf. Ensign Harlow said: "By alternately drifting and struggling to keep the boats' heads to the wind, their bows deeply loaded with the dead, shipping gallons of water that smashed with broken ice floes nearly to the thwarts, we finally got alongside" the *Thetis*. The cutter smashed into the hull of the *Thetis*, and two of the bodies were washed overboard. An alert seaman hauled the bodies back in just before they sank.

Aboard the *Thetis* Commander Greely had been stripped of his fetid clothing, and wore new heavy flannels. He sat upright in ice pilot Norman's berth in the wardroom, revived by spirits of ammonia and eating minced "teaspoons of fresh raw beef." He was pleased to learn that all the tin boxes containing his dutiful scientific records, as well as the Peirce pendulum the men had refused to abandon, had been recovered at Stalknecht Island and brought on board the *Thetis*. Greely felt proud of his expedition's two years of scientific labor and was relieved that their records and observations would be committed to polar history.

When first brought onto the *Thetis*, Greely had vomited and then fainted. The doctor attending him reported that "his skin hung from his limbs in flaps, shriveled and sallow . . . his face, hands, and scalp blackened with a thick crust

---

* In the official report, submitted by Schley, Colwell makes the following statement: "Found the bones of a man about 75 yards from hut. No head. Tied him up and took on board." Henry's body was later found to have one bullet hole in his chest. As to his headlessness, there remains speculation. It could have been removed by the blast had a shotgun been one of the weapons used during his execution. It might have been dragged away by foxes or a bear. (See also Stein, "An Arctic Execution," 410).

of soot." His weight was recorded at 120 pounds. He had lost nearly 50 pounds since retreating from Fort Conger, but with food, medicine, and rest, he slowly began to recover. The rest of Greely's men, being fed, bathed, and gently cared for, were also steadily improving.

Schley ordered the ships to rendezvous at Payer Harbor and remain there until the next morning, giving his men a chance to rest after their arduous rescue mission. Late on the afternoon of June 23, the ships fired their boilers and coursed southeast toward Littleton Island. When the *Thetis* and the *Bear* blew their whistles, the remnants of the Lady Franklin Bay Expedition—both the living and the dead—steamed away from the rocky desolation of Cape Sabine forever.

∽∾∽

At Littleton Island five of the bodies of the dead explorers were transferred from the *Thetis* to the *Bear*. Henry's body was already on board. Schley gave instructions for their care and preparations. They were undressed, and then identified either by a group photograph taken prior to their departure in 1881, or "by some characteristic mark or peculiarity, so that identification in the case of all of them became a matter of absolute certainty." On each ship the bodies were fully examined, then wrapped in cotton cloths and placed in preserving tanks containing a mixture of salt water and alcohol.

Ensign Harlow was assigned to assist in these preparations. "It was a hideous job," he said. In preparing the bodies "it was found that six, those of Lieutenant Kislingbury, and of Jewell, Ralston, Henry, Whisler, and Ellis, had been cut, and the flesh removed." Of the discovery Harlow would say little else, adding only: "I refrain from details, thinking it best not to be put into writing." With this necessary but macabre business concluded, on the afternoon of the twenty-fourth, the flagship *Thetis* signaled the *Bear*, and the rescue ships struck south.

Commander Greely was improving rapidly, being fed at four-hour intervals the following strict diet: "Oatmeal, broiled steak, beef extract, soft boiled egg, milk toast, raw minced beef and onions, and beef broth again as a 10 PM nightcap." He became strong enough to sit up and read letters from Henrietta and look longingly at pictures she had sent along of herself, Antoinette, and Adola. After another two days Greely stood and made his way to the deck of the *Thetis*, "to the delight of everyone on board." He took a seat out in the open air and sunned, well bundled up. It was the best he had felt in many months. Encouraged by the doctors, Greely began a regimen of daily strolls around the decks.

With the exception of Elison all the other survivors had also regained much of their health. But since the rescue, the physicians had been concerned about the corporal. On the first night out at sea Elison awoke in terrified delirium, sobbing from a nightmare of being left behind, alone at Camp Clay. The next night he had become so agitated that the doctors sedated him with a morphine injection so that they could carefully examine his wounds, which had been treated by Doctor Pavy and hospital steward Biederbick in the toxic conditions of the stone hut and tent on Sabine. The tibia and fibula bones protruded from his leg stumps, and both feet were gone. The stump ends were infected and oozing. Two of the fingers on Elison's right hand were missing, and a doctor "removed the remaining fingers and thumb with bone pliers." The doctors agreed that further amputation of Elison's legs would be necessary to thwart blood infection, but they chose to wait a few days to see if he might improve.

On the afternoon of June 30 Schley came upon the *Alert* and the *Loch Garry*, both beset in the ice pack north of Upernavik. The *Thetis* and *Bear* "immediately broke their way through and released them," and the fleet of four continued south along the Greenland coast, reaching Upernavik on July 2. Here Commander Schley and his fleet received a warm welcome from the one hundred or so villagers and their governor, Elborg. Schley told him the sad news of their countrymen, Jens Edward and Thorlip Frederik Christiansen (Eskimo Fred), and agreed to convey Christiansen's body to nearby Godhavn at Disko Island for burial. Schley also asked Governor Elborg to alert the whalers of the Dundee fleet to the rescue, and to thank them again for their assistance during the friendly rivalry north.

On July 4 the ships continued south, dressing the decks with American flags in honor of the day. The men drank rum punch and brandy in celebration.

Greely and his men told stories of the baseball games played at Fort Conger, everyone laughing good-naturedly at the image of the Greenlanders dashing wildly around with no notion of the rules.

Late that night Elison's gangrenous condition deteriorated, and the surgeons decided to attempt amputation the next morning to prevent his blood sepsis from spreading. On the same day that the body of Greenlander "Eskimo Fred" Christiansen was being unloaded at Godhavn for burial by his countrymen, surgeons sedated Elison with ether and whiskey, and then amputated both of his legs. But it was no use. Elison hung on for three more days, then died on July 8, weighing just seventy-eight pounds.

Before Elison was committed to the saltwater-and-alcohol tank alongside his cohorts, Greely spoke of his tremendous courage and "indomitable will-power" during the terrible months on Cape Sabine, remembering him as "an honest, faithful man who never spared himself when the interests of his comrades or the expedition could be advanced. He was equally valuable in the workshop, or field, as botanist, carpenter, or sledge man."

During the next days of steaming, Greely spent much time with Commander Schley, learning about the efforts of Secretary Chandler, President Arthur, and Henrietta to ensure the rescue mission. In turn Greely told Schley in great detail of their triumphs at Fort Conger and their trials on the ice and at Camp Clay. The squadron of rescue ships reached St. John's on the morning of July 17, the harbor barely visible through dense fog. When they anchored, the wharves were already crowded with curious onlookers. The world anxiously awaited news of the Greely Expedition, and now it had arrived. Before landing Schley had read a general order to all his men that no information of the mission was to be conveyed to anyone on shore until his official telegram had been sent to Washington. Schley handed an officer his report, as well as a personal message from Commander Greely to Henrietta, both of which his emissary rushed to the telegraph office.

Schley's telegram to Washington was lengthy, containing many of the details transcribed from his own and Greely's reports, but the first paragraph contained the news that was most important:

ST. JOHN'S, N. F., JULY 17, 1884.

HON. W. E. CHANDLER, SECRETARY OF NAVY, WASHINGTON, D. C.:

THETIS, BEAR, AND LOCH GARRY ARRIVED HERE TO-DAY FROM WEST GREEN
LAND, ALL WELL, SEPARATED IN GALE FROM ALERT YESTERDAY 150 MILES
NORTH. AT 9 P.M., JUNE 22D, FIVE MILES WEST OF CAPE SABINE IN SMITH
SOUND, THETIS AND BEAR RESCUED ALIVE LIEUTENANT A. W. GREELY,
SERGEANT BRAINARD, SERGEANT FREDERICK, SERGEANT LONG, HOSPITAL
STEWARD BIEDERBICK, SERGEANT ELISON, AND PRIVATE CONNELL, THE
ONLY SURVIVORS OF THE LADY FRANKLIN BAY EXPEDITION.

    W. S. SCHLEY, COMMANDER.

Greely's telegram to Henrietta was concise and devoid of the emotion he
must have been feeling when he wrote it aboard the *Thetis*. But he knew there
would be plenty of time to fill her in when they were reunited, and also, he was
distrustful of the prying eyes and gossipy inclinations of the telegraph office
workers who would read it. Greely's telegram read simply:

MRS. A.W. GREELY, SAN DIEGO, CA—PERFECTLY WELL BUT WEAK. FIVE MEN
ONLY SURVIVE, NO OFFICERS. REMAIN HERE FOUR DAYS. LOCKWOOD BEAT
MARKHAM LATITUDE. SUIT YOUR CONVENIENCE COMING EAST. SHALL TAKE
LONG SICK LEAVE.

    A.W. GREELY

In the nation's capital, the offices, halls, and corridors of the ornate State,
War, and Navy Building on Pennsylvania Avenue became frenzied as the wires
poured in. Messengers were sent to the White House, where President Arthur,
eating breakfast, received the news of the triumphant and tragic Greely Expedition and its successful rescue. Secretary Chandler was out of town at West
Point, but Schley's lengthy dispatch was instantly forwarded to him there, and
he read it carefully, page by page. He paused on one passage and read it over a
few times, wondering at its seriousness and import. Near the end of the telegram, Schley had stated: "I would urgently suggest that the bodies now on board

be placed in metallic cases here for safer and better transportation. This appears to me imperative."

From the beginning, Secretary Chandler had given Commander Schley full discretion and powers in all matters of the rescue mission, and he trusted his judgment now, whatever the circumstances. As soon as he had finished reading, he sent Schley the following reply:

COMMANDER W. S. SCHLEY: JULY 17, 1884

RECEIVE MY CONGRATULATIONS AND THANKS FOR YOURSELF AND YOUR
WHOLE COMMAND FOR YOUR PRUDENCE, PERSEVERANCE, AND COURAGE IN
REACHING OUR DEAD AND DYING COUNTRYMEN. THE HEARTS OF THE
AMERICAN PEOPLE GO OUT WITH GREAT AFFECTION TO LIEUTENANT
GREELY AND THE FEW SURVIVORS OF HIS DEADLY PERIL. CARE FOR THEM
UNREMITTINGLY AND BID THEM BE CHEERFUL AND HOPEFUL ON ACCOUNT
OF WHAT LIFE YET HAS IN STORE FOR THEM. PRESERVE TENDERLY THE
REMAINS OF THE HEROIC DEAD; PREPARE THEM ACCORDING TO YOUR
JUDGMENT AND BRING THEM HOME.

WILLIAM E. CHANDLER, SECRETARY OF THE NAVY

36

"Home Again, Home Again"

Immediately after Commander Schley received the telegram from Secretary Chandler, he ordered a dozen metallic caskets, each weighing seven hundred pounds and made of boiler iron, all coated in black paint and secured with fifty-two bolts for permanent sealing. It would take a week for them to be readied, and until then the Greely Expedition's dead would remain in their saltwater-and-alcohol baths, the tanks on the decks of the *Thetis* and *Bear* shielded from view by dark canvas curtains.

Despite hordes of prodding newspaper reporters and curious townsfolk, Greely and his men managed, in the first few days at St. John's, to slip from the *Thetis* and take short walks around the port township. One of the first things Greely did was visit the home of Mr. and Mrs. Joseph F. Rice, the parents of photographer George Rice. Commander Greely paid his respects and told them of their son's heroism, explaining how he had perished on the ice while trying to bring in food to save the others. Greely heartened them with stories of their son's selfless courage, and with the knowledge that his photographs—which had been saved with all their scientific records—were unique and unprecedented in Arctic exploration. No one had ever before made such comprehensive images capturing those far-northern frozen lands and sea.

Greely's rescue caused an instant global sensation. When the ships landed at St. John's, *The New York Times* had requested six thousand words for its Sunday edition, and Commander Schley granted Ensign Harlow permission to "send all you can as soon as possible" about the rescue. Both Schley and Secretary Chandler fully understood the international acclaim this would bring the U.S. Navy.

On the morning after his arrival, Greely learned that nearly every major newspaper in the United States had run stories, the coverage highlighting both the dauntless courage and the devastating tragedy. Bold headlines lauded Greely's attainment of Farthest North and his unprecedented explorations of Grinnell Land. James Gordon Bennett of *The New York Herald* ran an extensive piece, including quotes from Arctic veterans praising Greely's "unparalleled, remarkable and heroic achievement," with Sir George Nares writing that Commander Greely had taken "the longest stride yet toward a knowledge of the Arctic mysteries. Mr. Greely's achievement has placed America in the vanguard of Arctic research up to the present moment." President Arthur even received a cable from Windsor Castle, which was made public: "The Queen heartily congratulates the President and the People of the United States on the rescue of Lieutenant Greely and the gallant survivors of the Arctic Expedition." Queen Victoria was proud that her Royal Navy had been able to loan the United States the *Alert* for the rescue mission.

But for Greely these accolades were overshadowed by the stark truth that nineteen of his men had died. A headline from the *Chicago Tribune* read: "FROM THE JAWS OF DEATH—Lieutenant Greely and Six Brave Companions Rescued in the Northern Sea—A Graphic Tale of Terrible Privation." Greely knew that soon he would be besieged by even more sensational stories and questions—both official inquiries and prying queries from salivating reporters—about exactly what had happened to his men and how they had managed to survive.

By the morning of July 26, 1884, the dead men of the Lady Franklin Bay Expedition had been transferred into the coffins belowdecks. The lids of the metallic caskets were bolted shut, each one mounted "with a silver identification plate with the name and death date of its occupant." Flags in

St. John's flew at half-staff as the four-ship relief flotilla left the harbor and steamed south, escorted by tugboats flying their pennants and blowing their whistles.

As he sailed toward home, Greely read the mounds of mail, telegrams, and official reports from Washington, as well as letters from home. He learned that Henrietta was on her way east from San Diego and, barring any delays, would be at Portsmouth, New Hampshire, by the time of his anticipated arrival around the first of August. This pleased the commander beyond words. Many times he had resigned himself to never again seeing Henrietta or his daughters. A flood of telegrams and correspondence underscored for Greely the growing and feverish interest in his story. The publishers Harper & Brothers wanted to know if Greely would write a book, or at the very least "favor us with an article with sketches for *Harper's Weekly*" describing his expedition. A prominent lecture circuit agent was nearly frothing at the mouth, writing with a directness that Greely found off-putting under the circumstances: "Want you for two hundred lectures. See me at Portsmouth before making any engagements."

On the morning of Friday, August 1, 1884, the *Thetis*, the *Bear*, and the *Alert* emerged from thick New England fog and stood ten miles off the Isles of Shoals lighthouse, on the border between Maine and New Hampshire. Greely and his men went abovedecks and saw the naval sloop *Alliance* arriving to lead them into port. Greely's pulse quickened as he recognized familiar landmarks of his native shores, near his boyhood home of Newburyport, Massachusetts, just twenty-five miles to the southwest. As they proceeded into the harbor a few hours later, Commander Greely and his five remaining men stood on deck, awed by the scene before them. The entire North Atlantic Squadron of the U.S. Navy lay in the lower harbor, foremost among them the massive five-thousand-ton flagship, *Tennessee*, accompanied by nearly a dozen other warships. It was a humbling display.

Navy Secretary Chandler had spared no expense or detail; for both personal and private reasons he wanted the U.S. Navy to shine on this important day. Greely's arrival would be documented by the world's press, and Chandler had orchestrated the movements down to the final docking. "The shores of the river on both sides," wrote Schley proudly, "were lined with people, and the harbor was filled with steamers, sailboats, and small craft of every description, all of them dressed in flags and streamers."

Once inside the harbor, Greely pressed close against the rail, trying to recognize friends and family and looking anxiously for Henrietta. As they passed each grand warship in succession, "their crews swarmed in the rigging," cheering loudly and waving. The decks of these naval ships teemed with national politicians and dignitaries from Portsmouth, and somewhere among the crowds were Greely's wife and family—though he could not yet locate them among the exultant throng.

Secretary Chandler and General Hazen stood in formation with admirals and other high-ranking officers on the quarterdeck of the *Tennessee*. Henrietta Greely was near Secretary Chandler, trying keenly to find her Dolph's tall and angular outline. As the relief ships finally came alongside to anchor, the flagship's band played "Home Again," with thousands of people waving handkerchiefs and singing along, many with tears streaming down their faces and their voices harmonizing, with equal parts joy and grief:

> *Home again, home again,*
> *From a foreign shore,*
> *And oh, it fills my soul with joy,*
> *To meet my friends once more;*
> *Here I dropped the parting tear,*
> *To cross the ocean's foam,*
> *But now I'm once again with those,*
> *Who kindly greet me home.*

As soon as the relief ships were landed and standing at anchor, Secretary Chandler took Henrietta by the arm and led her to the boarding ramp of the *Thetis*. Chandler had issued strict orders that "no one, not even Commander Schley's wife" would board the *Thetis* until after Henrietta Greely—flanked on either side by her twin brothers, Loring and Otto Nesmith—was escorted aboard Schley's flagship. Henrietta and her brothers—three of the chief voices that created the impetus for the rescue mission—strode proudly up the ramp and onto the ship.

Pacing impatiently and nervously inside Commander Schley's cabin waited Commander Greely. After what seemed an interminable period—a continuum of one that had lasted more than three years—Henrietta stepped quietly inside, and behind her the door of the captain's cabin clicked shut.

⌢⌢⌢

The day after the long-awaited reunion of Adolphus and Henrietta Greely, newspapers ran stories complete with illustrated engravings of the couple's passionate embrace. One piece, from *Frank Leslie's Illustrated Newspaper*, depicted Greely knocking over a chair in his ardent desire to embrace his wife. Another included their first words, with Henrietta exclaiming: "Oh Dolph!—my dear Adolphus," and his breathless reply: "Rettie . . . My wife!" In fact no one had been in the room, and it was only after the two had spent some quiet and tender moments together that they had opened Schley's cabin door and allowed others in, including Mother Greely holding Antoinette and Adola, General Hazen, Henrietta's brothers, and Secretary Chandler.

When Henrietta read the news articles about their reunion, she could only scoff and shake her head at the untrustworthy press. In fact she had been pleased to see that in the six weeks from her husband's rescue to his return, he had gained back all of the fifty pounds he had lost. She wrote a short letter to her father in San Diego to keep him informed of the truth: "Of course the published descriptions of our meeting were absurd, as there was no one anywhere about Captain Schley's cabin when we met. . . . Mr. Greely is improving perceptibly daily. His brain and nerves are in perfectly sound condition and his general physical health is good."

Secretary Chandler had organized a banquet, parade, and welcome-home rally for the coming days. Commander Greely and Henrietta were housed in a lovely cottage in an apple orchard, surrounded by a white picket fence, secreted away from the prying press. Sergeant Brainard and the other enlisted men were given berths aboard the USS *Constitution*, named by President George Washington for the nation's foundational document. The three-masted heavy frigate, nicknamed "Old Ironsides," was being used as a receiving ship at the Portsmouth Naval Shipyard, and Brainard and the other men were made comfortable there, proud to be housed on the fabled, nearly one-hundred-year-old warship, which had seen action in the War of 1812 and the Civil War.

Over the weekend, while awaiting the festivities, Secretary Chandler and General Hazen convened with Commander Schley aboard the *Thetis* to discuss a number of pressing matters. Greely had turned in some of his official reports of the expedition, and Schley now added his report of the rescue—which included mention of the six bodies that "had been cut, and the flesh removed." There had already been murmurings of cannibalism, leaked—while he was drunk—by the ice pilot James Norman back at St. John's. Hazen and Chandler discussed the future handling of the caskets, as well as the issue of Private Henry's execution, of which Greely had by now informed the general.

During the rest of the weekend, the streets of Portsmouth bustled with excited and curious visitors, many hoping to catch a glimpse of "the hardy six who had come back alive from their Arctic ordeal." Local citizens and sightseers alike were allowed to board the rescue ships. Many of them were particularly intrigued by a display of remnants—including the distress flag from Camp Clay and a sledge—brought back from the Lady Franklin Bay Expedition—being showcased aboard the *Thetis*.

On Monday, August 4, the streets of "the staid old New Hampshire town were transformed beyond all recognition" by some twenty thousand people. The toll bridge connecting Portsmouth, New Hampshire, and Kittery, Maine, was "choked with pedestrians and carriages, while from other directions people poured in by train and roads from surrounding towns." The captains of the relief ships—chief among them Commander Schley—who was by now being heralded as a national hero—were paraded through the streets in open carriages following brass bands and drum processions, waving to the cheering onlookers as they passed. The parade culminated at Market Square, where Greely and his men, on physician's orders, watched from the grandstand before retiring to their quarters for the remainder of the day and evening.

The celebrations culminated in an evening of speeches at the Portsmouth Music Hall, attended by fifteen hundred people. Attendees included the governor of New Hampshire, General Hazen, and several admirals, state senators, and representatives, as well as Portsmouth's mayor. Secretary Chandler, born and raised in the Granite State of New Hampshire, took full advantage of the limelight for himself—he was considering a run for the U.S. Senate— and for the navy. In a rousing speech he heaped praise on Commander Schley and the other rescue captains, as well as on Lieutenant Greely for his steadfast command and leadership. Secretary of War Robert Todd Lincoln was notably absent, having declined Chandler's invitations to the events, claiming he needed to review his militia at Gettysburg. More likely he wished to avoid embarrassment at being outshone by the navy. There was also widespread knowledge that Lincoln had been set against Arctic exploration from the start, and because of his years of bureaucratic foot-dragging and the army's inept and ill-fated rescue attempts, Lincoln had been partially blamed for the disasters and tragedy.

Commander Greely and his men had been advised by the Portsmouth Navy Yard surgeon general not to attend the event. They thought it too much activity for the survivors' weakened nerves and constitutions. In Greely's place Otto Nesmith, Henrietta's brother, took the stage and read prepared remarks from Greely as the crowd grew hushed and absorbed:

> *I am now unable to fittingly express how deeply we feel the honor done us by your assembling here to greet with kindly words of welcome the living, and to give voice to tender sympathy for the dead. During our service in the North we tried to do our duty. If in our efforts aught is found of work accomplished or of actions done which touches the heart of the people, we shall feel that our labors and hardships are more than rewarded. . . .*
>
> *Never for a moment in our darkest or gloomiest hour did we doubt that the American people were planning for our rescue. . . . From day to day, as food failed and men died, that strength and that certainty gave strength to us who lived. . . . We thank you for your kind deeds, thoughtful consideration and tender sympathy to and for us all—the living and the dead.*

After a few moments of silence, the crowd erupted in applause, then settled into a respectful murmur. The rally concluded, and the assembly dispersed, filtering out of the music hall.

The next day the relief squadron sailed for New York. On August 8, 1884, the ships arrived and "the batteries of the 4th and 5th Artillery were drawn up on the wharf at Governor's Island to receive the dead." After a brief service, "all but two of the caskets were delivered to friends and families of the deceased." Private Schneider had requested that his remains be shipped by steamer to his family in Germany. Private Henry—for whom no family came—was transported to and interred at Cypress Hills National Cemetery in Brooklyn, New York. Ironically, given his inglorious death, he was buried with full military honors. The exact details of the manner of his death were still under scrutiny by the U.S. Army, which felt it most prudent to lay the soldier to rest immediately.

When the relief squadron reached Fort Columbus, Schley and his gallant men were greeted with a patriotic twenty-one-gun salute. But while Greely prepared to be honored and feted at his home town of Newburyport, Massachusetts, he was to receive a very different kind of welcome. Newspaper headlines in bold black ink shouted out shocking headlines: "SHAME OF A NATION"; "PROOF FROM THE GRAVE"; "THE MUTILATED ARCTIC HEROES!" The rumors had gone to print, reporting that in their final weeks of starvation at Camp Clay, some members of the Greely Expedition had been driven to consume human flesh.

Commander Schley *(fourth from left)* and rescuers aboard the *Thetis*. *(Courtesy of Naval History and Heritage Command)*

The *Thetis*, the *Bear*, the *Alert*, and the *Loch Garry* during the Greely Rescue Mission. *(Courtesy of Naval History and Heritage Command)*

Survivors and rescuers aboard the *Thetis*. Greely is #22. *(Courtesy of Naval History and Heritage Command)*

Commander Adolphus W. Greely on the *Thetis* after the rescue. *(Courtesy of Naval History and Heritage Command)*

37

"No Law, Human or Divine"

Commander Greely's hero's welcome was short-lived. While he was recuperating at the cottage on Seavy's Island near the Portsmouth Naval Shipyard, getting reacquainted with Henrietta and playing with Antoinette and Adola, scandalous news stories were being printed daily. One of them was particularly hurtful to the Greelys and felt like a personal betrayal. The editor of *The New York Times*, Charles R. Miller, had been a college classmate of Henrietta's brother Otto. Miller had earlier been helpful with editorials championing Henrietta's Bounty Bill. The Greelys and the Nesmiths certainly did not expect Miller to contribute to the rabid sensationalism surrounding Greely's return. But the enticement of publishing a salacious story he knew would sell thousands and thousands of copies prompted him to print a story on August 12, 1884, with the following headline:

HORRORS OF CAPE SABINE—*Terrible Story of Greely's Dreary Camp—Brave Men, Crazed by Starvation and Bitter Cold, Feeding on the Dead Bodies of their Comrades . . .*

The article went on to claim—with lurid detail that suggested the reporter had been on the scene scribbling furiously in a notebook—that after the men had run out of food in early February, "they were kept alive on human flesh." This piece, and scores of others like it printed from shore to shore across the United States, were basing their news primarily on the rumors started by the ice pilot James Norman from a barstool in St. John's, and the leaked reference in Commander Schley's initial report that some of the bodies had had flesh removed. The article also implied that Private Henry had been murdered and then eaten.

Things got even worse over the following days. On August 14, while Greely and Henrietta were enjoying a festive homecoming celebration at his birthplace in Newburyport, Massachusetts, Lieutenant Kislingbury's body was being exhumed at Mount Hope Cemetery in Rochester, New York. The editor of the *Rochester Post Express* had relentlessly pressured Kislingbury's family to allow him to pay for Lieutenant Kislingbury's exhumation in exchange for an exclusive story. Kislingbury's three brothers finally agreed. The casket was raised, the fifty-two iron bolts were removed, and after the lid was lifted, two physicians carefully examined the body. They gave a sworn statement that was published the next day: "In our opinion, the flesh was cut away with some sharp instrument."

Commander Greely was initially devastated and sickened by the news. He and his men had been through hell and back already, and now this. He convened the surviving men and asked them if they knew about, or had seen, any cannibalism. Each man in turn looked Greely in the eyes and swore that he was innocent. Greely took them at their word, and from Portsmouth issued a lengthy statement denying any personal knowledge of the act, adding: "If there was any cannibalism . . . the man eating was done in secrecy and entirely without my knowledge. I can give no stronger denial." He concluded by saying: "Perhaps those who died last fed upon the bodies of those who died before; but all of this is supposition. I can but answer for myself."

Reporters hounded the other survivors, who echoed Greely's denials. Julius "Shorty" Frederick, visited by a local journalist, said only: "There might have been some cannibalism. I saw no instance." Sergeant Brainard, also interviewed, answered definitively: "I know nothing of cannibalism."

It was a painful period for Greely and the other survivors. Only they knew the privation and anguish they had endured at Camp Clay. What wasn't being reported was the selflessness and sympathy they had all shown to Private Elison, who was unable to feed himself for nearly eight months. How on numerous occasions Greely had given his own rations to men during their last days and held dying men in his arms as they took their final breaths; how during the entire ordeal, as Greely put it, "the weak and helpless had naught but kindness and consideration from the stronger."

A few reputable papers, such as the *New-York Tribune*, refused to stoop to the sensational stories and criticized those that did, calling them "vultures who have been gloating over these exaggerated and revolting stories." Greely was heartened by the words of the highly respected explorer Sir Clements R. Markham, who was then secretary of the Royal Geographic Society in London. In Europe the polar exploration and scientific community cared little about fabricated and salacious stories with shocking headlines; they were interested in what Greely and his men had achieved and what they had discovered. Markham was quoted in the *New-York Tribune* piece: "The accusations of murder and cannibalism made against the Greely party is a disgrace to American journalism. Decency would have suggested silence until Lieutenant Greely had submitted his report to the government."

Greely's report was, in fact, forthcoming. So was the official rescue report from Commander Schley. Schley had met with Secretary Chandler and War Secretary Lincoln in Portsmouth, and also communicated with President Cleveland about the shameful stories and accusations. Commander Schley's final report included a phrase that, when published, cast some doubt that there had been cannibalism at all. Schley reiterated that six of the bodies "had been cut and the flesh removed," but added a possible explanation that the flesh had been taken "no doubt to use as shrimp bait."

Mercifully for Greely and everyone involved, after a few weeks the stories began to fade away. Unfortunately enough damage had been done that his expedition, whatever its achievements, would forever be associated with the ultimate taboo of the consumption of human flesh. There would be lasting comparisons to the tragic Donner Party episode of nearly forty years before. Commander Greely tried his best to end public speculation about the last days of his expedition. When Greely published his personal account of the expedition, *Three Years of Arctic Service*, he had one last thing to say on the subject:

As to other matters which have engaged an undue share of public attention, while having no official knowledge of the facts in the case, yet the responsibility for all action in connection with such an expedition rightfully and properly rests on the commanding officer. In assuming that responsibility I know of no law, human or divine, which was broken at Sabine, and do not feel called on as an officer or as a man to dwell longer on such a painful topic.

For Commander Greely there remained one other controversy to deal with: the execution of Private Henry. During the press onslaught in the first few days following the rescue, stories questioning the details of Private Henry's execution had been published, some accusing Greely of murder. Others were calling for Lieutenant Greely to face trial by court-martial. Secretary of War Lincoln, concerned about how this might reflect on the army, sought an explanation, and put the matter before the adjutant general's office at the War Department for official review.

Commander Greely had always maintained that Henry's execution was right and warranted, his only regret being that he had not done it himself and much earlier. He felt he had been too lenient and allowed Henry's thieving to persist for too long. He had given Private Henry numerous chances to desist. So Greely was relieved but not surprised when the adjutant general's letter arrived from Washington supporting his actions. The War Department had carefully considered Greely's own report, as well as the diaries of several members of the expedition—including Private Henry's—and concluded: "The Secretary of War entertains no doubt of the necessity and entire propriety of your action in ordering the execution of Private Henry under the circumstances." No further inquiry would be necessary, and the matter was officially closed.

∽∽∽

In 1881, when A. W. Greely boarded the *Proteus* as commander of the Lady Franklin Bay Expeditionary Force, he had been acutely aware that he was embarking on a dangerous mission, and that in Arctic expeditions, crew losses of 50 percent were common. Confident in his abilities to lead, he of course had never expected that the disasters associated with his mission would result in the loss of nineteen of the twenty-five men on board. But despite this tragic loss of American soldiers, Greely's belief in exploration and discovery never wavered.

Commander Greely's so-called "expeditionary force" was unusual. Greely landed at Lady Franklin Bay with two officers, a French-Creole physician, two native Greenlanders, a Canadian-born photographer, and a nineteen-year-old meteorologist. The enlisted men were mostly from the Signal Corps and cavalry, hardscrabble men plucked straight from their posts in the southwest American plains. In many ways this corps appeared unsuited for work in the Arctic, one of the most inhospitable places on earth even for those experienced with its icebound environment. Yet Greely had managed to lead this unlikely unit in one of the epic expeditions in the history of Arctic exploration and scientific discovery. It was remarkable.

In his book *Three Years of Arctic Service: An Account of The Lady Franklin Bay Expedition of 1881–84 and the Attainment of Farthest North*, Greely closed with a strong call for his great and proud nation to continue to strive forward into the unknown, for all its danger and cost, for only in such quests could the United States enlarge its standing in the world:

> *Our great country in these days asks not in vain for its sons to venture their lives for any idea which may subserve its interests or enhance its greatness. I trust that posterity may never mourn the decadence of that indomitable American spirit which in this generation fought out to the bitter end its great civil war, and made it seem an easy thing in time of peace to penetrate the heart of Africa, to perish in the Lena Delta, to die at Sabine, or to attain the Farthest North.*

38

꧁꧂

"A Blue-Ribboned, Star-Shaped Medal"

A few months after his return the United States, Greely was invited by the Royal Geographic Society of London, and the German and French geographic societies, to come to Europe and give lectures. Feeling fairly well recovered, he accepted graciously. While abroad in 1886 Greely was thrilled to meet "the distinguished men of Europe, the crowned heads of various countries," and become intimate with some of the world's "great scientists, geographers and explorers." He was now a part of that elite fraternity and was awarded the Founder's Medal of the Royal Geographical Society of London and the Roquette Medal of the Société de Géographie of Paris.

While in the Arctic, Lieutenant Greely had missed a promotion to captain, but was advanced two years after his return. Recognizing Greely's achievements, in 1887 President Cleveland promoted him to brigadier general and appointed him chief signal officer. Remarkably, Greely, who had enlisted as a teenager in 1861 in the Nineteenth Massachusetts Volunteer Infantry, had become "the first private soldier of the Civil War to reach Regular Army general officer rank."

Greely headed the Signal Corps for the next twenty years, his commands taking him all over the world—though never again, to Henrietta's great relief, to the high Arctic north. His energies, especially given what his mind and body had been through in the polar regions, seemed boundless. Between 1899 and 1903, he supervised the construction of more than ten thousand miles of telegraph lines in the Philippines, Puerto Rico, Cuba, and Alaska, and during the Spanish-American War, he "invented a secret code for telegraphic communication."

Shortly afterward Greely, still with the Signal Corps, oversaw balloon and aerial experiments. He became involved in the Smithsonian Institution's race for manned flight. Greely dispersed fifty thousand dollars of congressionally appropriated funds toward tests of the steam-powered *Aerodrome*, conceived by the Smithsonian's secretary, Samuel Langley, and supported by Langley's friend Alexander Graham Bell. The *Aerodrome* made a number of unmanned flights of up to a mile, but the project was scuttled after the aircraft crashed into the Potomac River on December 8, 1903. Nine days later Orville Wright flew 120 feet at Kitty Hawk, North Carolina.

By 1906 Greely had been promoted to major general and assigned to command the Pacific Division, headquartered at the Presidio in San Francisco. He was on leave and was traveling east to attend his daughter Adola's wedding in Washington when the San Francisco earthquake struck on April 18. Hearing the news, Greely disembarked in Chicago and sent a telegram to Secretary of War William Howard Taft, requesting to take the first train available and return to San Francisco. Once back at the Presidio and in command, he "skillfully organized a military response to a major catastrophe," helping to control the chaos and manage the displacement of more than 250,000 people.

Greely retired in 1908, at the age of sixty-four, though he did not remain idle. He immediately took Henrietta, and two of their daughters—Gertrude and Rose (by now he had six children)—on a round-the-world journey. They sailed to the Philippines, Japan, and China, then went to Europe via the Trans-Siberian Railway, taking nearly two weeks to cross Siberia. After spending the winter in Europe, visiting Florence and the Austrian Tyrol, they returned to their home in late 1909 and settled in at their house on G Street, between Nineteenth and Twentieth, just two blocks from the State, War, and Navy Building, which had played such a significant role during Greely's Arctic expedition.

In Washington the Greelys enjoyed an active and vibrant social life, mostly at the urging of Henrietta, who had become intimate with Mrs. Grover Cleveland and many other politicians' wives. For his part, Greely preferred reading and writing, visiting their summer home in Conway, New Hampshire, and taking long walks among the white birches. Greely devoted a great deal of his time to writing, producing four books in retirement: *A Handbook of Alaska* in 1909; *True Tales of Arctic Heroism*, in 1912; *Reminiscences of Adventure and Service: A Record of 65 Years*, in 1927; and *Polar Regions in the Twentieth Century*, which he wrote in 1928 at the age of eighty-four. His mental and physical energies remained remarkably prodigious.

When not writing, Major General Greely gave some lectures on his decades of adventure, and although he was offered thousands of dollars for appearances, he would never accept money to speak about the winter at Cape Sabine, "in deference to the memory of those who did not come back." Greely was one of the founders of the National Geographic Society and the Explorers Club, both prestigious organizations. Henrietta was an active member of the Daughters of the American Revolution until her death, in March 1917, just before her seventy-third birthday.

Greely mourned the loss of Henrietta deeply. She had been his companion, ardent supporter, and fierce champion for thirty-nine years of marriage. Her faith in him, coupled with her persistent and vociferous efforts with the press and with politicians, had raised a national cry for his rescue. He would never forget how instrumental she had been in saving his life and the lives of the other five survivors of the Lady Franklin Bay Expedition.

After Henrietta's death Greely lived for a year with his daughter Rose in Cambridge, Massachusetts, where she was studying architecture. When she finished her studies, they moved back to Washington, and, beginning in 1920, he took up residence at the famous Cosmos Club, an exclusive club for individuals who had distinguished themselves in science, literature, the arts, and public service. Greely was certainly qualified. There he remained for seven years, vigorously reading and conversing with some of the most influential thinkers of the early twentieth century. He eventually settled, with his daughters Rose and Antoinette, into a house on 3131 O Street in Georgetown. Greely kept up daily exercise, walking around the city streets well into his ninetieth year.

March 27, 1935, was Greely's ninety-first birthday. Four of his six children and two of his grandchildren were there, the grandchildren eager to start on the cake. But otherwise it was unlike any other birthday he had ever celebrated. Outside his Georgetown home, Troop F of the Second Cavalry had halted, and Greely could hear the neighing and snorting of horses. A military band was playing. Neighbors came out of their houses and lined the streets to see what was happening. A line of automobiles rolled up slowly and stopped in front of Greely's brick house. Out of the lead car stepped George H. Dern, the secretary of war. As the band played the national anthem, Dern strode up the steps and into Greely's home.

Within minutes Major General Greely was flanked by officers at attention. Standing proudly next to Greely was Brig. Gen. David L. Brainard, his dear friend and confidant who had been at his side fifty-one years before on that miraculous, storm-tossed day when they had crawled from the tent at Camp Clay and been liberated from that desperate shoreline. Brainard and Greely had remained close for the next five decades. Now Greely beamed, overcome with emotion at the presence of Brainard. The two had made it a point to have dinner together every chance they could on June 22, the anniversary of their rescue. On those occasions he and Brainard would reminisce about their experiences in the Arctic and recall stories about the men, and they often ordered the elaborate meals that Lieutenant Lockwood had conjured in his imagination and fantasized about.

Secretary of War Dern leaned forward and pinned on Greely's left lapel "a blue-ribboned, star-shaped medal." It was the Congressional Medal of Honor. Dern read a citation: "For conspicuous gallantry and intrepidity in actions, at the risk of his own life above and beyond the call of duty, and a life of splendid public service." Behind his glasses Greely's eyes were dewed with emotion. The military men then marched out the front door and down the steps, the cavalrymen reined their mounts and trotted away in formation, and the band marched after them.

Seven decades after joining the army, Major General Greely had finally been recognized as an American hero and a national treasure, honors he had long deserved. It was only the second Congressional Medal of Honor to have been awarded for service during peacetime, the first having been given to Charles A. Lindbergh.

In early October 1935 Maj. Gen. Adolphus Washington Greely, commander of the Lady Franklin Bay Expedition, grew weak. His doctors had him admitted to the Walter Reed National Military Medical Center. His mind was sharp, but his body was finally failing. For the next few weeks, attended by nurses and doctors and his children, Greely received a constant stream of visitors. One retired soldier came every day. It was Brainard, Greely's dutiful second in command in their final days at Cape Sabine: "I have seen Greely much worse than this and get through it," Brainard said, "and I am sure he will do it again."

But his old friend's time was up. Greely died on October 20, 1935, at the age of ninety-one, surrounded by his family. Last respects were paid two days later. Gen. William "Billy" Mitchell was there. In 1898, during the Spanish-American War, Mitchell had served under Greely with the Signal Corps, and had become like a son to him. Said Mitchell of the funeral procession: "The caisson bearing his body moved slowly up the Fort Meyer Road toward Arlington Cemetery, where he was laid to rest with the others of the nation's brave and distinguished servants. It was a day brilliant with sunshine and the bright, flaming colors of the autumn leaves." Greely was lowered into the ground next to Henrietta, with soldiers saluting and the low, mournful trumpet notes of "Taps" carried away on the wind.

Greely as chief Signal Corps officer. *(Courtesy of Naval History and Heritage Command)*

EPILOGUE

Weyprecht's Dream

The original purpose of the Lady Franklin Bay Expedition was the fulfill-
ment of a revolutionary idea conceived by the Austrian explorer Karl
Weyprecht. Weyprecht had discovered Franz Joseph Land in 1873 and had
dreamed of establishing an international cooperative of a dozen weather stations, "a girdle of stations around the entire Arctic region to record simultaneously observations relating to various branches of physics and meteorology,
and also botany, zoology, and geology."

Greely's was to be the northernmost station of this "girdle." Greely had been
honored to be part of this revolutionary scientific mission—named the International Polar Year (IPY)—a global effort to record data at the farthest reaches
of the world to better understand the Earth's climate. Commander Greely, of
course, also secretly wanted to either reach the North Pole or attain Farthest
North, but at no time did he ever forget Weyprecht's dream and the unprecedented purpose of his own expedition to the Arctic.

In 1888 Lieutenant Greely proudly presented his formal International Polar Expedition report to the House of Representatives, Forty-Ninth Congress,
First Session. The monumental two-volume document was thirteen hundred

pages long and contained scrupulously detailed scientific data and descriptions and accounts of every sledge journey made from Fort Conger—highlighted by those of Lockwood and Brainard to Farthest North and Farthest West. It featured the dramatic, unprecedented photographs taken by George Rice; the meticulous sketches made by Lockwood; numerous maps of the expedition's discoveries on Ellesmere Island and Greenland; as well as hundreds of charts and numbered, orderly records of all of the artifacts and relics brought back to the United States. They had protected these specimens and records even through the perilous fifty-one-day, five-hundred-mile boat, sledge, and floating iceberg retreat from Fort Conger to Cape Sabine.

Supplemented by several of the expedition members' diaries, the report reflected the expedition's collective, collaborative experience in the Arctic, and it was heralded as a shining tribute to the First International Polar Year. Greely took great solace in knowing that all of those thousands of hours of observation—taking as many as five hundred readings per day—had not been in vain. In fact their work and his report would serve as a standard for all subsequent International Polar Year observations. Greely and his men had helped the world to better understand the general tide patterns of Arctic waters and had elucidated some of the "mysteries of the earth's magnetism."

David Brainard had been instrumental in assisting Greely during the writing of the report, sitting with his commander for countless hours organizing the materials. Greely would also never forget Brainard's tireless, selfless efforts from the day they landed at Fort Conger in 1881 to the day they were rescued in 1884. Greely wrote so glowingly of Brainard's "extraordinary service, his manhood, courage, and self-sacrifice displayed on the polar sea," that in 1886 President Grover Cleveland promoted Sergeant Brainard to second lieutenant in the U.S. Cavalry. Brainard went on to have a long and distinguished military career, retiring as a brigadier general and later receiving the Purple Heart in 1933. He was the last survivor of the Greely Expedition, and in 1936—on his eightieth birthday—he was bestowed the award of First Honorary Member of the American Polar Society. Brainard remained vibrant and active in business up until his death of a heart attack in Walter Reed Hospital on

March 22, 1946. He was laid to rest in Arlington National Cemetery, not far from his old friend Adolphus Greely.

∽∽∽

The frozen north that Adolphus Greely, David Brainard, and all the men of the Lady Franklin Bay Expedition explored, mapped, charted, and measured was so cold much of the year that the mercury in their thermometers routinely froze (it must be −37.89° for this to happen). Greely and his men recorded an annual mean temperature of −3.93° for the duration of their stay at Fort Conger, the lowest verified for any known spot on the globe. So Greely could probably never have conceived that just a century and a quarter after his return home, global temperatures would have risen to such an alarming rate that Greenland would be losing on average 260 billion tons of ice each year, raising sea levels around the world and imperiling coastal communities with increased erosion, storm surges, and violent weather patterns bringing hurricanes, cyclones, and flooding at rates and intensities never before chronicled.

The contributions of Greely and his team were significant and would have a lasting impact that still resonates today. They provided a comprehensive and precise baseline for subsequent scientists to consult and compare against. The scrupulous records of Greely's astounding official report included two consecutive years (1881–83) of readings and observations—in some cases hourly, but also daily, monthly, and annual—including atmospheric, air, and water temperatures; barometric pressure; precipitation; magnetism; tidal movements; wind direction and velocity; evaporation of ice and water; ice and snow depths; and pendulum observations. They had advanced human knowledge and understanding in auroral phenomena, meteorology, and especially climate. The researchers Kevin Wood and James Overland, in their 2006 article, "Climate Lessons from the First International Polar Year," state: "That notable climate change has taken place in the Artic in the years since the first IPY is beyond dispute." By studying and comparing Greely's observations (and those of the other nations involved in the First IPY) with current data, Wood and Overland concluded that "evidence of the impacts of climate change is widespread.

Northern seas have become warmer and the extent of sea ice has diminished. Glaciers have declined. Permafrost has thawed, leading to the long-lasting transformation of eco-systems."

∞∞∞

Analyzing data collected by Greely, the members of the International Polar Year 2007–9 determined that there is now "abundant evidence of changes in snow and ice: reductions in extent and mass of glaciers and ice sheets, reductions in area, timing, and duration of snow cover, and reductions in extent and thickness of sea ice."

Greely and his team demonstrated that, properly equipped and under the right leadership, it was possible to conduct laboratory-quality science in the field, and in the harshest environments on the planet. Greely—ever mindful of Weyprecht's original goals—helped set in motion concerted scientific study of the polar regions and helped show that the Earth's complexities could be simultaneously surveyed by researchers from numerous countries and disciplines, all in the pursuit of shared human knowledge and understanding.

Greely's efforts also shifted considerably the very way science would be conducted, and by whom. Until that time, according to Dr. E. Fred Roots, a noted Canadian polar scientist, science was "an exclusive or elitist pursuit, often jealously guarded for reasons of national or institutional prestige." Greely helped show that a well-organized group of army soldiers could contribute to science at the highest levels of inquiry. Dr. Roots went on to say that in carrying out Weyprecht's grand vision, Greely and the participants in the First IPY had prodded science "into an open activity, in which everyone qualified could take part and in which the results belonged to the whole world and the quality of the science was judged by criticisms of other knowledgeable scientists, not by patrons or clients."

The Lady Franklin Bay Expedition helped to initiate a series of later IPYs. Forty-four nations participated in the IPY of 1932–33. The 1957 installment—expanded to include and acknowledge worldwide advances in computing, radar, and rocketry—involved sixty-seven countries simultaneously studying all manner of the Earth's phenomena. Both the United States and the Soviet Union launched satellites to coincide with the event, with *Sputnik 1* being the world's first "artificial" satellite.

All this work and impetus culminated in the Fourth IPY of 2007–9. With an estimated fifty thousand researchers and observers involved, it was the largest and most complete coordinated field campaign ever mounted to study the Earth's polar regions. Today's extension of previous IPYs continues through the National Oceanic and Atmospheric Administration (NOAA), which in 2007 undertook the painstaking but important task of amassing and analyzing all the original data. At last the meteorological records of the First International Polar Year—including an extensive documentary image collection thanks in part to Greely's photographer, George Rice—have been collected in one location in digital format at noaa.gov. The data continues to be compiled and compared at the International Polar Year Collections Database, a cooperative global endeavor that identifies and describes all publications that have resulted from any of the IPYs undertaken so far, and those that will be conducted in the future. Subsequent IPY conferences were held in Oslo, Norway, in 2010 and in Montreal, Canada, in 2012, with the ongoing goals to steward sustainable development and environmental protection of the polar regions.

Additionally, Greely was a pioneer in understanding and coping with the devastating psychological effects of extended stays in polar regions. Having spent years studying the logs and journals of expeditions to the high Arctic, Greely knew that long periods of isolation and confinement resulted in so-called "cabin fever" and "polar madness." These were the expressions used to describe bouts of depression and mood disturbances, insomnia, irritability and violence, memory loss and cognitive impairment, and even suicide. Knowing that his men would face months at a time of darkness and would be working together in close quarters under the harshest conditions imaginable, at Fort Conger Commander Greely kept his men constantly active—both physically and mentally. He instituted daily lectures and developed a triweekly "school" with regular courses in mathematics, English grammar and spelling, and geography as well as meteorology. He demanded daily exercise in addition to the required work, encouraging the men to hike among the hills and mountains around the fort. To maintain morale and thwart depression, boredom, and anxiety, he organized games, festivities, competitions, and evening entertainment through participation in music, singing, and even performances in skits. Greely continued his one-to-two-hour-long lectures during their seven harrowing months in the cramped confinement of Camp Clay at Cape Sabine.

Greely painstakingly documented the behavior of his men in his daily reports and journals, and his records demonstrated that a rigorous practice of continuous physical and mental activity reduced the symptoms of a variety of conditions and syndromes for which psychologists now have names, among them clinical depression, winter-over syndrome, Polar T3 syndrome (caused by a decrease in the thyroid hormone T3), and seasonal affective disorder (or SAD, recurring major depression with a seasonal pattern, caused by decreased exposure to sunlight). The results of Greely's observations have helped leaders of future expeditions to both the Arctic and Antarctic regions realize the importance of integrating regular, diverse, non-work-related exercise and mental acuity regimens both in preparation for and during long stays at the poles. Greely's work has been vital and far-reaching, its legacy seen in the nearly one hundred polar research stations (some drifting on ice and some permanent) that exist in the world today. The knowledge gained and practices employed by Greely have also benefited teams training for and conducting lengthy tours on space flights and living on manned space stations.

⌀⌀⌀

Fortunately for history, the legacy of Adolphus Washington Greely, and of the men of the Lady Franklin Bay Expedition, lives on. Fort Conger, where the vast majority of the scientific work was done by the members of the expedition, is now part of Quttinirpaaq National Park of Canada, Nunavat, and has been designated a Canadian Federal Heritage building. This important historical classification was awarded for the fort's close connection to Arctic exploration and discovery. After Greely and his men departed the fort in August 1883, it was subsequently used by Robert Peary in his three separate attempts to reach the North Pole in 1899, 1905, and 1908.

Thankfully, modern science has preserved the site, which has been threatened by thawing permafrost, erosion, and "bio-fungal growth caused by the warming microenvironments in wooden structures." Due to the efforts of Peter Dawson, a University of Calgary archaeologist, Fort Conger has been "digitally preserved" by means of terrestrial laser scanning to make a 3-D model and interactive website, which can be visited at the Virtual Museum of Canada, http://fortconger.org/index. Visitors can take 3-D animated virtual tours of Fort Conger, complete with a visual time line of the construction sequences, photo galleries, videos, and interactive exhibits. The science-minded Greely would no doubt be impressed and humbled by this enduring testament to the fort he built and the harsh and dramatic landscape he inhabited for two years of his remarkable life.

Adolphus Greely was ambitious and dedicated, a complex figure with a powerful intellect; he was equally versed in science, mathematics, language, cultures, history, and the arts. A true polymath. A man of destiny. But it was his leadership, perhaps above all else, that should be remembered. History has at times judged him unfairly; there are plenty of critics who claim that if he'd only remained at Fort Conger, none of his men would have experienced the horrors they did and perished at Cape Sabine. They had enough food for another year, the argument goes, and there was no reason to leave.

But for Greely staying at Fort Conger was never an option. A plan had been put in place, multiple contingency plans had been considered and accounted for, and military orders had been agreed upon and signed. A breach in such orders, from a man who had enlisted in the army at age seventeen (after being rejected twice!), was unthinkable. Following orders was too deeply ingrained in him, and he had enough experience to know that not following orders led to chaos and even anarchy. In the end, ill-planned and botched rescue attempts, sluggish and cumbersome bureaucracy, and the vicissitudes of the unforgiving Arctic north sealed the fate of many of his men. But only through his astute leadership did any of them have a chance to survive. He understood how to delegate, how to read personalities for their strengths and weaknesses, when to push, and when to relinquish. Adrift and imperiled on the ice floes in the deadly Kane Basin, Greely showed a capacity for change, and he adjusted his leadership style to become more diplomatic and democratic, keeping his men focused on common goals for the preservation of all, until at last, time simply ran out for some of them.

Throughout his 720-page book *Three Years of Arctic Service*, Greely's attention to and appreciation for his men is palpable. He held many of them in his arms as they whispered their final words and breathed their last breaths. The pages of his book and journals reveal a profound sense of caring and humanity, a deep responsibility for those he was destined to lead. The dedication he wrote at the beginning of his book offers insight into the man, and it seems fitting to close this book with that same dedication, to serve as a reminder of what grace looks like:

> *To the Lady Franklin Bay Expedition*
> *These volumes are dedicated:*
> *To its dead who suffered much—*
> *To its living who suffered more.*
> *Their energy accomplished Farthest North*
> *Their fidelity wrought out success;*
> *Their courage faced death undauntedly;*
> *Their loyalty and discipline in all the dark days*
> *Ensured that this record*
> *Of their services should be given to the world.*

ACKNOWLEDGMENTS

Writing books often feels like a solitary endeavor, though of course it's really a collaboration in the truest sense of the word. I want to thank my literary agent, Scott Waxman, for remembering my research on the Greely Expedition of some years ago and encouraging me to resurrect it. Scott has been a trusted supporter of my work since 2003, and I rely greatly on his sagacity and knowledge of the book-publishing industry. He's notorious for his hands-on approach to book projects from their conception to proposal to finished work. He has represented me on six books so far, and I hope to partner with him on a dozen more at least.

Scott Waxman introduced me to my editor, Marc Resnick, at St. Martin's Press, and Marc has been an absolute joy to work with. From our initial half-hour phone conversation, I could tell he was a kindred spirit. When I started relaying the story of the Greely Expedition to him, he said, "Just tell it to me like you are telling it to someone in a bar." I knew then we were going to get along fine. Marc has a deep respect for authors and understands the hard work involved; he is also a strong reader with a sharp eye and ear for what makes great storytelling. He is a consummate professional and terrific teammate, and I hope to work with him on future books. Ditto his editorial assistant, Hannah O'Grady, who is fast, furious, and efficient. Thanks for everything, Hannah!

Also a big shout-out of appreciation to copy editor extraordinaire Susan Llewellyn, whose astute inquiries, fastidiousness, enthusiasm, and inquisitiveness helped make this a better book.

Two students of mine, Sarah Perry and Cheryl Aarnio, desire to work in book editing in their careers. They proofread my first pass pages, doing a great job at finding a few of my residual typos and punctuation errors. Thanks and "Go Cougs!"

My dear friend John Larkin has been my first reader on most of my books, providing insight, excellent questions, and a wealth of historical and especially nautical knowledge that has proved indispensable. His marginal notes are often hilarious and have been vital sustenance during the laborious drafting process. John, you've helped more than you can ever know. I'd go to the North Pole with you anytime.

I have such love and admiration and appreciation for my dutiful and intrepid Free Range Writers: Kim Barnes, Collin Hughes, Lisa Norris, and Jane Varley. A tip of the glass to the ammo box! But not yet, not yet.

The Washington State University College of Arts and Sciences, and especially the Department of English, has supported (both spiritually and financially) my research and travel, helping me to pull off a full-time teaching load while also writing books. Many thanks.

Finally, to my loving family: My beautiful wife, Camie, and my dear children, Logan and Hunter—your support and trust are constant and unwavering, buoying me in the rough seas that come with the writing of every book. You make me try to be a better man.

AUTHOR'S NOTE ON THE
TEXT AND SOURCES

⟨≈≈⟩

I have been mesmerized by the wilds of the Great White North since reading Jack London as a boy. Much later, in 2003 I had the great good fortune to visit Greenland as a journalist to cover an expedition adventure, and I was riveted by the place, its ruggedness, its isolation, its people, and its history. On my return home I began reading widely about the many storied Arctic expeditions (and their frequent disasters), and I simply could not get enough of them, representing as they do some of the most compelling stories of human endurance and tenacity, in the most uninhabitable places, in history. When I discovered the story of the Greely Expedition, I was enthralled. Like nearly all great stories from the past, it had been told before, but I knew I wanted to tell it in my own way. So I have tried to provide an interpretation that focuses on the adventure and triumphs, on the unity, brotherhood, and patriotism of the men.

The literature on the history of Arctic exploration, and especially works concerning the search for the Northwest Passage and the quest for the North Pole, is rich, varied, and fascinating. For readers who wish to explore further the worlds of the explorers, selected works are listed below and in the bibliography that follows—works that have been cited, quoted directly, or consulted as references in the writing of *Labyrinth of Ice*.

In part because the Greely Expedition and the subsequent relief and rescue operations were military endeavors, a wealth of material is available at the National Archives and Records Administration (NARA) in Washington, D.C., the United States Army Historical Institute in Washington, D.C., and the Library of Congress. Other superb resources are the Explorers Club in New York City and the National Geographic Society Library and Archives in Washington, D.C. The miracle of electronic databases and archives now permits online access to much of the information related to the Greely Expedition. Of particular interest is the Greely Polar Collection at the National Geographic Society. Greely was one of the society's founders, and he donated a stunning sixteen hundred volumes to the library in 1918.

As with my previous narrative histories, I have drawn significantly from the primary works of the participants themselves. In the case of the Lady Franklin Bay Expedition, we are fortunate to have detailed diaries, letters, and narrative accounts of numerous members of the original expedition party of 1881, as well as official documents and reports written by participants in the subsequent relief and rescue missions. In my interpretation of the Greely saga, the three principal figures are Adolphus W. Greely, David L. Brainard, and Winfield Scott Schley—though there were of course scores of other people who figure prominently in this remarkable series of events and period in our nation's history.

I relied heavily on two main documents written by Adolphus W. Greely, and they were vital contributions to my telling of the story. The first is his thirteen-hundred-page, two-volume *Report on the Proceedings of the United States Expedition to Lady Franklin Bay, Grinnell Land,* which he presented to the House of Representatives in 1888. The report records—in concise and detailed month-by-month summaries—the weather, work, exploration, and scientific activities and operations of Greely and all his expedition members from the moment of Greely's assumption of command in March 1881 until its return in July 1884. The report also includes all of the commander's written orders during the period, as well as his officers' field reports from the numerous explorations—most notably those to Farthest North in northern Greenland and Farthest West on

Ellesmere Island—originating from their base at Fort Conger on Lady Franklin Bay.

Greely's official report also contains entries from Lt. James B. Lockwood's journal, Sgt. David L. Brainard's journal, and a portion of Pvt. Roderick R. Schneider's journal (miraculously discovered on the banks of the Missouri River in 1885, but that's definitely another story). Because Fort Conger was a weather station and observation outpost, the report provides daily temperatures, wind speeds and direction, barometric pressure, tidal observations, and descriptions—along with maps, drawings, and photographs of the flora and fauna—allowing us to know with incredible accuracy the conditions that Greely and his men were experiencing on a daily basis. It is an extraordinary document and was indispensable in helping me to describe the landscapes and seascapes in the high Arctic.

Greely's published book *Three Years of Arctic Service: An Account of the Lady Franklin Bay Expedition of 1881–84 and the Attainment of Farthest North* was an equally essential resource. Considerably shorter at just 720 pages, the book contains much of the information of the report but has a more narrative style, as it was written for a more general reader. The work provides tremendous insight into the personalities and characters of Greely's men, and chronicles their daily interactions and the triumphs of their achievements as well as their tragic misfortunes. In *Three Years of Arctic Service*, Greely also intersperses personal diary entries that provide insight into his thoughts about his wife, Henrietta, his children, and the government under whose aegis he was operating. The descriptions of life at Fort Conger, the retreat to Cape Sabine, and their time at Camp Clay provide a great sense of his command, his leadership style, and his personality. *Three Years of Artic Service* also afforded me the opportunity to quote Greely and the other men, whose conversations he recorded and relayed daily in his diary and journal.

David L. Brainard played a major role in the expedition. Along with James B. Lockwood, he participated in the two most significant explorations of discovery undertaken. Brainard was also among the most prolific and dutiful diary and journal keepers, writing until his fingers could literally no longer hold his pen or pencil. His book *Six Came Back: The Arctic Adventure of David L. Brainard* was published in 1940. It is essentially a replication of his diary, recording dated entries from July 7, 1881 (the date of their departure from Newfoundland), to June 21, 1884, and comprising the entirety of the expedition. Brainard's sarcasm and sense of humor often shine through, and there are interesting insights to be gleaned from his responses to Greely's command and from his unfiltered observations about most—if not all—of the other men. Remarkably, given the difficult conditions in which he was writing, he missed very few days. Brainard's focus on the minute details of their daily work, of who was doing what, and his precise recounting of nearly every meal—often down to the ounce—was unbelievably helpful.

Brainard's other book, *The Outpost of the Lost: An Arctic Adventure*, was published in 1929 and differs essentially in that it summarizes in narrative form the stay at Fort Conger and the expeditions emanating from there, focusing more on the retreat from Fort Conger, their arduous journey to Cape Sabine, and their subsequent seven-month ordeal there. For those wishing to dig more deeply into the compelling life of an American hero, consult the Papers of David L. Brainard in the Dartmouth College Library. A transcript of Brainard's diary from March 1 to June 21, 1884, written while at Camp Clay, is available among these papers.

Last of the most useful published works by key players is Cdr. Winfield Scott Schley's *The Rescue of Greely* (coauthored by Professor J. R. Soley), published in 1885. Schley's comprehensive work not only details the rescue mission he commanded but gives thorough accounts of the previous relief attempts in 1882 and 1883. As a naval commander, Schley was particularly adept in providing a nautical point of view, and I benefited greatly from his expertise and his descriptions of the ships, their outfitting, and their movements. Schley offers a crow's nest view of the northern waters and the challenges they presented not only to him but to the other captains attempting to reach Greely. Schley's affinity for and knowledge of the Dundee whaling fleet also helped me (I hope) to add texture, nuance, and verisimilitude to the telling.

One other primary document was particularly useful, though it is something of a mind-numbing read. This is the *Proceedings of the* Proteus *Court of Inquiry on the Greely Relief Expedition.* Presented to the Forty-Eighth Congress, First Session, in 1883, the 250-page report (single-spaced!) includes every distinct correspondence (military orders, letters, telegrams) comprised by the lengthy inquiry into the *Proteus* disaster. Every item on every ship is listed and tabled, down to the last can of pemmican. There are also recordings of the court proceedings attendant to the inquiry, which allowed me to come away with a good sense of exactly when (though not always exactly why) certain actions were taken (or not) by the commanders of the relief effort of 1883, and what role these actions played in the fate of the Greely Expedition.

A few popular narratives deserve mention for the heavy research lifting they did long before I decided to take on *Labyrinth of Ice.* The first of these, and the most recent, is Leonard Guttridge's *The Ghosts of Cape Sabine: The Harrowing True Story of the Greely Expedition*, which was published in 2000. Guttridge's book (he incidentally also authored a book on the disaster of the USS *Jeannette*) is excellent, prodigiously researched, and comprehensive. I am indebted to his scholarship, especially his sleuthing out of many letters and correspondences among some of the other significant members of the expedition—particularly those of Lt. Frederick Kislingbury and Dr. Octave Pavy. Guttridge has a keen eye for some of the discord among Greely and his men. Guttridge also includes considerable background and context on Karl Weyprecht and the origins of the International Polar Year, which I found valuable. Similarly, Guttridge spends time on the failed Howgate Colony that preceded—and in ways precipitated—the Greely Expedition.

Alden Todd's *Abandoned: The Story of the Greely Arctic Expedition 1881–1884* came out in 1960 and is terrific. This was the first "popular" account of the Greely story I read, and I owe Todd for getting me hooked. Todd had the good timing to be writing at the time that the Greely family was releasing a wealth of previously unpublished materials (as was Brainard's family, it turns out—most of which is now housed at Dartmouth College). Todd's book does a fine job of integrating diary entries and personal letters into his narrative, and I have in instances followed his lead.

Coincidentally, Theodore Powell's *The Long Rescue* also appeared in 1960. Powell's book dispenses with Greely's time at Fort Conger and concerns itself with the retreat from there and the aftermath. *The Long Rescue* is a strong supplement to Schley's *The Rescue of Greely* and helped me to comprehend the complicated chronology of the various movements of ships at sea and men on land. My only caveat is that Powell adopts an approach that resembles an historical novel, in that he invents dialogue.

As with all my books, the libraries and library networks of Washington State University have aided my research tremendously.

The bibliography that follows represents much of the other material I consulted while writing *Labyrinth of Ice*. There is enough material listed to keep you reading for a year or two, anyway.

BIBLIOGRAPHY

❦

Books

Amundsen, Roald. *My Life as an Explorer.* Garden City, NY: Doubleday, Page, 1927.

Annual Report of the Chief Signal Officer, 1883. Washington, DC: U.S. Government Printing Office.

Annual Report of the Secretary of War, 1883. Washington, DC: U.S. Government Printing Office.

Baldwin, Hanson. *Admiral Death: Twelve Adventures of Men Against the Sea.* New York: Simon & Schuster, 1939.

Beattie, Owen, and John Geiger. *Frozen in Time: The Fate of the Franklin Expedition.* New York: MJF Books, 2004.

Berens, S. L., and John E. Read. *Nansen in the Frozen World.* Chicago: National Publishing, 1897.

Bessels, Emil. *Polaris—The Chief Scientist's Recollections of the American North Pole Expedition, 1871–73.* Alberta: University of Calgary Press, 2016.

Brainard, David L. *The Outpost of the Lost: An Arctic Adventure.* Indianapolis: Hobbes, 1929.

———. *Six Came Back: The Arctic Adventure of David L. Brainard.* Indianapolis/New York: Bobbs-Merrill, 1940.

Breton, Pierre. *The Arctic Grail: The Quest for the Northwest Passage and the North Pole, 1818–1909.* New York: Viking, 1988.

———. *Prisoners of the North.* New York: Carroll & Graf, 2004.

Brown, Stephen R. *The Last Viking: The Life of Roald Amundsen.* Vancouver, BC: Douglas & McIntire, 2012.

Caswell, John Edwards. *Arctic Frontiers: United States Explorations in the Far North.* Norman: University of Oklahoma Press, 1956.

Clark, Geoffrey E. *Abandoned in the Arctic: Adolphus W. Greely and the Lady Franklin Bay Expedition, 1881–1884.* Gretna, LA: Pelican Publishing Company, 2015.

Damas, David. *Handbook of North American Indians.* Vol. 5, *Arctic.* Washington, DC: Smithsonian Institution Press, 1985.

Dick, Lyle. *Muskox Land: Ellesmere Island in the Age of Contact.* Alberta: University of Calgary Press. 2001.

Dolin, Eric Jay. *Leviathan: The History of Whaling in America.* New York: W. W. Norton, 2007.

Feeney, Robert F. *Polar Journeys: The Role of Food and Nutrition in Early Exploration.* Fairbanks: University of Alaska Press, 1997.

Fleming, Fergus. *Ninety Degrees North: The Quest for the North Pole.* London: Grove Press, 2001.

———. *Off the Map: Tales of Endurance and Exploration.* New York: Atlantic Monthly Press, 2004.

Greely, Adolphus W. *Handbook of Alaska: Its Resources, Products and Attractions.* New York: Charles Scribner's Sons, 1909.

———. *Handbook of Polar Discoveries.* Boston: Roberts Brothers, 1896.

———. *The Polar Regions in the Twentieth Century.* Boston: Little, Brown, 1928.

———. *Reminiscences of Adventure and Service: A Record of Sixty-Five Years.* New York: Charles Scribner's Sons, 1927.

———. *Three Years of Arctic Service: An Account of the Lady Franklin Bay Expedition of 1881–84 and the Attainment of Farthest North.* New York: Charles Scribner's Sons, 1894.

———. *True Tales of Heroism in the Arctic World.* New York: Charles Scribner's Sons, 1912.

Guttridge, Leonard. *The Ghosts of Cape Sabine: The Harrowing True Story of the Greely Expedition.* New York: G. P. Putnam's Sons, 2000.

———. *Icebound: The Jeannette Expedition and the Quest for the North Pole.* Annapolis, MD: Naval Institute Press, 1986.

Henderson, Bruce. *Fatal North: Murder and Survival Aboard the U.S.S. Polaris, The First U.S. Expedition to the North Pole.* New York: New American Library, 2001.

Herbert, Wally. *Noose of Laurels: The Race to the North Pole.* New York: Macmillan, 1989.

Jones, Huw-Lewis. *Imagining the Arctic: Heroism, Spectacle and Polar Exploration.* London/New York: I. B. Tauris, 2017.

Kobalenko, Jerry. *The Horizontal Everest: Extreme Journeys on Ellesmere Island.* New York: Soho Press, 2002.

Lanman, Charles. *Farthest North; or, The Life and Explorations of Lieutenant James B. Lockwood of the Greely Arctic Expedition.* New York: D. Appleton & Co., 1889.

Larsen, Edward J. *An Empire of Ice.* New Haven: Yale University Press, 2011.

London, Jack. *The Sea Wolf.* 1904. Reprint, New York: Bantam, 1960.

Loomis, Chauncy C. *Weird and Tragic Shores: The Story of Charles Francis Hall, Explorer.* New York: Knopf, 1971.

Lopez, Barry. *Arctic Dreams: Imagination and Desire in a Northern Landscape.* New York: Bantam, 1986.

Lotz, Jim. *Canada's Forgotten Hero: George Rice and the Lady Franklin Bay Expedition, 1881–1884.* Sydney, Nova Scotia: Breton Books, 2009.

Lourie, Peter. *Whaling Season: A Year in the Life of an Arctic Whale Scientist.* New York: Houghton Mifflin, 2009.

Markham, Albert Hastings. *The Great Frozen Sea: A Personal Narrative of the Voyage of the* Alert: *1875–76.* London: C. K. Paul, 1880.

———. *The Life of Sir Clements R. Markham.* London: Murray, 1917.

McGhee, Robert. *The Last Imaginary Place: A Human History of the Arctic World.* New York: Oxford, 2005.

McGoogan, Ken. *Fatal Passage: The Story of John Rae, the Arctic Hero Time Forgot.* New York: Carroll & Graf, 2002.

McMillan, Miriam. *Green Seas and White Ice.* New York: Dodd, Mead, 1948.

Mitchell, William. *General Greely: The Story of a Great American.* New York: G. P. Putnam's Sons, 1936.

Mowat, Farley. *The Polar Passion.* Salt Lake City: Peregrine Smith Books, 1973.

Nansen, Fridtjof. *Farthest North.* Sverdrup, Norway: Otto Neumann, 1897.

———. *The First Crossing of Greenland.* London: Longmans, Green, 1890.

Neil, Christopher. *Unikkaaqtuat: An Introduction to Inuit Myths and Legends.* Toronto: Inhabit Media, 2011.

Nourse, J. E. *American Explorations in the Ice Zones.* Boston: D. Lothrop, 1884.

Nurminen, Juha, and Matti Lainema. *A History of Arctic Exploration: Discovery, Adventure, and Endurance at the Top of the World.* London: Conway, 2010.

Palin, Michael. *Erebus: One Ship, Two Epic Voyages, and the Greatest Naval Mystery of All Time.* Vancouver, BC: Greystone, 2018.

Parry, Richard. *Trial by Ice: The True Story of Murder and Survival on the 1871 Polaris Expedition.* New York: Ballantine, 2001.

Powell, Theodore. *The Long Rescue.* New York: Doubleday, 1960.

Putnam, William Lowell. *Arctic Supernovas.* Sedona, AZ: American Alpine Club, 2001.

Revkin, Andrew C. *The North Pole Was Here: Puzzles and Perils at the Top of the World.* New York: Kingfisher, 2006.

Robinson, Michael F. *The Coldest Crucible: Arctic Exploration and American Culture*. Chicago: University of Chicago Press, 2006.

Schley, Winfield S. *Report of Winfield S. Schley, Commander, Greely Relief Expedition of 1884*. Washington, DC: U.S. Government Printing Office, 1887.

Schley, Winfield S., and J. R. Soley. *The Rescue of Greely*. New York: Charles Scribner's Sons, 1885.

Sides, Hampton. *In the Kingdom of Ice: The Grand and Terrible Polar Voyage of the USS Jeannette*. New York, 2014.

Simmons, Dan. *The Terror*. New York: Little, Brown, 2007.

Streever, Bill. *Cold: Adventures in the World's Frozen Places*. New York: Little, Brown, 2009.

Todd, Alden. *Abandoned: The Story of the Greely Expedition 1881–1884*. Fairbanks, AK: University of Alaska Press, 1960.

Toll, Ian. *Six Frigates: The Epic History of the Founding of the U.S. Navy*. New York: W. W. Norton, 2006.

Walker, Paul. *Adolphus Washington Greely: A Man of Indomitable Courage*. Gretna, LA: Pelican Publishing, 2015.

Watson, Paul. *Ice Ghosts: The Epic Hunt for the Lost Franklin Expedition*. Toronto, Ont.: McClelland & Stewart, 2017.

Williams, Glyn. *Arctic Labyrinth: The Quest for the Northwest Passage*. Berkeley: University of California Press, 2009.

Winchester, Simon. *A Crack in the Edge of the World: California and the Great Earthquake of 1906*. New York: HarperCollins, 2005.

Articles

Barr, William. "Geographical Aspects of the First International Polar Year, 1882–1883." *Annals of the Association of American Geographers* 73, no. 4 (Dec. 1983): 463–484.

Bertulli, Margaret M., Lyle Dick, Peter C. Dawson, and Panik Lynn Cousins. "Fort Conger: A Site of Arctic History in the 21st Century." *Arctic* 66, no. 3 (Sept. 2013): 312–328.

Boas, Franz. "The Configuration of Grinnell Land and Ellesmere Island." *Science* 5, no. 108 (Feb. 27, 1885): 170–171.

C. A.S. "The Magnetic and Tidal Work of the Greely Arctic Expedition." *Science* 9, no. 213 (Mar. 4, 1887): 215–217.

Caswell, John Edwards. "Materials for the History of Arctic America." *Pacific Historical Review* 20, no. 3 (Aug. 1951): 219–226.

England, John. "The First Expeditions to Lady Franklin Bay, Northeast Ellesmere Island, N.W.T., Canada." *Arctic and Alpine Research* 5, no. 2 (Spring 1973): 133–144.

Greely, A. W. "The Scientific Results of the Lady Franklin Bay Expedition." *Science* 5, no. 115 (Apr. 17, 1885): 309–312.

Harlow, Charles H. "Greely at Cape Sabine: Notes by a Member of the Relief Expedition." *Century Illustrated Monthly Magazine* 1 (May 1885).

Keenleyside, Anne. "The Last Resort: Cannibalism in the Arctic." *Explorers Journal* 72 (1995).

Nares, G. S., A. H. Markham, and H. W. Feilden. *Proceedings of the Royal Geographic Society and Monthly Record of Geography* 6, no. 4 (Apr. 1884): 221–226.

Noble, Dennis L., and Truman R. Strobridge. "The Arctic Adventures of the *Thetis*." *Arctic* 30, no. 1 (Mar. 1977): 2–12.

Palinkas, Lawrence A., and Peter Suedfeld. "Psychological Effects of Polar Expeditions." *The Lancet* 371, no. 9607 (Dec. 2008): 153–163.

Pavy, Lilla May. "Dr. Pavy and the Polar Expedition." *North American Review* 142, no. 352 (Mar. 1886): 258–269.

Salmons, Kim. "Cannibalism and the Greely Arctic Expedition: A New Source for 'Falk.'" *The Conradian* 36, no. 1 (Spring 2001): 58–69.

Stein, Glenn M. "An Arctic Execution: Private Charles B. Henry of the United States Lady Franklin Bay Expedition, 1881–84." *Arctic* 64, no. 4 (Dec. 2011): 399–412.

———. "General David L. Brainard, U.S. Army: Last Survivor of the United States' Lady Franklin Bay Expedition." *The Polar Times* (July 2008).

———. "Sledging into History: Belated Recognition for David L. Brainard." *Orders and Medals Research Society* (Dec. 2009): 229–237.

Ullman, Bruce L. "This Wonderful Man: A. W. Greely, a Father of Military Aviation." *Air Power History* 38, no. 2 (Summer 1991): 49–55.

Wamsley, Douglas W. "The Arctic Exploits of Dr. Octave Pavy." *Arctic* 68, no. 1 (Mar. 2015): 1–15.

Weslawski, Jan Marcin, and Joanna Legezynska. "Chances for Arctic Survival: Greely's Expedition Revisited." *Arctic* 55, no. 4 (Dec. 2002): 373–379.

Wood, Kevin, and James E. Overland. "Climate Lessons from the First International Polar Year." *American Meterological Society* (Dec. 2006): 1685–1697.

Ziobro, Melissa. "Adolphus W. Greely." *On Point* 21, no. 2 (Fall 2015): 18–21.

Films

The American Experience. "The Greely Expedition," Written, produced, and directed by Rob Rapley. Boston: WGBH/PBS, 2011.

Special Collections

Collection of the Lady Franklin Bay Expedition, 1881–1884, arranged and described by Clare Flemming, M.S., C.A. Explorers Club Research Collections (46 East Seventieth Street, New York, NY, 10021).

Web Resources

https://archive.org/.

www.armyheritage.org/75-information/soldier-stories/270-fire-a-ice-adolphus-w-greely.

International Polar Year 2007-2009 https://ipy.arcticportal.org/about-jpy

Historical sketch of the life of David Brainard by Glenn Stein
https://dragonhistory.com/2008/08/10/a-historical-sketch-of-the-life-of-general-david-I
   -brainard-us-army/

INDEX

〜〜〜

Alaina Mullin

BUDDY LEVY is the author of eight books, including *Conquistador: Hernán Cortés, King Montezuma, and the Last Stand of the Aztecs* and *River of Darkness: Francisco Orellana's Legendary Voyage of Death and Discovery Down the Amazon.* He is coauthor of *No Barriers: A Blind Man's Journey to Kayak the Grand Canyon* and *Geronimo: Leadership Strategies of an American Warrior.* His books have been published in eight languages. He lives in Idaho.